Preface

There are two distinct views about the Indian woman. One is the typical old Indian viewpoint of the Indian woman being a symbol of purity, faithfulness and submission and devotion to her husband (or *patideva*). Sita and Savitri happen to be the archetypes of this view. The other view, mostly typical of western scholars, is that the Indian woman is backward, suppressed and treated almost as a chattel.

These two extreme views or myths have forced many serious scholars to explore and explicate the realities about the womenfolk, and consequently, a considerable body of literature on the Indian woman has burgeoned, especially during the last two-three decades. Thus women's studies, as in the West, has emerged as a very fascinating area of research in the realm of social sciences in India. Nevertheless, works based on rigorous research with a clear theoretical framework are still very few and far between. Our knowledge of the Indian woman continues to be quite inadequate and in some ways superficial, too. The fact that issues relating to women are quite vast and of bewildering complexity has greatly hampered our understanding of the womenfolk. Furthermore, considerable variations between different regions, between rural and urban areas, between classes and also between different religions, ethnic and caste groups, have made our task enormously arduous, if not impossible.

Considering the facts stated above, over two hundred experts from various disciplines, both from India and abroad, were invited to contribute a detailed and scholarly account of the Indian woman on any of the topics listed below. The contributors were requested to identify the real issues about the Indian woman, focus the attention upon them bring evidence to bear upon the situation, and investigate the whole matter in a logical and rigorous way. For obvious reasons, they were free to follow their own perspective in the treatment of the subject to unravel the myth and reality about the Indian woman.

Section-1

1. Women's Studies in India: a Review of Facts and Theories.
2. The Woman Down the Ages.
   (A) Ancient Period,
   (B) Medieval Period,
   (C) Modern Period.
3. The System of *Devadasi*/Nautch girls.
4. The Reformation Movements and the Woman.
5. The Woman and the Nationalist Movement.
6. Virgins in *Tantra*.
7. The Woman in Ancient Scriptures.
8. The Concubine System.
9. Images of the Woman in Society.
10. Gender Bias in Indian Culture.

Section-2

1. The Hindu Woman.
2. The Muslim Woman.
3. The Harijan Woman.
4. The Tribal Woman.
5. The Sikh Woman.
6. The Christian Woman.
7. The Woman in India and the West: a Comparative Conspectus.

Section-3

1. Patriarchy and the Woman.
2. The Feminist Movement: a Search for New Identity.
3. Gender and Feminism.
4. Social Constructions and Representation of Gender in Society.
5. Gender Divisions in Food Production and Food Consumption.
6. Gender Issues in Production and Reproduction.
7. The Woman: a Marxian Perspective.

THE INDIAN WOMAN
Myth and Reality

8. The Woman as Sita or Savitri: Myth and Reality.

Section-4

1. Sociology and the Woman.
2. Anthropology and the Woman.
3. Demography and the Woman.
4. The Woman in New Household Economics.
5. The Woman and Development.
6. The Woman in Indian Literature.
7. Sexism in Research.
8. Non-sexist Methodology of Research.

Section-5

1. Marriage, Dowry and Divorce.
2. Facets of the Woman: Mother, Sister and Widow.
3. The Woman and Home.
4. The Woman and Work.
5. The Woman in Informal Sector.
6. Female Education.
7. The Woman in Public Life.
8. Prostitution: Harem, Hotel and Redlight.
9. The Woman: Rural-urban Contrasts.
10. The Woman and State: Atrocities on the Woman.
11. Neglect of Female Child.
12. Poverty and the Woman.
13. The Woman: Past, Present and Future.

Now let me present a summary view of different contributions. Since the focus of attention, theme of discussion, source materials and authors' ideological bases vary markedly from paper to paper, most papers are independent of one another to a great extent. And so it is difficult to find a common thread connecting all the contributions but for the fact that all of them relate to social images or *locus standi* of the Indian woman. However, a perusal of this book would throw enough light on the current position of the womenfolk and develop new insight into certain social realities of India.

Since time immemorial men have been harbouring various kinds of prejudices against women. The Shakespearean aphorism: 'Frailty thy name is woman' is one of the most striking reflections of man's bias against woman. Clarice A. Auluck-Wilson's paper is a clear negation of this age-old prejudice. A woman can possibly work harder and provide better leadership than men, if need be. This is clearly evident in Auluck-Wilson's vivid anthropological account of the emergence of grassroots women's organisation in rural Maharashtra. Herein it has been shown that the illiterate, poor and the under-privileged womenfolk can make remarkable contributions to the development of their community.

Based on the census and the National Sample Survey materials, the editor of this volume in his paper entitled 'The Sociology of Women and Work' has found that women have a lesser economic participation than men. They are mostly engaged as manual and semi-skilled workers and often paid less than their male counterparts. Females are not usually encouraged to work outside their homes, as the working of female is not a valued activity. The women who can enjoy leisure at home have a better social status than those who work outside their homes. Women are so marginalised in the job market that they need constitutional provisions for reservation in jobs. Such provisions would help them enhance their social and economic empowerment. It would be a useful measure both for the upliftment of women's status and population control. Work participation provides an alternative identity to motherhood roles.

There is yet another paper on women's activities where P.K. Majumdar and Saswati Dutta have observed that female's economic activity continues mostly in the traditional sector. More then 20 percent of the working females is found engaged in agriculture and agriculture related activities. The nature of involvement in this sector is such that female workers are subjected to a high degree of deprivation. Since the agricultural sector is expected to remain static as a main provider of employment to women, they are going to face more or less a similar level of deprivation in future as well. Mass illiteracy among women is believed to be a crucial reason for their continuing deprivation in the job market.

Sabita Guha has contended in her presentation that Indian society is highly patriarchal and patrilineal. It is because of this fact that the abortion of female foetus and neglect of female child are continuing in our society. The birth of a female child is rarely taken as a happy event. The preference for male issue is quite strong both among men and women. Such a strong pro-son mentality or outlook has been greatly responsible for the lower status of women in Indian society. There is yet another paper on girl child written almost on a similar line by Godavari D. Patil and Madhumati Patil wherein the authors have opined that in India, same as in other societies characterised by patriarchy, females, whether kids, adolescent or adults, are taken as inferior beings. Sons are always preferred to daughters. Being an economic burden, they are made to grow in an apathetic and hostile environment. They are socialised to bear with all sorts of neglects and discriminations within the family of origin. Our age-old system of beliefs or the value system is such that the women are divested of their individuality and are socialised to grow as submissive and self-sacrificing daughters and later as wives and mothers.

A. Shariff has drawn our attention to some socio-economic issues relating to widows and their survival in South India, particularly in rural Karnataka. Widowhood continues to be taken as a curse on woman for her sins in the earlier life and widow remarriage is considered a very inferior kind of social ritual. Since the lack of general practice of widow remarriage creates social problems, the author has emphasized the need for certain specific programmes and legislations to tackle the problem of rehabilitation of widows in society.

Sandeep Parmar and S.B. Singh Parmar have argued that women's educational attainment and future career are greatly hampered by the special role they have to play in the process of reproduction at an early age. This is greatly responsible for the subordination of women in society. The deprivation of woman from education and consequent blockade of professional career combined with various social handicaps force them to remain occupied with the household chores throughout their life.

Vibhuti Patel's paper is related to issues associated with rape of women in India. The theme of her paper covers such aspects of amended rape laws as the ideological undercurrents in the definitions of 'rape'; wilful consent' and 'past sexual history of the complainant'; the *modus operandi* of the criminal justice system and women victims of sexual assault; the state of enforcement machinery; police, hospital and legal administration and the rape victim; experiences of efforts at gender-sensitization of the government apparatus to deal with cases of rape and the recommendation of the National Conference of Rape (1990).

Raj Mohini Sethi in her paper on women, technology and development has argued that the development of technology has adversely affected women's expectations, opportunities and behaviour. In her views industrialisation and agricultural mechanisation have greatly contributed towards increase in women's dependence on men. In addition, they have been further relegated in the occupational hierarchy. Nevertheless, she is not opposed to development of science and technology; rather, she suggests the inculcation of a scientific temper among women to help them become independent and self-reliant.

Some of the issues which have been conceptualised and formulated by Ms Sethi have been addressed by Meera Basu and her research team on the basis of empirical evidence from selected electronic and food processing industries in Maharashtra, Karnataka and Himachal Pradesh. It has been argued in the paper that the restructuring of economy under the New Economic Policy might provide fresh economic opportunities to women, but the net result might cause their further exploitation as cheap labour.

Part II of this volume begins with an article on the changing role status of women written purely in a historical perspective by N.V. Jagannath Rao and Godavari D. Patil. The authors have contended that a flexible social structure which existed in ancient period became rigid in the medieval period. The women who once enjoyed freedom and equality were subjected to a subordinate status following the development of various evil practices. They are made subordinate and dependent on men. Women's age-old inferior social position tended to change for better only with the efforts of social reformers of the 19th Century. Certain legislations passed during the post-independent period also helped women improve their social images. Now more and more women are consequently able to enter into different walks of life and are in a better position to claim equality with them.

R.N. Nandi has offered a very thorough discussion on matrilineal rights in early South Indian society, and has contended that the matriarchal character of the old Dravidian family was substantially compromised under the influence of Brahmin-dominated partriarchal culture. In this study he has tried to establish that despite the heavy influence of partriarchal culture, the vestiges of matriarchy remained in the familial system of the peninsular region. This paper has given enough clue to the reason why the position of women in South has been superior to that in North India.

Awadh Kishore Singh has offered a vivid description of the rise and development of the *Devadasi* system in South India. According to the author, the system of nautch girls developed from the ritual dancing which was prevalent in the peninsular region in the early century of the Christian era. In the course of time temples developed as very rich institutions with a large of body staff consisting of priests, accountants and dancing girls. The association of nautch girls with temples attracted gradually more and more people and wealth which led to various kinds of degenerate practices in and around temples. Some serious efforts were made to weed out the evil practice of the *Devadasi* system in the beginning of this century, but the remnants of this system are still noticeable in adjoining parts of Karnataka and Maharashtra.

In this volume four papers have been based on the analysis of published books of either religious or literary nature. The paper of J.S. Grewal is based on the *Adi Granth* of the Sikhs. In this paper the author has given a scholarly account of the system of patriarchy among the Sikhs based on their religious treatise, following a historical perspective. Papers by Mridula Garg, Ravindra Rajhans and S.N. Prasad, on the other hand, are based on purely literary works in Hindi and English literature.

In her paper entitled the metaphors of womanhood in Indian literature Mridula Garg has opined that authors in most Indian literature have portrayed very partial images of the Indian woman. Most of the early literatures mainly dealt with traditional images of woman, but with the lapse of time the writers' theme, though gradually, underwent change. The situation changed somewhat more drastically form 1950 onwards with the advent of feminism in the field of literature. Despite this most contemporary literatures generally cover the problems of middle class women and rarely the problems of the poor rural women. But at the same time a small number of literary works have appeared very lately wherein women have been portrayed as thinking beings with a distinct world view and not just as victims, supporters or avengers of men or as sources of inspiration for them.

Ravindra Rajhans has examined how during the last hundred years the attitude of Hindi writers towards female characters have gradually changed from idealistic to realistic treatment. The women in the contemporary fictions appear to be more conscious of their rights and clamour for equality with men in all walks of life. The search of self-identity shows great departures from their traditional image which had a halo of divinity around them. They now strongly desire to be treated just as human beings. This is clear reflection of the changing value system of the Indian society.

Based on certain English fiction S.N. Prasad has offered a detailed discussion on the rise of women against the tradition-bound, male dominated society in India and the West in a comparative fashion. In author's opinion it is the woman endowed with greater sensitiveness than man, who is more intensely aware of the malaise in all man-woman relationships. Indeed, she need not waste away her womanliness for nurturing the feminist movement. Ultimately every woman, in the East or the West, or anywhere else for that matter, is more precious than the movement known as feminism.

Sangeet Kumar and Dilip Kumar Singh in collaboration with J.P. Singh have collated latest available data on women from various published sources. On the basis of these data one can readily. understand the existing realities about the position of women objectively and can plan further research. The book ends with comprehensive bibliographical survey of the relevant literature by Prabhash Kumar Singh. Experts interested in women's studies would find it highly useful in pursuit of their research. Entries have been made in an alphabetical order so that both generalists and specialists can easily find out the reference of their choice. Lastly, I must add that since there are different authors with varying ideological foundations, subject biases might have crept into this book. As an editor I have made no effort to twist facts to suit my ideological stance.

At the end of the thematic summary of this volume, let me quote certain thought-provoking observations of Swami

Vivekananda, a social-philosopher of modern India: "There is no chance for the welfare of the world unless the condition of women is improved. It is not possible for a bird to fly only one wind.... Women must be in a position to solve their problems in their own way. No one can or ought to do this for them. And our Indian women are as capable of doing it as any in the world".

This book is a somewhat new venture in cross-disciplinary studies of the Indian woman. As far as possible each contributor has offered an original account of the current dialogue on the subject covered, giving sufficient empirical or historical depth. This volume will have achieved its purpose, if it provokes the students and researchers alike to engage in serious and concerned reflection upon the Indian woman.

I am deeply grateful to all the contributors of this volume. I am no less indebted to those who took interest in the collaborative exercise but whose papers could not be included in this volume. I beg apology to all such collaborators. I must express a deep sense of gratitude to late R.C. Prasad, former Professor and Head of the Department of English at the Patna University who always encouraged and inspired me to edit this volume. His untimely death in 1993 has deprived me of his final guidance in the completion of this work. Therefore, this book is a special homage to the memory of late Professor R.C. Prasad.

A word of special appreciation is due to Ms. Shruti Shukla, a senior journalist of the Hindustan Times, Patna and Ravindra Rajhans, Professor of English at College of Commerce (M.U.), Patna for their extensive help in the preparation of the manuscript and proof- reading. Finally, as the editor of this book I hold myself personally responsible for the shortcomings of this volume and not those who have assisted me in their various capacities.

Patna J.P. SINGH

[illegible] Western [illegible] superior modern India. "There is no chance for the welfare of the world unless the condition of women is improved. It is not possible for a bird to fly on only one wing. ... Women must be put in a position to solve their own problems in their own way. No one can or ought to do this for them. And our Indian women are as capable of doing it as any in the world."

This book is a somewhat new venture in cross-disciplinary studies. [illegible] As far as possible, each contributor has offered an original account of the current discourse on the subject covered, [illegible] depth. This volume will have achieved its purpose if it provokes the students and readers to engage in serious and concerned reflection upon the Indian woman.

I am deeply grateful to all the contributors of this volume. I am also grateful to those who took interest in the whole exercise but whose papers could not be included in this volume. I tender apology to all such scholars. I must express a deep sense of gratitude to late K.C. Prasad, former Professor and Head of the Department of English at the Patna University, who always encouraged and inspired me to edit this volume. His untimely death in 1993 has deprived me of his final guidance for completion of this work. Therefore, this book is a special homage to the memory of late Professor K.C. Prasad.

A word of special appreciation is due to Ms Shruti Singh, a senior journalist of the Hindustan Times, Patna and Ravindra Kumar, Professor of English at College of Commerce (M.U.), Patna for their extensive help in the preparation of the manuscript and proof-reading. Finally, as the editor of this book I hold myself personally responsible for the shortcomings of this volume and not those who have assisted me in their various capacities.

Patna J.P. SINGH

Contents

PART—I

SOCIAL, ECONOMIC AND DEMOGRAPHIC PROFILE

1

"With All of Us Together, There is Hope"

Profiles of Five Women Activists

*Clarice A. Auluck-Wilson**

The purpose of this chapter is to profile five women who have been instrumental in the growth and development of a remarkable grassroots women's organisation, the Samaj Vikas Mahila Mandal,[1] which is located in the village of Peth in the State of Maharashtra. It is my hope that an examination of the highlights of these women's life stories and of their current situations will contribute to an understanding of how and why they have become such capable and confident leaders and that this understanding, in turn, will prove helpful to those committed to the development of grassroots women's organisations.

My husband, Arvind Kumar Auluck-Wilson, a native of Maharashtra, and I, a citizen of the United States, have had the privilege of serving as consultants to the Samaj Vikas Mahila Mandal since October, 1989. We moved to Peth at this time at the request of several women friends who lived in the village. They were interested in organising a strong Mahila Mandal and they asked for our help in doing so. My husband and I agreed to move to the village for six months on the condition that we would serve as facilitators of the development of the Samaj Vikas Mahila Mandal, but that the agenda we would facilitate would have to be the women's own. We agreed

* The author is at the University of Minnesota, 757 Raymond Avenue, Suite 316, Saint Paul, Minnesota 55114, U.S.A.

to help the women organise, but insisted that they set their own priorities and make their own plans. Our job would be to help the women take action on these priorities, to help them put these plans into effect. Together with the women of the Samaj Vikas Mahila Mandal, we undertook a feminist participatory research project,[2] the documentation and analysis of which was to become the basis for my Ph. D. thesis, *"When All the Women Lift, the Mountain Will Move": Case Study of a Grassroots Women's Organisation in Rural Maharashtra, India"*.

This title came from a letter I received in October, 1990, from the Samaj Vikas Mahila Mandal. I had received many communications from the members of this organisation since I had left their village to return to my home in the United States. But this letter was special. It was the members' evaluation of the first year of our collaborative research project. The women wrote of the difficulties they had faced, many of which they had been able to overcome; of the concrete services they had brought to their village; of the confidence and capacities they had gained in the process; of the acceptance and respect their organisation had earned in the community; of the many positive changes they had been able to bring about in their lives and those of their family members; and of their hopeful vision of the future. In large letters across the top of the first page they had written: "When All the Women Lift, the Mountain Will Move".[3]

When Arvind and I returned to India in January, 1991, to stay in Peth for six more weeks and once again interact with the members of the Samaj Vikas Mahila Mandal, I asked them to tell me more about the "mountain" they were so confident they could lift by working together. I received a variety of responses, but they all focused on the oppressions that these women have experienced because they are poor and female, and in some cases, because they are also members of one of the Scheduled Castes. In the words of one member of the organisation:

> This mountain of poverty, this mountain of never-ending work, this mountain of violence, of despair. It weights me down and bows my back, so I can't even see the sky...I've struggled against it all my life. Alone, it's far too heavy to move ...But together? With all of us together, there is hope.

The catalyst for the hope-filled beginnings of activism in the Samaj Vikas Mahila Mandal was, unexpectedly, a tragic event. The dowry related torture and murder of a young woman, Ranjana-bai, who had been married into the village just four months before her death. Arvind and I happened to be visiting friends in Peth on the day that Ranjana-bai's body was found in the well. That evening we were asked to join the meeting 20 local women had called among themselves to discuss the murder. At first there was only silence. A sense of shock pervaded the room. No one knew what to say. Then, just as the women began to open up and speak about Ranjana-bai's death, one woman's husband walked in, sat in the back, and said, "You can't talk about this murder. It's still a police matter and if the police think you know something, they' ll make you testify. They'll take you away, too".[4] We all sat in silence for several minutes. Finally, one women spoke, expressing what many later said they had wanted to say, but had not been able to put into words:

> The police can come take me away if they want to; but I won't be quiet. I have something to say and I'am going to say it...We can't bring Ranjana-bai back to life. It's too late to save her. But it's not too late to save ourselves... Ranjana-bai had been in Peth for four months and none of us knew she had such troubles. If we'd known, we could have helped her. If she'd had a place to come for help, she might be sitting with us now. If we'd been united, we could have helped her. But we weren't united, so it's too late for Ranjana-bai. But it's not too late for the rest of us. There may be other women who are being tortured; but how can we know if we're not united?...We must work together to protect ourselves. Women are not garbage to be used and thrown away. We are human beings. We have rights...We must be strong and united...We must build a strong Mahila Mandal. If we don't, things will remain the same, and someday we may be the ones pulled from the well.

Ranjana-bai's murder brought the wide range of vulnerabilities and resultant fears many women in Peth live with daily into sharp focus. As a result, the women present at this seminal meeting agreed that they needed to take action to create a more secure environment for women. They decided that the most effective way to accomplish this would be to establish a strong women's organisation. Instead of being immobilised by the shock of this dowry-related murder, these women used it as a focal point for mobilisation of collective strength.

As the women began to organise for action, they identified four major issues they felt demanded immediate attention: violence against women; lack of access to healthcare for the entire community; limited opportunities for education for girls and women; and women's relative lack of political power. Due to their commitment, hard work, courage and vision, the 114 members of the Samaj Vikas Mahila Mandal have made remarkable progress in a relatively short time toward addressing these four priorities. For example, coping with violence against women led to the members' creation of a women's centre in February, 1991, a place of safety and retreat where any woman from Peth or the surrounding areas can take shelter in times of crisis. It also led to a system of domestic crisis intervention in which Mahila Mandal members go the home where abuse is under way to publicly confront the abuser(s) and to protect the victim(s). Recognising the link between alcohol abuse by men and violence against women in the village, the members persuaded the main local seller of illicit liquor to close down his business in March, 1990. Concern for provision of healthcare led members to approach the director of a private hospital in Pune, which is within 30 kilometres of Peth, for support. As a result, the Mahila Mandal has been to sponsor day-long medical camps or clinics in the village quarterly since the first one in December, 1989. Doctors from the hospital approached volunteer their time, offering medical care free of cost to everyone in the area. Addressing the limited opportunities for education of girls and women, the Mahila Mandal opened its own high school for girls in June, 1990, with plans for adjunct literacy and technical classes for women. The organisation also opened a pre-school in February, 1991—to encourage early childhood education and to free mother's time for educational and economic activities—and plans are under way for the addition of infant care. Finally, attention to women's relative lack of political power has led to the Mahila Mandal's involvement in local politics and plans to back an all-women panel for the upcoming Gram Panchayat election.

In order to even begin to transform their village and their lives, the women of the Samaj Vikas Mahila Mandal have had to grapple with tremendous difficulties created, in part, by the organisation's lack of material resources; the problems members experience trying to find adequate time to meet due to their heavy workload at home and in the fields; an insufficient number of members with literacy skills combined with the large amount of paperwork required for the organisation to qualify for government assistance; opposition of some family members to women's participation in activities outside the home or the fields; and caste-based divisions within the organisation.

Many factors have contributed to the ability of the members of the Samaj Vikas Mahila Mandal to work collectively to overcome these difficulties. But one of the most important has been the exceptional leadership provided by the five women profiled in this chapter. Each has made her own unique contributions to the Mahila Mandal that have strengthened the organisation and facilitated the extraordinary achievements of its members. Examining the common elements in these women's backgrounds and in their present situations helps explain what has made these contributions possible.

Each profile begins with the women's own words describing herself, self-introductions prepared specifically for inclusion in the text of my Ph.D. dissertation during my visit to Peth in early 1991. I then describe each woman's current situation in the village and outline her life story, often using her own words. I have taped extensive life stories of each woman in this chapter, but have included only limited selections here due to constraints of space. I have consulted with the five women profiled and we have worked together to chose the selections included.

Mahadevi-bai

Mahadevi-bai introduces herself:

> Tell the people in America that I am a woman with dignity. Tell them that I hold my head high. I live my life honestly. Every *paisa* [one hundredth of a *rupee,* the basic unit of Indian currency] I borrow, I pay back—with interest. I owe no one. No one has a claim on me. If I had to leave my home today, I could choose to go to any one of a hundred villages. I'm well known in this area and well trusted. I'll never go hungry. The people in a hundred villages know me and respect me and will shelter me anytime. But no, I won't leave. The birds come and go over the river each season, but I remain. This is my home.

> These fields are a part of me. I love them as a mother loves her children. Tell the people in America that I am a farmer who nurtures these fields that are her children. Tell them that I cannot write my story, so I give it to you [Clarice] to write. I cannot write, but the sunlight and the moonlight of Peth are a part of me and in my words, I send this light to America to illumine the stories of the women who live here. Oh, and also tell them that if they come to Peth, we'll play *fugady* [a boisterous traditional game] and I'll win!

Mahadevi-bai is the individual perhaps most responsible for our move to Peth. Long before Ranjana-bai's murder, Mahadevi-bai tried persuasively to convince Arvind and me to move to the village and study the lives of the women there. She was very persistent, confident that we would come eventually; she is a woman long accustomed to succeeding in whatever task she undertakes. She is strong and forthright, very bold in both what she says and the way she says it. She is highly respected in Peth and the surrounding areas.

Mahadevi-bai is a Maratha, a member of Peth's dominant caste. She is currently a member of the Gram Panchayat [the elected village-level administrative body of nine] and has been for the past eight years. However, she has only recently begun to take an active role in its deliberations—since becoming involved in the Samaj Vikas Mahila Mandal. Mahadevi-bai is also one of the three presidents of the Samaj Vikas Mahila Mandal,[5] something she tells long before she mentions her position on the Gram Panchayat. She is proud of the women's organisation, its accomplishments and her role in its activation, and these subjects are often the focus of her conversation. She is over 60, with pure white hair, a ready smile, no teeth and an out–rageous sense of humour. Mahadevi-bai exudes self-confidence and, unlike most other women in the village, she comes and goes to Pune and neighboring areas completely on her own. When asked how she manages to travel so freely when most women in the area are either hesitant to do so or are not allowed to do so by family members, Mahadevi-bai responded:

> I earned my freedom to come and go as I like when I was young. For years I was a slave in my husband's house—and he was the master. I was beaten, degraded, spat upon, starved... I was so thin that when people came to

> visit from Peth and saw my wretched condition, they were shocked. I'd been beautiful, but not any more. They hardly recognised me. They would hide a quarter of a *bhakri* [unleavened bread made out of millet or sorghum flour] under their plate so I would find it when I cleared the dishes—and would have at least something to eat. But then the problem was-when could I eat it? I would hide it in my *sari* and wait until I went to wash dishes outside the house...When I left my husband and his family and returned to Peth, I vowed I would never be a slave again....So now I am a free woman. I go where I like, when I like, and no one has a right to question me.

Raised in Peth, Mahadevi-bai was married at the age of 11 to a boy seven years her senior with whom she had grown up in the village. The boy and his family, however, had moved to Bombay, and Mahadevi-bai joined them there immediately after the wedding. At 11, she was already accustomed to hard work. She had been working in her parent's fields since she was eight and when she was even younger, she had been forced to drop out of first grade after only a few months of classes in order to take care of younger siblings and cousins. But she had never known the amount of work demanded of her in her in-laws' home:

> From the time I got up in the morning—at four o'clock—until the time I nearly collapsed late each night, I worked constantly. And I worked hard, but I never got all the work done and my mother-in-law was never satisfied. As time went by I got weaker and weaker and couldn't do as much work as before because I never had enough rest or enough food. Then the beatings got worse. Then I couldn't work because of the beatings, which was justification for even more mistreatment.

Badly abused by both her husband and her mother-in-law for five years, Mahadevi-bai resolved when she was 16 to start her own business selling vegetables door-to-door. She felt that if she became a wage earner and contributed directly to the family income that she could create a more secure place for herself in her in-laws' family. The business was successful and Mahadevi-bai continued it for six years, until she returned to Peth to care for her ageing parents. Gradually, Mahadevi-bai's situation in her husband's family improved, but her relationship with her husband remained difficult. Before her menstrual cycle even began, her husband had started seeing other women. Consequently, her marriage was never consummated:

> I was such a little girl when I moved to my husband's house. I was at the age when I should have been carefree—laughing and playing and running about...Instead, I was working endlessly, always tired, exhausted. So my body never really grew as it should have and my time of the month came very late—I was nearly fifteen...In the early years of my marriage, I wasn't ready to be with my husband and my mother-in-law was very strict those first few years that he not come near me at night. But then even my mother-in-law became impatient when I'd been in the house so many years and my time still hadn't come...But I don't think it really would have mattered if my time had come earlier, because my husband had already been with other women. He was often gone nights and he bragged about his time with other women...My mother-in-law blamed me because my husband couldn't be with me at night. But I knew that it wouldn't have mattered. The only change would have been that he would have been with me *and* with other women. It's a blessing that didn't happen. At least I didn't have to suffer that humiliation...Since I left him, he's "married" over 20 other women and lived with them. But he soon leaves them. He doesn't know how to be faithful. He wanders from one women to the next even now that he's in his seventies.

When she was 22 Mahadevi-bai's parents began to have health problems and they asked her to come home to Peth to care for them. Her father was losing his sight and her mother suffered from a degenerative disease that led to bouts of senility. Mahadevi-bai took care of their needs for the next 20 years, until they died, and she never returned to her husband's house in Bombay:

> I don't miss my in-laws' home. Never. Why would I ? Who would miss being abused and mistreated ?...But I do miss Bombay. I loved the days there when I had my business and so many people knew me and depended on

me. Everyone in the neighbourhood knew me and respected me. I'd deliver vegetables to the fancy apartments on the fifth or sixth floor—claiming all those stairs—and when I'd knock on the door, sometimes the women of the house would say, "Oh, Mahadevi-bai you've come.

You must be tired. Sit down. Have a cup of tea. Tell us what the news is today." These women loved to hear the news, to hear about what people were talking about in the streets...They had money and fancy apartments and silk *sarees* and every nice thing you could want, but they didn't have freedom like I did. I came and went freely and they were always curious what was happening in the outside world.

But then when I came back to Peth, I remembered that my mother had also suffered like I had when she was very young. She was only eleven when she was married, too, and her husband's mother had already died. So she was in charge of the household—at eleven! Then her husband's brothers married and do you know how old their wives were ? One was nine, and the other, hardly seven. So at eleven my mother was as good as a mother-in-law to these younger girls. And my mother's father-in-law was a very tough person. He made life very hard for her. My mother had no experience running a household, but she took on all that responsibility...As soon as my father and mother could build a house of their own, they did. And then my mother had some good years. But she had suffered so much already—just like I had at my in-laws' house. I thought, "Why should she suffer now as well? I'll serve her now as she served me when I was a child, and I'll make her last years happy."...

I learned so much from serving my parents. That was my real education. I learned so much from spending time with my mother. Most women who live our Marathi way of life only get to see their mothers for a few days now and then once they've grown and married and moved away...I'am so grateful that I got to spend so much time with my mother. She was my teacher, my inspiration...She

> was such a remarkable person. And she was strong. She taught me how to endure... Now, in my old age, I'm sustained by memories of my mother's strength and my parents' good wishes are supporting me.

Mahadevi-bai still lives in the house her parents built when they separated from the extended family. She heads a household consisting of two younger brothers—one who is a practising alcoholic whose wife has left him, and the other who is mildly mentally retarded; an eleven-year old niece named Manda whose mother died in childbirth and whom Mahadevi-bai has raised as if she were her own daughter; and a nephew, his wife and their infant son. Mahadevi-bai's oldest brother lives in Pune and seldom visits the village. Mahadevi-bai has three sisters who live in neighbouring villages with whom she keeps close contact. The family owns several acres of prime farmland, but can no longer make enough money farming it to live solely off the profits. As a result, the brothers have begun to sell it off in parcels to industrialists wanting to build factories in the area.

The brothers sold their first parcel of land during the first few weeks Arvind and I lived in Peth. Once all the papers had been signed and all of the financial transactions completed, the three brothers refused to give Mahadevi-bai and her sisters their rightful shares of the profits as they had earlier promised. At first, hurt and saddened by her brothers' betrayal, Mahadevi-bai felt she could do nothing to change their minds. She sat for hours in our room, recounting all she had done for her brothers over the years only to be repaid in this way.

But gradually she began to get angry and eventually, due to great extent to the moral support she received from the Samaj Vikas Mahila Mandal, she decided to take decisive action. She went on strike. She refused to cook or clean or gather fuel wood. She did go to the fields, because she is the one who sells the crops and distributes the income among the family members. But she made it clear that there would be no distribution of income until she and her sisters received their fair share of the profits from the land sale. Her brothers were forced to recognise the great amount of work that Mahadevi-bai had always done for them and that they had hitherto taken for granted. They also had to confront the very real possibility of being cut off from the profits from the fields.

After two months the brothers capitulated, but only after Mahadevi-bai threatened to take them to court. Her brothers knew that Mahadevi-bai was serious about this threat. They knew that she was familiar with the workings of the court since she had sued her husband for alimony long ago and had returned to the court whenever he had not paid it on time. They also knew that Mahadevi-bai had access to the free legal aid now offered through the Mahila Mandal. After receiving her rightful share from the land sale, Mahadevi-bai began cooking, cleaning and gathering fuel wood again, in addition to her farming work. But she did it with a new spirit, knowing that she could walk out on this work anytime and that she would not be the one who would suffer if she did.

Mahadevi-bai learned how to write her name for the first time in my apartment in Pune, before I moved to Peth. I had shown her a picture of my mother in a graduation cap and gown, explaining that she had gone back to school after raising her children and had received her college degree when she was 50. Mahadevi-bai had responded, "If it wasn't too late for your mother, then it's not too late for me," and had asked for a pencil and a sheet of paper. She glows with pride now when she tells people that she no longer has to rely on her thumb print to validate Gram Panchayat or Mahila Mandal documents. Now she can sign her name herself. She can neither read nor write—beyond her name—but is eager to learn to do both. Whenever the Samaj Vikas Mahila Mandal lists its priorities, Mahadevi-bai is the first to speak and her priority is always the same—adult literacy education for women:

> I tell people I want to learn how to read and write and they laugh at me. They say,"Old woman, what use is reading and writing at this point in your life. Go back to making *bhakri*." But I don't listen to them....They say I'm crazy to want to learn how to read and write because they already know how and they take it for granted. They don't know what it's like to go to Pune and not be able to read the street signs or the bus signs. They don't know how helpless it makes me feel that I always have to ask someone where I am or what bus to take...There is power in knowing how to read. And I want that power.

Mahadevi-bai is, above all, a farmer. She regularly spends ten to twelve hours a day in the fields planting, weeding and harvesting.

The only thing she does not do is the plowing, which is considered men's work. Her main crop is flowers for the Bombay market, but she also grows staple grains and a variety of vegetables for family consumption. She is respected for her knowledge of farming and others—often men—come to her for advice when they are having agricultural problems. She hopes to have a nursery of her own some day where she can make a living grafting fruit trees. In the meantime, she is the manager of the 10,000-tree nursery that the Samaj Vikas Mahila Mandal has started as part of its reforestation effort.

Mahadevi-bai was one of the first women from Peth to become active in the series of day-long retreats or *shivirs* held for rural women in Pune, and she was one of the women at the meeting after Ranjana-bai's death who asked Arvind and me to move to the village. She has played a key role in the beginnings of activism in the Samaj Vikas Mahila Mandal. She is one of the most innovative members of the organisation, often offering new ways of approaching difficult problems. Because she is also one of the oldest members of the organisation—in a society where age is respected—she has frequently been the one to help others see the value of breaking with restrictive traditions. When I asked Mahadevi-bai how she came to be so open-minded, she laughed:

> At this point in my life, what else can I be? The world around me is changing so fast that if I don't change, too, I'll get left behind or run over!...When I was young, the only vehicles we had in the village were bullock carts—slow and easy. You could see them coming a half hour away. Now trucks race through on the main road. They appear out of nowhere and before you know it, they're gone. Now if I were to stand in the middle of that road thinking like we used to when we only had bullock carts, what would happen? The trucks would probably run right over me...Well, I'm not one to let much of anything run over me...I figure the trucks aren't going to change. They're going to keep on coming. So that means it's my thinking that has to change, right?...And besides, what do I have to lose by listening to new ideas? Nothing. And what do I have to gain? Who knows? Maybe something. So I'am willing to try most anything. And why not? Life isn't predictable. Who could have known that I'd leave my husband and return to Peth? Who could have known

that Manda's mother would die and I'd become like a mother to her? Who could have known that you [Clarice] and Arvind would come to the village? Life is full of change...

Should I let everything around me change and cling to the old ways just because I'am old, so they're what I know best? Maybe someone else knows a better way...I'm the biggest fool of all if I think I know the best way to do everything...I used to think I knew everything. Now I know I have so much more to learn

Saraswati-bai

Saraswati-bai introduces herself:

How can I tell people who have never met me who I am? How can I tell those who have never stood at the well near the river at dawn—watching the sunrise and listening to the birds and smelling the smoke from the morning cooking fires—what my life is like? Perhaps I'll start with the things we may have in common.

I'am a married woman—a happily married woman. My husband is good and kind. He never beats me. He doesn't drink. He helps me when I have too much to do. He works hard for our family. He appreciates the Mahila Mandal. I'am proud to be his wife. I'm a mother. I have a four-year-old daughter, Savita-bai, and a one-year-old son, Kailash. My children are a blessing and a joy.

I'm a daughter-in-law. I love my in-laws very much and it's an honour to serve them. My father and mother are both gone now. I never had a chance to serve them in their old age. I'am grateful that I can at least serve my husband's parents.

I'm a member of the Samaj Vikas Mahila Mandal. This is very important for me. When I first came to this village, I didn't have much hope that things would ever change. I'd lived in the city, and I'd never lived in such poverty and in a place where there is so much backwardness. I didn't know any other women outside this area of this village, except for a few women I'd met at the factory. I

> didn't do much other than work and eat and sleep. But now I have hope. The Samaj Vikas Mahila Mandal gives me great hope. Our work together gives me hope that my children will have a better life.
>
> I am one of the secretaries of the Samaj Vikas Mahila Mandal, although even I have trouble reading my writing because I'm so out of practice. I'm now teaching in the Mahila Mandal's pre-school and I like it very much. I wanted to be a teacher when I was young, but I never though I'd be able to be one after I had to quite school after third grade. But I'm a good teacher. I'm good with children. I like them and they like me.
>
> That's about all I can say about myself now. My life is really very simple. It's full of hard work and love.

Saraswati-bai has a graceful, polished presence. She speaks deliberately and thoughtfully when making an important point. Although she is only 24 years old, she speaks with the voice of experience. Born on the edge of Pune, she wears a city-style six-yard "circle" *sari,* unlike the traditional nine-yard sarees worn by most of the women in the village, and this sets her apart.

Saraswati-bai is a Buddhist, a member of the Mahar caste, which is one of the Scheduled Castes. She lives in the Buddhist community on the southeastern fringe of the village. But she spent most of her childhood on an Air Force base just outside Pune where her parents were servants in the homes of Air Force officers. She remembers very little about her mother, who died when Saraswati-bai was five. But she remembers very clearly how difficult her life became once her mother was gone:

> My five brothers and my sister were much older than I and most of them were married by the time my mother died. My father often worked at night, so I started moving from one brother's house to the next. I'd stay as long as they'd let me, then find another place to stay. They'd let me stay as long as I was useful...
>
> Once when my second brother's wife was pregnant, he asked me to stay with them, and I worked so hard. My brother's wife had a difficult time her last two months and I was the only one around to take care of her... I had

> to take care of everything. I was barely seven years old at the time. Once the baby came, I looked after him, too...I remember that no one had ever taught me anything about cooking. But somehow or other, I managed to cook something edible...
>
> Another brother lived right next door with his wife and family and they knew how much trouble I was having, but they never once came forward to offer any help...
>
> After my second brother's wife recovered, instead of being appreciative of all the work I'd done for her, she started fighting with me. So I had to move again...
>
> Then once my father and I were both living with another brother because his wife was pregnant for the first time and she needed help. After the baby came, I did all the housework—the washing and cleaning and cooking—and then I had to go to the officers' houses and do the same kind of work, too, for pay. Then I would come home and stay up half the night protecting the baby because my brother had started drinking heavily and he kept threatening to harm the baby because it was a girl... My brother's wife died when the baby was just four or five months old...My brother eventually stopped drinking and he married again and his new wife threw my father and me out of the house, so again we had to go looking for a place to stay.

Saraswati-bai managed to stay in school until she had finished third grade, washing dishes in several officers' homes before and after school to supplement the family income. But when she was eight, she had to drop out of school to move to Bombay to take care of her elder sister's children. Her sister became ill soon after Saraswati-bai arrived and never recovered. The responsibility of caring for her sister as well as for her sister's children fell upon Saraswati-bai until her sister died nearly two years later. When her sister's husband remarried, Saraswati-bai returned to live with her father at the Air Force base near Pune. She was ten at the time. She began working for a family who made a significant impact on her life:

> This family, the Nagars, was from Punjab. I looked after their children and helped in the kitchen. I worked for them for seven years, from the time I was ten until I

married... They were such good, kind people and they treated me as if I were part of the family. Mrs. Nagar was like a mother to me. I never had to work as hard for Mrs. Nagar as I did for all my sisters-in-law! When she knew I was tired, she made me rest. And she always made sure that I ate what the rest of the family ate...Mrs. Nagar taught me the importance of cleanliness and good manners and self-respect. She taught me how to dress correctly and fix my hair so that I looked well-kept and orderly. She taught me so many things...She was an English teacher and she tried to get me to learn English, but I would never have any time back at home to study because I always had so much work still to do at home once I had finished at the Nagars ...I would say, "I left school so long ago that my mind doesn't work any more, "and then she would say," Never stop trying to learn. You're never too old to learn." I'll always remember that...

The sweetest time of my life was when the Nagars moved back to Punjab and they took me with then. I stayed there for four months and I loved it. There was so much affection in the house. Everyone in Mrs. Nagar's family liked me and praised my cooking. They even taught me how to make Punjabi food! Asha was my name before I married[6] and Mrs. Nagar's family would say," Asha, why don't you just stay with us forever? Since you've come to our house, we're all so comfortable and happy. You've settled in, too, and we feel as if you're one of our family." I never once thought of coming back to Pune the whole time I was in Punjab because the people were so lovely there and all I had back home was brothers who were selfish and sisters-in-law who used to harass me...

But my father worried about me while I was gone and he decided to arrange my marriage. My uncle and my father-in-law took care of all the details and my father never even met the man they'd arranged for me to marry, or his family...Then soon after my marriage, my father came to visit me here. He found the house so small and dirty and everything in it so inadequate—not even a glass for drinking water...He was shocked by what he saw. It made a serious impact on him and finally he died with the worry that he had ruined my life. After my father died, his best friend told me something—that my father had come to him after visiting me here and had wept and wept, saying, "I've ruined my daughter's life."...

I wish my father could see the house now. It's just as small, but it's clean and neat...When I first came to this house, I nearly burst into tears. The house was so filthy. Everything was spread all over the room. The utensils were unwashed—they just kept eating off them like that. And my God! The stench! No one had taken a bath for at least a week. I felt like vomiting. Somehow or other I managed to change things, bit by bit. First I made them take a bath every day. And I taught them the importance of cleanliness. But it took me nearly a year to improve the situation...But once everything was in order, everyone started praising my efforts and I felt good that I'd been able to make these changes.

Saraswati-bai now lives with her husband, their two children, her parents-in-law and two sisters-in-law, one of whom has recently been sent back for good to her parents' home by her husband of just six months. They all live in one room that is so small that it is difficult to maneuver around the family's only piece of furniture, a metal-framed single bed. They own a small parcel of unproductive farmland and financially, the family has trouble making both ends meet. When Saraswati-bai first moved to Peth, she worked in the small aluminium utensil factory in the village and this helped the family income. But she finally quit when she miscarried. She is convinced that the chemicals used in the factory led to her miscarriage. She describes coming home every day with her hands and arms inflamed from the acids in which she was required to dip the utensils to polish them. Until recently, the factory supplied no gloves or other protective equipment to its employees.

Saraswati-bai says that after the difficult time during her adjustment to Peth the first year after her marriage, the only other major problem occurred when her first child was born—a girl:

I was so disappointed when I miscarried. Everyone was. My mother-in-law wanted a grandson in the family so

> badly. So she was delighted when I got pregnant again. But when Savita-bai was born and my mother-in-law found out that the she was a girl, she refused to even see her. She didn't even want to see her face. She just cursed her fortune and wailed and wept. She said, "You took so long to get pregnant, we thought you were barren. Now I wish you had been. It's better to have no child than to have a girl child..."She carried on and on like this for six days...She cursed the day I'd joined the family. She reminded my father-in-law and my husband and me repeatedly that she'd wanted her son to marry someone else—her sister's daughter—and how it would have been better if he had... Then my mother-in-law's brother came to see the baby—six days after she was born. And he got angry and said, "What's all this snivelling and whining? I was married 25 years ago and we still don't have any children. God has at least blessed you with a grandchild. So accept what God has given you and be grateful. Stop talking nonsense. This is a beautiful child."So my mother-in-law stopped cursing her fate and blaming me and with time she's come to love Savita-bai... They've become almost inseparable companions. But I wasn't completely accepted by my mother-in-law until Kailash was born and she finally had the grandson she wanted.

Saraswati-bai was one of the first Buddhist women to join the Samaj Vikas Mahila Mandal. The first meeting she attended was the one in which the members decided to ask for volunteers to fill the nine positions of the Executive Committee they had decided to form. Saraswati-bai volunteered to be one of the three secretaries, a step she was later amazed she had taken:

> I don't know where I found the courage to volunteer. Somehow, I just though it was a good idea and I raised my hand. There I was with all those women I'd never met before and I raised my hand!...I wanted to be a part of the organisation and when I heard that the Executive Committee would be trained in how to run a meeting and how to keep minutes and accounts, I thought, "This is a good way to learn more, just like Mrs. Nagar always used to tell me to do". But as soon as I'd volunteered I thought,

> "How can I be a secretary? I haven't even written anything in years." I was so worried I'd make a fool of myself... Remember when they asked me to take attendance at that meeting? My hand shook so much when I tried to write everyone's names as they said them out loud that I couldn't even read what I'd written. I finally said. "I'm afraid I can't do this well enough. I haven't written in years." And no one laughed at me. Instead, someone said, "At least you know how to write. I don't even know how to sign my name." So I felt like I should at least try to write ...And now I keep a journal every day. I write down what I've done and what I've thought. Becoming a secretary has been a very good thing for me.

Nearly three years after the meeting mentioned above, Saraswati-bai is still one of the secretaries of the Samaj Vikas Mahila Mandal. She is an excellent organiser and hers is often the voice of reason when other members of the organisation decide to take on more than they have the time or energy to accomplish. She is also one who is able to quite accurately gauge possible repercussions of different strategies when the Mahila Mandal is planning its activities; she has a very analytical mind. She has been instrumental in keeping the organisation from dividing over issues of caste. This has meant that she has been accused of being disloyal to her caste by some of her fellow Mahars, and has also been accused of trying to disrupt the traditional caste hierarchy by some members of the higher castes. But she has stood firm in the face of opposition and, over time, this has earned her considerable respect within the Mahila Mandal. When asked how she managed to develop such fortitude, she responded simply, "Strength is the reward for suffering."

Usha-bai

Usha-bai introduces herself:

> If I'd had to introduce myself a few years ago, or even last year, I wouldn't have known what to say. I was dead then, or just barely alive. I worked. I ate. I slept. That's all. The only thing that kept me going was that my mother and Sushma [her niece] depended on me. What would they do if I were gone? Who would care for them? How would they eat?

Back then, I worried every day about what people were saying about me. I know that they called me a loose woman and worse behind my back—not because I ever did anything to deserve being called such names, but because there hasn't been a man in this house since I left my husband years ago. I'd think, "What a terrible way for Sushma to grow up, to have people calling her mother—which is really what I am to her—a loose woman."

But look at me now. People treat me with respect. They come to me for advice. They listen when I speak—even important people like the Collector. The Mahila Mandal has given me new life. I never thought I'd get the chance to show the village who I really am. My husband's family has told so many lies about my character and my behaviour. Now I have the chance—and I am going to make the best of it. The Mahila Mandal has given me back my honour. So say that to the people who will read your book. Say that this woman who once had nothing now has honour and dignity.

I love to serve. It's in my bones. It makes me happy. Serving my mother and Sushma has kept me going all these years. Now I have the chance to serve others. I've tried my best as the village health worker to serve others, but I don't think I've accomplished much. But I know I've done a lot through the Mahila Mandal. Now we have a high school for girls, and medical camps, and a pre-school and a tree nursery. Peth never had these things before. And I helped make them happen. This is how the Mahila Mandal changed my life. It gave me the chance to show that I could help. This gives me hope that the Mahila Mandal can change other women's lives, too. So tell the people who read your book this, too—that I am a woman with hope for the future, a woman who only a few years ago had no cause for hope.

I've suffered a great deal in my life. And I've always wondered, "When will the time come when the suffering will end and I'll have peace of mind?" That time has finally come.

Usha-bai is a Maratha who is in her late forties. Like most of the older women in the village, she does not know exactly when she was born. She was raised in Peth for many years, although her family also lived in a nearby village for some time. Like Mahadevi-bai and Saraswati-bai, her memories of childhood are of hard work:

> I was my parents' first child. After me, my mother had seven children—two boys and five girls—and they all died. My poor mother was always exhausted from pregnancy and grief...And I remember that I was always working—washing clothes, cooking meals. But it wasn't an unhappy time... My father had a good job, so we didn't have to worry much about money, and I got to go to school through fourth grade. I really liked school. But then my mother had a child who lived—my sister—then two more girl children who lived and I took care of them all... Our school only went to fourth grade, so there wasn't really any question of more schooling. And I was happy to have sisters to play with...Our life was good until my father began to drink, and then everything began to fall apart.

Before she reached puberty, Usha-bai's parents arranged her marriage to a young man she had known since childhood whose family home was in Peth. Soon after her marriage, part of the family moved to Bombay to start a wholesale onion business and Usha-bai and her husband joined them there:

> Bombay was so big and exciting after growing up in a village. There was always something new to see, something new to talk about. At first I was frightened by all the new sights and sounds—I couldn't even sleep at night... But then I got used to all the new things and really began to like the city life. I especially liked all the markets with all the pretty things. I never had any money to buy them, but at least I could look. And two or three times I even saw a movie in a theatre... Life in Bombay was nothing like life in Peth.

Usha-bai recalls that her relationship with her husband and her in-laws was good in the beginning, but that it became increasingly difficult with time:

> When we first married, my husband was good man and he was kind to me. Affection grew between us....My in-laws

were good to me when I first married. I had to work hard in my in-laws' house, but no harder than I'd worked at my parents'...I don't remember how old I was when I married, but it was before I'd reached puberty...We didn't have dowry then—we had a bride price. And my father-in-law gave my father quite a lot of money when I married. I somehow remember that it was a few thousand *rupees* and back then, that was a huge amount of money. I remember I was very proud that the bride price was so high. I felt so important. I felt special that someone had given so much just to marry me...

After a few years or so, I got pregnant and I came to my mother's home to deliver...The delivery went fine and I bore a daughter who seemed healthy...Then suddenly, when she was just two months old, the baby got a high fever. There weren't any paved road or trucks going by at that time. My parents went to my in-laws' family and begged my brother-in-law to take the baby to the doctor. But he said he didn't have any time and he went away... I think things would have been different if the baby had been a boy...Three days later, the baby died and a few weeks later, I returned to Bombay...

My husband was very kind to me after the baby died. But he'd changed somehow during the four or five months I'd been at my mother's home for the delivery. He'd started drinking and using drugs and gambling. He'd fallen in with the wrong crowd.. Once he gambled away all the money he was supposed to use to buy a shipment of onions and the whole family was furious with him; but I was the one they really yelled at. They said, "Can't you even keep your husband home and out of trouble?"..Then he got all wrapped up with moneylenders and men began to come late at night, banging on our door demanding payments. I began to always be afraid.

Then I got pregnant again and this time I had a healthy son. I thought this would make my husband so happy that he'd forget all of the bad ways he'd taken up. But one night he came home and said, "I want to marry again. I want a second wife." I was so upset that I took my son and came back to my parents' house here in Peth...My father was angry that I'd come home. He was drinking a lot then and always arguing...He said, "How can you come to your parents' house when your in-laws live here in the same village. What will people think? Why do you want to bring shame to your parents' home? You should go stay with them." So he made me go to my in-laws' house...

My mother-in-law tried to pressurise me to tell my husband that he could marry again. And my father-in-law did the same... They told me that my husband had wanted to marry this girl—his cousin—long before he'd married me. But his parents had said no because the girl's father wouldn't help them in the onion business. Now he was ready to help them, so all of my in-laws wanted my husband to marry again...What could I do? I was being pressed from all sides. My father-in-law said, "If you say yes, he'll marry her. If you say no, he'll marry her. So say yes and keep peace in the family, instead of saying no and making everyone miserable. Suppose he marries her and she stays with you in Bombay. What's the harm? At least she'll cook your meals on time." I said, "If he marries and she becomes his wife, then who will I be?" But everyone said, "Don't worry. You will always be his first wife." In the end, I said, "Go ahead, marry her."...

My husband left for Bombay to marry her. But when he arrived, he found she'd married someone else a few days earlier. He was devastated...Then everyone began to blame me because I'd taken so long to say yes, and now my husband couldn't marry into this family that had promised to help in the business. That was the beginning of bitter relations between us...

At some point, when my son was about a year old, my husband started to go crazy. I don't know how it started or why. Maybe it was too many drugs...He would start talking to himself and lose his temper and forget all about the business...Then he started to beat me. When he was clear-headed, he'd say, "I'am so sorry. I don't know why I acted like that." Then I'd hope that he'd recover; but he

> didn't...This went on for a long time. He'd beat me, then say he was sorry, and I'd think he was going to recover; but he never did.
>
> My in-laws kept telling him that my father and I were doing something to make him crazy. I don't know why they said that. But when he was really out of his mind, he'd grab me and shake me and say, "Tell me what you and your father have done to me, "But since we hadn't done anything, what could I say? I'd say, "You're my husband. Why would I want to drive you mad?" But then he'd accuse me of mocking him, and he'd beat me again.

Usha-bai's husband became increasingly violent and beat Usha-bai more and more frequently. She was hospitalised three times due to the severity of these beatings, once because he had fractured her arm. During this period, Usha-bai's in-laws forcibly took her son away without explaining why and six months later, he died. He had fallen sick and Usha-bai's in-laws had not sought medical help. Usha-bai believes that he died of neglect and says the grief over losing him devastated her, that she did not recover for many years. Usha-bai describes the time immediately after her son's death as almost unbearably painful for many reasons:

> In Bombay, we moved in with my husband's uncle, in a room he rented. Often, there was no food at all to cook and no money to buy food—because no one would give my husband work. They all knew he was out of his mind... My husband would wander the streets during the day then come home and demand food. And what could I give him? There was nothing. This was just one more excuse for him to beat me. I tried to get work so I could earn and we could eat, but then my husband would say, "Where have you been? You've been with another man." And again he would beat me...My husband's uncle finally got tired of all the fighting and he threw us out. And for weeks we had nowhere to sleep but the sidewalks...
>
> Finally, I decided that it would be better to go back to Peth than to bear the shame of living like this. I knew at least we'd be able to eat there and I could get work in the fields...But we didn't even have enough money for

> the bus fare all the way to Pune, and we only made it halfway before the conductor threw us off...Then I had to do something I'll never forget. I had to beg. I had to beg for the money to pay for the bus to Pune. I thought I'd die from the humiliation. I stood in the bus stand, weeping from humiliation, and I begged. What else could I do? I've never known such shame...I vowed I'd never beg again, even if I were starving. And I never have. I've had times when all I've had to eat for days on end has been cold, stale rice, but I've never again lowered myself to begging.

Back in Peth, Usha-bai separated from her husband. She moved in with her parents and made it clear to her in-laws that she was no longer willing to be responsible for her husband or to be involved with him in any way. He was eventually diagnosed as mentally ill and was institutionalised for several years.

Usha-bai tried to start a new life for herself in the village, but her attempts to do so were hampered by the revival of an old incident that had happened one evening soon after she had married. She had been working in the fields on her in laws' farm with her brother-in-law and his wife. Her brother-in-law had sent his wife home early and then had approached Usha-bai on the pretext that he wanted to discuss something involving her husband. But when he came near her, he pulled her into the bushes and attempted to rape her. Usha-bai escaped and ran to the village where she told her in-laws and her parents what had happened. They all told her to keep quiet, that if others heard this story, her reputation would be ruined, and they privately censured her brother-in-law.

For years, no one else in the village knew what had happened, but her brother-in-law had been so angry at the time that Usha-bai had told anyone at all that he had vowed to ruin her life. Consequently, when she returned to Peth and separated from her husband, her brother-in-law began spreading his version of this early incident. He said that Usha-bai had seduced him that evening in the field, that she had always been a loose woman and that this was the reason her husband had lost his mind and her marriage had failed. Usha-bai reports that those who knew her well dismissed this all as pure fabrication. They knew that she had been only eleven or twelve years old at the time, had not reached puberty and had not yet even consummated her marriage with her husband. In Usha-bai's words, "I knew nothing about the reality of the relationship between a husband and a wife. Even though I was married, I was still a little girl." But many people believed the rumour and Usha-bai has had to bear the weight of the negative public opinion it created for years.

Usha-bai now lives with her aging mother and her eight-year-old niece, Sushma. It is the only all-female household in the village, and this has made it particularly hard for Usha-bai to clear her reputation. The whole household has been ostracised over the years because there is no "man of the house" something that is almost unheard of in this area. Usha-bai has drawn strength from the example given her by her long-term friend, Bhave-bai, who also lives in an all-female household in a nearby village:

> Sometimes I carried on only because of Bhave-bai's encouragement...I'd go to her when I thought that my life was too difficult to bear, and she'd remind me of her own suffering and how she's persevered...In spite of all the hardships she's faced, she's still managed to make a place for herself in society...She was married at the age of eleven and her husband died just a few days later. So she was a widow when she was still just a child. Her in laws and her parents wanted to shave her head—which is the custom for widows—and she refused. So she ran away to her uncle's house and begged him to help her. He sent her to a boarding school and she learned to be a teacher..She's made it through her life alone. She's been a good friend and has given me courage to hold my head high, no matter what people say.

Usha-bai has training in tailoring and she has survived economically for years by sewing *sari,* blouses and petticoats. In spite of the fact that she is always looking for ways to increase her income, there are only limited opportunities to expand her business in Peth; only a few women in the village can afford to have new *sari,* blouses and petticoats sewn for them with any frequency. The family lives on the edge of poverty, supported mainly by a small pension Usha-bai's mother began to receive after her husband's death. Usha-bai says she does not know how she and Sushma will survive when her mother dies and the pension stops. Her mother owns a small parcel of farmland in Peth that Usha-bai will inherit, but it lies unproductive for most of the year because the family cannot afford to have the well drilled that is necessary for irrigation.

Usha-bai is an extremely articulate woman with a remarkable memory for details. She always carries a small notebook in her bag in which she records all of her income and expenditures. She has kept a diary over the past 30 years of important events in her life. She is an avid reader; she reads the newspaper regularly and is always eager to discuss the day's news.

She is the government's village health worker, a position she finds frustrating at times because she feels she has not been given enough training to do the job well—and because she is only paid Rs. 50 a month. But she also acknowledges the benefits of the job, the biggest of which she identifies as the opportunity to travel once a month to meet with other health workers from all over the *taluka* [the government's administrative unit that is a subdivision of a district which, in turn, is a subdivision of a state]. She is very outgoing and enjoys this kind of interaction:

> Here in Peth when I talk to someone on the road, I always think to myself, "Has this person heard the rumors about my character?"...Often I've had people just ignore me, walk by me and pretend they don't see me—afraid their reputation will be hurt by being seen with me... But when I go to the meetings for the health workers, no one treats me badly. They haven't heard these rumours, so they listen to what I have to say. They think I have good ideas...Now, with the help of the Mahila Mandal, I'm beginning to be listened to in Peth...I want to clear my name and be respected. And this is already happening with my work in the Mahila Mandal.

Usha-bai is a powerful public speaker and she utilises her oratorical skills often as one of the three current presidents of the Samaj Vikas Mahila Mandal. She is also a thoughtful organiser and planner. She is a dominant force in the women's organisation, often the one to persuade those less vocal than she is to speak. Her dominance has strengthened the organisation in many ways, but it has also been the cause for dissension. Several times she has taken the initiative to make decisions on her own that others in the group felt should have been collective decisions. However, when they have questioned her right to make these decisions, Usha-bai has readily admitted her mistakes and has made her desire to learn how to act more collaboratively clear:

> For years I've had to fight for every good thing I've got, and I've had to fight alone. No one has been there to help me. So the only way I know how to act is to take charge and fight for what I think is right...I've suffered so much and this is the only way I've survived, by taking charge ...Now, in the Mahila Mandal, I'am learning that I don't have to fight for everything alone, and that it's better if we work together. But it's hard to change after all those years alone...I want to change. I want to learn how to work together. I don't want to be alone anymore.

Vimal-bai

Vimal-bai introduces herself:

> Tell the people who will read your book that I may be old, but I still have plenty of fighting spirit left. I have a lot of battles left to fight, and I'am not about to give up. I'll probably be fighting them until the day I die—and enjoying it!
>
> I've seen a great deal of change in my [Mahar] community in my lifetime. Do you know Godse-bai whose husband works in Bombay? Her father-in-law and mother-in-law [who are Marathas] used to rush off and take a bath every time a Mahar's shadow fell on them. But now things have changed so much that two of my nephews are married to Brahmin women because my nephews are well educated and have good jobs. They're engineers.
>
> Babasaheb [Ambedkar] changed everything for my people. He taught us so many things. He told us to work hard and get a good education. It was too late for me to get an education, but I educated all six of my children as best I could. I've tried to lead my life in a way that would make Babasaheb proud. I never got to meet him while he was alive, but I attended his funeral. I wasn't well at the time, but I felt I just had to go anyway. The trains were flooded with people going to Bombay to go to his funeral. Extra trains came from all over India. I had to

walk so far to get there that my feet were raw and bleeding by the time I arrived. But it didn't matter. At least I made it there. He'd done so much for my people. What else could I do but go and pay my respects?

I've fought for the rights of my people, and I've lost my voice many a time shouting for justice. And I'm not done shouting yet. You've probably noticed that, haven't you? I do my share of it in the Mahila Mandal and I know some people don't like it. And they're not shy about telling me so, are they? They think people will only listen if we're all polite and chat about our problems in a ``civilised" way over a cup of tea. But I know better. I'm a hot-tempered woman and sometimes I get a little wild and everyone tells me to quiet down and be patient, that I can rant and rave in Pune, but it doesn't work here in Peth. But they're wrong. Sometimes it does work here when nothing else does. Sometimes if you ask nicely, the officials will smile and say, "Yes, we'll connect your electricity soon," and then years go by while you sit and wait. But if you yell, sometimes they jump and get it done right now.

I am all for the whole village coming together and deciding to do good work. That's really the only way the conditions in the village will get better and stay better, isn't it? We used to all work together in Shanti Nagar—people from all castes—and that's how we got so many things done. But sometimes in order to get everyone to agree on what to do, first you have to poke them and prod them—and sometimes shout at them. Everybody can tell me to keep quiet all they want, but I won't. When I get mad, I just have to shout. And injustice makes me mad. When all the injustice is gone, maybe I'll quiet down. Maybe.

Vimal-bai is a tiny woman, barely four and a half feet tall, and she has a fierce inner strength. She has been fighting for the rights of her people, the Mahars, for most of her life. She does not remember in what year she was born, but judging form her recollections of factory work during the British rule, she must be over 60 years old. She was born in a village not far from Peth and her parents were farmers who managed to make a fairly good living off their land. She was married into a family in Peth when she was six or seven years old and moved to the village soon after the wedding. There is bitterness in her voice when she talks of her years in Peth just after her marriage:

> Life at my parents' house was good. There was always enough to eat and I didn't have to work. I played. What else should a six or seven-year-old girl do? But then I was married...I don't know why I was married to such a poor person. There's an old saying that goes, "A poor woman may marry into our house, but our daughter should marry a rich man. "But it didn't happen that way with me...I never asked my father why he chose my husband...Maybe it was because Peth was so close to my parents' village, or because there was hope that my husband would get work in the ammunition factory in Pune, which he finally did...I don't know. But I do know that while my father had the money to hire two labourers to work in his fields, I had to take any work I could get in order to earn. My mother-in-law used to send me out of the house every morning saying that if I didn't find work, we'd all starve. And I was still such a little girl.

When Vimal-bai was 15, she and her husband moved to Shanti Nagar, which was then little more than a squatters' settlement on the edge of Pune. They left Peth because there were so few opportunities for them to earn a decent living, whereas there were many factory jobs available in Pune. They stayed in Shanti Nagar with one of Vimal-bai's brothers and his wife. Then, when Vimal-bai's mother died a few years later, her father and three more of her brothers and their families joined them. At first, they all shared one small mud hut that they rented. But eventually, when they all found work in factories, they were able to save enough to build a small house. However, they built it on land belonging to a government factory and when the government decided to expand the factory facilities, the family was evicted.

Vimal-bai led the fight to get the house back. She gathered a crowd from her neighbourhood and marched to one of the local politician's offices where she demanded her rights. Vimal-bai recalls that she said to him, "There are eleven voters in my family, and if you want our eleven votes, you're going to have to earn them," She threatened the politician that she would convince all the Mahars in Shanti Nagar to vote against him, and her tactic worked. Although she never got the house back, she did manage to pressure the politician into giving her family the title to a piece of land in Shanti Nagar where they began again. Eventually were able to build another larger house.

Vimal-bai gave birth to six children in Shanti Nagar and over the years, it was also here that she received much of her political education. Shanti Nagar developed a large, active Mahar women's political organisation. Vimal-bai joined and was befriended by women who were to become her role models. These politically astute women, who had long been active in the movement for the rights of the Scheduled Castes, taught her the importance of organising, of working together and of developing effective strategies. Vimal-bai relates that it was generally due to these women's efforts that Shanti Nagar developed into a thriving community. Now, years later, when the Samaj Vikas Mahila Mandal is confronted by a particularly difficult problem, Vimal-bai often recalls the advice of these women, or she relates the way this early women's, organisation in Shanti Nagar once resolved a similar problem.

At some point not long after Ambedkar's death—Vimal-bai cannot recall exactly when—the Mahar women's organisation in Shanti Nagar resolved to join a march of women going on foot from Pune to Ambedkar's house in Bombay to meet his son. The march was called for the general purpose of publicising the plight of Scheduled Caste persons living in poverty. The women from Shanti Nagar wanted to bring attention to the fact that the Mahar residents in their settlement were being denied the right to use the only public well because of their low caste status. En route to Bombay, they were stopped by the police:

> There were over a hundred of us, and they made us sit in a tight circle, and they put an iron chain around us and told us not to cross it. They kept us like that for three days. We got so restless from sitting there, idle...When the police asked where we were going, I was the one to speak. I said, "We're marching to Babasaheb's house. His son will show us the right way. People in our area won't let us take water from the well. How can we survive

> without water? Water is necessary for a human being to live."...After three days, they let us go—without ever telling us why they'd stopped us, and having given us just barely enough food and water to get by...We finally made it to Babasaheb's house where his son and two nephews welcomed us and told us the whole story of Babasaheb's life. That day, more than a hundred of us became Buddhists.

Vimal-bai's entire family converted to Buddhism, and several times they went together to the city of Nagpur in northeastern Maharashtra to visit the Buddhist temple built on the spot where Ambedkar and tens of thousands of Mahars first converted to Buddhism on October 14, 1956. Vimal-bai recalls the effects of one of these trips to Nagpur that she took with a large group from Shanti Nagar:

> It was so exciting to all be together that when we returned, we just went wild. It seemed that everywhere we looked there was injustice. We couldn't contain ourselves. We were violent. We broke windows in government offices. We cornered the officials. We demanded our rights...We succeeded in getting public latrines constructed in Shanti Nagar, and a road. And we got about 25 water taps installed, too...We took the power into our own hands and we got things done!

Vimal-bai worked in several different factories before she found a job doing cleaning in the government hospital in Pune, which she kept for 20 years. Her father was a patient in this hospital for the last two months of his life. During this time, Vimal-bai visited him every day and came to know the cleaning staff, and they found her a job. Vimal-bai, in turn, found jobs in the hospital for many members of her family. Today, two of her nephews, two of her sons and one of her daughters-in-law still work in the hospital.

Vimal-bai has never had any formal education, but she explains that she has learned a great deal in her life through her participation in different organisations:

> I've learned more in one caste meeting than my children have in years of school! I never miss a caste meeting if there's one called. That's how I've educated myself over the years. I can't read or write, but I can get a protest

march together in no time, and I know how to work the system...My daughter-in-law used to say, "Why do you go to the caste meetings? When you take leave for the day to go, it's deducted from your salary. "Every time for I'd tell her, "Babasaheb spend his whole life trying to improve the lives of our people. So why should I be concerned about losing one day's salary to try to do the same?"..

I never missed a union meeting either. It's true that most of the time the leaders just collect the dues and get fat on them; but when you need the union, it's there for you...During the Emergency, if it hadn't been for the union, most of us would have been out of a job. But we all rallied together, and didn't let that happen...There's lot of power in sticking together in hard times...

The first women's organisation in Shanti Nagar taught me a lot, too...I left my mother's house so young, and my mother-in-law was so overworked that she never had any time for me. But the leaders in the women's organisation treated me like a daughter. They taught me how to organise and how to get things done...They taught me to never be intimidated by someone just because they have a big name or a big office—especially if they have a big name or a big office!..They taught me how much power there is in numbers and how we all have the same rights, but that some of us may have to push harder than others to get them.

Vimal-bai and her husband moved back to Peth four years ago, after they both retired. Her husband is losing his hearing and was also losing his sight until he underwent a cataract operation arranged by the doctors whom the Samaj Vikas Mahila Mandal had brought to Peth to conduct medical camps. Her husband is a quiet, good-natured man who at times seems almost in awe of Vimal-bai's brashness. She says he has never been politically active himself, but that he has never interfered with her own activism. These days, he encourages her participation in the Samaj Vikas Mahila Mandal, saying he is happy she still has a good cause to keep her lively.

One of their sons-who is mildly retarded-and his wife and child have joined Vimal-bai and her husband in Peth. They all live in one room, barely surviving on the small pension that Vimal-bai's husband receives and whatever their son can earn when he can find work, which is not often. Vimal-bai does not have a pension, although she could have had one. She opted instead to trade her right to a pension for a guaranteed position in the government hospital for one of her daughters-in-law, assuming that she would benefit directly from this arrangement. But this daughter-in-law now claims that all of her income is necessary for her own immediate family, and Vimal-bai receives nothing.

Vimal-bai one of the most vocal members of the Samaj Vikas Mahila Mandal. Her history of activism has often contributed to her frustration with other members who believe in the effectiveness of more subtle means of change, and she seldom restrains herself from expressing this frustration. At times this has caused dissension within the organisation, but at others, it has forced the more conservative members to re-examine their tactics. There have been incidents when they have agreed to more overt methods due to Vimal-bai's insistence. There is certainly little danger that the Samaj Vikas Mahila Mandal members will settle into complacency as long Vimal-bai is an active participant.

Many years after Vimal-bai's initial participation in the Mahar women's political organisation in Shanti Nagar, a Mahila Mandal was formed in the same area with members from many different castes. In this second organisation, Vimal-bai learned a great deal about the government's Mahila Mandal programme, and this knowledge has been very useful to the Samaj Vikas Mahila Mandal. Her awareness of the responsibilities of the different government offices, which she learned through participation in various organisations, has also been quite helpful. Vimal-bai frequently visits Shanti Nagar and when she returns, she always reports on the activities of the Mahila Mandal there, which is older and whose members are therefore more experienced than those of the Samaj Vikas Mahila Mandal. This networking has helped give women in Peth new ideas for their organisation, as well as inspiration. It is Vimal-bai's fond hope that the members of the two organisations will one day meet and undertake activities collectively.

One of the most important assets Vimal-bai brings to the Samaj Vikas Mahila Mandal is her willingness to talk straightforwardly about caste issue. When the organisation first became active, many of the members from a variety of caste backgrounds were uncomfortable with discussions of inter-caste tensions. Even other Mahar members made it clear that they preferred to avoid such discussions, if possible, perhaps hoping that doing so would make the tensions fade away. But experience showed them and others on several occasions that ignoring these tensions often tended to exacerbate caste-related problems within the organisation. Thus, the members have come to appreciate Vimal-bai's frankness and are trying to follow her example of addressing caste issues directly and openly.

Kalu-bai

Kalu-bai introduces herself:

> I've been the president of the Samaj Vikas Mahila Mandal since it began in 1984.[7] At first, that meant nothing at all because the Mahila Mandal never met or did anything. It was just a name on a piece of paper. But now it means a great deal. The Mahila Mandal is active all the time now. The women have elected me and I've tried to do my best. I didn't know anything about being a president at first, but I've learned so much. After our first meetings, I could barely get the courage to speak out loud, but now look at me. I'm introducing myself to the people in America and my voice isn't even shaking!
>
> I've always thought that I'd make something of my life. Not in a big, fancy way, but in a simple way—lead a good, clean life and raise my children well, and always make sure they'd have enough to eat and that they'd get a good education. But I never dreamed I'd be doing the kind of things I'm doing now—like going to see the Collector, who called me "sister" once, and meeting with the BDO [Block Development Officer]. The BDO knows who I am now when he meets me and where I'm from, too. He always asks what's been happening in our Mahila Mandal.
>
> My life used to be the same from day to day. Now I never know who will come to see me or what will happen because of the Mahila Mandal. Last week the Member of Parliament came to Peth and he sent a message ahead saying he wanted to meet the Mahila Mandal. Then when

we met him and someone said that I was one of the presidents, do you know what he did? He bent down and touched my feet. He gave me that much respect. The Member of Parliament touched my feet-in front of my husband and his friends from the temple and the *sarpanch* [the head of the elected village administrative body, the Gram Panchayat] and everyone. I was so embarrassed, but at the same time I was so proud. My life has changed because of the Mahila Mandal. If it weren't for the Mahila Mandal, do you think the Member of Parliament would have even thought of touching my feet? I would have been just another woman in the crowd.

What else can I say about myself that's anything special? I'm really just a woman like any other woman. I cook. I carry water from the well. I work in the fields. I take care of my family. I love my children. I belong to the Mahila Mandal. That's all. That's what's important in my life.

Kalu-bai is a woman with tremendous dignity and an equal amount of humility. She walks with her shoulders back and her head high. She recalls that her father often told her when she was young, "We may be poor, but we still have each other and our dignity. We don't need anything else. "Her face has a leathery, worn look, even though she is only thirty six years old. It reflects the difficulties she has endured. She speaks quietly but with authority and can be quite intimidating in public when her face is stern and her jaw set. But in private, she is the first to laugh at her own humorous stories-which she delights in telling. She says she is not afraid to laugh at herself and that this is one of the ways she has kept up her courage when times have been hard.

Long ago, Kalu-bai began to ignore many of the restrictive norms of caste relations in Peth. Her house is located near where the Maratha neighbourhood ends and the Buddhist area begins. She is a Maratha herself, but she has friends from many different caste backgrounds and some of her closest friends and neighbours are Buddhists. When Kalu-bai first moved to Peth as a girl of 15 soon after she was married, it was the Buddhist women who gave her shelter when her husband and sister-in-law beat her. It was also the Buddhist women who helped her find work on the government's local dam project when her husband lost his job because of drinking.

Kalu-bai has been elected one of the three Samaj Vikas Mahila Mandal presidents for the three years since the organisation has become active and she often uses this position to promote inter-caste unity. While others often talk of the importance of unity, but continue to socialise only with their own caste, Kalu-bai provides and example by welcoming Buddhist and other Scheduled Caste women into her home and by frequenting theirs.

Kalu-bai was born in 1955 and raised near Pune in a settlement built up along the highway to Bombay. Her memories of her childhood are vivid. When Kalu-bai was quite young her mother became chronically ill. Because her mother was unable to do the housework, for years her father worked in a factory during the day and when he came home at night, he did all the cooking and cleaning. Kalu-bai remembers that every morning her father would comb her hair and braid it neatly and make sure that she had a clean dress to wear. She has very fond memories of the loving attention her father gave her during this time. When her mother's health became worse, the whole family moved in with her mother's parents so that there would be more money available for medical care. This proved to be the beginning of a difficult period. Almost all of Kalu-bai's father's salary went to pay for medical treatment for her mother, so there was little left to contribute to the common family fund to buy food. This was the source of a great deal of friction in the household; Kalu-bai remembers never feeling free to eat her fill at her grandparents' house because the issue of who was to pay for the food was such a source of controversy.

Another cause of difficulty while living at her grandparents' house was Kalu-bai's aunt, a woman who had lived with her parents since she was widowed in her teens:

> My aunt used to drink liquor all the time and smoke dried hemp flowers. This would go on all day. She'd just sit and drink and smoke and stare out the window and never do any work...Once in a while, she'd go out and come back with groceries or a new bottle. She'd charge everything on my father's account and never share anything with the rest of us. This kept my father constantly in debt and he was so honest he always paid her bills...She was always picking fights. The minute my father would come home at night from the factory, she'd try to start an

> argument with him. It was always about the same thing. She wanted my father to marry her, but he didn't want to have anything to do with her...Sometimes she'd leave the house angrily when he'd tell her one more time that he was already married and didn't want a second wife and then sometimes the police would bring her home later. I never knew why she was in trouble with the police, but my father always told me, "I don't want you to grow up to be like your aunt. Lead a clean life. Don't follow her ways."

After three years of living like this, Kalu-bai's father decided that he could no longer tolerate raising his children in such an atmosphere. He rented a room for himself and his two children and moved out. He had wanted Kalu-bai's mother to come as well, but she refused on the grounds that she did not want to burden him. She died soon thereafter.

When Kalu-bai was eight years old, her father remarried and this changed her life.:

> You'll hear all sorts of stories about how step mothers treat their step children badly, but that was never the case with me. My step mother treated me as if she one who took an interest in my studies and made sure I did my homework and that I went to school. At my grandparents' house, no one ever bothered if I went to school or not, so often I didn't go. I didn't know how important it was. So I'd leave home in the morning then spend the day playing with my girl friends...My father was working two jobs and he was too tired when he came home to pay much attention. If he'd known I wasn't going to school, he would have made me go. But no one bothered to tell him...
>
> The main reason I didn't want to go to school was that there was a teacher there who used to slap us hard across the face whenever we'd make a mistake-or for any reason at all, or for no reason-and I was really afraid of him. We used to call him the Wolf Master because he was so mean...I told my stepmother that I was afraid to go to school because of him, so she went with me to make sure that I got a different teacher. And this time it was a

> woman teacher, Bhosle-bai. She took a special interest in me. I don't know why, but she really liked me and she still does. I go to visit her whenever I go to my father's house and tell her everything that's been happening in my life and she gives me advice...When I was in school, if I'd forget my lunch at home, she'd share hers with me. And if she was going to be gone so I'd have to go the Wolf Master's class all day, she'd always warn me ahead of time so I could stay home. If I'd miss a day, sometimes she'd even come to my house to find out if something was wrong...She didn't have any daughter of her own, so she treated me like a daughter.

Kalu-bai stayed in school until she had completed seventh grade. She wanted to continue her education, there were no schools nearby that offered classes beyond seventh grade at that time. She did well in her studies and now laments the fact that she did not have the opportunity to go on:

> Who knows what I might have become if I'd been able to stay in school? I was very good at all my subjects-except math because the Wolf Master taught math and I always skipped his classes. I might even have done well in math with a good teacher...Instead of going on in school, I took training in tailoring for a year and a half. My stepmother gave me lots of encouragement, but I never got very good at tailoring. I was always dreaming of becoming a teacher or a nurse or something important and was never really interested in tailoring enough to work hard enough to learn it...
>
> My oldest daughter dropped out of school after seventh grade and she took a tailoring class just like I did. And she's not very good at it either....I tried everything to get her to stay in school. I kept saying to her, "You'll be sorry later if you don't get more education. I would have given anything at your age to stay in school. You just don't see the value of it now, but you will later. It's not too late to go back." But she's determined not to go to school. She says it's just too boring and she'd rather stay home...My husband and I both want a good education for our children. I especially wanted both our two girls to stay

> in school. Hopefully Lata [Kalu-bai's younger daughter] will. Life for girls is so uncertain these days that they have to be prepared to fend for themselves in case anything goes wrong in their marriages.

When she was 15, Kalu-bai's father arranged her marriage to her first cousin:

> My father felt sorry for his sister and her family. They were so poor that all they ever had to eat was whatever vegetables and grain they could manage to grow. They didn't even have enough money to buy salt...My cousin was my aunt's only son and my father helped him as much as he could. We didn't have much, but we had more than his family. So my father made sure that he went to school and later he got him a factory job...My father knew that if he married me outside the family that it would be very expensive for the wedding costs and the dowry and all. He was afraid that to pay for all that, he'd have to sell his land and then what security would he have left? So it was decided that I'd marry my cousin.

Kalu-bai married at the beginning of the severe drought in Maharashtra that lasted from 1970 to 1973. Many of her memories of her first years living in Peth with her in-laws are of difficulties compounded by the drought:

> My husband started to drink soon after we married—or maybe he used to drink before we married and I just didn't know about it. Anyway, he drank so much that he lost his job—just when we needed the money more than ever because we didn't have any crops because the rains never came...Finally, I joined the work on the dam—carrying dirt. It was the only work around since all the crops had dried up...I'd never done work like that before. I'd never really done any hard work before at all because my stepmother wouldn't let me. She always made me study instead and she took care of the house....Work on the dam was back-breaking; but it was better than starving, I guess....I used to think, "So this is what marriage is all about. You get married and your husband turns into a drunkard and you have to stoop to hauling dirt and rocks all day so you don't starve. Great."..

> My father came to visit me the very day I started work on the dam. He went to my in-laws' house and they told him I was working on the dam and he walked all the way out there to find me When I ran to meet him, he started crying and I'd never seen him cry before. He'd taken such good care of me all my life, working hard so I wouldn't have to, and there I was doing that kind of work...He gave me a 20 rupee note and after that, he'd send money whenever he could and that's what pulled us through.

Kalu-bai's early troubles in her in-laws' house were more than financial. Her husband began to beat her soon after they were married whenever he was drunk and he was goaded to do so by his sister.

> My sister-in-law's husband sent her back to my in-laws' house for good and she just couldn't stop being mad about it. She'd pick a fight with anybody, even her mother, but she was especially mean to me. I don't know why she decided to take it out on me in particular. Maybe it was because I was still with my husband and she was jealous. Anyway, she'd spend all day making up lies and when my husband came home, she'd meet him up lies and when my husband came home she'd meet him at the door and say something like. "your wife didn't go to work on the dam today. She stayed home and ate all the rice we had in the house, so now there's nothing left for you to eat." He'd be so drunk, he'd believe her. So he'd shout and knock me around. He used to beat me every other day or so, and she'd beat me sometimes too. I'd have to run out of the house and hide in the cowshed or at some neighbour's...
>
> For seven years I put up with her harassing me and with my husband's drinking and his beatings—seven years...Finally, my stepmother gave me the idea of going to my sister-in-law's husband and convincing him to take her back. But then we found out that he was a drunkard, too, so what good would it do to talk to him? So I found out where his brother worked—at the Thakur mill—and every week or so, I'd go see him there and try to convince him to send for my sister-in-law. And he finally did ...After my sister-in-law left, my life improved tremendously.

Kalu-bai's husband eventually became active in the revival of the Varkari religious tradition [a Hindu tradition related to pilgrimage to Pandharpur] in the village, which strongly opposed to the use of alcohol, and he stopped drinking completely. He now attends the *bhajan* [devotional singing] sessions every evening in one of the local temples and he has become a well-respected man in the village. He is both the chairman of the local Cooperative Credit Society and the Congress(I) Party representative in Peth and he has political ambitions for himself and for Kalu-bai. In 1990, when Congress(I) Party officials were looking for a woman to head the local women's wing of the party, he submitted his wife's name. Although the party officials did not ask Kalu-bai to serve, she was delighted that her husband had demonstrated his belief in her capacities by nominating her.

These days, Kalu-bai and her husband get along much better than before, although she says there are still occasions when he loses his temper and beats her. But these occasions have become increasingly rare as Kalu-bai has become active in the Samaj Vikas Mahila Mandal:

> He knows that if he beats me and I call for the Mahila Mandal and all the women come that he'll look like a fool. He talks a big line in public about how the Mahila Mandal is doing such good work stopping all the violence in other homes, and then he comes to his own home and beats one of the presidents—me! The Mahila Mandal members never let him hear the end of it whenever he hits me these days, and it's had an effect. I know he thinks twice before he hits me—that is, it he's not so mad he's senseless. Then nothing can stop him...
>
> There's another reason he's treating me with more respect these days... I've started speaking my mind more and he sees that I have some pretty good ideas...Last month we went to a wedding in Pune and when we were coming back, a policeman blew his whistle and waved us over. My husband stopped and told me to wait with the motor scooter, that he'd handle it. But I just couldn't wait. I went over and heard the policeman saying that we'd run a red light. But I knew we hadn't. I knew he was just trying to get money out of us, so I said, 'You think you can take advantage of us because you see that I'am wear-

> ing a nine-yard sari so you know we're village folks. You think you can intimidate us because we're not from the city. But you're wrong. That light wan't red when we went through it and you know it. So we're just going to go on our way and you should feel lucky that we're not going to report you for trying to get a bribe out of us." And then I just walked away and my husband followed me, and the policeman didn't say a thing....My husband was angry with me then for opening my mouth; but later I heard him bragging to his friends about how much courage I'd had and how I'd saved us at least 25 rupees!.

Kalu-bai's husband is generally supportive of her work in the Mahila Mandal, although there have been times when he has either refused to let her leave the house to attend a meeting or has sent for her in the middle of meeting. According to Kalu-bai, this is just his way of reminding her that his word is supposed to be law in the house—in his opinion. She takes these reminders in her stride; sometimes she does what he says and sometimes she does not . At times, she manages to do what he says and still get her own way. For example, during one Executive Committee meeting, Kalu-bai's husband sent for her and she sent back a message saying, "Better make a big pot of tea because we're not done with our business here, so if I have to come, everybody else comes, too. "We all went and that was the last time her husband interrupted a meeting. Whenever she suspects that her husband might insist that she stay at home on the night of a scheduled meeting, Kalu-bai simply asks all the Mahila Mandal members to meet in her house. This way she can obey her husband and still attend the meeting. Although it makes him angry when she does this, he always has to leave halfway through these meetings because he works the night shift in a factory near Pune. Kalu-bai says that by the time he comes home in the morning, he has usually forgotten his anger.

Kalu-bai's husband has helped the Samaj Vikas Mahila Mandal in many ways. For example, he used his influence to get a local weekly newspaper to publish an announcement of the Mahila Mandal's first medical camp, and on the day of the camp, he helped organise the patients. When the Mahila Mandal convened a *gram sabha,* village-wide assembly meeting, he convinced all the men active in the Varkari revival to attend. These are some of the most powerful men in the village and at times, they have opposed the Mahila Mandal. Consequently, members of the Mahila Mandal took their attendance at the *gram sabha* as a sign of substantial progress in the process of the acceptance in Peth of the women's organisation and its activities.

Kalu-bai and her husband have four children. Their two oldest, a girl of 16 and a boy of 14 are "just ordinary kids" in Kalu-bai's opinion. But she sees special potential in her two youngest children. Her son, Ram, who is 11 had polio when he was young. One of his legs is withered so badly that he has a great deal of trouble walking. But he has an indomitable spirit, a quick mind and a charming sense of humor. Kalu-bai believes he will find a special place for himself in the world.

A few years ago, Kalu-bai tried to apply for the government stipend available to help disabled children. But the clerk in the *Zila Parishad* [the district-level elected administrative body] office obstinately refused to process her application. Although he would not give her any explanation for his refusal, Kalu-bai suspects that he was waiting for a bribe—which she was not willing to even consider. Now, through the Mahila Mandal, Kalu-bai has compiled a list of all the 14 disabled children in the village and she has organised all the parents to file stipend applications together. The Mahila Mandal members have agreed to send a cover letter with the applications, giving them the organisation's support. In addition, several Mahila Mandal members plan to form a delegation to personally deliver the applications to the *Zila Parishad* office. Kalu-bai is hopeful that the stipend will help Ram get as much education as possible.

Lata is Kalu-bai's ten-year old daughter and it is in her that her mother sees the greatest potential:

> Lata isn't like other children. She doesn't seem to think like a child. She knows things far beyond her years...She doesn't respond to authority—not in school or even here at home. She just does what she wants to do when she wants to do it. In a way, she's a lot like me. She thinks for herself. And we women aren't supposed to think for ourselves, are we ? Not if we want a peaceful home life.

> She has a strong will and I worry about what that will bring her in life....Sometimes I have the funny feeling that she'll never marry but that she'll do something great with her life. If any of my children make it to college, it'll surely be Lata. I dream about her being a doctor or an engineer...She's bright and determined and she'll have to do something different because she just doesn't fit in here.

These days, Kalu-bai and her husband are fairly stable financially. He works in a factory and she works in the family fields. Through the efforts of both the family gets by. They own a motor scooter, one of the few in the village, and her husband uses it to commute to his work near Pune. They live in one room with their four children and Kalu-bai's ageing mother-in-law who is losing both her sight and her ability to walk on her own and who requires a great deal of care-which is Kalu-bai's responsibility.

Kalu-bai loves to read and she laughingly admits that her favourite reading material is her husband's mail:

> He gets so mad when he finds out I've opened his mail; but I still just can't seem to resist. It comes and sits there and I try to keep working, but I can't. I keep thinking, "What if there's something imprortant in there that I should know?"...He gets so much interesting mail—from the Congress Party and about the Cooperative Credit Society, and from lots of other places. I've learned a great deal over the years from reading his mail—things I'd never have a way to learn otherwise because he never tells me what's in his mail and I rarely get any mail at all...So these days, I've learned to steam the envelopes open and glue them shut again before he comes home so we're both happy. I get to read his mail and he gets to think I don't.

Her high level of literacy is one of the important assets that Kalu-bai brings to the Mahila Mandal. Many of the members who have had some schooling have not used their reading and writing skills much over the years and consequently, no longer have as high a level of literacy as they may once have had. But a few members, including Usha-bai and Kalu-bai, are comfortable enough with reading that they go over government documents and other Mahila Mandal-related papers carefully, working to find out how the organisation can benefit from the resources available.

Another asset that Kalu-bai brings is her reputation for being scrupulously honest as well as balanced in her judgements. She has earned the trust of the villagers over the years; thus her support of the Samaj Vikas Mahila Mandal has helped increase the organisation's membership and its general acceptance in Peth.

Her key role in the Mahila Mandal has been to link the various caste communities represented in its membership through bonds of friendship. She has set an example of intercaste unity by befriending members of all castes. She has particularly strong ties with the Buddhist community, the community many of the more traditional Maratha members privately say they wish would withdraw from the Mahila Mandal. Kalu-bai has been persistent in her work to eliminate caste prejudice within the Mahila Mandal and her efforts have definitely shown results.

Conclusion

The five women profiled in this chapter have all made substantial contributions to the development of the Samaj Vikas Mahila Mandal by assuming strong leadership roles. There seem to be common factors in their lives and perspectives that have made this possible. First, all of these women, as well as other leaders within the organisation, are remarkably open-minded. Before I moved to Peth, I often heard rural Maharashtrian women described as "guardians of traditional culture." This suggested a conservatism that might preclude ready acceptance of new ideas. But I found this description did not fit the majority of the women I worked with in the Mahila Mandal at all. On the contrary, the women are very open to new ideas. One of the factors contributing to this openness seems to be the women's development of a high level of flexibility in response to the need to adjust to their in-laws's homes after marriage.

Kalu-bai explains that when a woman moves to her husband's home, "almost everything changes." She and others describe moving to their in-laws' homes and how the most basic features of their lives changed literally overnight: their eating and working habits; their schedule of sleeping and waking; the time they were allowed to got to relieve themselves in the fields; and even their names. Coming from situations of relative freedom in their parents' homes, as new daughters-in-law, they were suddenly subject to a wide range of restrictions. Kalu-bai describe the changes that came about in her own situation:

> In my father's house, I hardly had to work. My step-mother took care of everything and my "work" was to study. But when I moved to my in-laws' house—what a shock! Life was nothing but work—up at four in the morning to grind the grain, then straight through until ten at night or later, until all the work was done... Suddenly nothing was the same, even though my mother-in-law and father-in-law were my aunt and uncle, so I'd known them all my life...In Pune I'd come and go as I pleased and no one worried much about it, as long as my stepmother knew where I was...I went to the market along alone and to school and to my girl friends' houses...But with my in-laws, I had to ask permission for every little thing and I could never go out alone-never!...I was used to the city life and all of a sudden, here I was in a village, not knowing anything about farming or taking care of animals; but I had to do it anyway. It was all so different... I was lucky that at least I got to keep my own name. Every other women I know has been given a new name by her in-laws along with her new life.

Kalu-bai's descriptions and those of others, of the tremendous adjustments a new bride often has to make, indicate that if a woman is not flexible in her in-laws' house, she may well suffer. Women are expected to accommodate themselves to their in-laws' living habits, not vice versa. Consequently, many women learn to be flexible quite quickly because it is in their own interests to do so. Kalu-bai explains that this flexibility does not necessarily mean that a woman sublimates her own personality to the expectations of her role as a daughter-in-law or a wife, although this certainly happens in some cases. It is just as possible that she learns the system of expectations at her in-laws' house carefully in order to determine how to make that system work best for her. This seems to have been the case in the lives of all the five leaders profiled. They learned to use flexibility as a means both of surviving and of promoting their well-being in their in-laws' homes. They then carried this asset of flexibility into other areas of their lives such as their work with the Mahila Mandal.

In addition to flexibility, another factor that has contributed to the open-mindedness of the women in this chapter is that they have all had extended life experiences outside of Peth. Mahadevi-bai and Usha-bai both lived for many years in Bombay, where they learned to cope with the exigencies of a fast-paced urban life very different from that of Peth. Likewise, the remaining three woman all lived for many years in or very near Pune, where they had a substantial amount of independence and exposure to different ways of life. Vimal-bai, for example, commuted to work every day by herself using public transportation; and the whole atmosphere on the air force base where Saraswati-bai was raised was quite cosmopolitan because of the mix of people living there from all over India. Saraswati-bai was also exposed to a very different life-style when she travelled with the Nagars to Punjab for four months.

The five women profiled have had a broader range of experiences than most women in the Mahila Mandal; thus, they have become more accustomed to dealing with new ideas and different perspectives. But it is important to note that nearly all of the women in Peth have had extended experiences living outside the village. It is the local custom for women to marry into a village other than their own. Therefore, very few women—only those exceptions born in Peth and married into families in Peth—have stayed in one village all their lives. Women who have married into Peth have brought with them the unique experiences and often different ways of doing things from their natal homes. Women who were raised in Peth, married outside the village, and now have returned to their parents' homes have also experienced life in another place—their husbands' homes. The fact that almost all women in Peth have lived outside the village for at least some time is in direct contrast to the reality of the majority of men in Peth. Most of these men were born in Peth and have always lived in this village, usually even in the same house. Except for those who have travelled to Bombay to find work, most men have never had extended experience living outside the village. This may account in part for the general tendency in Peth for women to be more flexible and more open to change than the men in their families.

A final factor in the open-mindedness of the five women profiled is that they have all suffered a great deal. They have all had times in their lives when they have not had enough to eat for long periods of time; they have all known extreme poverty. Mahadevi-bai Usha-bai and Kalu-bai have been subjected to sustained domestic violence. Saraswati-bai and Vimal-bai have borne the brunt of derision based on caste prejudice. The relationship between suffering and open-mindedness is clarified by Usha-bai:

> When you're tired and hungry and aching and you're not sure you can go on, what's the use of clinging to old ways? You ask yourself, "Where have they got me so far anyway?" And the answer is, "At the very bottom of a deep, dark well." And when you're at the bottom, you'll take any help that gets you out, you'll try almost anything. Believe me. I've been down there so many times, I know.

All the five women recall breaking with conventions many times when they were pressed to do so by necessity of suffering. For example, when Kalu-bai's husband and sister-in-law began to beat her soon after she moved to Peth, Kalu-bai frequently took shelter in the homes of Buddhist women. These were homes other members of her caste would not even go near. When Mahadevi-bai was not given enough to eat at her in-law's home, she started her own business selling vegetables even though she was expected to stay home and tend to the house. When Vimal-bai's family was evicted from their house in Shanti Nagar and forced to live in the streets, it was Vimal-bai who led the fight to try to get the house back when her brothers said they felt helpless to change the situation. These and other examples illustrate that necessity has often encouraged in the women profiled a relatively high level of openness to new ideas and innovative tactics.

One of the factors that has given all five of these women strength over the years is their knowledge that they can support themselves financially if they must. At some point in their lives, they have all had a source of income outside their families and this is relatively rare among women in Peth. Most women in the village work on family farms for no wages and do not have access to the profits when the crops are sold by the men in their families. By contrast, Vimal-bai worked either in factories or in the government hospital in Pune from the time she was 16 until she retired and she received regular salary cheques drawn in her name throughout. Saraswati-bai worked in homes on the air force base for years for payment. For a limited time, she also worked for daily wages in the aluminium utensil factory in Peth. Kalu-bai was the main wage earner in her family during the drought years after her husband lost his job. Mahadevi-bai had her own successful business in Bombay and she still supports herself by farming her own family fields and managing the sale of the crops. She is the only woman in the village who has this much control over the sale and profits of agricultural produce. Usha-bai has supported herself, her mother and her niece for years with her tailoring business. All five women report that knowing that they can support themselves has given them a strong sense of independence, stronger than that of the majority of the women in the village. This has contributed to the ability of these five to serve as leaders of the Mahila Mandal.

Support given by family members has also been a critical factor in the five women's ongoing participation in the Mahila Mandal. Saraswati-bai was able to take part in all of the organisations' activities only after her mother-in-law joined the Mahila Mandal as well and recognised the merit of these activities. While Saraswati-bai's husband has been supportive of her organisational activities all along, in the beginning his was a fairly passive type of support. But over time, he has come to place an increased value on Saraswati-bai participation, both because of the improvements the Mahila Mandal have brought to the village and because of the respect these improvements have, in turn, brought to his wife and thus to his family, Recently, he has even begun to stay home to do the housework and care for the children on nights when Mahila Mandal meetings are held so that his mother and Saraswati-bai are free to attend. Vimal-bai's husband has encouraged his wife to assume a leadership role in the Mahila Mandal. He speaks of Vimal-bai's leadership skills with pride, often referring to their various role in the women's organisations in Shanti Nagar and how these organisations have succeeded in improving the lives of the residents there. Although Kalu-bai's husband has troubled Kalu-bai from time when she goes to meetings on evenings he would rather have her stay home, he is generally supportive of her leadership in the organisation. He speaks of it as a source of increased status for the entire family. He also sees it as a stepping stone to Kalu-bai's involvement in local politics, which he has encouraged. Support from their spouses (as well as from other family member) has been essential for the involvement in the Mahila Mandal of these three women.

The remaining two women profiled, Mahadevi-bai and Usha-bai, head their own households and, therefore, do not have to have permission form any men in their families to take part in the Mahila Mandal. They also both have supportive women family members who encourage their participation. Mahadevi-bai's sisters who live in neighbouring villages have watched the growth of Mahadevi-bai's leadership in the Mahila Mandal with great interest. They have even asked Mahadevi-bai to help them start Mahila Mandals in their own villages. Usha-bai's mother is one of the Mahila Mandal's most ardent supporters and she willingly takes on the extra responsibilities at home when Usha-bai is too busy to attend to them because of her work for the organisation.

A final common thread that runs through the lives of these women is that they all have had at least one strong women mentor or role model who has given them inspiration and encouragement, particularly in difficult times. For Mahadevi-bai, this role model was her mother—whom she was able to spend considerable time with as an adult, contrary to the situation of most mothers and daughters in the village. When she was in her teens, Saraswati-bai received guidance from her employer, Mrs. Nagar. Kalu-bai had two sources of moral support when she was young-her stepmother and her teacher, Bhosle-bai—and they are both still very much a part other life. Usha-bai's ongoing friendship with a teacher many years her senior, Bhave-bai, has sustained her through many trials. Vimal-bai found many mentors among the women active in the women's organisations in Shanti Nagar. All five of the women profiled report that these special individuals have had a tremendously positive impact on their lives that has been responsible, at least in part, for the strength and self-confidence that has helped them become leaders of the Mahila Mandal.

In summary, a few of the common factors that have contributed to the development of leadership qualities in the five women in this chapter are: their open-mindedness, which is due in part to the flexibility required to adjust to life in their in-laws' homes, their broad range of experiences living outside the village, and the breaks with convention that necessity has sometimes forced upon them; their knowledge that they have the ability to financially support themselves; the encouragement of their families; and the inspiration and support they have drawn from their mentors and role models.

References

* Much of the text of this chapter is drawn from my Ph.D. thesis: Clarice A. Auluck-Wilson, "When All the Women Lift, the Mountain Will Move: Case Study of a Grassroots Women's Organisation in Rural Maharashtra, India" (Ph.D. thesis), Minneapolis: University of Minnesota, 1992.

1. This is not the actual name of the women's organisation, nor is Peth the real name of the village where this organisation is located. When I first decided to make the Samaj Vikas Mahila Mandal the focus of my Ph.D. research, the women involve said that they wanted me to use the names of both their organisation and their village in my dissertation because they are proud of their accomplishments. But as they became increasingly open about their lives over time, relating views and information that I thought might have negative consequences for them if made public, I began to be seriously concerned about protecting their privacy. Consequently, as I neared the completion of my dissertation, I wrote to the members of the women's organisation expressing this concern. They responded that the circumstances had changed considerably since our original agreement to use the names of their organisation and village and they asked that I use pseudonyms instead, which is what I have done. In addition, all individuals' names have been change, except for mine and my husband, Arvind's, again as a step to protect privacy.
2. I have given the methodology used in Peth this label because it utilised the basics of both " feminist" and "participatory" research. Sandra Harding ["Introduction: Is There a Feminist Method" in Sandra Harding (ed.), *Feminism and Methodology: Social Science Issues*, Bloomington Indiana: Indiana University Press, 1987] states that while there is no one feminist method, there are three characteristics of feminist research: 1) "it generates its problematics from the perspective of women's experiences" (p.7); 2) "the purpose of research and analysis are not separable from the origins of the research problems" (p.8); and 3) "it insists that the inquirer her/himself be placed on the same critical plane as the overt subject matter, thereby recovering the entire research process for scrutiny in the results of research" (p.9).

The three basic elements of participatory research are social investigation, education and action.

3. I have translated this letter and all of the quotes included in this chapter into English from the original Marathi.
4. Ranjana-bai's husband, parents-in-law, brothers-in-law and sister-in-law had already been jailed by this time. Later, in a plea bargaining agreement, her husband entered a guilty plea and in exchange, charges against the others were dropped—although it is generally believed in Peth that all of the in-laws played a part in Ranjana-bai's torture and murder. The husband served only one year in prison before being released and is now preparing to remarry.
5. The members of the Samaj Vikas Mahila have adopted a unique internal administrative structure. Instead of the conventional structure with a president, vice president, secretary and treasurer, the organisation has an Executive Committee of nine which is composed of a presidium, a secretariat and a treasury, each of which has three members. The members of the Executive Committee have no authority individually; they only have authority when working in consultation with the other members of the Committee. This reduces the possibility that any one member will dominate the organisation and promote her own agenda instead of that of the Mahila Mandal. The purpose of the Executive Committee is primarily to facilitate the implementation of collective decisions made by the broader Mahila Mandal membership. Its function is to serve, not to dominate, the Mahila Mandal.
6. In Peth and surrounding areas, a women's first name is commonly changed by her husband or her in-laws at the time of her marriage and she also takes on her husband's last name. All but one member of the Samaj Vikas Mahila Mandal—Kalu-bai—had their first names changed at the time of their marriage, Many women who have left their husbands, such as Mahadevi-bai and Usha-bai, have returned to using their first names given at birth.
7. The Samaj Vikas Mahila Mandal was started—at least on paper—in 1984 when the project officer of the government's Integrated Child Development Services (ICDS) headquarters in the *taluka* in which Peth is located undertook registration of a Mahila Mandal in every village in his jurisdiction in which ICDS had established its services. The paperwork required to register the Samaj Vikas Mahila Mandal was processed at this time, but there were no grassroots initiatives to activate the organisation until after Ranjana-bai's death.

2

The Sociology of Women and Work

*J.P. Singh**

Women in most countries are an integral part of the labour force, but their level of participation in productive processes varies quite considerably across societies. Numerous are the factors which determine the nature or level of economic involvement of women in a society. The most important determinant of economic role of women in any society is possibly the traditional division of labour by sex which has further been influenced by numerous factors varying from one historical phase to another. Partly because women are perceived differently in different societies and partly because the term 'work' has no standard definition, marked variations in the level of workforce participation rate (henceforth WPR) are noted across countries.[1] For instance, Islamic countries like Bangladesh, Iraq, Pakistan, Niger and Tunisia tend to record a very low level of WPR (Appendix I). The Islamic society probably represents an extreme form of patriarchy where women generally are able to exercise a fairly low level of autonomy in their life[2]. The household heads (or benevolent dictators) never allow or encourage female members of the family to work outside their homes to earn a livelihood unless the very survival is really threatened. The onus of providing economic support to the family usually rests with the men.

Based on the nineteenth century European experiences, Patai has contended that as socio-economic development takes place, activity rates for females tend to increase. Women tend to shift

* The author is Reader in Sociology, P. U., Patna and Chairman (Hon.), Institute of Population and Integrated Development, 25 Ram Krishna Path, North S.K. Puri, Patna-800 013.

gradually from primary to secondary and tertiary sectors of the economy.[3] The validity of this generalisation seems to be somewhat doubtful in the case of contemporary India. Despite the fact that different censuses employed different definitions of work, it has become quite evident from the census data that the general activity rates of females have shown a declining trend during 1911-1991. The work participation rate has shown an increasing tendency only from the 1971 census onwards. But the work participation rates at both 1981 and 1991 censuses are less than those recorded at all other earlier censuses between 1911 and 1961 (see Table 1). This has happened even when the pace of development, more especially during the post independent era, was faster than that during the colonial period. The continuing downward trend reflects a tendency towards diminishing participation in the labour force. This is said to be true of many developing countries.

Table 1 : Distribution of Working Female Population in India, 1911-1991

Census Year	*Percentage of female workers to total female population*
1911	33.7
1921	33.7
1931	27.6
1941	N.A.
1951	23.3
1961	28.0
1971	14.2
1981	19.7
1991	22.7

Note: The 1951 Census figures do not include the State of Jammu & Kashmir.

Sources: Census of India, 1961, Paper No.1 of 1962, *Final Population* and Census of India, 1991, Series-1 *India, Provisional Population Totals: Workers and Their Distribution,* Paper-3 of 1991.

There are two main reasons why India presents a different scenario. First, economic development could not be fast enough to absorb the rapidly growing population, ensuing from a faster rate of decline in mortality than fertility in the country. Second, as a result of recent industrial development, the spread of modern education, westernisation and urbanisation a new class of people has started to emerge in Indian society. Those who have been successful in climbing up from the lower socio-economic strata to higher ones do not favour the idea of sending females outside homes for work. "They in general, like most upper castes and class people, consider women's involvement in work indignified or ignonimous. Such people tend to withdraw the women from work. The idea is widespread that working for wages is a mark of low status....."[4]. It may also be the case that increasing male incomes lessen pressure upon females to act as a supplementary income earners, especially where family loses social status if the wife works outside the home. Women are the locus of family honour. The notion of honour and shame is very much attached with the activity of women in society. Jeferry's observation aptly describes the existing Indian value system relating to women and work: "... the ability to keep women in seclusions and uninvolved in economic activity outside home is an important index of relative wealth.... The seclusion of women is a function of a family's worth, in an economic sense, but it also becomes indicative of their social worth, or their honour"[5].

Durand has argued that women's participation falls in the early stages of economic development and rises again at a later stage. Thus the total picture supports a U-shaped relationship between development and female's participation rates[6]. Evidence from the Indian census is more on the line of Durand's view than on Patai's. The workforce participation of females started to decline gradually from 1911 to 1951 and then made an upward swing from 1971 to the 1991 census (see Table 1). If the Durand's view is accepted, it can well be expected that females workforce participation will keep on increasing still further or at least until it reaches the level of male workforce participation.

It is well-known that men's attitude towards women or the general images of woman in any society can also be gauged and understood from the nature of involvement of women in economic pursuits. According to the census definition of 'work', females constitute a much smaller proportion of the workforce than males. Despite some improvement in the level of workforce participation of women over earlier censuses at the 1991 census, female workers constitute merely 23 percent of their total population against 52 percent for males at the 1991 census. This fact is a clear indication of the subordinate position of women in Indian society.

Regional and Ethnic Variations

The female WPRs vary not only across the countries, but also within the same country depending on the level of economic development, type of family, system of religious belief and level of female education and the nature of political system. For these reasons the level of female participation varies markedly from one region to another and also between rural and urban areas within the same region in India. For example, it will be evident in Table 2 that States of South India (Andhra Pradesh, Karnataka and Tamil Nadu) (except for Kerala), western zone and eastern region (except for Tripura) (see Table 2) have claimed a higher proportion of women in the workforce

Table 2 : Percentage of Workers by Sex at 1981 and 1991 Censuses

States	*Males*		*Females*	
	Percentage of workers		*Percentage of workers*	
	1981	*1991*	*1981*	*1991*
INDIA*	52.6	51.6	19.7	22.7
1. Andhra Pradesh	57.7	55.4	33.5	34.8
2. Arunachal Pradesh	58.6	54.2	45.7	39.6
3. Bihar	50.2	47.9	13.5	15.7
4. Goa	48.5	49.5	21.9	20.5
5. Gujarat	52.9	54.3	20.7	27.1
6. Haryana	49.9	47.9	10.6	11.3
7. Himachal Pradesh	52.6	49.7	31.9	34.8
8. Karnataka	54.6	53.9	25.3	29.3
9. Kerala	44.9	47.8	16.6	16.9
10. Madhya Pradesh	54.5	52.1	30.6	32.5
11. Maharashtra	53.7	52.0	30.6	33.0
12. Manipur	46.8	45.4	39.5	37.5
13. Meghalaya	54.0	49.1	37.5	36.7
14. Mizoram	52.5	54.4	37.7	43.9
15. Nagaland	52.6	48.6	43.2	39.2
16. Orissa	55.9	53.7	19.8	20.8
17. Punjab	53.8	53.3	6.2	6.8
18. Rajasthan	50.9	49.1	21.1	27.0
19. Sikkim	57.2	53.6	37.6	52.7
20. Tamil Nadu	56.6	57.0	26.5	30.9
21. Tripura	50.7	47.5	12.8	14.3
22. Uttar Pradesh	50.8	49.4	8.1	12.9
23. West Bengal	50.3	51.4	8.1	11.7

*Excludes Assam and Jammu & Kashmir.

Source : Same as for Table 1.

than those of other regions of the country. Furthermore, Punjab has recorded the smallest proportion of female workers (about 7 percent), while the State of Sikkim has recorded about 53 percent of female workers at the 1991 census. The States of Tripura, West Bengal, Uttar Pradesh, Orissa, Kerala, Haryana, Bihar and Goa have recorded a much smaller proportion of the working female population than the national average of about 23 percent (see Table 2). In other words, variations in economic participation at the state level are marked more in the case of females than males.

The states of Northern India show a lower level of female activity rate than other regions, since they have a long tradition of feudalism coupled with an obdurate kind of patriarchal and patrilineal family system. According to Boserup, a larger tribal population in the South where women generally play a very important subsistence role as well as greater influence of Islamic culture in the North largely account for a lower female activity in the northern parts of India.[7]

Under the traditional division of labour in a patriarchal society characterised predominantly by agricultural economy, women are usually expected to engage themselves in work within or near the homestead (food processing and preparation, household maintenance, animal husbandry and petty agricultural activities) depending upon the economic condition of the family, while men work outside the homestead (fieldwork, trading, wage, labour and employment in industries).

It is not to be construed from the above that all the segments of the Indian society are under a similar type of patriarchal system. The reality of patriarchy in India has always diverged from the ideal. Women from different castes and classes have been subjected to different levels of patriarchal authority. Women belonging to lower castes or class are usually less subjected to patriarchy than those belonging to the well-to-do agricultural households. Similarly the Hindu and the Christian women experience much less patriarchal control than the Muslim women. The tribal women, irrespective of religion, experience still far less amount of patriarchal control. Men and women function under the egalitarian ethos. Within this framework of contrasts, the position of women varies quite considerably in the country. It is not our intention here to offer a discussion on the full range of regional, religious, caste and socio-economic differentials. The level of patriarchal control depends not only on the age-old system of beliefs and social practices or historical circumstances, but also on the level of economic contributions made by females to the sustenance of family vis-a-vis those made by males of the family. Economic condition is in fact more important than other factors, for economic condition provides a material base for patriarchal domination. Work makes a woman worthy in the household. A study of Bangladeshi women has shown that increasing poverty in rural areas has greatly eroded the system of patriarchy among the poor. The poorer-households generally have more egalitarian relationships and responsibilities between the sexes. Despite similarities in the patriarchal structure, patrilineal descent and inheritance and patrilocal system of residence after marriage, women in India, compared to those in Bangladesh, are less dependent on men and less vulnerable in the absence of a male.

Economic empowerment of women is one of the most vital conditions for the upliftment of women's social status. Unless the women become economically independent or make nearly equal economic contributions to the family for its sustenance, they cannot be equal to men in the decision-making process. The problem of gender-based discriminations or subordination of women is very much rooted in the economic dependence of women. Possibly realising this fact the Government of India has launched several schemes for economic empowerment of women such as support to training and employment programme for women (STEP), opening of employment-cum-income generating production units, condensed courses of education for adult women and vocational training programme, national credit fund for women, *Mahila Samriddhi Yojana* (MSY) and various support services for women like ICDS and creches. Impact of these schemes and strategies are, however, yet to be felt in our society.

Rural-Urban and Educational Variations

The share of workers is two to three times larger than that of female workers in India. The disparity between male and female workforce participation is in fact much greater in urban than in rural areas. In urban areas females form a very small proportion of workers to their total population. During 1971-91 the share of female workers, for instance, was somewhere between 7 and 10 percent, while male workers constituted about 49 percent of their total population (Table 3). This is contrary to the general expectation that women in urban areas are more likely to be involved in work outside their homes than in rural areas.

Table 3 : Percentage of Workers to the Total Population by Sex During 1971-1991 Census

Year	*Total* *Rural* *Urban*	*Persons*	*Males*	*Females*
1971	Total	34.2	52.7	14.2
	Rural	35.3	53.8	15.9
	Urban	29.6	48.9	7.2
1981	Total	36.7	52.6	19.7
	Rural	38.8	53.8	23.1
	Urban	30.0	49.1	8.3
1991	Total	37.7	51.6	22.7
	Rural	40.2	52.5	27.2
	Urban	30.4	48.9	9.7

Notes : 1. Excludes Assam where the 1981 Census could not be held and Jammu & Kashmir where the 1991 Census was not held.

2. The 1971 Census figures include workers and non-workers with secondary work. The 1981 and 1991 Census figures include main workers and marginal workers.

Source: Same as for Table 1.

There are marked variations in workforce participation between the sexes by place of residence at the state level. In the case of urban areas the proportion of working females is much less than that of the national average in Rajasthan, Bihar, Punjab, Haryana, Uttar Pradesh, West Bengal, Tripura and Kerala. But for Rajasthan, these states show a similar trend in the case of rural areas, too (Table 4).

The detailed classification of workers by different categories for the 1991 census is not yet available; nevertheless, some idea about the latest situation can certainly be had from the 1971 and 1981 censuses. An analysis of these census materials reveals that of all those employed in organised sector, about 11 percent are in public sector and 18 percent in private sector. In urban areas most working women are surprisingly concentrated in agriculture, hunting, forestry and fishing (28.7%), manufacturing (27.4%), community, social and personal services (26.4%) and wholesale and retail trade (10%),

Table 4 : Percentage of Workers to the Total Population by Sex and Place of Residence and States, 1981 and 1991

States	*Rural*				*Urban*			
	1981		*1991*		*1981*		*1991*	
	M	*F*	*M*	*F*	*M*	*F*	*M*	*F*
INDIA*	53.8	23.1	52.5	27.2	49.1	8.3	48.9	9.7
Andhra Pradesh	60.2	40.0	58.0	42.9	49.6	11.8	48.5	12.5
Arunachal Pradesh	58.5	47.6	53.6	42.9	60.2	11.6	58.1	14.0
Bihar	51.1	14.6	48.9	17.1	44.3	4.8	42.2	5.9
Goa	47.4	24.9	48.8	23.8	50.7	15.1	50.5	15.5
Gujarat	54.2	26.8	55.8	36.5	50.2	6.5	51.7	8.8
Haryana	49.8	12.3	47.7	13.2	50.3	4.4	48.5	5.4
Himachal Pradesh	52.4	33.4	49.4	36.6	54.3	11.3	52.3	14.1
Karnataka	57.2	30.7	55.9	36.3	48.4	11.8	49.5	13.1
Kerala	45.2	17.7	48.0	17.9	43.4	11.8	47.2	14.0
Madhya Pradesh	56.4	35.8	53.9	39.1	47.3	9.6	46.6	10.3
Maharashtra	55.4	40.8	53.0	45.8	50.9	10.1	50.5	11.6
Manipur	48.4	43.4	47.4	41.4	42.2	28.6	39.9	27.4
Meghalaya	55.4	42.0	50.6	41.1	47.5	16.1	42.6	17.1
Mizoram	54.1	42.8	55.6	47.7	47.8	21.9	53.0	39.6
Nagaland	52.8	48.3	48.3	42.6	51.5	10.9	50.1	21.8
Orissa	56.7	21.1	54.6	22.7	50.1	9.5	48.4	8.3
Punjab	54.4	6.9	54.0	7.0	52.0	4.2	51.7	6.2
Rajasthan	52.2	25.0	49.9	32.8	46.2	5.9	46.4	7.1
Sikkim+	56.6	41.4	53.5	55.8	60.1	15.6	54.8	19.1
Tamil Nadu	59.2	33.5	58.7	39.2	51.2	12.0	53.8	14.5
Tripura	51.3	13.3	47.4	15.2	45.6	8.7	47.7	9.4
Uttar Pradesh	51.5	9.0	50.1	14.7	47.5	3.5	46.3	5.3
West Bengal	50.6	8.9	52.1	13.5	49.6	5.6	49.5	6.5

*Excludes Assam and Jammu & Kashmir.

+ Decline in number of workers in urban areas of Sikkim may be due to the reorganisation of five major towns by excluding certain portions from them which were added to the adjoining villages after the 1981 Census.

Source : Same as for Table 1.

While most male workers are concentrated in manufacturing (27.4%), community, social and personal services (21.3%), wholesale and retail trade (10%), agriculture, hunting and fishing (10%) at the 38th round of the National Sample Survey. A nearly similar pattern existed in the cases of 27th and 32nd rounds of the NSS (Table 5). Worker's classification by broad categories at the 1991 census suggests that females compose a relatively bigger proportion as agricultural labourers and household industry workers. This does not vary much by the place of residence—rural and urban (see Table 6). Here it is evident that the women are marginalised equally in both rural and urban areas.

Table 5 : Percentage Distribution of Workers (Main & Marginal) According to the Usual Industrial Divisions by Sex in Urban India Based on the NSS

Industrial Category	*Males*			*Females*		
	Survey round number			*Survey round number*		
	27th	*32nd*	*38th*	*27th*	*32nd*	*38th*
(1) Agriculture, hunting, forestry & fishing	10.7	10.6	10.3	32.8	31.9	28.7
(2) Mining and quarrying	0.9	0.9	1.5	0.7	0.5	0.7
(3) Manufacturing	26.9	27.6	27.4	25.0	29.6	27.4
(4) Electricity, gas and water	0.8	1.1	1.2	0.1	0.1	0.2
(5) Construction	4.3	4.2	5.1	3.3	2.2	3.6
(6) Wholesale and retail trade, etc.	20.1	21.6	20.1	9.4	8.7	10.4
(7) Transport, storage and communication	9.0	9.7	10.2	0.9	1.0	1.5
(8) Financing, real estate, etc.	3.0	2.9	3.1	0.4	0.6	1.1
(9) Community, social and personal services	24.0	21.4	21.3	26.7	25.3	26.4
(10) Others	0.3	0.1	0.0	0.8	0.1	0.0

Source: Sarvekshana (1986), Vol.9, No.4, S-112 and 113.

Table 6 : Distribution of Workers by Broad Categories, Place of Residence and Sex in India, 1991

Place of Residence	Sex	Total Main Workers	Percentage	Cultivators	Agricultural Labourers	Household Industry Workers	Other Workers
*INDIA**							
Total	Persons	285,422,913	100	38.7	26.1	3.6	31.5
	Males	219,233,479	100	40.0	20.9	3.3	35.8
	Females	66,189,434	100	34.5	43.6	4.6	17.3
Rural	Persons	221,590,657	100	48.5	31.8	3.1	16.7
	Males	164,159,136	100	51.2	26.1	2.8	19.3
	Females	57,431,521	100	39.0	47.9	3.8	9.3
Urban	Persons	63,832,256	100	5.0	6.7	5.6	82.8
	Males	55,074,343	100	4.9	5.3	4.8	84.9
	Females	8,757,913	100	5.5	14.9	10.3	69.3

*Excludes Jammu & Kashmir where the 1991 Census was not held.

Source: Same as for Table 1.

It is generally believed that the rise in the level of female literacy would cause greater female participation rates, but this does not seem to happen even in urban areas despite the fact that urban areas offer numerous kinds of jobs for both skilled and non-skilled people. Since leisure has status, middle—and high-income educated women often choose not to work. Further, where it is difficult to combine child care with wage employment outside the home, women often withdraw from the labour force after marriage or the start of child-bearing.

Rise in the level of education has unexpectedly resulted in a lower level of female participation in India. Females who are able to receive modern education mostly belong to upper castes and other privileged sections of the society. They are often discouraged by their husbands to work outside the home. People who make enough money to support family rarely favour the idea of working women, no matter how high is their education. "The obvious reason is that the educated women are usually married to better educated men than themselves who are well-placed in society, and, therefore, the female members of such households are in much less economic need or much less encouraged to seek jobs, or the jobs appropriate to their social status are not available"[8]. For many people it is not dignified to allow their women to work outside. A strange kind of sexual morality is attached to the woman in India irrespective of religion. The women who are frequently seen outside their homes are often considered 'loose and immoral'.

Female's work is generally not a valued activity in India. While participation in certain professional categories may be on the increase and while more and more women are entering or ready to enter non-traditional occupations, there are still many barriers to female work participation. For an average Indian woman, work participation is a status-relegating rather than status-enhancing activity. Highly educated professional women represent an exception to this general pattern. This notion may not prevail uniformly throughout the country. In South India, for instance, a higher level of education of women means a higher encouragement for them to work.

But throughout the country, metropolises or big cities present a situation conspicuously different from the rest of urban areas. The new metropolitan milieu has effected numerous changes in the status and role of women. A large member of educated women have come out of their homes to work with men in office and industry. In cities like Calcutta, Delhi, Bombay, Bangalore, Madras, Hyderabad, Ahmedabad and in numerous others women are always seen freely travelling and working with men. Most of these women are, however, from 'westernised'/urban families generally with high levels of education. Women are more and more keen to enter the public services, professions and earn regular salaries. This is partly because of the increasing cost and the demands of higher standard of living and partly because of the increasing tendency among women to get rid of male subordination and endless drudgery of housework. But in terms of the overall picture such women create forms a very tiny part of the working population. It is worthwhile to note that a new kind of urban scenario impelling greater participation of women has been emerging fast since the early sixties, and there is absolutely no chance of reversal from this new trend.

The Female Child Labour

Under the Article 29 of the Constitution of India, no person below the age 14 can be employed in a factory, mine or any hazardous work. The exploitation of children is also protected by the

Factories Act, 1948 and the Minimum Wages Act, 1948. But very often young children are seen engaged in a variety of activities. The law is bound to be ineffective when poverty keeps people face-to-face with death. Poverty forces starving households to send their children to work for a living rather than to schools for learning. A sizeable proportion of working children are parentless or homeless as well. Those who need cheap labour tend to employ poor children for a very low wage or sometimes for two square meals and treat them as inferior humans. This makes a mockery of democratic ideals and the concept of welfare state as enshrined in the Constitution of India.

At the 1981 census, the working male population below 15 constituted about six percent in rural areas and about three percent in urban areas. The practice of child labour is more common among boys than among girls both in rural and urban sectors. But the practice of female labour is lesser still in urban areas. Both at the 1971 and 1981 censuses working female population below the age 15 constituted less than one percent of the total female working population. This is much less than most of the developing countries in the world. This is mainly because most parents do not allow their young daughters to go outside their homes to work even in the case of economic hardships. Protection of virginity of young girls is always the upper most in the mind of parents. Young girls, compared to women, are most likely to fall prey to sex abuse, especially when they are away from their parents. This is one of the seminal reasons why rural to urban migration is highly selective of males in India[9]. The young girls often tend to work along with their parents—usually mothers. Poor parents want their young daughters to stay behind to mind the domestic affairs and younger siblings, and thus they release their mothers for wage earning work[10]. A report of the National Commission on Self-Employed Women and Women in Informal Sector also provides similar evidence.

It is socially and economically advantageous for parents to keep their daughters at home. The poor parents are not able to realise the fact that they play havoc with their daughters' future by keeping them at home at the expense of their schooling. Because of the increasing practice of dowry and the lack of any material return from their daughters in future, parents often treat them as their liability. It is usually easier or cheaper for parents to find suitable grooms for illiterate or semi-illiterate than well-educated daughters. Neglect of education to female children is well reflected in the fact that the level of female literacy is 39 percent, contrary to 64 percent for males, in India according to the 1991 census. It is really a pity that the Indian women is devalued as a child, denied equal access to education and often devoid of skills, she carries into her womanhood all the accumulated burdens of her past.

Concluding Observations

It is usually argued that males work more than females, but in reality this is not the case. Female's economic contribution to family or the society in general has always remained misrepresented because of the bias inherent in the definition of work. The term 'work' has been defined in such a way in Indian censuses or surveys that male's work get over-represented or female's work remain underestimated. As female's household work is always unpaid, their work is not recorded in economic terms. The domestic or household work is not recorded in the censuses or surveys also because that work does not bring in a wage and whatever a woman does is not considered productive in traditional sense. The basic contradiction is that housework performed for one's own family is not regarded as an economic activity, unlike housework performed for somebody else for wages. It is really strange that women who work inside homes or take care of family business are enumerated as non-workers, whereas men who work on their own or family land are enumerated as workers. It is not really understandable why such a significant contribution of women continues to remain unquantified in India or elsewhere. This conceptual problem with work is in fact characteristic feature of most censuses and surveys in the world. The women all over the world, and still more so in the Third World, are victims of old-fashioned statistics[11]. Women's household work has to be recognised on par with any other work performed by men. The age-old myth that men produce and women consume has to be demystified. Recognition of women's contributions to the household economy in particular and society in general would greatly alter and improve the women's image in society.

It is true that there are a number of occupations and industries where women are invariably preferred, but their economic participation, as said before, is still much less than that of men. Women as professionals continue to be marginalised. For the purpose of social and economic empowerment, the Constitution of India should be suitably amended to provide reservation in jobs for women same as the *Dalits* or the OBCs. There are many professional areas or activities such as teaching, nursing, pediatrics and nutrition, community health services, social education and welfare, book-keeping, secretarial services, manufacturing, construction, trade and commerce, transport and a host of white-collar jobs where women are in a position to prove themselves more efficient and useful than men. Increasing female employment is needed also because it exerts a negative influence on the fertility of women which is important for population control. Work participation provides an alternative identity to the motherhood role.

References

The paper was largely written while the author held a UNDP Fellowship at the Institute of Social Studies, the Hague (the Netherlands) during 1989-90.

1. As the term 'workforce participation rate' (WPR) is the equivalent of the 'labour force participation rate' and 'general activity rate' or 'activity rate', they are used interchangeably in the paper. The term is defined as the number of working people per 100 of the total population.
2. Patriarchy is used in a general sense to suggest a socio-sexual system in which males exercise a superior authority and economic privileges in the family.

3. R. Patai, *Women in the Modern World,* New York, Free Press, 1969.
4. M.N. Srinivas, *The Changing Position of Indian Women,* Delhi, Oxford University Press, 1986.
5. Patricia Jeffery, *Frogs in a Well: Indian Women in Purdah,* Delhi, Vikas Publishing House, 1979, p.25.
6. J. Durand, *The Labour Force in Economic Development,* Princeton, Princeton University Press, 1975.
7. E. Boserup, *Women's Role in Economic Development,* St. Martin's Press, New York, 1970.
8. J.P. Singh, *Patterns of Rural-Urban Migration in India,* New Delhi, Inter-India Publications, 1986, p.190.
9. J.P. Singh, 'Age and Sex Differentials in Migration in India', *Canadian Journal of Population Studies,* 1988, 15(1): 87-89.
10. Malavika Karlekar, *Poverty and Women's Work: a Study of Sweeper Women in Delhi,* New Delhi, Vikas Publication House, 1982.
11. M. Fong, 'One reason that women are too easily excluded from national development planning is because they are victims of old fashioned statistics', *Ceres,* May-June, 1980, pp.28-32.

APPENDIX I

Female Workforce Participation Rates in Selected Developing Countries

Countries	%	*Countries*	%
ASIA		Ghana (1984)	45.8
Bahrain (1987)	10.3	Lesotho (1976)	21.7
Bangladesh(1984-85)	5.6	Madagascar (1985)	31.6
China (1982)	47.0	Mauritius (1987)	29.3
Cyprus (1985)	33.4	Niger (1977)	4.4
Hong Kong (1986)	37.8	South Africa (1985)	26.7
India (1987)	19.8	Sudan (1973)	10.0
Indonesia (1985)	32.6	Swaziland (1976)	54.6
Iraq (1988)	11.6	Togo (1981)	28.3
Israel (1983)	26.8	Tunisia (1984)	13.3
Japan (1987)	39.1	Zimbabwe (1982)	25.4
Republic of Korea (1987)	32.3	*LATIN AMERICA*	
Kuwait (1985)	18.1	Argentina (1987)	20.0
Nepal (1981)	32.4	Bahamas (1980)	36.0
Pakistan (1984-85)	5.8	Barbados (1987)	58.4
Singapore (1987)	36.3	Bermuda (1980)	51.3
Thailand (1984)	50.1	Bolivia (1987)	14.5
AFRICA		Brazil (1980)	27.9
Benin (1986)	23.9	Colombia (1987)	34.3
Botswana (1984-85)	36.0	Costa Rica (1987)	20.8
Burkina Faso (85)	48.2	Cuba (1986)	30.6
Burundi (1986)	56.9	Chile (1986)	20.6
Cameroon (1985)	30.3	Equador (1988)	20.4
Egypt (1984)	13.5	Guatemala (1986-87)	16.2
Gambia (1983)	43.6	Guyana (1987)	21.0
		Jamaica (1985)	41.1
		Mexico (1980)	18.2
		Peru (1989)	33.6

Source : Yearbook of Labour Statistics, Geneva, International Labour Office, 1988:13-38.

3

Women's Participation in Economic Activities in India

*Prasanta K. Majumdar and Suswati Dutta**

Female labour force, as a part of the total labour force, is an important component of the economic development of a country. Fertility depends on economic activities of the population especially of the female population. In most cases a negative correlation is to be found between females' participation in economic activity and the fertility rate. This relation varies widely from one socio-economic context to another: that it appears to be closer in developed than in underdeveloped areas, in urban rather than in rural areas and in industrialised sectors in comparison with non-industrialised sectors (Mitra et al.,1980). Thus it is interesting to make a study of rural-urban differentials as well as inter-industry variations in female participation over the intercensal period. This paper examines changes in the pattern of females' participation as main and marginal workers in different industries in India during 1961-91 and intends to highlight the rural-urban differentials in female labour force participation, if any. It also proposes to analyse the whys and wherefore of these changes despite the fact that the data from census reports and the quinquennial surveys of employment and unemployment conducted by the National Sample Surveys (NSS) are subject to several kinds of limitations.

* The authors are respectively Associate Professor and Project Assistant in Population Studies Unit, Indian Statistical Institute, Calcutta.

In the census, there is a possibility of not only over—or under-estimation of workers, particularly female workers, but also a possibility of females reporting the occupation of their husbands as their own occupation. There is another problem of identifying the 'unpaid family workers' and determining the amount of work required for the inclusion of 'unpaid family workers' in the active population. Most of the unpaid family workers are female. What is interesting is that the amount of work done by them is often ignored in surveys and censuses. Moreover, females are more often left out of reckoning than males when they are in the marginal workers' category. The problem of comparability of available data for different censuses is yet another serious problem for the researchers.

In 1961, 1971 and 1981 censuses , the data on workers were collected on the basis of labour force approach—i.e., classifying a person according to his status as worker or non-worker by verifying his participation in some economic activity during a specified reference period. The reference period for seasonal workers employed in agriculture, agriculture-related activities and household industries was the last working season in 1961 and last one year in 1971. The reference period for workers in regular employment in trade, profession, services, business, etc. was reduced from a fortnight in 1961 to a week in 1971. One more change was introduced in 1961, that is, in the case of regular work, a person was to return himself/herself as a worker or a non-worker, whereas in 1971, a person was to be considered as a worker according to the type of the main activity which s/he was engaged in most of the time. Accordingly, many persons who were workers only marginally might have been counted as 'workers' in 1961 and as 'non-workers' in 1971. In the 1981 Census, the definition of a worker required that a person spends at least 183 days per year in one activity, while a person who worked for some time during the last year but not for 183 days, was treated as a marginal worker. This approach was adopted with the expectation that a partial comparability of 1981 census economic data with that of 1971 as well as 1961 would be possible. It was expected that the main workers of 1981 would correspond to the workers of 1971 and the main workers and marginal workers together of 1981 would correspond to the workers of 1961 (R.G., 1981). Thus the main and marginal workers of 1961 and marginal workers of 1971 are to be estimated separately.

The concept of 'work', as adopted in the 1981 Census, has been by and large continued in 1991 Census for comparability, the definitions of main and marginal workers remain the same. There is only one exception in the 1991 Census. That is the extension of the reference period from one year to any time before the date of enumeration in case of non-workers 'seeking or available' for work so as to know the number of entrants to the labour force for the first time. Moreover, special care has been taken to ensure that the economic activity of unpaid workers, especially females and children, is properly enumerated in the 1991 Census. The final economic tables of 1991 Census are yet to be published and only workers under four industrial categories, namely cultivators, agricultural labourers, household industry and other workers are available.

Since the analysis chiefly covers data from four consecutive censuses (1961-91), the scope and limitations of the National Sample Survey (NSS) estimates on 'worker' are not discussed in detail here. The NSS data from the three surveys, i.e., 1972-73 (27th round), 1977-78 (32nd round) and 1983 (38th round) are used to supplement the analysis of census figures.

Method of Estimation

In order to measure the possible extent of the effect on data, ensuing from differences in the definition of worker between 1961 and 1971 censuses, the Registrar-General of India conducted a sample survey during December 1971 and July 1972 where the 1971 economic questions were canvassed in one sample and the 1961 questions in the another (R.G., 1974). Thus an adjusted labour force participation rates in 1971, according to the 1961 Census definition and vice versa, were obtained by sex, by residence and by three categories of main activity, viz cultivators, agricultural labourers and other workers.

For arriving at the comparable estimates of the number of workers under each category, the ratio method used by the Central Statistical Organisation (CSO) has been followed (CSO, 1980). Now, on the assumption that the estimated effect of conceptual difference in the participation rate for each of the three categories of main activity is fairly stable and uniform in the different industry-groups falling within each main activity, the revised estimates of workers at the industry level by sex separately for rural and urban areas have been worked out. In the 1961 Census, Standard Industrial Classification (SIC-1960) was used for the industrial category of workers whereas in the 1971 Census, National Industrial Classification (NIC-1970) was used for the same. For the purpose of comparison, the 1961 actual figures of workers have been reclassified into NIC-1970 and then re-grouped into nine industrial categories of workers adopted in 1971.

Table 1 : Workers of 1961 by Sex and Industry, Adjusted According to the 1971 Concept of 'Worker'

(in ' 000)

*Industry**	*Total*			*Rural*			*Urban*		
	Persons	*Males*	*Females*	*Persons*	*Males*	*Females*	*Persons*	*Males*	*Females*
I	84,674	65,430	19,244	83,240	64,230	19,010	1,432	1,198	234
II	27,975	16,859	11,116	27,059	16,274	10,785	916	585	331
III	6,869	5,230	1,639	6,043	4,529	1,514	825	701	124
IV	850	724	126	650	551	99	199	172	27
V(a)	8,184	5,463	2,721	6,455	4,315	2,139	1,729	1,147	582
V(b)	7,591	6,994	597	2,257	1,974	283	5,335	5,020	315
VI	2,367	2,094	273	1,342	1,166	176	1,026	929	97
VII	7,751	7,108	643	3,312	2,900	412	4,439	4,208	231
VIII	2,916	2,866	50	860	848	12	2,057	2,019	38
IX	16,169	13,151	3,018	9,484	7,505	1,979	6,685	5,646	1,039
Total	165,346	125,919	39,427	140,702	104,293	36,409	24,643	21,625	3,018

*I. Cultivators;
II. Agricultural Labourers;
III. Livestock, Forestry, Fishing, Hunting and Plantations, Orchards and Allied Activities;
IV. Mining and Quarrying;
V. Manufacturing, Processing, Servicing and Repairs.;
VI. Construction;
VII. Trade and Commerce;
VIII. Transport, Storage and Communication.; and
IX. Other Services.

The main worker of 1961, according to the 1971 Census, was estimated by multiplying the main worker of the 1961 Census by the ratio of actual labour force participation rate of the 1971 Census and the labour force participation rate was estimated from 1971 Census according to the 1961 Census definition. These ratios were worked out for 'cultivators', 'agricultural labourers' and 'other workers' by sex for rural and urban areas separately. For estimating the number of workers in the industry, livestock, forestry, etc., the ratio for 'agricultural labourer' is used, keeping it in mind that these activities are basically seasonal in nature, whereas for other industries, the ratio for 'other workers' is used, since work in these industries is principally regular in nature. Thus, the estimated main workers of 1961 by sex, industry and residence are shown in Table 1. Now subtracting these figures from the corresponding 1961 actual figures, the marginal workers are estimated and are given in Table 2.

Table 2 : Estimated Marginal Workers by Sex and Industry, India, 1961

(in'000)

	Total			*Rural*			*Urban*		
Industry	*Persons*	*Males*	*Females*	*Persons*	*Males*	*Females*	*Persons*	*Males*	*Females*
I.	14,946	1,034	13,912	14,648	987	13,661	298	47	251
II.	3,546	465	3,081	3,543	555	2,988	93	**	93
III.	500	46	454	574	154	420	35	35	**35
IV.	69	23	46	58	19	39	11	4	7
V(a)	1,168	174	994	990	146	844	179	28	151
V(b)	384	191	193	178	67	111	205	124	81
VI	157	62	95	108	39	69	48	23	25
VII	424	202	222	260	98	162	164	104	60
VIII	93	78	15	34	29	5	60	50	10
IX	2,072	1,023	1,049	1,034	254	780	409	140	269
Total	23,359	3,298	20,061	21,427	2,348	19,079	1,450	718	982

* For description refer to Table I.

** Conceptually there are no male marginal workers.

Table 3 : Estimated Marginal Workers by Sex and Industry, India, 1971

(in '000)

	Total			*Rural*			*Urban*		
Industry	*Persons*	*Males*	*Females*	*Persons*	*Males*	*Females*	*Persons*	*Males*	*Females*
III.	500	46	454	574	154	420	35	35	**35
I.	3,524	937	2,587	3,442	883	2,559	82	54	28
II	7,223	1,290	5,933	7,330	1,601	5,729	204	**	204
III	344	51	293	429	160	269	24	**	24
IV	40	18	22	28	11	17	12	7	5
V(a)	347	112	235	268	83	185	79	29	50
V(b)	369	224	145	146	65	81	223	159	64
VI	79	45	34	42	22	20	37	23	14
VII	308	215	93	126	74	52	183	142	41
VIII	120	97	23	33	26	7	87	71	16
IX	675	306	369	329	151	178	345	154	191
Total	13,029	3,295	9,734	12,173	3,076	9,097	856	219	637

\+ Excluding Sikkim

* For description refer to Table 1.

** Conceptually there are no male marginal workers.

In the estimation of the 1971 labour force according to the 1961 concept of worker, the adjustment factors are the ratios of actual 1961 participation rates and participation rates adjusted according to the 1971 Census concept. Then, for estimating the number of workers by sex and industry for rural and urban areas separately, the same method, as for the 1961, is used. Thus, the estimated total workers, i.e., main and marginal together in 1971, are obtained. Now subtracting the actual 1971 Census figures of main workers from corresponding estimated figures for total workers, the marginal workers in 1971 are estimated, as shown in Table 3.

Female Work Force

In the 1981 Census, 222 million persons were main workers of which 45 million were females, constituting 20 percent of the total main workers of whom 66 million are females. Total main workers in 1971 were 180 million of whom females accounted for 17 percent. The estimated figure for female main workers in 1961 was 39 million constituting 23 percent of the total estimated main workers. In the rural areas the female main workers constituted 26 percent, 22 percent, 19 percent and 25 percent in 1991, 1981, 1971 and 1961 respectively, whereas the respective figures for urban areas were 13, 11, 10 and 12 percent.

Table 4. Distribution of Female Main Workers by Broad Industrial Category and Sex Ratio, India, 1961-1991+

*Industry**	*Rural*								*Urban*							
	Percentages of female main workers				*Sex ratio (females per thousand males)*				*Percentages of female main workers*				*Sex ratio (females per thousand males)*			
	1961	1971	1981	1991	1961	1971	1981	1991	1961	1971	1981	1991	1961	1971	1981	1991
I	52.2	32.6	37.1	39.0	296	135	194	263	7.7	4.2	4.6	5.5	195	93	118	180
II	29.6	54.4	50.2	48.0	663	501	605	642	11.0	17.5	16.6	14.9	566	437	470	442
III	4.2	2.6	1.8	N.A	334	235	211	N.A	4.1	2.0	1.8	N.A	177	145	129	N.A
IV	0.3	0.3	0.3	N.A	180	179	N.A	0.9	1.0	0.7	N.A	157	114	82	N.A	
V(a)	5.9	0.6	3.8	3.8	495	265	382	464	19.3	10.0	10.5	10.3	507	264	328	340
V(b)	0.8	1.6	2.1	N.A	143	147	161	N.A	10.4	13.9	14.6	N.A	63	62	74	N.A
VI	0.5	0.4	0.6	N.A	151	108	140	N.A	3.2	3.9	3.1	N.A	104	94	96	N.A
VII	1.1	1.0	1.1	N.A	142	84	98	N.A	7.7	8.2	8.9	N.A	55	45	55	N.A
VIII	0.0	0.1	0.1	N.A	14	33	24	N.A	1.3	3.2	2.2	N.A	19	35	30	N.A
IX	5.4	3.4	2.9	9.3	264	140	157	169	34.4	38.1	37.0	69.3	184	190	228	130
N=	100.0	100.0	100.0	100.0	349	232	289	350	100.0	100.0	100.0	100.0	139	116	132	159

\+ The 1991 Census figures have been calculated from Provisional Population Totals: Workers and their Distribution, Series -1, Paper -3.

* For description see Table 1.

N.A= Not available.

Table 4 presents the percentage distribution of female main workers in rural and urban India by industrial categories at the 1961, 1971 and 1981 censuses. It is not possible to include 1991 data in this table because the general economic tables for 1991 Census are yet to be published. In Table 4, some marked changes in females' economic activity, particularly in the rural sector, are seen. Some important facts which emerge from this table are: first, the high sex ratio, i.e., females per thousand males, of workers was mainly concentrated in agricultural activities. Secondly, there was a large shift towards agricultural labourers at the expense of cultivators between 1961 and 1971 and this is true of both rural and urban sectors. Thirdly, the 'non-household manufacturing' is the only industry where a gradual upward trend is observed. And lastly, the service sector predominates the females' employment in the urban areas.

Table 5 : Distribution of Female Marginal Workers by Broad Industrial Category and Sex Ratio India, 1961-1981+

Industry*	Rural						Urban					
	Percentage of female main workers			Sex ratio (females per thousand males)			Percentage of female main workers			Sex ratio (females per thousand males)		
	1961	1971	1981	1961	1971	1981	1961	1971	1981	1961	1971	1981
I	71.6	28.1	49.0	13841	2898	6112	25.6	4.4	16.5	5340	518	3108
II	15.7	63.0	42.3	5384	3578	6680	9.5	32.0	26.0	**	**	3258
III	2.2	3.0	1.6	2727	1681	2564	3.6	3.8	2.4	**	**	1333
IV	0.2	0.2	0.1	2053	1545	1617	0.7	0.8	0.1	1750	714	280
V(a)	4.4	2.0	3.3	5781	2229	7712	15.4	7.8	21.1	5393	1624	6601
V(b)	0.6	0.9	1.6	1657	1246	2988	8.2	10.1	12.0	653	402	1106
VI	0.4	0.2	0.3	1769	909	1514	2.5	2.2	1.5	1086	608	328
VII	0.8	0.6	0.8	1653	703	1586	6.1	6.4	9.1	577	289	927
VIII	0.0	0.1	0.1	172	269	267	1.0	2.5	0.6	200	225	123
IX	4.1	1.9	0.9	3071	1179	1825	27.4	30.0	10.7	1921	1240	1084
N=	100.0	100.0	100.0	8125	2857	5756	100.0	100.0	100.0	1368	2909	1714+

\+ Marginal workers by industrial category for 1991 are not available.

* For description see Table 1.

** Conceptually there are no male marginal workers.

The sex ratio for cultivators and agricultural labourers was highest in 1961, decreased substantially in 1971 and then again went up considerably. There may be some economic reasons behind it. Certain states had made remarkable progress in agriculture during

1961-71 which might have prompted the rural women to withdraw themselves from work. Here, prosperity in agriculture does mean higher productivity through investment of capital and greater use of modern technology. It needs more skilled labour and it might be cheaper to hire suitable labour from outside than to employ the inefficient unpaid female family labour (Mitra et al., 1980). The higher sex ratio in agricultural sector between 1971 and 1981 could be accounted for by the fact that in some states like Punjab, Haryana, Orissa, Andhra Pradesh, Tamil Nadu, etc., it went up considerably.

Table 4 shows the percentage share of cultivators in rural area in 1961 was 52, while the percentage share of agricultural labourers was 54 in 1971. An attempt was made to find out the reasons by the Registrar-General in the survey conducted during 1972-73. "It was found that roughly around 6-10 percent had remained unspecified and 60-70 percent of the changes were due to either retirement or non-workers coming to take up employment" (R.G.,1974). Among other reasons 5 percent of the changes were due to adverse economic conditions like natural calamity, loss of jobs, selling of land due to adversity, etc. The reason, `seeking better prospects', was accounted for by roughly 15-20 percent. No specific differential by sex was observed in rural and urban areas.

Outside the agricultural activities, women are mostly engaged in the manufacturing industry. Over the period of 1961 to 1981, the percentage share of the non-household manufacturing industry has gone up and in urban areas particularly this share is remarkable, the share being 10 percent, 13 percent and 15 percent in 1961, 1971 and 1981 respectively. Females' employment in household manufacturing industries increased steadily during 1971-81 both in rural and urban areas whereas males' employment in this industry was growing slowly, the percentage share of male workers in this industry remaining stagnant during 1961-81. The sharp decline in females' activity in household manufacturing industry, from 6 percent in 1961 to almost one percent in 1971 and from 19 percent in 1961 to 10 percent in 1971 in rural and urban areas respectively was partly due to under-enumeration in 1971 and partly due to real decline in the work participation rate which occurred between 1961 and 1971.

This is dealt with in a greater detail in the subsequent section. The sex ratio in the household manufacturing industry has been increasing consistently over the period of 1971 to 1991, the ratios being 265, 382 and 464 in 1971, 1981 and 1991 respectively in rural areas and 264, 328 and 340 in 1971, 1981 and 1991 respectively in urban areas. This type of change in sex ratio reveals the fact that females are joining this industry at a much faster pace than males.

A very small fraction of Indian women are employed in the mining and quarrying industries. They constitute less than one percent of the total workers in this sector. This is because in certain economic activities which require hard manual labour involving greater risk, male workers are preferred to female workers. Construction is a big industry which is expected to absorb a large number of unskilled female labourers, but only less than one percent of female main workers participate in this industry.

Table 6 : Distribution of Female Workers by Services and Sex Ratio, India, 1971 and 1981

	Number of female workers (in '000)		*Percentage of female workers*		*Sex ratio (female per thousand males)*	
	1971	*1981*	*1971*	*1981*	*1971*	*1981*
Public and Admn. Services	162	332	5.6	8.4	3	6
Sanitary Services	97	91	3.4	2.3	43	41
Education,Scientific and Res. Services	691	1151	24.1	29.0	28	36
Medical and Health Services	223	372	7.8	9.4	31	35
Community Services	33	55	1.2	1.4	7	10
Recreational and Cultural Services	19	24	0.7	0.6	7	7
Personal Services	829	878	28.9	22.1	23	25
Domestic Services	400	496	39.9	12.5	60	88
Laundry Services	282	283	9.8	7.1	42	53
Services not included elsewhere	133	286	4.6	7.2	16	15
Total	2869	3968	100.0	100.0	-	-

Source: Census of India, 1971, Series 1, pt II B(III), General Economic Tables B-IV, 1977; Census of India, 1981 Series I, pt II, Special Report Based on 5 Percent Sample Data, Tables B-12.

The service sector is the only sector where around 30 to 40 percent of the urban female main workers are employed. Of the total urban female main workers 34, 38 and 37 percent were employed in 1961, 1971 and 1981 respectively in this sector. In rural areas agriculture is the largest industry in respect of females' employment and a few female workers were engaged in service sector. Of the total rural female main workers only a little less than five percent were employed in services.

Table 6 shows that around 25 percent of female workers are employed in educational services while it had been increased by about 67 percent between 1971 and 1981 Censuses. A large section of females is engaged in medical and health services, public and administrative services, personal and domestic services. In all the services except personal services, the movement is in the upward direction. Another notable feature is that the sex ratio is steadily increasing in almost all the services indicating a faster rate of growth of females in the service sector compared to their counterpart. The service sector being such an important sector with a large number of urban women indicates the greater attainment of female education.

Marginal Workers

Only in 1981 and 1991 censuses were workers split up into main and marginal workers. However, for the purpose of comparison, workers have been estimated for the 1961 and 1971 censuses as well under some specified assumptions.

The first thing to be noted in Table 2 is that conceptually there were no marginal male workers in two industries, namely 'agricultural labourer' and 'livestock, forestry, etc., and agriculture allied activities' in 1961 and 1971 in urban areas. Two factors are responsible for this. First, in 1961, the enumerators were instructed to record principal and secondary activities where economic activity was recorded against cultivator and agricultural labourer, cultivation was treated as a principal activity. Secondly, questions on cultivation were asked first and as a result the probability that the persons owning small plots but subsisting basically on agricultural labour might have been treated as cultivators was not insignificant. This was also reflected in a sharp decline in the percentage share of female cultivators from eight to four in urban areas and from 52 to 33 in rural areas between 1961 and 1971, whereas a sharp increase appeared in the percentage share of female agricultural labourers, as is depicted in Table 4. Thus the adjusted 1961 Census figure for males in agricultural labourer which should have been lower than the original figure of 1961 appeared to exceed the original figure of 1961. On the other hand, the adjusted 1971 figure for this industry appeared to be less than the 1971 original figure. The number of workers in agriculture allied activities being adjusted using the same adjustment factor used for agricultural labourer, the same trend had been seen for this industry also.

In 1981, total number of marginal workers was enumerated as 22 million, females constituting 84 percent. The respective percentages for 1961 and 1971 were 88 and 75. According to the provisional report of the 1991 Census, total number of female marginal workers is 25 million constituting 85 percent of the total marginal workers (R.G., 1991). Thus females' activity as marginal workers are increasing steadily over the census period 1971-1991. It also appeared that for marginal activity the females dominate the males during the observation period and even this time for both rural and urban residents.

In rural areas, in all the three censuses (i.e., 1961, 1971 and 1981), agriculture is the only industry where most of the females are employed both as main workers and marginal workers. Whereas in urban areas females are coming more and more into the manufacturing industry replacing the service industry. The number of female marginal workers in service sector decreased drastically from 30 percent to about 11 percent over the decade 1971-81 as is depicted in Table 5. The sex-ratio in transport, storage and communication industry is very low in rural and urban sectors. However, the sex ratio in these sectors remained stable in rural areas but decreased considerably in urban area during 1971-81. Manufacturing industry, especially in urban area, is taking an important role in employing a large section of total urban female marginal workers, the share increasing from 18 per cent in 1971 to 33 per cent in 1981. A very negligible part, out of the total female workers, is engaged in mining and quarrying industry and no significant rural-urban difference is observed among these workers. This is due to the fact that the nature of work in the mining industry demands special skill or greater risk and the employers may have some discrimination against female workers. The sex ratios of marginal workers in different sectors reveal the important fact that the primary sector, comprising cultivation, agricultural labour, livestock, forestry, hunting, fishing and allied activities, mining and quarrying; the secondary sector, comprising manufacturing, processing, servicing and repairing and construction and the tertiary sector, comprising trade and commerce, transport, storage and communication and other services were dominated by female workers over the observation period.

The sharp increase of 9 million in the number of marginal workers over 1971-1981 may be considered as an indication of the increase in the number of unemployed mandays rather than the number of persons unemployed. In the absence of census data on unemployment, the National Sample Survey (NSS) estimates on unemployment are considered here. In all the three quinquennial surveys of the NSS, the workers were classified according to their status into three categories: (i) usual status approach with a reference period of 365 days preceding the date of survey; (ii) current week status approach with a reference period of 7 days preceding the date of survey and (iii) current day status approach, reference period being each day of the 7 days preceding the date of survey (N.S.S.O., 1987). A person 'seeking and or available for work' was considered as unemployed. Accordingly, in the usual status approach if a person was unemployed for the majority of days in the previous year is categorised as unemployed whereas by the current week status approach a person is categorised as unemployed if unemployed for a majority of days in the previous week and by the current day status approach a person is considered as unemployed if he was unemployed just the previous day. Consequently, in all the NSS surveys of unemployment for both in rural and urban sectors, a relatively steeper increase has been observed in unemployment, irrespective of sex, as one goes from the usual status to weekly status as depicted in Table 7. The gradual increase in casual wage labourer over the period of 1972-83 might be the reason behind it, as shown in Table 8. From Table 7, it appears that the percentage of female unemployed increased between 27th and 32nd rounds and decreased in the 38th round irrespective of the area. It may account particularly in the rural sector for the fact that the share of 'self-employment' along with 'regular wage/salaried work' have declined from 69 percent to 65 percent between 27th and 32nd rounds and then marginally increased in the 38th round. The rate of growth of unemployment by the usual status for males indicates the extent of chronic unemployment of people willing but unable to work. On the other hand, females tend to withdraw from the labour force in case work is not available and do not report themselves as unemployed. The increase in proportion of marginal workers to total female workers from 24 percent to 29 percent during 1971-81 does indicate the extent of under-employment in female labour force.

Female Work Participation Rate

It was discussed in the previous section that the inconsistency in the data for female workers in 1961 and 1971 was principally due to conceptual differences in categorising a person as worker or non-worker and accordingly the Registrar-General of India made a re-survey in 1972-73 (R.G., 1971).

Table 7 : Unemployed as Percentage of the Total Labour Force by Activity Status: All India

Type of Activity Status	*Males*			*Females*		
	27th round (1972-73)	*32nd round (1977-78)*	*38th round (1983)*	*27th round (1972-73)*	*32nd round (1977-78)*	*38th round (1983)*
Rural						
Usual	1.2	1.3	1.4	0.5	2.0	0.7
Current Weekly	3.0	3.6	3.7	5.5	4.1	4.3
Current Day	6.8	7.1	7.5	11.2	9.2	9.0
Urban						
Usual	4.9	5.4	4.6	6.0	12.4	4.8
Current Weekly	6.0	7.1	6.7	9.2	11.0	7.5
Current Day	8.0	9.4	9.2	13.7	14.5	11.0

*Activity status is defined in the text.

Source: National Sample Survey Organisation, 'Report on the 3rd Quinquennial Survey on Employment and Unemployment', June, 1987, No.341, Table 8, Table 15, Table 18.

Table 8 : Percentage Distribution of all Workers (Main and Marginal) According to Usual Status by Category of Employment Separately for Males and Females in Rural and Urban India

Category of Employment	*Males*			*Females*		
	27th round	*32nd round*	*38th round*	*27th round*	*32nd round*	*38th round*
Rural						
Self Employment	65.9	62.7	60.4	64.5	62.1	62.2
Regular Wage/Salaried Work	12.1	10.6	10.8	4.1	2.8	3.1
Casual Wage Labour	22.0	26.7	28.8	31.4	35.0	34.7
Urban						
Self Employment	39.2	40.4	40.7	48.4	49.5	46.5
Regular Wage/ Salaried Work	50.7	46.4	44.6	27.9	24.9	26.2
Casual Wage Labour	10.1	13.2	14.7	23.7	25.6	27.3

Source: NSSO,'Key Results of Last Three Quinquennial NSS Enquiries on Employment and Unemployment, 1983', 38th round, No 315, Table 2.

Table 9 : Participation Rates of the 1961 and 1971 Censuses Adjusted for Conceptual Differences - All India

Description		Rural		Urban	
		Males	Females	Males	Females
Adjusted	1961	57.0	25.7	51.6	32.1
Census	1971	53.5	13.1	48.8	29.1
Census	1961	58.2	31.4	52.4	33.5
Adjusted	1971	54.7	18.8	49.7	30.7

Source: Ashok Mitra et al.,'The Status of Women- Shifts in Occupational Participation, 1961-71', I.C.S.S.R., 1980, p-26.

The adjusted and original participation rates of 1961 Census adjusted according to the 1971 Census concepts and vice versa from Mitra's work (Mitra et al., 1980) are reproduced for rural and urban areas separately in Table 9. It shows that even after making adjustment the 1961 participation rates are considerably higher than 1971 and it indicates nothing but a general decline in the work participation rates during the decade 1961-71. The decline in participation rates in 1971 may be due to increase in 'students' and 'others' categories in the case of males and in the case of females largely by the 'housewife' category and to some extent by 'student' category. It is also found that between 1961 and 1971 females' employment in the 'housewife' category had increased by 24 percent and in 'student' category by 4 percent. However, the female participation rates of 1981 are much lower than that of 1961 rates because a large proportion of females who were reported as housewives in 1971 or 1981, described themselves as engaged in some kind of economically productive work in 1961. Therefore, the over-enumeration in 1961 must be due to insertion of 'one hour a day' as the basis of 'regular work'. The reason for insertion of 'one hour a day' of work as a regular worker is probably due to the inclusion of unpaid female family labour in the category of workers.

The work participation rates of rural females are much higher than those of urban females as reflected in Table 10. This may be explained by several factors: (i) agricultural sector is the single largest source of females' employment and it does not need any skill or education for its operation; (ii) female agricultural workers are not required to go away form home while in urban areas the working place may be far way from home; (iii) agriculture is the largest industry in rural India providing maximum job opportunities especially for females, while the urban females face the problem of less job opportunities; and (iv) the urban jobs require some skill or education in most cases. The female literacy rates, according to the 1981 Census, was 25 percent while for men it was 47 percent and, therefore, it is obvious that urban women had to face a tough competition for obtaining a job against their male counterparts.

Table 10 : Work Participation Rates by Sex in the Age Group 15-59 India, 1961-81

	Rural		*Urban*	
Census Year	*Males*	*Females*	*Males*	*Females*
1961	93.8	50.8	83.2	18.3
1971	89.5	21.7	78.2	11.0
1981	87.7	39.7	78.3	19.1
1961-71	+4.3	+29.0	+5.0	+7.3
1961-81	+6.11	+11.0	+4.9	-0.8

Source: Ashok Mitra et al.., The Status of Women—Shifts in Occupational Participation, 1961-71', I.C.S.S.R., 1980, P-27.

It is observed from Table 10 that the female participation rate is declining over time. Since the 1981 Census rate is much lower than that of the 1961 Census, it can be said that there is a tendency to rise in dependency ratio which will ultimately depress per capita income.

Another important observation is that if one adds the marginal workers to main workers, the result will be a sharp increase in females' participation rate. The female participation rates by considering both main and marginal workers were 28, 16, 20 and 23 percent in 1961, 1971, 1981 and 1991 respectively. Whereas, by considering only main female workers the respective participation rates were 19, 12, 14 and 16 percent. Thus, more or less it confirms the findings of NSS estimates based on 27th and 32nd rounds.

The census data reveal that the participation rate, particularly the female participation rate, varies considerably from state to state, from 50 percent in Arunachal Pradesh to 27 percent in Kerala in 1981. The census data also reveal that the rate of increment varies by a significant extent, from 58 percent in Arunachal Pradesh to 29 percent in Kerala, over the period of 1971-81. Recent studies on the subject have shown that on the whole, the observed interstate variation in female participation rate explains 90 percent of the observed interstate variation in the overall labour force participation rate among states.

A study, based on the 1971 Census data, was conducted on the factors which govern the regional variation in female participation rate (Dholkia and Dholkia, 1978). The interesting result which emerged from the study was that the observed deviation in female participation rate from the national average are determined principally by the socio-economic and cultural factors in the case of each and every state.

Conclusion

Accurate and reliable statistics on the basis of sex are important in a given population for analysing any kind of trend or for evolving policies. The existence of the problem of under enumeration in data for females reflects the subordination and under-evaluation of women in Indian society. Assessment of females' contributions to society and estimation of the extent of their deprivations are essential for eradication of existing inequality and subordination.

The NSS provided significant improvement in the estimates of female participation rates in the labour force by covering both rural and urban areas. Still there is scope for further improvement. The experience of the our neighbouring country, Pakistan, in this respect may be mentioned here. In India, the female work participation rate, based on main and marginal activity given by the population census, is higher than the census-based activity rate for Pakistan. The estimates from the NSS of India also show a higher activity rate for females. But the 1980 agricultural census of Pakistan provided a figure of 73 percent participation rate for all female workers, i.e., full-time and part-time female workers engaged in agricultural and non-agricultural work of their own households as well as for others which is much higher than the Indian rates based on the census data and NSS data (Bose and Premi, 1992). This indicates that the actual rate for Indian females would also be higher than the rates reported by the census and NSS if the data-base could be improved. Thus, improvement of the data-base is the pre-requisite for any kind of meaningful policy prescription for them.

Females' employment, even after four decades of independence, is traditional in nature. More than 80 percent of the working females are either in agriculture or in agriculture related activities. The agricultural workers are more unorganised and as a result the extent of deprivation is more acute. Since a large section of female workers are associated with agricultural work, these females are found to suffer over a long period of time. It is expected that agriculture will continue to remain the largest single sector for employment generation, especially for women indicating that the principal task is to get them organised through some awareness generation programmes.

The tertiary sector possibly be another sector generating employment for females. However, the high rate of drop-outs from school, low rate of literacy, lack of facilities for attainment of technical education and other causes make it impossible to bring about possible improvements in the sector in this regard.

References

1. Ashish Bose and M.K. Premi, *Population Transition in South Asia,* Delhi: B.R. Publishing Corporation, 1992.
2. Ashok Mitra, Lalit Pathak and Shekhar Mukherji, *The Status of Women:* Shifts in Occupational Participation, 1961-71, New Delhi : ICSSR, 1980.
3. Bakul H. Dholkia and Ravindra H. Dholkia,'Interstate Variations in Female Labour Force Participation Rates in India', *Journal of Man Power,* 1978, Vol. 20, No. 4, p. 290.
4. Census of India, 1981, *Primary Census Abstract, General Population,* Series I, Part II, B(i).
5. Census of India, 1991, *Provisional Population Totals,* Series-I, Paper I, New Delhi : Office of the Registrar General of India, 1991.
6. Central Statistical Organisation, *National Accounts Statistics*-Sources and Methods, New Delhi, C.S.O., 1980.
7. National Sample Survey Organisation, *Report on the Third Quinquennial Survey on Employment and Unemployment,* 38th round, No. 341, 1987.

4

The Girl Child is Not a Lesser Child

*Sabita Guha**

Two elderly women are waiting anxiously in the lounge of a posh nursing home in a Calcutta suburb. They are the mother and mother-in-law of a young girl who has been taken to the labour room of the nursing home. A nurse come out and announces the birth of a healthy baby, much to the relief of the two women and then hurriedly disappears. This is the first child of the young girl. How nice to be a grandmother, the ladies exchange pleasantries. Is it a boy or a girl? They did not ask for it, neither did the nurse care to reveal the sex of the child. On enquiry, it was found that the nurse had deliberately avoided the issue. As it was a girl and she was afraid to disclose the news which she felt would upset the grannies. This is a common experience which speaks for the normal reaction of a family towards the arrival of a girl child, specially if it is a first issue. The experienced nurse knew it and, hence, she was cautious. The discrimination begins at birth and the child grows up into womanhood with an inferiority complex.

Normally, Indians are fond of children. Because of the existence of a more or less strong family tie and a low divorce rate, children are not regarded as a burden. But there is a strong preference for a male child. Attitudinal survey data on sex preference collected by

* The author is Senior Statistician, State Planning Board, Government of West Bengal, Ab/2, B. Abasan, Salt Lake, Sect. III, FB Block, Calcutta-700091.

individual demographeres in selected areas reveal widespread preference for sons over daughters. Ethnographic literature also provides evidence of son-preference in the form of negligence toward daughters in food allocation, medical-care and other aspects of life.[1]

The explanation of such a behaviour pattern is to be sought in the social outlook and family environment. In India, there is a long tradition of male dominance. The menfolk are the bread-winners and masters of the family. Women and children are to be protected from the rough and tumble of everyday life. This protective attitude has ultimately led to some sort of a situation where women appear to be a burden, both financial and social. Women are housekeepers and that house-keeping also needs the approval of male-earning members. Most of the women also accept the man's status, and encourage sex discrimination in the family as mother, sister and wife. This is the general tendency but there may be some exceptions. One significant development in recent times is women's entry into labour market. Her household services are non-remunerative and her hard work at home is scarcely appreciated. But when she starts earning and contributing to the upkeep of the family, her status changes vis-a-vis the family.

Reverting to the traditional attitude, the common experience is that women are not treated as equal partners by their male counterparts. They play a subordinate role. Their upbringing makes them adore a boy and abhor a girl. They hurl their bitterness on girls because the birth of a girl means an addition to a life of struggle and subordination. Hence a mother disapproves the birth of a girl child more than a father.

The subordinate role of women is best illustrated by an ancient Indian scholar, Manu: 'Father protects a women during childhood, husband during youth, sons during old age, so a woman deserves not freedom for sooth'.[2] Women's professional career is not to be encouraged since the household will then suffer. The housewife ideology nurtured by the patriarchal society appears to have stood in the way of proper development of a woman's personality. The male dominance is not a unique feature of Hindu society in India. The gender bias is even stronger among Muslims. It is also present among other religious groups. Christian girls may be in a slightly better position because of the Western influence. But local conditions influence the attitude of all people irrespective of socio-religious background. In some of the tribal societies of North-East India where some sort of matriliny still prevails, the situation may be a bit different. So, one factor leading to male preference is the belief that the boy will take up both financial and social responsibility of the family when he grows up.

The second factor which leads to male preference is the family lineage. It is the son who carries the family name and so he is more important to the family. He inherits property and assumes family liability. An All-India Family Planning Study by the Operation Research Group finds that a great number of couples believe that one must have a son to carry on the line and support the family.[3]

The Hindu Law of Inheritance was changed in 1956, allowing daughters a share in the father's property. But married daughters usually do not put forward their claims. This is somehow regarded as indignified. In an Indian family a daughter is a *parayadhan* (other's property) to be nurtured at home and then gifted away with a dowry. Since a lump sum investment is needed at marriage, some savings is to be made during upbringing. A son is an asset for the future, while a daughter is a liability to be disposed off with a dowry. The Dowry Prohibition Act of 1961 has done precious little to discourage the practice. The condition of the girl child is perhaps worse among Muslims where religious strictures are more unfavourable to women and the inheritance law also discriminates against women.

The Behaviour Pattern

The psychological barrier against accepting a girl child influences behaviour pattern of the society. A deplorable tendency in present-day Indian society is to take advantage of a quick abortion after pre-natal sex determination tests. Till now there is no reliable statistics on amniocentesis or female infanticide. But it is obvious that such pre-natal tests are expensive and ordinary people are not expected to know much about such tests. One can easily guess that relatively rich and educated people take recourse to such methods. Newspapers reports on the wide acceptance of amniocentesis in states like Maharashtra is alarming. There is a general impression that the practice is spreading to different regions of India with varying intensity. Social workers are voicing the need for a Central Government enactment to fight the evil. While the enactment will be made at the all-India level, the states will be responsible for its implementation. But such a legal step is not enough to fight a social evil. A transformation in our attitude towards bearing and rearing a girl child is more important.

The problem is gradually getting media attention. An interesting observation is referred to in this section based on a survey of media coverage of five women-related issues, one of them being sex determination test.[4] The following English language dailies are consulted—The Hindustan Times (North), The Hindu (South), The Statesman (North-East), The Times of India (North-West), and the Indian Express (almost all regions excepting East). So the area coverage is wide. Among women related issues attracting media attention, the debate on misuse of sex determination test is not much. However, according to this survey, during the 80s, within four months the issue was dealt with 51 times in different newspapers. Judged by the nature and relative obscurity of the issue, the media coverage is significant.

Leaving aside the issue, the treatment that a girl child is expected to get in the family once she is born may be analysed. The persistent unfavourable sex ratio in India causing concern among demographers. In-depth surveys of small communities reveal discrimination against daughters in health-care and food allocation. This leads to higher mortality among girls. Discrimination begins at the stage of lactation. A male child is more willingly breast-fed and for a longer period than a female child. As brother and sister grow up together, the brother gets better food, medical-care and education. It is rather difficult to prove all these views empirically. But now-a-days a number of micro-studies are being made to find concrete evidence.

One evidence in support of this contention is the fact that female babies are more often underweight. As for boys and girls in the same age group, boys are taller and healthier. It is a common knowledge that in Indian families, boys get preferential treatment in respect of consumption of fish, milk, egg and other delicacies. Girls become habituated to biased treatment and after marriage she still continues it. We forget that the baby's health depends on the mother's health. And babies are both boys and girls.

Let me now quote a few observations from some micro-studies undertaken in different regions of India. A study probing into the causes of malnutrition among rural children in Punjab revealed a definite sex bias in nutritional norms. The differentiation was more acute among the low caste and low income group people, i.e., economically and socially backward classes.

Another study undertaken on health-care in South Indian villages testified the data that expenditure on treatment of first born girls was as low as 35 percent of that incurred on first born boy. A study in rural Karnataka came to the conclusion that breast feeding of boys lasted longer.

In Gujarat, a survey was undertaken on child mortality in ten villages. Out of 58 deaths, 17 children were dead within one month and there was no sex bias found in the mortality pattern. But of the other 41 cases as many as 27 happened to girls and the cause was malnutrition and diarrhoea which could be easily treated. Out of the critically ill babies only 22 percent girl children were taken to hospital while the figure was 80 percent in the case of boys. The results of these studies are often quoted in journals and periodicals. But systematic all-India coverage is yet to be done. Otherwise, such studies may not be convincing. In fact, in December 1990 I myself made a small study to find out the attitude of women on the treatment of girl child within the family. The result showed that women themselves are not so conscious about the issue.

The plan and findings of the survey are briefly stated here. Fifty-two families in urban areas of Calcutta and its newly developed satellite city, Salt Lake, were visited and in each one of these families a married woman in the 20-40 years age group with at least one child was approached with a simple questionnaire. The responses are analysed mainly to throw light on the issue of how a girl child is treated in her family. The families belonged to three income classes—low (monthly income less than Rs. 1000), middle (monthly income 1000 to less than Rs. 6000) and high (monthly income above Rs. 6000). While in the low income group all are working and in two other groups we have two sub-classes-working and non-working women. Let us first analyse the sex preference for the first child. I posed the question separately for the respondent, her husband and her elderly relations.

It appears from Table 1 that, out of 52 respondents, only 14 wives (26 percent) and 12 husbands (23 percent) desired a girl child at the time of the birth of the first issue. In rural areas the situation may be worse. In case of husband, the number is the same for each income class. But poor females largely preferred a male child both in regard to their first and second issues. A detailed probe revealed that in case of working women belonging to two other groups the usual answer was 'no preference' indicating no desire for a second child. Working women feel it is tough for them to bear and rear a child.

Table 1: Sex Preference for the First Issue

Income Class	*No. of respondents*	*Wife* M	*Wife* F	*N.P.*	*Husband* M	*Husband* F	*N.P.*
1. Low	10	7	2	1	5	4	1
2. Middle							
(i) Working	10	1	2	7	2	3	5
(ii) Non-working	12	5	4	3	10	1	1
3. High							
(i) Working	10	3	2	5	3	3	4
(ii) Non-working	10	4	4	2	2	1	7
Total:	52	20	14	18	22	12	18
Second Issue							
1. Low	10	6	1	3	5	2	3
2. Middle							
(i) Working	10	4	—	6	4	1	5
(i) Non-working	12	4	3	5	3	3	6
3. High							
(i) Working	10	1	4	5	—	4	6
(ii) Non-working	10	3	5	2	4	4	2
Total	52	18	13	21	16	14	22

N.B: M— Male; F — Female; N.P. — Non-Preference.

So far as the attitudes of relatives are concerned specifically asked for the reactions of grand parents. Almost 90 percent of the grand parents showed a preference for a male child as the first issue. In fact I found only six instances of distinct preference for a female child among nearly 52×4, i.e., 208 individuals. Compared to the earlier generation, we find that a girl child is more acceptable now in an urban nuclear family. In fact, when the first issue is a boy, couples expressed a preference for a girl child in the second case and vice-versa.

While noting the family size in pre- and post-marital stages of my respondents the number of boys and girls in the family were counted separately. Table 2 presents and average number of boys and girls per family.

Table 2 : Family Size by Sex

Income Class	*No. of boys per family*		*No. of girls per family*	
	Present	*Pre-marital*	*Present*	*Pre-marital*
1. Low	1.3	3.2	0.8	3.5
2. Middle				
(i) Working	0.6	2.2	0.8	4.3
(ii) Non-working	1.3	2.0	0.6	2.7
3. High				
(i) Working	0.8	1.0	0.2	1.6
(ii) Non-working	0.8	1.0	0.7	1.8

Thus the families interviewed have a larger number of male than female children at present. The situation was different in pre-marital families of the respondents. However, the respondents in general did not speak of discrimination between brothers and sisters in their families. They were asked to state their views under three heads—food, education, household work. As far as food is concerned there was no report of wilful descrimination. Regarding education, the respondent under the low income group flatly stated that neither boys nor girls had any opportunity for education. In the higher income bracket, some ladies complained that their families did not allow much freedom of choice in respect of higher studies. Two ladies were quite critical on this issue. Fortunately, they could pursue higher studies after marriage because of their husbands' cooperation. Regarding household work, it appeared that every one agreed that discrimination in this sphere is quite natural.

Table 3 : Response to Incidental Questions

Income Group		No Reply				
	Yes	*Marginal*	*No.*	*Female*	*Male*	*N.P.**
1. Low	3	1	6	2	6	2
2. Middle						
(i) Working	8	1	1	6	2	2
(ii) Non-working	8	2	2	4	7	1
3. High						
(i) Working	7	3	-	5	3	2
(ii) Non-working	5	5	-	4	4	2
Total	31	12	9	21	22	9

* N.P.— No Preference.

Two extra-observations by plotting two of the answers provided against two questions—(A) Whether you enjoy your present status of life as a woman (B) if you are to be born once again whether you like to be a male or a female—are presented in Table 3.

There is a consistency in the answer pattern of the first group. Those who do not live under male dominance would like to be born as male child. Life is not so uncomfortable for other ladies, still, a good number of them preferred a male life. They stated that men have more freedom, more security, and better scope for enjoying life. Some of these who said they would like to be born as women stated that they enjoy most their role as mother. As females can attain motherhood, they would like to remain women for all times to come. Otherwise, life is softer, more enjoyable for males. This is the universal attitude.

I have analysed the responses in an objective manner as far as possible. But now I cannot hold back the temptation to make a few comments. The coverage is quite small, but I have tried to involve women belonging to different socio-economic classes. So far as the educational standard is concerned, only seven respondents were literate in the low income group. In the middle-income group working category, there were two post-graduate degree holders, six graduates and two under-graduates. They work as teachers, office assistants and nurses. Among the non-working women in this class, two have post-graduate degree, three women have read upto class X and the rest are graduates. In high income group all are at least graduates. There are three Ph.Ds, two MBBS and one LL.B. and one Diploma in Journalism. So, we may conclude that educational opportunities enjoyed by females in higher income bracket are not negligible. A substantial number of the respondents were highly educated and half of them are engaged in different occupations. But most of them appeared to be not so specific about what they want for themselves or for improving the conditions of women in society.

The answers obtained against the last question of the questionnaire is most unsatisfactory. The question purported to the issue of improvement in the condition of the respondent as well as of other women in society. The women in the low income group were more categorical in their answers. They wanted more money, their own house and better living conditions for their children. The educated women had in most cases no comment to make. On insisting, they would say perhaps they would like to bring up their children in a much better way than they were brought up. This is a vague answer, when they appear to be satisfied with the life that they have spent so far. Altogether only four respondents in the high income groups spoke of equal status of male and female. But what they actually wanted to convey through the concept of 'equal status' is not clear. A good number of women stated that they did not like to have more than one child. But is this a healthy sign, when economically one can afford to have two children? Strangely enough, working women did not ask for having creche facilities and the like. It appears to me that the upbringing of girl children in our society shows a serious gap. It makes women mentally dependent on men for decision-making, discouraging independent thinking. This is a more serious drawback than merely allowing a shorter period of breast-feeding to girl child.

The Indicators

It is the general impression that a girl child occupies a position in the family which is below that of a male child. This view finds support in many sections of our society. Let me start with the definition of a child. A child means every human being below the age of 18 years unless under the law applicable to the child, majority is attained earlier. Now human beings within this group being themselves proteges can hardly protect their own rights under adverse circumstances. Hence, the World Body prepared a long list of child's rights and chalked out a plan for their implementation. The Indian Council for Child Welfare, in a meeting convened in December 1991, demanded early ratification of the UN Convention on the Rights of the Child and also proposed to examine the ways and means of reaching the norms laid down in the World Summit (1990 September). Miss Mamata Banerjee, the then Union

Minister for Women and Child Development, while inaugurating the ICCW meeting, gave an assurance that the government was taking steps to formulate a National Programme of Action in the light of the recommendations of the Summit. Such steps are expected to go a long way in improving the condition of a girl child.

The span of life upto 18 years is very important. It is the formative stage. Health, nutrition and education of a child are to be taken care of at this stage so that society gets a good stock of people. Neglecting girls at this stage means bringing woe to the society of the future. But there are indications that women do not receive adequate care and attention in the family. This negligent attitude has an adverse effect on their health which influences their longevity.

Let me start with the issue of declining sex ratio. It is a continuous trend of twentieth century with a single exception in 1981. But again the ratio dropped in 1991 (Table 4). Thus from a sex ratio of 972 in 1901, it has dropped to 929 in 1991. Because of stonger biological resistance power of women, the picture is different in most other. countries.

Table 4 : Sex Ratio in India, 1901-1991

Census Year	*Sex Ratio (F/M)*
1901	972
1911	964
1921	955
1931	950
1941	945
1951	946
1961	941
1971	930
1981	934
1991	929

Source: Office of the Registrar General, *Census of India* 1991, Paper 1, *Provisional Population Totals.*

Of course, in India there are regional variations. In general, the southern part has a larger number of females compared to the north. But except Kerala which has a sex ratio of 1040 females per 1000 males, no other state or union territory has a ratio with a higher number of women. The Union Territory of Chandigarh has the lowest sex ratio (793). However, it has increased from the level of 1981 (769). In between 1981 and 1991, the sex ratio improved in Assam, West Bengal, Sikkim, Jammu Kashmir, Himachal Pradesh, while it went down in Bihar, M.P., Gujarat, Manipur. The census report suggests that the composition of the population is affected by the differentials in the mortality conditions of males and females, sex selective migration and the sex ratio at birth.[5]

The sex ratio at birth is calculated by the number of live male issues per 100 female issues. Due to biological reasons the number of male births is slightly higher than female births all over the world. The figure varies between 102 and 107 males for every 100 females. From available data on sex-wise live births (United Nations, Demographic Year Book, 1986), the sex ratio at birth is calculated to be 105 for Japan (1985) and USA (1984). It is difficult to get year-wise and sex-wise data of live births in most other countries. In India also, hard data on sex ratio at birth is not available. However, from various estimates, demographers guess the ratio to be near 105 and assume that it has remained almost at the same level during the last 40 years. A reference to a higher sex ratio at birth based on Civil Registration and SRS data (115/110 in 1986; 1987-88) has been made in a recent study which the author himself rejects as spurious.[6]

Sex differential in the infant mortality is quite low, though a ten year period of sex-wise infant mortality rate presented in Table 5 shows that it is slightly higher for female issues most of the time. In 1981, the figure for males was 110 per 1000 births and for females, 111 per 1000. In 1987, the corresponding rates were 95 and 96 respectively. The early childhood (0-4 years) mortality per 1000 population at the all-India level is higher for female than for male babies. The rates were 43.3 for females and 39.2 males in 1981. They came down to 36.8 and 33.6 for females and males in 1986.[7] The under-5 age group mortality rate in India was 121 females and 116 males per 1000 live births[8] (World Development Report, 1992).

Table 5 : Infant Mortality Rate in India by Sex, 1971-80

Year	*Male*	*Female*
1971	129	129
1972	132	148
1973	132	135
1974	128	119
1975	140	140
1976	124	134
1977	126	135
1978	123	131
1979	120	121
1980	113	115

Source: A.K. Jain & P. Visaria (eds.), *Infant Mortality in India*, New Delhi: Sage Publications, 1988 : 95.

A relatively higher incidence of mortality among females in the early childhood suggests that female issues are not properly looked after. The discrimination in respect of food and medical care has been discussed in earlier sections. In fact, women enjoy a longer span of life in most other countries of the world because the advantage of males at birth gets neutralised by about 20 years of age. After that, comes a period of higher mortality among males than females as the latter have greater resistance power to diseases.

Table 6 : Sex Ratio of the World Population, 1985

		Total	*Age Group*		
			Upto 15	*15-64*	*65+*
World Population (in Million) 1985	Male	2434	826	1487	122
	Percentage of total male	100	34	61	5
	Female	2403	789	1450	165
	Percentage of total female	100	33	60	7
	Sex ratio (M/F)	101	105	102	74

Source : United Nations, Demographic Year Book, 1986.

The age-wise breakup of sex ratio for the world as a whole in 1985 (Table 6) shows that the ratio is favourable to females in 65 age group (U.N.O. 1986). Hence, sex ratio unfavourable to women is not a unique demographic feature of India. Nonetheless, it is a disturbing feature. The reason must be in higher incidence of mortality among females in different age groups. The figures for expectation of life at birth for both males and females presented in Table 7 bear witness to the higher incidence of mortality among females. Though the difference is marginal in SRS based data, the figures presented in World Development Reports is more disturbing. However, while expectation of life is lower for females in the countries of the Indian sub-continent, it is higher in some other Asian countries (Table 8). It is recently claimed that in India female life expectancy has slightly exceeded that of male. But the maternal mortality rate is still 500 per lakh, mothers, which is a source of some concern.

One of the factors thus contributing to the high mortality rate among women is death at childbirth. Mother-care should start not simply at the time of pregnancy, but from the day of the birth of a girl child. Malnutrition and diarrhoea are two common causes of child mortality. Girls fall easy victim to these. They are underweight at the time of birth and their growth is retarded due to lack of proper nutrition. They do not receive adequate medical-care at the time of illness. So a female issue grows into a sick girl with retarded growth. She reaches puberty at a late age and her menstruation starts late. But then again, marriages take place early and then starts procreation. Because of her under-developed body she suffers more during child-birth and gives birth to underweight babies. Again, a high premium is attached to male issues and the relatively high level of child mortality induces couples to go for a larger number of issues. The undernourished, weak mother thus gives birth to several under-weight children, some of whom are females and have the same prospect of life ahead as their mothers. The vicious circle moves on. One of the major health deficiencies among Indian women is the prevalence of acute anemia. This depends on quality of food intake as also food habits.

Table 7 : Expectation of Life at Birth by Sex in India, 1970-75; 1976-80 and 1981-85

Period	*Male*	*Female*
1970-75	50.5	49.0
1976-80	52.5	52.1
1981-85	55.4	55.7

Source : India, Office of the Registrar General, 1989. Occasional Paper No. 1, SRS Based on Abridged Life Tables, 1981-85, New Delhi.

Table 8 : Expectation of Life at Birth by Sex (a few Asian Countries), 1990

Country	*Male*	*Female*
India	60	58
Bangladesh	52	51
Pakistan	56	55
Sri Lanka	69	73
China	69	71
Japan	76	82

Source : World Development Report, 1992, Table-32.

There is no denying the fact that the food intake of poor people lacks vitamin, iron and proteins. The women-folk get a smaller quantity, too. However, a proper knowledge of nutrient qualities of different food items can improve the quality of food intake at a low cost. Fruits, vegetables and pulses can go a long way in fighting nutritional deficiency. Poultry-keeping and consumption of eggs is also a good habit. But not only poor women, women of relatively well-to-do families, because of lack of knowledge of nutritive values of food items, tend to take unhealthy food. Another bad practice among women in general is irregular food habits which cause indigestion. Here also, when boys are served food more regularly girls are encouraged to take food with their mother. Anemia follows weak health. The weak, undernourished girl becomes dull and slow.

Like health, girls' education is also neglected. The sex-wise literacy figures as available from census data shows the gap between male and female literacy level from 1901 to 1991 (Table-9).

Table 9 : Literacy Rate in India by Sex, 1901-1991

	Literacy Rate		*Change in Percentage Points*	
Year	*Male*	*Female*	*Male*	*Female*
1901	9.8	0.6	...	...
1911	10.6	1.1	0.8	0.5
1921	12.2	1.8	1.6	0.7
1931	15.6	2.9	3.4	1.1
1941	24.9	7.3	9.3	4.4
1951	25.0	7.9	0.1	0.6
1961	34.4	12.9	9.4	5.0
1971	39.5	18.7	5.1	5.8
1981	46.6	24.8	7.1	6.1
1991	52.9	32.6	6.3	7.8

Source: K.G. Jolly 'Strategies to Attain Universal Literacy in India by 2001', *Demography-India*, Vol. 20 No.1, Jan-June, 1991: 142.

The literacy rate is lower by nearly 20 points for females all through. The rate of increase is also slower compared to that of the opposite sex. The situation has shown some improvement after 1971. But more effort is necessary in this sphere.

Formal education starts at school level. The latest figure for 1991-92 regarding enrollment at the elementary level is disappointing (Table-10). Actual enrollment shows that girls constitute nearly 40 per cent of the total enrollment. The additional target for enrollment envisaged for the 8th Five Year Plan is 4.38 crores, of which girls are 2.24 crores, i.e. 51 percent, a slightly better picture. However, much depends on actual fulfillment of the target. In the field of higher education and professional courses, girls' participation is not at all satisfactory. The country is committed to attain Health for All and Education for All by 2001 A.D. Accordingly, it has chalked out policies like the National Education Policy (NEP) of 1986 and the National Health Policy of 1982. To look after women's interests a National Commission for Women is also operating. Its performance is yet to be thoroughly appraised.

Table 10 : Enrolment at School Level

(in crores)

	No. enrolled upto 1991-92		
	Total	*Female*	*p.c. to total*
Elementary Education	13.5	5.5	40.9
Primary (Class I-V)	10.0	4.2	42.0
Upper Primary (Class vi-viii)	3.4	1.3	37.8

Source: Eighth Five-Year Plan 1992-97, Vol-II Govt. of India, Planning Commission.

A few comments may be made here on women's employment, because the woman must be self-reliant in order to look after herself better. The girl child starts life as an all purpose assistant of her emaciated mother. From quite an early age she starts helping her mother in household work and looks after younger siblings. A girl cannot afford to go to school but she has to prepare her brother for school. In poor families, the girl goes out with her mother to work in the informal sector. This is a common sight: mothers working as daily maids bringing their daughters to do part of the work. Small girls are preferred for household work as they can be more easily exploited.

Table 11: Work Participation Rate in India, 1971-1991 by Sex and Residence

Year	*Male*			*Female*		
	Rural	*Urban*	*Total*	*Rural*	*Urban*	*Total*
1971	53.78	48.88	52.75	15.92	7.18	14.22
1981	38.79	29.99	52.62	23.06	8.31	19.67
1991	52.50	48.95	51.56	27.20	9.74	22.73

Source : Provisional Population Totals, Paper 3 of 1991, India, Office of the Registrar General, Census of India 1991.

In India the formal entry of women in the labour market is not upto the mark. In fact, in 1991 Census the work participation rate (i.e. the proportion of total workers in the population expressed as a percentage) shows wide sex variation. While the rate is 51.56 for males, it is only 22.73 for females. No lower age limit for worker is specified in India. Table 11 presents a sex-wise and residence-wise data. The rate here stands for proportion of total workers (which includes both main and marginal workers) to the total population.

In India, female WPR has increased from 14.22 in 1971 to 19.67 in 1981 and then 22.73 in 1991. In between 1981 and 1991 the percentage increase in the number of female workers is much higher in urban areas (60.99) compared to rural areas (40.25). The WPR is nearly steady for male workers. While in the organised sector, no discrimination is made between males and females in respect of wages and other service conditions, it is not so in unorganised sector. In fact, girls are employed in small factories and offices at lower wages and they are found to work for longer hours. The owners prefer girls because they are less demanding and they cannot organise themselves to fight for their rights. Thus, the girl is exploited at home as well as at the work place.

Finally, while going out for work, girls often fall victims to sexual abuse. This is a common experience in the informal sector. While women in general are exposed to this sort of risk the danger is greater for young girls. They are more attractive and less alert. Girls working in brick kilns, in forest areas as contract labourers, etc., suffer most.

In India, child prostitution is yet another social menace. Young girls from poor rural families, or from squalid *bustee* areas are lured into this profession. But the evil is spreading among middle-class families of urban areas also where young girls are sometimes induced to play the role of part-time call girls. Of course, this sort of practice prevails in other countries also. India was largely free from this evil due to the conservative upbringing that middle class families gave their daughter.

However, another bad practice is of girls being often exploited through the institution of marriage. Young girls are given to marriage to rich old ruffians who use them as sex objects. A practice is growing among Muslims to resort to match-making with oil-rich Arab men. The demand is great for young beautiful girls. Nobody knows for certain what happens to these girls once they leave their home country with their foreign consorts. Stray cases appearing in the media convey doleful stories. These young girls are sacrificed for the well-being of the family with full knowledge of the guardians and are often sold for a price. No amount of legislation and deliberations can prevent such evil. Persistent efforts should be made to rouse social consciousness.

Role Difference

There is a hue and cry for achieving equal status between men and women all over the world. The staunch feminists appear to be in favour of physical equality of the gross kind, and in this they disregard the qualitative difference between men and women as ordained by Nature. This, to my kind, is a bit illogical. There is no dearth of studies on sex difference and women of developed countries also take great interest in such studies. The recent scientific investigations suggest that the brains of men and women work differently from early life as a result of the influence of sex hormones. The apptitudes of girls and boys are different and their skills often develop in different directions. These genetic differences does not, however, prove a superiority complex among men, nor do they justify discrimination in providing basic needs like food, medicine and education.

Theoretically, India provides an ideal social and legal set-up for her women-folk. The Constitution of India has granted equal status to men and women through Articles 14, 15, 16. India has also signed the UN Convention granting political rights to women. There are hardly any legal disabilities from which they suffer now. And the Indian women do not have to fight for these rights like the Western women. But the Report of the Committee on the Status of Women in India (1975) observed, "Our investigations have revealed that large masses of women in this country have remained unaffected by the rights guaranteed to them by the constitution and the laws enacted since independence."[8] When grown-up women themselves are not conscious about their legal rights, little can be expected of immature girls.

Indian society is changing. The joint family system is breaking up and with this, the dominance of elderly people is receding. Earlier, the status of girls in large families was more unsatisfactory. They were scolded, ill-treated and always put on a subordinate plane to boys. The outlook is changing. It is also a natural instinct that girls are more attached to families than boys. The girls often themselves like to work and stay indoor. Of course, in our society, the choice of sphere quite often does not depend on their free will. It is relegated to them by tradition. But attending to household and pseudo-household chores is not an inferior job. Proper training is also necessary for doing these jobs efficiently. Moreover, predominance of agricultural activities and prevalence of household-based small production units, particularly in rural areas, offer engagement without wage to women and girls. Carrying food to the field for male relations is an important responsibility for girls. After meeting all the demands of the family a girl gets relatively little time to look after herself. Even if she tries to make some time for self-development, she is discouraged.

No amount of legislation or official intervention can remove these evils. The change of outlook should come from within. Non-Government Organisations (NGOs) can help the effort if they work seriously in this field. Small steps may work wonders. Various women's organisations have done commendable work and earned recognition for it. Most of them are trying to provide poor women with some remunerative work.

There should be a system of free medical check-up and health investigators should be appointed for regular family visits, so that minor ailments get attended at home. Finally, girls should be brought up with a sense of dignity. They should be made to understand that self-effacement and cowardice will make them more vulnerable to the evils of society. They should be strong both mentally and physically to be able to face better challenge of future life.

Sex discrimination is not an evil associated with Indian society alone. In fact, the second sex, weaker sex is facing difficulties in almost every country. Developing countries are guilty of being negligent to women. Depending on the socio-economic and cultural environment of the country, women are reacting differently in different countries. Women are mere conscious of their interests in developed countries. In the U.S.A., where since the time of colonisation, women have been subjected to hardships and discrimination of worst type, the feminist movement gained ground quite early. For sometime, women strove for economic independence and ran after professional career neglecting family life. It is now felt that modern young girls in the U.S.A. are getting more interested in private lives. The situation is briefly stated by Ms. Sheryl Hatch (20), a broadcasting major at the American University in Washington D.C.—"In the 1950s women were family oriented. In the 1970s they were career oriented. In the 1990s we want balance. I think I can do both".[9] This attitude seems to be shared by modern Indian girls as well.

The natural difference that exists between a boy and a girl will persist. Each can excel in his or her own sphere. But a strict compartmentalisation of roles is not at all desirable. A girl child should get equal opportunity for developing her own self. But that does not mean that she will have to shake off her feminine qualities and softness to secure her rights. The Indian tradition of being respectful to womanhood in general is a good starting point. Since women are psychologically more attached to hearth and home, they tend to have a sacrificial attitude—which leads to self-denial. In private family talks we often come across the view that girls are more sincere and, hence, more dependable than boys. But while sharing family resources, they are being deprived unabashedly and the boys' claim is uppermost in each sphere of life.

The world seems to be getting more conscious about the future of children. Girls being more neglected should receive more attention. In September 1990, the World Summit for Children was held, bringing together leaders from 159 nations. They have devised 27 specific goals to be achieved by the year 2000, all relating to health, education and such other needs of children. It is to be hoped that the countries introducing these steps should not discriminate against girls. In fact, one of the ten propositions presented in the UNICEF report for serious consideration of different countries accepting the Summit's proposal is"... a new world order should oppose the apartheid of gender as vigorously as apartheid of race".

References

1. Moni Nag, 'Sex Preference in Bangladesh, India and Pakistan and its Effect on Fertility', *Demography India*, 1991, Vol. 20(2): 163-185.
2. *Manusmriti*, 9.148.
3. B.B.L. Sharma,'Demography: the Declining Sex Ratio, *The Economic Times*, 1991, Vol. XXXI (46), Friday 19, April.
4. Joseph and K. Sharma, 'Between the Lines: Women's Issue in English Dailies, *Economic and Political Weekly*, Vol. XXVI (43): 76-78.
5. The United Nations-*Convention on the Rights of the Child*, Part-1 Art-1.5.
6. Office of the Registrar-General India, New Delhi, Census of India 1991, *Provisional Population Totals*, Paper-1 of 1991.
7. Moni Nag, 1991, *op.cit.*
8. Pravin Visaria, 'Indian Population Problem: Emerging Perspective after the 1991 Census, '*Demography-India*, 1991, Vol.20(2): 280-281.
9. World Bank-*World Development Report*, 1992, Development and Environment Washington, D.C., USA.
10. *Phularence Guha, Report of the Committee on the Status of Women in India*, 1975.
11. Nancy Gibbs, *'A Turning Point'*, *SPAN*, May 1992, Vol. XXXIII (5): 2-5.
12. UNICEF-*The state of World Children* 1992 (The Ten Propositions).

5

Girl Child : a Study in Familial and Societal Negligence

*Godavari D. Patil and Madhumati Patil**

In ancient times, in all patriarchal societies the son was valued and desired more than the daughter because he was considered a permanent economic asset for the family, since he lived with his aged parents and did not migrate like the daughter to another family after marriage. He perpetuated the name of his father's family. He could defend his family from the attack by an enemy. The daughter had neither practical consideration nor fighting value. The son was both socially and ritually desirable because, the ancient Hindus believed, he could release the souls of his parents from bondage of bodies by offering oblations to God or deity and provide support to the parents in their old age. Therefore, in later years, the birth of a daughter was hardly welcomed. Sometimes, she was abandoned after her birth, at others she was even killed. Parents wished themselves accused on the birth of a female child.

Even today sons are seen to be qualitatively superior to the daughter. Ritual and practical considerations make a boy's birth essential whereas both in terms of rituals and practicabilities, a girl's birth is seen to entail expenses and problems in the future. She is also regarded as more susceptible to pollution and her re-purification is

*The former is Assistant Professor of Sociology and the latter is Assistant Agriculture Officer at University of Agricultural Sciences, Dharwad-580 005.

more difficult, as opposed to that of a son. Since she needs constant protection from male, she is visualised as a burden.[1]

In Hindu society the status and the position of the woman in the household and the community declines if she gives birth to daughters only. Indeed, they treat themselves as inferior as it is not realised that the sex of the child is determined by the chromosomes the man contributes. The woman is blamed for the fault of the man and often the man brings home another wife in the hope that she will bear him a son and the first wife is either ill-treated or deserted.

Girl Child in Ancient Hindu Scriptures/Society.

The position of women in India can be judged by the way in which the birth of a girl is perceived and how she is treated in the family and society. Since the Vedic period a girl child has been unwanted. In *Atharva Veda* one finds prayers for the birth of a son. One of the hymns says, "The birth of a girl grant it elsewhere, here grant a son."[2] A girl's birth is deprecated in this Veda.[3] Even in *Rigveda* one finds a frequent longing for a male child, although there are references to daughters being fondly caressed and affectionately brought up by parents. In certain *Samhitas* one also finds references to mystic charms used for undoing the effect of a female foetus and for changing it into a male one. In *Aitareya Brahmana* a daughter has been characterised as a misery, while in the *Brhadaranyaka Upanishada* there are certain rituals to be performed by the man who wants a learned daughter to be born.[4] Though she was lovingly treated by the parents, she was not regarded as equal to a boy. In the later periods of Hindu civilisation numerous passages about the undesirability of the birth of daughters are available. In Brahmin literature there is one passage which observes that while the son is the hope of the family, the daughter is the source of trouble to it. A similar idea occurs in *Mahabharata* also[5]. The custom of infanticide of girls crept into some sections of Hindu society during the mediaeval period. At this time the daughter was regarded as the root of all miseries and the source of unending troubles by the average householder. The temptation to do away with her became too irresistible in some sections of society.[6]

Even after the lapse of over a thousand years people's attitude has not changed. While they treat the birth of a son as an occasion for celebration, the birth of a girl is taken with sorrow and silence, since tradition and scriptural injunctions insist women to produce sons. Some women, therefore, fast and pray; others undertake arduous pilgrimages or visit seers and godmen while a few do away with their daughters. As Madan states, among Kashmiri Pundits, "sons are particularly auspicious and therefore greatly desired; a daughter's birth makes even a philosophic man (who has renounced the world) gloomy, whereas a son's birth is like sunrise in the abode of gods."[7] Shalini Bhogal says that none of the girls in her study was unwanted or abused, but she noticed the difference in the parental attitudes. This is because they genuinely believed that girls should not be treated the same way as boys, as they have to be trained for their difficult role as wife and mother. The socialisation of the traditional Hindu woman for her passivity begins from her birth—her birth itself being looked upon as a misfortune. She is a taker rather than giver and a perennial source of concern for the family in terms of finding her a match, getting her married early, maintaining her virginity (highly valued in Indian society), good character and reputation till marriage.[8] A female child does not usually receive the same attention and affection that is bestowed upon a male child in a Hindu family, and this attitude tends to intensify into indifference and coldness towards her. While some castes practising hypergamy have stopped at the intentional neglect of a female child, others have gone to the extent of practising female infanticide which is generally known to have been a practice with the Rajputs. There is little doubt that other castes like the Anavils and the Kulins resorted to it under the stress of economic pressure.[9] Parents, therefore, consider that a male offspring is a better investment since he is the potential bread-winner for them in future and rearing of a girl child is a burden. She takes away considerable money in the form of wedding expenses and dowry. She becomes an asset in the house of the in-laws. That is why the Telugu proverb says, "Bringing up a daughter is like watering a plant in another's courtyard". Economically a girl child is considered a drain on the family purse. This discrimination is born of cultural and religious values that spring from the patriarchal, patrilineal Indian ethos, which operate more powerfully in some parts of the country than in others. In all patriarchal societies females, whether kids, adolescents or adults, are believed to be and treated as being inferior to males. Even parents discriminate between daughters and sons.

In India the girl child is born into indifference and reared on neglect. She is caught in a web of cultural practices and prejudicies that divest her of her individuality and becomes submissive, self-sacrificing daughter and wife. She is entitled to much less than her brother. She is given less opportunity, less authority, less property, less status, less power and virtually no choice.[10]

The attitude towards the girl child is, of course, a reflection of Indian society's attitude towards women in general. Women here are broadly considered to be economically unproductive, dependent and expendable. The girl child is thus born into an apathetic and hostile environment. She faces prejudices in our society irrespective of caste, class and region. She is born to bear with the deliberate neglect and discrimination exercised by the parents and in-laws in particular and society in general. Today rejection of the girl child can begin even before her birth, if the foetus is female as detected by amniocentesis. The unborn girl child's normal course leading to a glorious birth is directed to a bloody and inglorious end. Stark terrorism haunts the female foetus growing in the safety of her mother's womb.[11] Attitude against a girl child is exploited by the bio-medical technologists for promoting techniques such as amniocentesis that can identify the sex of a foetus. Pranab Bardhan and Vimal Balasubrahmanyan have recently expressed the fear that scientific advances will lead to an even more unbalanced sex ratio in India.

The family of a girl child survives and achieves well-being because of her labour as a domestic servant, as an agricultural labourer or as a caretaker of her younger siblings. These domestic and non-domestic work robs her childhood and offers her only ignorance and weakness. The status of women in India has not changed much, though there are some social legislations and welfare schemes for women.

Indian population is predominantly male, since sex ratio is showing decline from the decades 1901 to 1991. The following facts depict the situation of girls in our society:

(i) Every year 12 million girls are born in India, 25% of them do not see their fifteenth birthday.

(ii) A large number of deaths occur in early childhood. The sex ratio at this stage falls to 957 per 1000, a figure that keeps declining gradually.

(iii) In most countries, the sex ratio is more than unity being favourable to women, but in India the 1991 census showed an excess of 23 million males.

Table-1: Sex Ratio in States and Union Territories of India (F/M. 1000)

India/States/Union Territories	*Sex ratio*
India	929
Andhra Pradesh	972
Arunachal Pradesh	861
Assam	925
Bihar	912
Goa	969
Gujarat	936
Haryana	874
Himachal Pradesh	996
Jammu and Kashmir	923
Karnataka	960
Kerala	1040
Madhya Pradesh	932
Maharashtra	936
Manipur	961
Meghalaya	947
Mizoram	924
Nagaland	890
Orissa	972
Punjab	888
Rajasthan	913
Sikkim	880
Tamil Nadu	972
Tripura	946
Uttar Pradesh	882
West Bengal	917
A & N Islands	820
Chandigarh	793
Dadar and Nagar Haveli	953
Daman and Diu	972
Delhi	830
Lakshadweep	944
Pondicherry	982

(iv) Despite the economic improvement and provision for basic services in India, the sex ratio has been declining every decade; from 972 in 1901 it dropped down to 929 in 1991.

(v) About one-quarter of India's population, i.e., 130 million are girls below the age of 20 years, almost 30,00,000 girls die annually. It has been estimated that every sixth death is due to the neglect of the female child.

(vi) Girls are at a greater risk of dying during infancy in the states of Haryana, Bihar, Gujarat, Jammu and Kashmir, Punjab, Rajasthan and Uttar Pradesh. There are remarkable regional contrasts within India in the female differential chance of survival.

(vii) A greater number of female foeticide could contribute significantly to demographic imbalances. In 1984-85, 40,000 female foetuses were aborted in Bombay. Hence, the Government of Maharashtra passed a bill prohibiting amniocentesis for detecting the sex of the foetus and inducing abortions on the ground of sex.[12] India is the only country in the world where the sex ratio has been declining over the years.

It has been observed that in South Asia, especially in India and Bangladesh, the male-female ratio is declining and the data also show a higher mortality rate among female children. This may be due to the discriminatory support to the female child. One doctor in Amritsar advertised his sex determination clinic with the slogan "invest Rs. 500 now and save Rs. 50,000 later." Data collected from six hospitals in Bombay revealed that out of 8000 foetuses aborted in 1990, 7999 were female.[13] The supporters of sex-detection tests argued that, based on the theory of demand and supply, an excess of males over females achieved with the reduction of unwanted and hence neglected women would actually raise the status of women.[14] But the proliferation of sex detection tests in Gujarat, Punjab, Haryana, Uttar Pradesh, Rajasthan and Delhi vouches for limitations of state legislation. A comprehensive single central legislation is of crucial importance for the girl and the future women.[15]

The South Asian countries have realised that there is need to create a critical awareness of the situation of girl child and an atmosphere of concern in favour of women. They gave a call for people's action, that is, organisation and mobilisation of people. With this objective the SAARC countries decided to observe 1990 as the Year of Girl Child.[16]

Girl Child and Health

In this country the discrimination begins right from birth. A girl is breastfed for a shorter period, less cared for and given the least priority in the matter of nutritious foods. The female child has to face neglect and poor treatment at every subsequent stage. It is evident from the problems of her health and nutrition as an infant. Though the average birth weight of boys and girls is more or less the same, the girls between 1 and 5 years of age are much more prone to severe malnutrition than boys because they are not fed properly. More than two-thirds of the girls are malnourished, growing slower. The mortality rate for females is consistently higher than for males in every age group upto the age of 35.[17]

It is generally true across the country that boys eat better food than girls even in privileged families. Sons are more likely to be given milk, eggs, meat and fruits in their diet. Working boys spend part of their earnings on food and snacks, while girls continue to eat the same unvaried diet, that is *chapati* and rice at home. Girls take much less food than their growing bodies need and, so, remain undernourished throughout their lives.[18] A study conducted by the Community Health Department (CHC), Ludhiana shows a wide difference between the nutritional status of male and female children. More female children are malnourished than the boys.[19] The girls are subjected to conscious and subconscious neglect. They get a lower allocation of food within the family and the time and money spent on their health and education is less compared to boys. Boys are seen as old-age insurance for parents and are thus fed well and protected from illness. Adolescent girls have fewer opportunities for recreation, healthy physical exercise and even exposure to fresh air.[20]

Malnourishment is caused not only because of the lack of food but also because of lack of access to food. Even mother discriminates in breastfeeding and in weaning. The impact of this discrimination is that as these undernourished girls enter into under-nourishment cycle, the chances of morbidity in the subsequent generation also increase.[21] Although girls eat less, they do much work not only at home but also in the fields. Her fragile nutritional status leads to anaemia and other nutritional deficiencies expose her to infection and she falls ill oftener than a boy. It has been observed that fewer girls are treated for illness than boys. Hospital records show that more boys are brought in for treatment than girls. This is even more marked for indoor admissions compared to outdoor patients. In most hospitals male admissions are around 65 percent and female around 35 percent of the total. In reports from different parts of India, the ratio varies from 2.1:1 to 1.3:1, the latter being mainly from the South. This in itself is an evidence of a bias against female children.[22] Hence, it is legitimately argued that attention to the mother must start not after she has become a mother, not even when she is just about to become a mother, but even when she is herself an infant and a child, because that is what happens to her during her own childhood which will eventually determine the adequacy of her maternal state.[23]

Besides all this, female infanticide is practised even today, though banned in 1870, by certain communities in Gujarat and in parts of Tamil Nadu. One of the methods followed is to put the child in a barrel containing milk to drown, i.e., death in a *'doodh peti'*. Those girls who survive the maladies of foeticide and infanticide are considered as a drain on the family income.[24] The polyandrous Toda of Nilgri Hills in Southern India practised female infanticide which maintained a certain demographic imbalance.[25]

Child Marriage

The root of the problem of discriminatory treatment being meted out to girls lies in the status of women in society and their expected roles. Males are seen as providers and the role of girls is circumscribed around marriage and motherhood, with little chance to attain individual identity outside the married identity. Girlhood is just a period when a woman is trained for the role she is expected to play. The role of home making and motherhood is assigned to them. Early marriage results in problems of health among women and children. Social reformers, even during the pre-independence period, therefore, advocated raising the age at marriage. The civil Marriage Act of 1872 was passed as a result of the efforts of Ram Mohan Roy. The most well-known legislation on child marriage is the Sarda Act of 1929 which fixed the marriage age for boys at 18 years and girls at 14 years. In 1949, the marriage age was raised to 15 years. The latest legislation, the Child Marriage Restraint Act of 1978, revised the age upwards to 18 years for girls. Marrying a girl earlier was for the first time made a cognisable offence. However, all these laws are more breached than followed. In many communities child marriage is practised even today.[26]

The census data of 1981 have shown that the mean age at marriage of "currently married women" in the country as a whole was 16.7 years. Child marriage affects both boys and girls. However, it affects girls more severely, since marriage spells the pre-mature domestic and child-care responsibilities. An immature body causes a higher infant mortality rate and the impulse for children results in physical weakness or depletion of strength. The fact is that a large proportion of girls, especially in rural India, is pushed into early marriage which is almost consummated after menarche at about the age of 14. In Bihar, Rajasthan, Madhya Pradesh and Uttar Pradesh about 50 percent of girls are married off before the age of 16. The data show that there is an increase in the mortality rate of teenage mothers in the age-group 15-19. It is not surprising, therefore, that the sex ratio drops from 944 in the 5-9 age group to 912 in the 15-19 age group.

Teenage mothers manage to cope with the trauma of pregnancy and the torment of giving birth with few facilities. But these are years when they could be playing with their friends, running about in a carefree way, playing the games children play. For a teenage mother having children herself is like a child playing with a doll. She is too old for toys perhaps but certainly too young to take up the responsibility of childcare. She bears ali that pain and anguish all alone. A suitable SAARC slogan goes thus," too old for toys, too young for babies".

Girls needs 4-5 years for full physical growth after they attain menarche. There is also evidence that adequate nutrition brings down the age at menarche. Whereas a girl who is malnourished experiences delayed menarche. Early marriage denies the girl an opportunity for development and increases the risk of higher number of low birth weight babies and child deaths and disabilities, maternal deaths, gynaecological problems and an increased number of pregnancies to replace the lost children. Unless more attention is focussed on the health of the woman, right from their birth, the cycle will not be broken. In addition, early marriage also deprives the girls of the opportunities of schooling; they are made to assume domestic and child care responsibilities early which hamper their intellectual and personality development. It, therefore, becomes obvious that the young mothers are not only physically inadequate but they become responsible for an intellectually poor population.[27]

Deaths related to childbirth and pregnancy claim a large proportion (upto 25%) of all adult female deaths. In India, 43% female deaths in ages 15-24 are due to causes associated with pregnancy and childbirth. In addition to death, many more women suffer from serious illness related to complications of pregnancy and child birth. The medical complications of adolescent pregnancy include first and/or third tremester bleeding, severe anaemia, labour complications, and toxemia of pregnancy.

However, a proper care of the girl is important from the point of view of society's future. As it is rightly said the health and nutrition of the girl today will affect the health and survival of the future generation, because she is the mother of tomorrow and no future can be built on an edifice that is not strong and healthy and which is corroded with discrimination and injustice at every level.

Education is Free, but Girls are not

The planners of independent India's future had a vision of education as the flaming sword that would shake the poor, the backward and the oppressed from their bonds of illiteracy and inequality. It is believed that education as the catalyst would give Indian women the equality, justice and dignity they had long been denied. The Fifth All-India Educational Survey reveals that there has been tremendous growth in educational facilities at all levels of education during the last 40 years of independence. The growth of enrolment and schooling facilities at the primary and post-primary stages if education was the result of the concerted government effort to implement the Directive Principles of State Policy stated in the constitution to provide free and compulsory education to all children upto the age of 14.[29]

The benefits of this major educational expansion have not reached the female children in any tangible way. Today's girls, tomorrow's responsible mothers, need to be provided with information about health, nutrition, economics and public affairs. For this they need to go to school, to learn, to socialise. But the girl children do not get time for all these, since they are over-burdened with the chores of household like caring for younger siblings, cattle, washing and assisting mothers in cooking.

Despite the continuous efforts towards the improvement in the educational system, the girl child has limited access. The child occasionally enrols out of drive and even attends school only to drop out very soon, since she finds herself unable to cope with both school and her domestic responsibilities. This is future reinforced by those parents who do not want to educate their girl in any way either, since he is going to be away from them after marriage.

Although she has the right to receive equal education, in reality only 18 percent of rural women and 48 percent of urban women are literate. The female literacy rate is only a little more than half that of the males. The gap between the level of education of males and females is gradually widening rather than narrowing. About 20 percent of children between ages 5 and 8 who are mostly girls from the lowest social and economic groups never go to school. While enrolment figures for girls tend to be much lower than those for boys in Scheduled Castes and Scheduled Tribes.

According to the mid-term appraisal of the sixth plan (1980-85) estimates, the total enrolment in the age-group 6-14, under both formal and non-formal systems, would be around 110 million as against the estimated child population of 140 million. This means that over 30 million children are not enrolled. This number consists mainly of girls belonging to Scheduled Caste and Scheduled Tribes in the state that are backward in primary education. In lower income families, education of girls is given the lowest priority. Even in many urban middle class families, cultural norms do not permit girls for higher education, though primary education is free, the cost of uniforms and learning materials is quite prohibitive for poor families.

The reasons for this lower literacy rate are suggested by the National Committee on the Status of Women in India as follows. It also revealed that about 17 percent of the respondents were against girls' education. Middle classes favoured education for girls for economic reasons. Girls in the lower income classes are required to contribute to family income while the affluent follow traditional customs.

The Committee identified the following causes behind social neglect and familial apathy to girls' education:

1. Lack of time, as girls have to attend to demostic work.
2. Poverty in families which forces children to work.
3. Parents view girls' education as being without utility.
4. Absence of schools within walking distance, absence of hostels, transport and security measures which make it much more difficult for girls.
5. Inadequate number of women teachers.
6. Absence of child-care facilities.[30]

The tyranny of household work takes over girls life as soon as they become able to perform the simplest tasks in the family. They shoulder upto 30 percent of the work of the household. Not only economic factors exclude girls from education but also cultural values do so. If the school is away they need to be escorted there. If their school is co-educational and teachers are male, girls may be withdrawn from the school around the age of puberty. Many a times their education is cut short by early marriage. Child marriage though prohibited by law is, still prevalent because parents are often anxious

Percentage of Children Attending Schools in Major States

India/State	*Age-group (in years)* 5-9			10-14		
	Total	*Boys*	*Girls*	*Total*	*Boys*	*Girls*
India*	38.45	44.33	32.21	50.45	62.07	37.47
1. Andhra Pradesh	40.51	47.04	33.88	41.12	51.64	29.78
2. Bihar	25.88	32.96	18.37	41.44	55.41	24.70
3. Gujarat	44.89	49.97	39.41	60.63	70.35	49.66
4. Haryana	39.14	46.57	30.70	54.89	71.12	36.23
5. Karnataka	43.25	48.71	37.78	48.07	58.14	37.80
6. Kerala	75.10	75.14	75.06	85.96	87.90	83.97
7. Madhya Pradesh	29.99	37.78	21.90	41.25	55.38	25.34
8. Maharashtra	54.46	57.60	47.12	62.59	73.07	51.23
9. Orissa	41.01	48.54	33.58	43.46	56.18	30.42
10. Punjab	52.00	54.36	49.33	62.85	69.20	55.58
11. Rajasthan	26.97	36.84	16.28	39.99	58.84	18.68
12. Tamil Nadu	59.53	63.93	54.61	55.47	65.93	44.62
13. Uttar Pradesh	23.35	32.08	17.41	43.60	58.46	25.05
14. West Bengal	36.85	40.77	32.83	52.86	60.18	45.11

**Excludes Assam.*

Source: Census of India, 1991, series, Paper 2 of 1993.

to discharge their responsibility early. In order to save the expenses of two marriages they may marry off two daughters at a time, even if the younger one is well below the legal age limit of marriage. The decision to send a girl to school or keep her at home is influenced by the preceived relevance of educatin as it is available today, which is not more responsive to individual and societal conerns. In India every third girl in the age-group of 6-11 years is not enrolled, in spite of the fact that the overall enrollment of girls has increased. Regional variations are quite tremendous. According to 1991 census, in Kerala and West Bengal 49 girls enrolled for every 51 boys, while in Bihar just 33 girls enrolled for every 67 boys. Non-formal education was started in this country, keeping in view the special needs of those who cannot attend formal schools.

The National Policy on Education (1986) states that the provision of incentives would be necessary for the initial involvement of parents and opinion leaders and these incentives can take many forms depending on local needs and conditions, like loan, subsidies or food compensation for families who send a girl for schooling or awarding a school building, handpumps or television set to a community which enrols and retains all its girls in school, since it is thought that education effects every other aspect of her own life and that of her family and has wider implications for the development of her community.

Work More, Paid Less

The involvement of young children in household work and family occupations constitutes an important part of their training for life and work. Such work training helps them develop skill and enhances their family income, but deprives them of schooling, recreation and rest. Girls put in greater number of hours in domestic work compared with boys. By the age of 10-12 years, girls may be engaged in demostic work for about eight hours per day and by age of 15 years, they work for at least 10 hours per day. Moreover, there is a close association between the work of young girls and that of their mothers. The mother might utilise her daughter's help in a part of her work in order to increase efficiency or wages. This may be especially true in female-headed households. Because a daughter is of high utility to her mother in alleviating the heavy load of household work, childcare has the potential for paid labour, the mothers have a somewhat negative attitude towards their education.

The contribution of the girl child in looking after younger siblings and doing household chores have never been taken seriously and viewed in terms of money value. Young girls work for long hours at home and in the fields, but their work is either not visible enough or is given such a low value that they are not considered as an economic asset. She tends to provide the family with free labour of about 9 hours everyday on an average of 315 days in a year. Her annual contribution to the family costs at least Rs. 2200 and it comes to about Rs. 40,000 per girl till the time she gets married. Parents differentiate the domestic labour extended by boys and girls and justify the contribution as an unproductive member's contribution to her own survival. Girls must earn their bread, while for boys it is not necessary. A report on the status of Indian women produced by the National Institute for Public Cooperation and Child Development reveals the following:

(*i*) The percentage of rural working girls in the age-group of 5-14 years shot up from 4.6 percent in 1971 to 7.8 percent in 1981,while the percentage of working boys declined from about 11 percent to 10 percent in the same period.

(*ii*) In the 15-19 age-group, the number of female workers has gone up by 17 percent, while the figure for males has decreased.

(*iii*) Age-wise girls tend to enter the workforce earlier than boys. Eight percent of the girl workers were below 14 years of age, while their boy counterpart constitutes just four percent. About 20 percent of the girls below 20 are 'main' workers, while only 14 percent of the boys are main workers.

From these statistics it can be said that in the last ten years a large number of female children have started going to work,while the number of boys going to school has increased. It seems most of the programmes instituted during the International Children's Year in 1979 were aimed at male children only.

Girls are found to work in rural, urban and metropolitan areas, though mostly in rural area. The condition of work in the cities and metropolis are very different from those in rural areas. A major contrast among girls and boys engaged in domestic and non-economic work is that while boys eventually move on the fulltime agricultural or wage labour, young girls continue to shoulder the burden of household tasks, from where they are relegated to their role as wives and mothers[32] more than half of the girls do household work whereas only a few boys do this, but boys mostly do outside work like shopping, marketing and helping business. Among non-working children boys constitute about 44 percent and girls only 15 percent. As Aparna Subrahmaniam says most of the girl children are doing domestic work. A combination of domestic and wage work is found to be high. Only a few children are occupied for a major portion of the day with non-domestic work.[33]

At home, a girl engages herself in cleaning, cutting of vegetables, washing clothes or actually cooking. These are the tasks of girls in the working-class and middle-class families. In the poorer families she has to look after her younger siblings depriving her of the opportunity of going to school. In rural areas her tasks extend to looking after domestic farm animal such as cows, buffaloes or poultry. Her work would also include collection of fuel, water and fodder, sometimes from far-off places. Often, this work goes completely unaccounted. In urban areas, a girl child is mostly busy in earning for her family. She indulges in works like washing vessels as a domestic servant alongwith her mother, *beedi* and *agarbatti* rolling, garment making, *papad* rolling, rag picking, construction work, brick-making, making pickles and numerous other odd jobs.[34]

SEWA's Ahmedabad project, co-ordinated by the ILO, reveals that (1) there are a million home-based piece-rate workers but they are not accounted for by the census. (2) The wage for such work is very low, usually Rs. 5 or 6 per day and sometimes as low as Rs. 2.(3) the piece-rate basis could work out Rs. 10 to Rs. 15 to roll 1,000 *beedis* or Rs. 8 to stitch a dozen petticoats. Of course in most of the cases, it is the woman of the house who is the main worker, with her daughters. In most big cities it is found that a large majority of the girls work in factories, workshops, hospitals, building construction and domestic services.

According to the 1981 census, about 8 percent of girls under 14 years of age were 'main' workers and 9 percent were marginal workers (part-time). In rural areas girls go for grazing animal on a payment of Rs. 10 per cow or per buffalo per month which could help them in buying only *meeth* and *mirchi* (salt and chillies). Such rural girls easily escape the long arm of the low and are beyond the reach of all requirements of the law. Child Labour Prohibition and Regulation Act of 1986 states that 'there must be an identifiable employer and an identifiable employee.'

In Karnataka, rural work "in disguise" at the employment place, since, if the employer sees that she is below 14, he will not employ her there. The thin, frail girl covering here face in a *pallu* works alongside her parents for just Rs. 3 to Rs. 5 per day. Child labour is exploited not only by their employers but parents have a major role in it too. The poor and the deprived sections of the society that contribute to child labour since engagement in labour denies opportunities of development, it means that continuance of child labour contributes to the perpetuation of social evils such as untouchability, bonded labour and poverty in general.

Childhood is the stage of personality development. Children in exploitative work are likely to suffer permanent adverse psychosocial consequences of the physical and emotional stress of work, combined with the denial of opportunity to play, explore and interact fully with other children. They also invariably undergo physical and emotional abuse, neglect and separation from the family and carry the burdens of precocious responsibility. Girls in domestic services are bored and have a risk of mental depression and sexual abuse. Working children are found to be frustrated; suffer from role conflicts and have low occupational, income and educational aspirations.[36]

One critical variable in girls' work setting is the degree of family support. Girls accompanying mothers from demostic service are likely to get more protection from parents than girls who put up with employees. Young girls in cities enter into a very different type of employer-employee relationship, which can give rise to a variety of exploitative practices. Girls are made to work much beyond their physical capacity; they are given low wages and at times they are sexually abused. The extent and forms of exploitation of girl-child labour are left to the individual employee's whims and fancies.[37]

Girl Child and Sexual Abuse

We often condemn the woman when she is steeped in prostitution; laugh at her when she does not send her children to school; for uncontrolled birth we hold her responsible and criticise her for not taking part in public, social and political life, while in many welfare schemes like 'Health for All', Universal Primary Education', and 'Literacy Year,...a girl child is not given any priority at all, since she remains at the bottom of social ladder, hidden in the home and often completely helpless. It is necessary for every one of us to realise that many aspects of society's progress depends on the improvement of her status and condition.

Among families of the poor classes in crisis, the girl child, besides being sent as domestic workers or sold into bonded labour to the landlords or the money-lenders, is also despatched off to fill the brothels of towns and big cities. She becomes a part of the process of getting bonded along with the rest of her family to the worst form of work and often exposed to sexual exploitation as well.There are an estimated 50,000 brothels in Bombay with over 1,00,000 prostitutes. It is estimated that about 20 percent of prostitutes in this country are teenagers.

It is found that in Bombay alone there are 20,000 child prostitutes. A child prostitute is very much a prized proposition and for virgin prostitutes a high price is tagged. Besides the sale of young girls to the rich pleasure-seekers is a growing business in cities like Delhi, Bombay, Calcutta and Hyderabad. The sexual exploitation of the girl child takes place both within and outside the family. The figures for within the family are lacking but often girls come into the flesh trade because they have been assaulted by a father, an uncle or a brother.

In the name of religion many poor girls are introduced to this profession through the *devadasi* system in South India. The *devadasis* are dedicated to God: they are first used by the temple priests and then become prostitutes. This system is still prevalent in parts of Karnataka, Maharashtra, Andhra Pradesh and Tamil Nadu. The practice of *devadasi* is well known in Karnataka, where the daughters of lower castes are dedicated, prior to puberty, to the goddess *Yellamma* and later actually made available to priests and other men (for sexual exploitation). As recently as February 9, 1990 on *Magh Poornima* over 2000 young girls were dedicated to goddess *Yellamma* at Saundatti Hill in the Belgaum district of Karnataka. A fairly high percentage of these girls are sold as prostitutes in the sex bazaars of Bombay. Among the prostitutes of Bombay are *devadasis*, unwanted daughters, rape victims, kidnap victims, women from extremely poor families or from the families of landless agricultural labourers of the perenially drought areas.[38] The daughters of such *devadasis* go into the same trade in order to pay back her mother's bondedness.

In the tradition-bound Indian society women are viewed as commodities. This commodification leads to a great exploitation of women, confining them to the background and to the less important jobs.[39] The girls of minority communities and destitute and abandoned girls are subjected to abuse, including forced prostitution.

Born with the stigma of being illegitimate, these children seem to be always shunned by society. They grow almost on the streets, exposed to every possible vice and in an environment which comprises pimps, brothel keepers, corrupt petty policemen, procurers, bootleggers, alcoholics, drug addicts, shady customers all of whom go to make their normal environment, most non-conducive for a child to grow.

In our social system, some persons have to survive by selling their body and offering sexual pleasure in the market. The children of the prostitutes become the innocent victims of the choice factor of having been born to a prostitute. They lead a life of deprivation and contempt. They have no choice. They are far from the minimum opportunities for fulfilment of their basisc material and emotional needs and even denied the ordinary opportunities of the life.[40]

Girl Child in the Media

For media the girl child is a non-entity, non-being untill she is 15 or 16 when she becomes ready for advertisement. As many as 1.5 million girls will never be the concern of media, since they will die before their first birthday. The media tend to reinforce cultural and traditional stereotypes that push the women in the background. In the print media there are stories of successful men and women in traditional roles. In advertisements, women are always shown with domestic appliances while men are shown going out, driving vehicles, taking decision, holding important positions in the offices.

Arun Bhattacharjee's analysis of the print media's coverage in seven newspapers published from different centres and in different languages is quite revealing in this regard. The findings of this analysis are as follows:

(*i*) Story of a criminal assault on female child.

(*ii*) A story of how a female child saved the life of a boy.

(*iii*) A study report of the status of women on the editorial page.

(*iv*) A study on the plight of women in the hill regions that also touched upon the girl child.

It is opined that the visual media could play a vital role in creating awareness among the people and in helping better the status of the girl child. The celebration of 1990 as the SAARC Year of the Girl

Child brought the girl child into more focus. New ideas and programmes are ventured to free her from the stereotypes which are internalised in her, that girls are weak, or that girls cannot do this or that and that they are inferior to boys; that their ultimate aim is marriage and giving birth to a son—possibly the greatest achievement of life. During this period efforts have been made in sorting out social priorities of women's struggle for their right and against gender discrimination.

Unless welfare measures are linked with the basic needs that are crucial to the development of the girl child and her parents, they will not be able to learn more and break the tentacle of poverty. She has to be given education and skills keeping in mind her needs of life. Our society and future depends on her. We can improve the situation of her and ourselves by creating consciousness among people. Overall development is possible only when women get an equal opportunity to work and advance themselves. For the realisation of a better deal for women the following points are noted:

(*i*) Banning of amniocentesis for sex-determination and sex-preselection in private hospitals.

(*ii*) Strict implementation of laws for banning infanticide.

(*iii*) Ensuring the protection of the girlchild's right to life by providing her with good education and treatment equal to her brother and restoring her childhood to her.

(*iv*) Ensuring free and compulsory education up to high school level, providing her opportunities in vocational training and guaranteeing her employment enabling her to contribute to the economy.

(*v*) Enforcement of property rights on par with those of her male counterpart.

(*vi*) The *Devadasi* system should be banned through strict implementation of the law.

(*vii*) Implementation of SITA and similar laws and rehabilitation of prostitute should be undertaken.

(*viii*) The Dowry Prohibition Act should strictly enforced.

(*ix*) Negative projection of women through the media should be stopped.

(*x*) Reinforcement of traditional gender based stereotypes and attitude towards women in textbooks should also be stopped.

(*xi*) Working girls should be rehabilitated by allowing them to learn, play and grow up.

Conclusion

The girl is not welcome in our culture which idolises sons. Today the rejection of the unwanted girl can begin even before her birth through prenatal sex determination. The girl who manages to survive is denied equal access to food, education, health care, employment and even basic human rights. It can be said that girls are discriminated against by their parents, by society and even by policymakers and administrators. This discriminatory treatment denies them their basic rights and the opportunities for full growth and development.

An integrated and holistic approach is essential for her fuller development. This could be done by creating new awareness among the people to value and nature her affectionately. The family and the community should allow her to evolve to her full potential. Formal schooling combined with non-formal education in accordance with local needs with the creation of new channels to reach adolescent and pre-adolescent girls, would create wide spread awareness about the rights of girl child. This way the girl child can be empowered to enter their mainstream of economic and social activity and can come out of the maze of neglect in which she has been confined for centuries. She can have an identity to her own.

References

1. S.C Dube, 'Men's and women's role in India: a Sociological Review' in Barbara Word (Ed),Women in the new Asia: The Changing Social Rules of Men and Women in South and South EastAsia, Amsterdam: UNESCO, pp. 190-192.
2. Atharva Veda, VI. 2-3.
3. *Ibid*, V111. 6.25, V. 11.3.
4. Brhadaranyaka Uprnishada. IV. 4.18. Quoted by B.S. Upadhyaya, *Women in Rigveda*, New Delhi: S.Chand and Co, 1974, p. 43.
5. A.S. Altekar, *The Position of Women in Hindu Civilization*, Delhi: Motilal Banarasidass, 2nd Edn., 1983, p. 5.
6. Ibid, p. 8.
7. T.N. Madan, *Family and Kinship*, Bombay: Asia Publishing House, 1965, p. 34.
8. Cormak Margret, *The Hindu Women*, Bombay: Asia Publishing House, 1961, p. 32.

9. K.M. Kapadia, *Marriage and Family in India* 4th Edn), Calcutta: Oxford University press, 1972, pp. 105-107.

10. Government of India, *The Lesser Child*, New Delhi: Ministry of Human Resources, Development 1990, p. 10.

11. M.M. Mascarchras, "Faminism Hijacked Down the Slippery Slope: Foeticide to Infanticide", in Sushma Sood (Ed.) *Violence Against Women*, Jaipur: Arihant Publishers, 1990, p. 93.

12. R. P. Ravindra, "Struggle against Sex Determination Techniques Unfinished Battle", *Economic and Political Weekly*, Vol. XXII (12) 1987, p. 490.

13. M.M. Mascarchras, op. cit. p. 94.

14. Kumar Dharma, "Male Utopia or Nightmares?", Economic and Political Weekly, Vol.VIII (III) 1983, pp. 63-64.

15. Lakshmi Lingam, "Sex-Detection Tests and Female Foeticide: Discrimination Before Birth ", *The Indian Journal of Social Work*, Vol. LII (1), 1991, p. 17.

16. Subhashini Channa, "Audio-Visual Review", *The Indian Journal of Social Work*, Vol. LII (1) 1991, p. 115.

17. A. Ramanamma, "Female Foeticide and Infancide A Silent Violence" in Sushma Sood (Ed.), *op. cit*, pp. 74-75.

18. Government of India, *The Lesser Child*, *op.cit*, p. 7.

19. *Ibid*, pp. 7-8.

20. Malini Karkal,"Visibility of the girl-child in India",The Indian Journal of Social Work,Vol.LII (1),1991,p. 9.

21. C. Gopalan and S. Kaur, *Women and Nutrition in India*, New Delhi: Nutrition Foundation of India, 1989, p. 2.

22. Shanti Ghosh, "Girlchild: A Life Time of Deprivation ", *The Indian Journal of Social Work*, Vol. LII (1), 1991, pp. 23-24.

23. C.Gopalan, "The Mother and Child in India", *Economic and Political Weekly*,Vol. XX (4), p. 166.

24. Dharma Kumar, *op. cit*, pp. 61-63.

25. Leela Dube, "Misadventures in Amniocentesis", *Economic and Political Weekly*, Vol. XVI (8), 1983, p. 280.

26. Malini Karkal and S.Lrudaya Rajan ,"Age at marriage: How much change",Economic and political Weekly, Vol. XXIV (10), 1989, p. 505.

27. Rayston, Erica and Sue Armstrong, *Preventing Maternal Deaths*, Geneva: World Health Organisation, 1989, p. 56.

28. Rami Chhabra, Veena Soni, Releigh and Anil Jindal, "Health and Demographic Consiquences of Early Marriage and Fertillity", *Social Change*, Vol. 17 (3), pp. 4-26.

29. ICSSR, "*Status of Women in India*", New Delhi, Allied Publishers, 1975, p. 52.

30. ICSSR, *op. cit*, pp. 41-42.

31. Usha S. Nayar, "Labour of Indian Girlchild: Multi-cure, Multi-Abuse and Multi-Neglect," *The Indian Journal of Social Work,* Vol. LII (1), 1991, p. 39.
32. Usha Nayar, *op.cit,* pp. 41-41.
33. Aparna Subrahmanian, "Work Pattern of the GirlChild", *The Indian Journal of Social Work,* Vol. LII (1), 1991, p. .58.
34. Govt. of India, *The Lesser Child, op. cit,* p.17.
35. Malini Karkal, *op. cit,* p.11.
36. Naidu V.S. and Parasuraman S, "*Health Situation of Working Children in greater Bombay*", Bombay: Tata Institute of Social Science, (Mimco) , p. 152.
37. Usha S. Nayar, *op. cit,* p. 11.
38. Priti Patkar, "GirlChild in Red Light Areas", *The Indian Journal of Social Work,* LII (1) 1991. p. 75.
39. Priti Patkar,"Girl Child in Red Light Areas", The Indian Journal of Social Work, LII (1),1991, pp. 73-74.
40. Priti Patkar, op.cit, p. 71 and 80.

6

The Practice of Widow Remarriage in South India

*Abusaleh Shariff**

Marital status is an important determinant of women's status in Indian Society. In a society where a woman has been assigned a subordinate position, her status and role tend to be determined by her age, marital status and number of children she has borne. Sometimes a combination of these three basic atttributes determine her autonomy and recognition within and outside the family.

A married woman is called *'sumangali'*. She carries the highest regards in terms of ritualistic privilege, social identity, preferential treatment in allocation of food, clothing, and health facilities. This doubtless is an appreciation for her inevitable role as the one who bears children for her husband and guarantees the continuation of the family lines and old age support through her progeny. In a village set-up she receives respect from co-villagers not because she is a valuable possession of one of its members, but because she is a daughter-in-law of the entire village community.

Within the family or kinship circle, the number of surviving

* The author is Associate Director, National Council of Applied Economic Research (NCAER), 11 Indraprastha Estate, New Delhi-110 002.

children, especially sons, she has given birth to grants her relative status; nevertheless, marriage is a sufficient precondition for her to attain this social dignity. However, a childless woman tends to lose much of her status both within and outside home. It is, nevertheless, certain that her social status is tied to her husband's occupation, education, economic standard and his health and survival status. A widow has been socially inferior to other women in the rural areas of South India since long.

Study Area and Perspective

This paper is an attempt to highlight some socio-economic issues relating to widows and their survival. Death of husband is regarded as a source of social and economic insecurity for a woman and her remarriage is viewed as a means to regain (at least partly) such security. The presentation in this paper is a part of an ongoing research work which is aimed at investigating morbidity and mortality patterns, nature and type of treatment by the people, old age and widowhood security.

The universe of this study is a cluster of four villages of different size, social and economic composition. They are sufficiently far from urban influence, yet the larger village carries signs of many of the modern facilities like transport services, telephones, electricity, schools, retail stores and so on. Three interior villages are exposed of different levels of amenities and government programmes. The smaller villages are relatively homogeneous both in social (caste composition) and economic standard, while the larger one has about 18 castes and is occupationally heterogeneous. In this paper, however, the inter-village and inter-caste variations will not be highlighted; rather, a general view, particularly relating to widows, is presented in a largely illustrative fashion.

The mode of data collection is unique to the demographic research tradition.The techniques hitherto known only to the anthropologists are appropriately modified to suit our purposes. Nevertheless, the village census and highly focused surveys have been used to present the quantitative dimension (not presented here). The author has paid frequent visits, often of a week-long duration, mixed with people, undertaken long probing conversations and in-depth interviews to extract information. Such an approach has come to be regarded as micro-approach in demographic studies. This method of investigation has many advantages over the other (survey) as far as the qualitative and substantive presentation is concerned.

Widowhood in South Indian Culture

Widowhood is a form of marital disruption. It is taken as a course on a woman for her sins in earlier life. She is normally the victim of a slanderous gossip for having 'eaten away her husband'. She is regarded vicious, unholy and inauspicious. From the time of her husband's death she is forced to do away with the worldly pleasures like wearing ornaments, colour garments, bangles, *mangal soothra* and *'kumkum'*. Certain castes even insist her to shave her head regularly. Her movements outside tend to be curtailed because the sight of a widow is inauspicious which brings ill-luck to others. She is also suspected to be defiled and unchaste. On becoming a widow she automatically loses most of her social, economic, spiritual and ritual privileges. Other spinsters and married women avoid to take blessings from her during marriage and on other auspicious occasions. The future of her life becomes gloomy and often without social and economic security. Since women mostly depend on husband's earnings and do not normally possess individual income of their own or own property in the absence of husband, they become a burden to their relatives who may push them to drudgery and physical hardships. For example, the marital-specific work participation rates for Karnataka from the 1971 and 1981 censuses show a disproportionately high work participation in all ages for the group of women categorised as widowed, divorced and separated. Although the Hindu Woman's Right to Property Act of 1937 and the Hindu Succession Act, 1956, recognise a widow's right to inherit a share in the property which was due to her husband at the time of his death from the joint family property, this is hardly found in practice at least in the study area. However, there are certain rules in existence to transfer a certain amount of property to the surviving son(s) of the deceased on his adulthood. The rules are, however, not very clear and standardised.

Because of the belief that marriages are performed in heaven and due to the social sanctions against promiscuity, a woman is excluded from having any kind of relationship with other men. No wonder the jocking relationship between a woman and her husband's brother is a subject for female gossip and an interesting topic to fill in the social anthropologist's notebook alike. A married man usually runs the risks of being ridiculed at his wife's movements outside home.

History is full of instances when a wife was customarily made to immolate herself with the dead husband, such customs were believed to be essential to attain *'moksha'* or salvation for both of them. When there were more than one wife, Dubois has observed that it was a privilege for the one who was selected by the community to be burnt alive on the husband's funeral pyre.[2] Nevertheless, the idea was that a woman could not have the pleasure of having another man either during her spouse's life or after his death. The question of a widow getting married never existed among the 'caste Hindus', although widow remarriage used to occur among certain low castes and untouchables.

Social and Economic Consequences of Widowhood

The traditional concept of marriage is 'gifting a woman' or *'kanyadaan'*. Thus the social context of marriage leaves a married woman under the complete control of husband or husband's family. Her contacts and the associated benefits are expected to be lost with her natal home and parents. This is very much true even today more in North than in South India due to the strict adherence to village and kin exogamy.[4] Nevertheless, after widowhood a woman is more likely to return to her parents or other surviving relatives (often brothers). This normally occurs because after husband's death, a widow is least likely to get adequate support and security, in spite of her right to inherit a share of property due to the deceased from the joint family as provided under the Hindu Succession Act of 1956. As a result, the social consequence of a woman's widowhood is more likely to be a change of residence, often to her natal home, thus adding to the responsibilities of her parents. The immediate consequences thus are the loss of security of her survival and after her return to her kin an economic burden on them. Besides, widowhood is bound to hamper the psychological balance as a woman as well.

It is clear from the interviews of villagers that the transfer of residence of a widow depends, among various others, on two main factors: (a) access to her deceased husband's property, and (b) the sex, age and number of living children the widow has. Nevertheless, the younger a widow is, the greater is her chance to return to her parent's home, and the older she is, the greater the possibility that she heads a nuclear family of her own with married or single sons.

Women normally do not own or control property. If her husband dies while living in a joint or undivided family, her chances of getting a share becomes remote. This is one of the reasons for the rise in early economic and family nucleation among the landed in rural areas[5]. In spite of smaller land holdings, the family nucleation is regarded viable in rural areas, but for a widow who is issueless or the one with very young children separate living is not promising. Thus, she is forced to seek support from her kinsmen who normally ask her to return home. However, if she has grown-up sons and some share in the property of her husband's joint estate, she is encouraged to keep in contacts with the affinal family.

The question is survival and security of widows is an important one, mainly because of the greater proportion of widows in the society than the widowers. In the research area the proportion of widows to widowers is 3:1 . This is for two main reasons: (a) Although the life expectancy at birth of males is slightly higher than that of females there is a greater number of widows in the society than the widowers because of substantial age gap between the husband and the wife of whom the letter is always younger. For example, the most preferred marriage in the South Indian family system is between a boy and his sister's daughter. Among such marriages the age gap is bound to be large sometimes 10 to 15 years. In this circumstances the most likely spouse to outlive the other is the wife. More recent evidence emerging from the census and other age specific mortality data is the fact that at older ages the life expactancy is merginally higher for woman which may also increase the proportion of widows in India's population. The second most important reason for a greater proportions of widows in the population is the greater incidence of widowers remarrying than the widows in this society.

One demographic and social consequence of a greater widowhood rate and fast increasing practice of family uncleation is that we have many of these widows left on their own and rendered helpless. Because of the absence of an effective social policy to extend them social security and alternative employment or pensions, their survival and modest living is not guaranteed.

Practice of Widow Remarriage

Widow remarriage has both social and economic implications in the society, yet the religious and spiritual considerations dominate restrictions on widows' remarriage. In the past widow remarriages were socially condemned and the religious texts did not sanction them because of the issues associated with female sanctity and deference. Although the practice of *'niyoga'* is believed to have existed in the ancient days, this was allowed only to enable a childless widow to beget upto children. Besides it is not known how prevalent this system was among the community at large. Even under this system, the intimacy between the sexual partners was probihited and the conjugal rights were sactioned only to secure an heir to the deceased. Nevertheless, more recently and especially after the abolition of *'sati'* in 1829 and the enactment of Hindu Widow Remarriage Act of 1856 there were instances of widow remarriage by the reformists and secular minded elites.

In the contemporary period widow remarriages are known to have been happening among the urban, high castes and elite sections of the society. Even in rural areas they do exist among those castes who are now ranked high in the caste hierarchy. The low castes among whom the practice was prevalent in the past now commonly tend to hide such occurrences. As a matter of fact such explicit arrangements are numerically insignificant. This development may possibly be treated a consequence of delayed Sanskritization process in which the low castes emulate a tradition which was followed by the high caste people over a generation ago.

The widow remarriages are considered inferior and entirely different rituals are followed to perform them. In the research area it is known as *'koodike'*. A *koodike* ceremony is normally performed at night, among certain castes, a night before the new moon where only widows and widowers gather for this ceremony. Spinsters and married women are discouraged to attend such occasions. The normal practice of giving bride price or dowry is not observed. A *koodike* may not follow a visit to temple or a holy place. After the *koodike* a woman regains her right to wear *mangal soothra,* bangles, colourful customs and *kumkum*. She may not, however, completely regain the same rights and status in ritualistic and social affairs. Yet she gets another opportunity to legally beget socially acceptable children, economic support and security of her husband. In the study area we noticed that a *koodike* bride was always taken as a second or succeeding wife.

There are instances of widows who have cultivated lasting relationships with men without explicit sanction of marriage. This sort of de-facto conjugal relationships have developed due to the restriction on remarriage of widows. It is emphasized that such associations can be also regarded as kind of remarriage.

Widow remarriage is neither universal nor is practised uniformly within the same community. Such marriages seem to be encouraged among the Brahmins and are also found among the Vokkaligas of Karnataka. The low caste Hindus who in the past used to allow widow remarriages now discourage the practice, although there are instances of such marriages in the form of elopement or becoming concubines. The Kurubas all over Karnataka appear to discourage this practice but they call those who practice as 'ketta Kurubaru', and regard such women as *'Basavis'* or the traditional prostitutes. Among Muslims this practice is encouraged and is regarded both a religious obligation and a social duty.

In a village situation, however, it is almost impossible to know an event of widow remarriage. Even others do not wish to disclose such occurrences because it is still regarded as an insult not only to a specific family or caste but also to the whole village. Widowhood is considered inauspicious and widow remarriage is regarded not so auspicious an event.

Factors Encouraging/Discouraging Widow Remarriage

Although it is difficult to establish the magnitude of the practice of widow remarriage, it can be said that it is not so widespread. Bhat and Kanbargi[6] have estimated using census data that about one-third of widows get remarried in India[6]. This estimate appears to be rather high, but in the absence of hard data on this social phenomenon, one has to accept the crude estimates and simulated projections. One indirect way of comprehending the magnitude of widow remarriage is to understand the social and economic factors which either support or suppress its practice in the society.

We will start approaching this problem with the determining variables which are demographic in nature, and their association with social and economic factors would tell us if the practice is widespread. Age is the most important attribute in determining the nuptiality status of a woman, this is as much an important factor in determining the widow remarriage. Although the incidence is low, a younger widow is more likely to remarry than an older one.

Nevertheless, the proportion of widows in younger ages is small; for example, it is less than two percent at ages below 25 and four percent at ages 25-29. But it is relatively large at middle ages about seven percent at ages 30-40 and 12 percent at ages 35-39. As expected the proportion increases substantially for women above 45 years reaching a peak of about 42 percent in the age group of 60+. A younger widow may not succeed in establishing her claim as the rightful owner of her deceased husband's property in a society where marriages are not registered. In spite of the fact that the law allows a share for a widow on her husband's death, in practice she may not get it. The only chance of her getting a share is through her son, who if, he does not survive she loses that claim. Under these circumstances she may not stay with her husband's relatives and is brought back to her parents' home. In her natal home she becomes both an economic and social burden. Parents fear the possibility of an extra-marital sexual indulgence which may prompt and encourage the parents to arrange another marriage for her. This is the most important reason why the villagers prefer to remarry their widow daughters/sisters.

However, a young widow in receipt of a share in her husband's property legally loses it upon marriage. It appears that the law discourages a widow from remarrying by severing her rights over the deceased husband's, property. The aim, however, of this law is to discourage wishful killing of husbands in a plot which a wife can execute with other man who can be her prospective husband. In one case the widow who inherited Rs. 10,000/- upon the death of her husband, who was a peon in the local school, could not remarry because she had to part with that money on her subsequent marriage.

Like her age, the sex, age and number of her living children also have bearing on the prospect of widows' marriage. With teen-aged children , especially sons, a widow may not choose to remarry rather she gets both social and economic incentives in grooming her children to adulthood. She also assumes the status of the head of a household which is customary in a family consisting of a mother and her married and single children. Nevertheless, in the process of the life cycle, the possibilities that she loses the security of her sons is also great especially when sons marry and become more obliged to their wives.

Thus the social and economic pressure on a widow and her close relatives is the motivating factor hehind a decision to arrange the remarriage of a widow. Other reasons like the effect of secularisation and education is only relevant with a minority of the population, particularly of the Brahmins and some other upper castes. The villagers, however, confirmed that the decision to arrange the marriage for widows is not a community or caste concern, it is purely the choice of an individual or an individual family. Many of the respondents were found opposed to widow remarriages but confirmed that such marriage did take place, though rarely.

Concluding Remarks

The women who got married after widowhood were feeling more secure and psychologically balanced than those who remained widowed for life. Two of them were so happy that they expressed their highest gratitudes to those who were involved in matchmaking. In fact they were not able to express adequate appreciations to their new husbands because of non-fulfilment of certain expectations. On both these occasions marriage ceremony was celebrated and there was explicit social recognition for marriage. With this one may clearly regard remarriage as a source of regaining economic security and social acceptance in a community.

In the light of above discussion it may be emphasized that a new look or rethinking is required to tackle the problem of rehabilitating widows, especially through specific programmes and legislations. The expectation that the social forces and consequent social change would take care of this disadvantaged group is too much to ask. Although the incidence of widowhood, particularly during young ages, is likely to fall in future due to falling age-specific mortality as well as due to narrowing gap between the age of spouse, the sheer size of widows in India is enough to warrant a serious thinking on their problems. One plausible solution is to popularise widow remarriage as a social service tied with both social and government incentives. In fact, a married man with a living wife, if feasible, may be encouraged to marry a widow under special circumstances. Yet another solution is to grant social recognition to de-facto conjugal relationships between a widow and single or widowed person.

References

The author wishes to thank P.M. Kulkarni and P.H. Reddy for their valuable comments on the earlier version of this paper.

1. See J.C. Caldwell, 'The Micro-Approach in Demographic Investigation: Towards a Methodology', presented in an International Seminar on 'Demographic Change in the Social Context, organized by the Population Centre, Bangalore, Sept.6-8, 1982 at Bangalore, and tabled at the IUSSP Workshop on the Micro-Approaches in Demographic Research, Canberra, Australia 1982. Abusalesh Shariff, *Fertility Transition in Rural South India*, Gyan Publishing House, New Delhi, 1989.
2. A. Shariff and K.N.M. Raju , 'The Relation Between Female Work Participation and Marital Status in Karnataka'(Mimcographed), 1984.
3. A.J.A. Dubois, *Hindu Manners, Customs and Ceremonies* (trans. by K. Beauchamp from the author's French version), (3rd ed.), Delhi: Oxford University Press, 1981.
4. A.M. Shah, *The Household Dimension of the Family in India*, Orient Longman, New Delhi, 1973.
5. J.C, Caldwell, P.H Reddy and Pat Caldwell, ' The Determinants of Family Structure in Rural South India' *Journal of Marriage and the Family*, 1984, Vol. 46(1): 215-229.
6. M. Bhat and R. Kanbargi, 'Estimating the Incidence of Widow and Widower Remarriage in India from Census Data' *Population Studies*, 1984, Vol. 38: 89-103.

7

The Litmus Test (Condition of Working Women in Industries)

*Meera Basu and Ekatra**

The New Economic Policy (NEP) is aimed at freeing market forces within the domestic economy and gearing it towards rapid export-oriented growth. This marks a complete turn around from the direction and policies which were pursued since Independence. The emphasis then was on a state-controlled economy and on self-reliance through import substitution. This major departure from the long-accepted policies and practices has generated intense debate.

Within the overall policy changes, the two components of immediate concern for women's studies with regard to the economic status and employment opportunities for women are the *New Industrial Policy* and the *New Trade Policy*. These policies, it is envisaged, would bring the necessary dynamism into the economy, encourage new entrepreneurship and give a boost to manufacturing industries and exports. This would also generate higher income and create more employment opportunities in the long run. This two-fold package, it is argued, is essential to extricate the country from

* The author is Consultant at Ekatra, 11-Amrita Shergill Marg, New Delhi-110003 and expresses sincere gratitude to the Ekatra team of experts consisting of Basil Basu, Rekha Bezboruah and Jayanti Banerjee for their assistance.

the 'balance of payments' (BoP) crisis and provide scope for rapid development. Opponents on the other hand see in NEP a loss of economic sovereignty, neo-colonialism through globalisation, the threat of de-industrialisation, enormous unemployment and increasing marginalization of the assetless, as market forces replace social state control of the economy. Exponents of women's studies warn that women being concentrated in lower rung of the labour market would be the *first* to face retrenchment.

The economic prospects for women under the NEP are highly debatable and are therefore being put to the following *litmus test* :-

(1) Will re-structuring empower women for easy and equal participation in the market or will the problems of women, especially poor women, worsen with the implementation of the NEP?

(2) Will the NEP offer better economic opportunities for a larger number of women or will job security and work conditions deteriorate as enterprises are freed from controls and are able to concentrate on cost-effective, profit-making management practices?

(3) Will women have equal access to training, technology and job mobility with the emphasis on modernisation and industrialisation being propagated by the NEP or will they continue to be used increasingly as cheap labour?

The seeds of the NEP area said to have been sown in the '70s (during Emergency), with results being manifested in the '80s, when the policy of import substitution made way for exports. A drastic fall in women's participation in the formal sector was observed in this period, particularly in the old manufacturing industries, followed by increasing induction into the informal sector. There was a growth in women's employment in some new manufacturing industries as wage workers. The move into the modern industries did not however mean a move into modern manufacturing processes. Women were in fact employed in the traditional processes at low wages and as casual, contract or piece-rate workers or in ancillary and small home-based enterprises. Since the NEP seeks to further promote rapid export-oriented growth, there is a broad agreement that the trend set in the '80s would intensify in the '90s.

The 'informalisation' of the labour-force, also termed 'feminisation' or 'flexibilisation' and 'casualisation' helped increase women's economic participation in the first instance. The effect of the 'decentralised' production processes, scholars feel, would not, however, be in women's economic interests in the long run, as they would be exposed to undue exploitation and discouraged from economic advancement.

Secondary sources indicate the following prospects in broad sectoral terms:

(1) 'Marginalisation' of women is predicted in the primary (agriculture) and secondary (manufacturing) sectors. Increase of women in the service sector (depending on the education and skill levels) and the informal sector is anticipated, these being the two poles of the labour hierarchy.

(2) Ever-growing interest rates of banks and suspension of government's affirmative action programmes due to cuts in social sector spending will be detrimental to the economic interests of women. Both self-employed women and women entrepreneurs are, therefore, likely to face difficulties in accessing institutional credit and would in turn be exposed to exploitation by money-lenders.

(3) Curtailment of extension services and input subsidies, as envisaged under the NEP, will have adverse effects on women, particularly those who are in need of special support services to overcome their various disadvantages in the economic sphere. Without these service supports, the existing gender inequality in the economic sphere will grow.

(4) Low level employment in small enterprises and informal labour relations militate against unionisation. Women workers are unable to bargain collectively for their rights or to get a better deal for themselves due to relatively small numbers per unit. Owners on the other hand prefer women for this very reason and for their aptitude in certain manufacturing processes.

In capital scarce and labour abundant economies, such as in India, small-scale industrial production has particular appeal, taking into account the broad-based social structure of the country. The Small Scale Sector (SSS) was favoured in the belief that it would generate more employment per unit of capital than larger units. Since a vigorous small industry sector is vital for industrial growth, it also received preferential treatment. Policy-makers expect that there will be a major expansion of the sector and hence increased employment of women who are the preferred labour force in many small-scale enterprises.

The controversy about the impact of NEP on women workers, specially in SSI, is obvious and must therefore undergo **The Litmus**

Test before the direction and the volume of impact are evident. This was the aim of the *Ekatra* research team in taking up a case *study* of women workers in SSI on which this paper is based.

Research Framework

Certain key assumptions based on the analysis of the global economy and gender studies in other developing countries that have undergone SAP provided the research frame-work of this study. Two possible outcomes of NEP, leading to two types of development are:

(1) Advent of the Multi National Corporations (MNCs) due to the attraction of a large supply of cheap-labour which would boost 'foot loose' industries such as electronics, with both short-term and long-term consequences, and

(2) Re-inforcement of the international division of labour through growth of agri-business which would be an extension of the old plantation industry with surplus crops being produced mainly for export, perhaps in the processed form (food processing).

The outcomes stated above are likely to have significant consequences for industries which employ a large number of women or have a potential to do so, such as electronics and food processing.

The new 'liberalisation' policies, contemplating large-scale expansions of the Export Processing Zones (EPZs) and Export Oriented Units (EOUs), affect women closely as a great number of them mostly young, single and semi-skilled or unskilled, are employed in the EPZ and EOU enterprises in labour intensive manufacturing of electronics, textiles, footwear, etc.

Food processing of the traditional kind has been the women's domain in their domestic role. Modernisation and commercialisation of food processing registered a substantial spurt with the setting up of a separate Ministry of Food Processing Industries in the mid '80s. Industrial and labour records show that in the small-scale, tiny and cottage sector, large number of women are working in the food processing industry. This has been designated as one of the thrust areas under NEP which ecourages export of value added products (processed foods, for example) instead of primary agricultural commodities.

Within the above context this study attempts to analyse prevailing work conditions and prospects for women's economic participation following the promulgation of NEP by GOI in 1991. The study focusses on women workers of SSS in selected electronics and food processing units.

Purpose and Scope of the Study

1) To analyse and understand the implications of the 'reform' measures, as they affect the economic participation of women in the productive sector, with respect to the electronics and food processing industries.

2) To identify strategies and interventions required to safeguard women's interests in the new economic environment.

Specific Objectives — To determine the range of employment opportunities for women in the electronics and food processing industries by examining:-

(1) Women's access to new technology;

(2) Opportunities for vertical mobility; and

(3) Conditions of work, job security and remuneration.

Three states, viz., Maharashtra, Karnataka and Himachal Pradesh, with varying degrees of industrialisation and diverse socio-cultural patterns which affect women's economic participation, were selected for the study.[1]

Maharashtra—a leading industrial state where both electronic and food processing and women's employment in them are well reflected and are increasing.

Karnataka—with its abundant natural resources and progressive industrial policy has achieved substantial industrial growth in recent years.

Himachal Pradesh—a far less industrially developed state but with potential for the electronics and food processing industries where women were reported to be present in large proportions.

Both electronics and food processing were identified as thrust areas in all the three states. Incentives for rural industrialisation were also available in the form of exemption from excise duties for a wide range of agro-based products.

Collection of Data

A combination of secondary and field-data were used. The secondary data provided an overview of the SSS and emerging trends in women's employment in previous decades which helped in sample selection for the field-study. The sources of secondary data were case studies, articles, debates, government policy statements, census figures, etc., collected from women's centres, libraries, documentation centres, journals, etc. Data documenting experiences of other countries which had undergone similar economic transformations were also considered.

The field-data collected were both qualitative and quantitative. The former were obtained through detailed interviews with officials in relevant government departments, training and financial institutions, while the latter were collected through well-structured questionnaires canvassed in the selected units of the electronics and food processing industries. The primary data gathered at two levels, the management and women employees, were so designed as to capture both the entrepreneurial and workers' views.

Lists of registered units in SSS of the electronics and food processing industries, available with various government departments and agencies, were initially used for selecting the sample units. The criteria for the sample selection identified earlier (See Appendix) had to be modified after the preliminary survey and pretesting. Many units did not have more than 4-5 women employees and the criterion of 'at least 10 women workers' had to be applied with flexibility. Selection of units was thus purposive and was based on preliminary visit to prospective units. The sample units were located in Thane, Bombay and Pune in Maharashtra; Bangalore and Mysore in Karnataka; Solan and Parwanoo in Himachal Pradesh.

Sample Size (Units and Women Employees) for the Study (April 1992)

S. No.	*State*	*Sample Size in the Industry Electronics and Food Processing*				*Total*
		Unit	*Women employees*		*Unit*	*Women employees*
1.	Maharashtra	11*	87	8	100	187
2.	Karanataka	10	105	10	117	222
3.	Himachal Pradesh	10	100	9	58	158
	Total	31	292	27	275	567

*Management/owner data for only 9 units are available as two of them refused to co-operate.

N.B.: Women entrepreneurs constituted 1 in electronics and 2 in food processing industries in Maharashtra, while there was only 1 woman entrepreneur included from the food processing industry in Himachal Pradesh.

Various difficulties with respect to field-work were responsible for the smaller sample size of 567 rather than the original size fixed at 600. The total number of units under study were 31 in electronics and 27 in food processing industries. The women workers interviewed therein were 292 and 275 respectively. The statewise distribution of the sample studied is given below:

The management or owners were mostly either hostile or had failed to co-operate with the investigators after an initial show of willingness. The sample may, therefore, reflect a bias as the employees of only co-operative and willing managements were interviewed.

The women were interviewed at their work-place mostly during break-times. Interviews with the women workers, very often, had to be conducted in the presence of the management/owners. This restricted the assessment of the *real* situation as the respondents were hesitant to reveal the truth.

Many units and products had to be left out since the selection criteria could not be matched by them; either only men were employed or women worked as seasonal labour and were not available at the time of the survey. Bakery units in Maharashtra, for example, did not employ women because it required working in night shifts.

In food processing, the criterion of at least 10 women employees per unit could not be adhered to and the number had to be reduced to 3-5 women employees. The main reason for this was the seasonal employment of women in fruit processing and the very limited number of permanent women employees in these units, specially in Himachal Pradesh.

In Himachal Pradesh, due to operational problems, the employees' data are available only in an aggregated form for both electronics and food processing units. Inferences have, however, been drawn on the basis of the investigator's qualitative report as well as from the distinctive characteristics which have emerged for the two industries in the other two states.

The study did not aim at comparability of data across the selected states and industries, though some standardisation and uniformity were attempted. The approach was to build up a data base from the field drawing on all the relevant qualitative and quantitative data available. In the process the diversity of the base, the variations in data sources and definitional discrepancies and contradictions were revealed and had to be addressed. The data accumulated had, therefore, to be interpreted and analysed within the limitations of the field conditions.

Analysis of Findings

Within the gamut of issues that arise from the NEP, the present study has looked at the likely direct effects on women workers in the SSS. Although there are general pronouncements about a rise in women's employment in certain sectors, policy-makers have not formulated any explicit employment generation measures for women in the Eighth Plan.

The study showed that women are employed in substantial number in both the electronics and food processing industries. They are carrying out a range of operations, spread across the skill levels. In most SSIs, however, they do not enjoy job security.

A majority of women in electronics are employed in unskilled and semi-skilled work. Their overall status in electronics is, however, better than those in food processing. Their educational levels are higher as also their socio-economic status. They belong by and large to a younger age-group, tend to be more conscious and aware of their rights and show potential for responding to organisational efforts (see Appendix for details).

Very few women have permanent jobs in the food processing industry. A large number of them work as casual or contract labour which usually brings them less than the stipulated minimum wage rates. It appears that women in this industry face greater exploitation and their work conditions are worse. In fish-based and cold storage units, investigators were denied access. It was found from other sources that women workers in such units are being brought through contractors from South India and are being kept like bonded labour. Most of these workers are young spinsters who do not speak the local language are not permitted to mix with local people and live in dormitory type accommodation close to the factories.

Sex Stereotyping of Jobs—No gender disparity in wages was apparent in either industry but sex stereotyping of jobs was obvious. While it may be agreed that women are better suited than men to perform certain jobs, the question arises as to why the "value" of what men do is greater than what women do and is rewarded with higher wages. Women worked on assembly line jobs in electronics and pre-processing functions in the food industry. Packaging was also typically undertaken by women. Men did the 'heavy' jobs and all the 'outside' work such as marketing, liaison, etc.

Most employers preferred to employ women for various 'inside' jobs in both electronics and food processing because they were committed, hard-working, loyal and patient with greater concentration. They did not waste work-time in unnecessary chatting, smoking or pan/tobacco chewing. They were perceived as less likely to leave since they are less educated and less skilled. What was not stated was the unlikelihood of union activity by women and their willingness to work for lower and uncertain wages.

Wages—Women stated that wages were the single most important issue. There were certain discrepancies regarding wages, as stated by the management and the workers. Wage averages were low. Despite industrialisation having started at an earlier period in Maharashtra, it was specially interesting to find that the wages of women employees in the electronics units, were as low as Rs. 350-600/- per month for almost 42% of these workers; the majority getting the lower limit of the income slab. Many of these were either the main bread-winners (their husbands/fathers being unemployed) or they made a substantial contribution to their family income. The provisions of Minimum Wages Act were often evaded.

Conditions of Work— Workers in either industry did not enjoy by and large the minimum benefits such as earned or casual leave, provident funds, medical or retirement benefits. Avoidance of such payments appears to be the reason for not having permanent women employees.

Women suffered from various occupational health hazards in both the industries. In several electronics units, they had to stand for long hours on the job even during pregnancy, or were given stools and not chairs to sit on during work. The argument of efficiency being used by the management for providing stools to women does not appear logical. Several women felt that they could work more more efficiently if they were more comfortable while at work. Women workers complained of backache, eye irritation, headache and other job related health problems. These problems were generally related to assembly line jobs.

In the food processing industry, the smell of spices and other food stuffs had overpowering effects as an eye and throat irritant. Women spent hours sitting on the floor bent over their jobs, rolling and packaging products, etc. Backaches were the most common complaints.

Most women workers unfortunately do not make the connection between their health problems and the nature of their jobs. 'Occupational health hazard' is only jargon known to them and their ill-health is accepted as a norm or at the most attributed to hard work and bad luck. It is only when the investigator spells out the possible health hazards due to the nature of their jobs that these women begin to perceive the reality. But do they have any option?

Worker-Management Relations and the Role of Trade Unions—Mainstream trade unions do not seem to have taken much interest in women workers of the SSS who are thus without an organisational umbrella. In the cases under study, however, wherever there were unions, the workers had better work conditions in terms of job security, wages, leave benefits, etc. A large number of the respondents felt that their condition was sure to improve if they had a union. Women's expectations from unions go beyond implementation of legal rights and wages. They feel that unions should also provide support services and help them get assistance from banks or start co-operative banks or loan giving societies.

An example from Maharashtra of untrained women workers taking up issues of women's welfare on their own, provided a refreshing example of worker's initiative and women's solidarity. In one of the concerns (Harniks), one woman had started a cooperative bank with workers' savings, lending out small amounts at 3% interest and sharing profits with the members. Similarly in another unit, women shared each other's work load in times of need so that the daily wage was not lost due to absence.

It was pointed out that even though there is no overt wage discrimination, traditional discriminatory attitudes still persist. Women felt that they had not only to fight against the management but also their male colleagues. The latter cooperated with the women against the management on common issues, but not when it came to special problems faced by women.

In the food processing industry, management-worker relations are still on patron-client lines and in a sense trade union activity has had a backlash, as in Chitale's in Pune. The union has enforced fixed hours and work output and wages. The management on its side has stopped giving sweets on Diwali and other festivals, as it has used to be before the union came into the picture.

The women on the whole felt 'grateful' to the managements—'without them we would not have our jobs. We need them and though they need us too, they have more bargaining power', they stated. Behaviour of the management e.g., respect for older workers and kindness were considered very important. Women in the Maharashtra and Karnataka samples were unanimous in their opinion that they were more comfortable working for women entrepreneurs, as they were more sympathetic and considerate towards their personal needs.

Access to New Technology—Changes in technology did not appear imminent and only in one case did it entail displacement of workers. Technology used in the food processing units was still at a simple level.

In electronics, women are receiving training and practising a new skill—albeit, manual one—in case of assembling. They are being inducted into a 'modern' industry and it represents a shift from their traditional occupations or skills. There also appears scope for their handling more highly skilled jobs in this sector—if they achieved the requisite skills. There is no significant gender bias here, the crucial factor being the level of education and technical training. Women can and are doing better than men, wherever they are on par—technically and educationally.

In theory, the possibility of vertical mobility exists but it is very rare in practice. A small SSI unit may not provide much scope within itself, but individual workers may change jobs and move up the grade. Their experience in one unit may not, however, equip them for work in another enterprise. Managements, prefers a stable (not formally permanent) work force and do not favour change.

Most of the units give on-the-job skill training to employees but only very few provide managerial training. Training has been identified as an important lacunae and a need in electronics. Women expressed a preference for training before joining rather than on-the-job training because it enables them to opt for better jobs.

Industrial Policy and the SSI—The industrial policies of the three selected states have in many respects a similar focus and thrust, viz., the development of hinterland areas through growth centres, incentives to entrepreneurs, promotion of electronics and agro-based industries among others and special incentives for the development of the SSIs.

Most of the entrepreneurs interviewed stated that it was too early to assess the impact of NEP on SSI. The effects so far have been felt only in the area of liberalisation of imports, custom duty exemptions and courier systems of purchase, which apply mainly to the electronics industry. Compared to their counterparts in electronics, the food processing manufacturers had little awareness or interest in NEP. As to the question whether procedural bottlenecks had been eliminated to any appreciable extent, there was still much uncertainty and some confusion. Fears were expressed that the implementing machinery would obstruct the new proposals.

All the units, without exception, expressed their problems with inspectors of various kinds and levels and harassment on account of clearances and documentation. Numerous stories were recounted about the corruption of government officers and lack of co-ordination in different departments. Irregular supply of electricity and lack of infrastructure were cited as important factors which affect the SSIs.

Both electronics and food processing entrepreneurs felt that they would have to 'export or perish'. They stated that government support was required in a much more organised way to help entrepreneurs with exports. Government credits and finance should also be liberalised and made more easily available to SSIs. Some entrepreneurs felt that small units could not survive in the face of competition and economies of scale vis-a-vis multinationals and large units. Others felt that ancillarisation was the only answer for them.

This, however, posed problems particularly for ancillary industries which supply to a single large unit. The buyers of their products (including government) did not release payments for several months. These companies had to buy raw materials with cash and pay sales tax in advanced and quite often an interest of 21% or above on the loan taken from banks or other agencies. The owners from middle-class backgrounds or as first generation entrepreneurs could not cope with these circumstances and were, therefore, forced to close down their units.

Nevertheless, it might be noted that about 820 items are reserved for production through SSI as per the Industrial Policy Resolution, 1991. The SSI entrepreneurs have high expectations and a tendency towards dependence on government. Many officials, however, believe and some studies undertaken recently suggest that eventually subsidies and protection to SSIs should be phased out and a natural interlocking of the SSI with Medium and Large Scale Sector be achieved through a process of ancillarisation. Observers suggest that the bigger companies should be statutorily obliged to pay SSIs within a month or pay interest on the amounts due.

While taking the due note of the constraints of SSIs, the present study has not attempted to find specific solutions for the sector as such. The concern here is only with women workers in relation to the sector. The point emerging very clearly is that with the closure of SSIs, the spectre of unemployment and hardships looms large for these vulnerable groups of women at a time when they can least bear it.

Implications for Women's Employment—Entrepreneurs expressed the usual view that they should not be hampered by labour laws which should also like to do away with unions, minimum wages and have the freedom to employ labour for short-term contracts without having to provide permanent employment. In the present climate of liberalisation in favour of entrepreneurs and management, statutory safeguards for working women may become a causalty. Even with the existence of laws governing wages and work conditions, the study shows that these are not a high priority with management or government. The SSS falls mostly outside the purview of these laws.

As the government is interested in expansion of the SSI, workers' interests should be taken into consideration. While measures to simplify procedural matters and curb corruption among government officers should be welcomed, the policy should not be used to further exploit workers. The trend to retrench workers, and convert regular workers to daily wages or contract labourers is visible. The standard of living of such workers is steadily deteriorating. If the NEP is to further sharpen the conflict between workers and industrialists, it would serve only the short-term interests of industry. The worst sufferers would be the workers, specially women employees.

No clear picture has emerged regarding increase in employment for women. In electronics and food processing, with the thrust on exports and incentives from the government, employment is expected to grow but with a greater degree of informalisation of labour. In electronics the nature of women's employment precludes much mobility or advancement even with re-training. The food processing industry at present offers scope for employment of unskilled and needy women but this could change if units went in for technology upgradation.

Maharashtra Government's policy of promoting industrial co-operatives for women in rural areas has encouraged technical training as well as entrepreneurship for women. Meltron's training programmes facilitate women's direct, indirect and self employment. Many trainees have formed electronics co-operative societies for manufacturing. Clearly, women are willing to avail opportunities that are offered.

Sick Units and Retrenchment—In the industrial estates visited, a large number of units could be seen lying empty. Many units are closing down while many others are sick. In this context, the issue of retrenchment and unemployment looms large.

A National Renewal Fund has been proposed for providing funds when an exit policy for public sector enterprises creates unemployment for a large number of workers. Originally conceived as a social safety net with a clear accent on alternative employment generation, training and re-employment, its scope is now being curtailed. In a proposal awaiting cabinet approval, the employment generation and employment insurance components have been shelved, narrowing its scope to the facility for providing assistance towards severance payments. For most workers this is likely to be a short-term solution.

It is clear in the surplus labour situation thus created, wages and the conditions in SSIs would become even more precarious as retrenched labour of the PSUs both men and women, become competitors for the SSI jobs.

When wages are already so low, inflationary trends will affect poor women and their families as consumers and nutrition levels are likely to fall. This kind of critical outcome must be viewed in the context of the already existing gender based inequality in family consumption patterns. A major goal of WID policymakers should, therefore, be to find ways of protecting the employment of these women.

Need to Safeguard Women's Interests—To sum up, the increase in insecure low-paid female employment and the credit squeeze on self-employed women makes it imperative to provide safeguards against women's marginalisation. If the SSS shows potential for growth, with the right inputs of technology, management skills and finance, women's concentration in the sector should become a positive factor in women's employment. This can be done by interventions that empower women so that their participation in SSIs is strengthened and brings them due returns.

Recommendations

The recommendations are grouped in various broad catagories. Some of them involve further studies, policy directions or changes, organisational structures, changes in perception, and training and access to resources. Otheres are remedial in nature and though relatively easy to provide, will yield quick results such as greater productivity, better morale and more continuity in the work-place.

It is recommended, within the industries which are declared thrust areas, priority must be given to those which employ a large number of women, e.g. electronics and food processing. This would enable women to contribute to and benefit from development plans and programmes. The recommendations which follow are designed keeping in view the duality of women's participation.

The study, though limited in scope, indicates clearly that if the NEP is to succeed and gender disparities to decrease, the state must play a more dynamic role for developing social sector programmes. This is critical for marginalised workers, often women, in the SSS, low skilled and low paid, with little margin to absorb the shocks of structural reforms.

Given the financial and other constraints of the government, however, all-out support is required on the part of multilateral and bilateral donor agencies. The role and importance of their assistance in the productive sector, which includes development of social sector activities, is crucial at this juncture.

This being a relatively new and unchartered field, further studies and surveys into specific problem areas are necessary for recommending meaningful and effective interventions. The following types of studies be supported by bilateral donor agencies and undertaken by research organisations, women's groups and individuals:

—studies of similar industries headed by women entrepreneurs to determine their sensitivity to gender needs vis-a-vis male entrepreneurs.

—study of sick industries and problems of women employees that are laid off with a view to their forming organisations to take over and run sick units (e.g. Kalyani Sharp).

The central and state governments and donor agencies should, by supporting NGOs, and concerned individuals, facilitate organisations of women workers (such as SEWA) which would in the absence of trade union protection, provide women with:

— a forum for getting together and expressing their opinions

— collective bargaining strength

— improvement of working conditions

— enforcement of minimum wages

— job security and benefits

— small loans or chit funds

— support services.

Provisions for training should be made in national and state allocations of funds as well as in WID policies and programmes of multilateral and of bilateral agencies.

(i) Technical and Vocational Training

—vocational guidance at a school level

—promotion of technical training after class X/SSLC

—retraining of retrenched workers for re-employment in new enterprises

—training for skilled and semi-skilled employment in electronics and other modern industries in rural areas

—advanced technical training during employment

—study leave to improve skills during employment

(ii) Training in management, leadership, organisational skills and in co-operatives (labour, producers, marketing, etc.)

(iii) Training in gender sensitisation of employers and male and female workers.

(iv) Training in entrepreneurial skills for rural women (i.e., how to start a business, obtain credit, collect information, conduct market surveys, identify needs of consumers and right products for manufacturing, quality control, etc.)

Women need access to credit as banks and other financial institutions are often not forthcoming. The government development agencies and other organisations should facilitate the flow of credit to women's co-operatives and to individual women to enable them:

—to improve their skills

—to undertake entrepreneurial activities

—to take up self-employment

—to obtain equipment and tools

—to organise support facilities which would enable them to undertake employment.

2. Credit should be made available enabling women workers of 'sick units' to take over and run them as co-operatives.

Entrepreneurs should be made aware by government, donor agencies and development groups of the importance of women's contribution in the two industries, as the value addition comes from their labour input. The overall efficiency and productivity of women workers would be improved if they were provided with:

—better and more comfortable working conditions (e.g., better work places, chairs rather than stools)

—better health and medical facilities

—frequent short breaks

—reasonable working hours

—minimum wages

—separate toilets for women workers

—job security during pregnancy

—maternity leave and benefits

—child care facilities

—nursing breaks.

Appendix

Criteria for Selection of Units and Women Workers

The sampled units and the women workers included:

(1) a range of ownership patterns, e.g., government, semi-government, public sector, private entrepreneurs, partnerships and

co-operatives;

(2) different sizes of SSS units across the investment range of Rs. 5 lakh to Rs. 65 lakh; the selected enterprise should fall within this sector even though the individual units investigated may not come under it by themselves;

(3) the sample should reflect a product mix and cover women engaged in various tasks at different levels—managerial, technical as well as wage-workers but not service staff; the selected units should have at least 10 women employees;

(4) at least two units, with women entrepreneurs as the head, should be selected from the electronics and food processing industries.

Some Demographic Characteristics of Women Employees Interviewed in Selected Electronics and Food Processing Units April, 1992

Table 1 Percentage Distribution of Level of Education of Women Interviewed in Selected Electronics and Food Processing Units, 1992

S. No.	*Level of Education*	*% of Women Employees Interviewed*		
		Maharashtra	*Karnataka*	*Himachal* Pradesh
1.	Illiterate	16.1	15.7	20.9
2.	Less than primary	14.0	—	4.4
3.	Primary	10.8	14.0	12.0
4.	Middle	20.4	8.1	8.2
5.	SSLC	24.7	36.5	—
6.	SSLC+/PUC	2.2	4.1	44.3
7.	ITI & Professional Diploma/ SSLC & ITI	4.8	4.5	—
8.	Graduate/Grad. & Professional Diploma	4.3	10.8	9.5
9.	PG & Above/BE	2.7	5.4	—
10.	Others	—	0.2	0.6
	Total	100.0	100.0	100.0

Table 2 (A) Percentage Distribution of Different Age Groups of Women Interviewed in Selected Electronics and Food Processing Units, 1992

S. No.	*Level of Education*	*% of Women Employees Interviewed*	
	Age Group	*Maharashtra*	*Himachal Pradesh*
1.	15-20	11.3	8.9
2.	20-25	18.2	37.3
3.	25-30	15.1	20.3
4.	30-35	17.7	17.1
5.	35-40	17.2	9.5
6.	40-45	10.2	1.9
7.	45-50	6.5	2.5
8.	50 & +	3.8	2.5
	Total	100.0	100.0

Table 2 (B)

S. No.	*Level of Education*	*% of Women Employees Interviewed*		
	Age Group	*Maharashtra*	*Karnataka*	*Himachal Pradesh*
1.	15-30	44.6	68.9	66.5
2.	30-45	45.1	27.0	28.5
3.	45-60	10.3	4.1	5.0
	Total	100.0	100.0	100.0

Table 3 Percentage Distribution of Marital Status of Interviewed in Selected Electronics and Food Processing Units, 1992

S. No.	*Level of Education*	*% of Women Employees Interviewed*		
	Marital Status	*Maharashtra*	*Karnataka*	*Himachal Pradesh*
1.	Unmarried	30.1	42.8	39.9
2.	Married	49.5	57.2	48.7
3.	Others*	20.4	-	11.4
	Total	100.0	100.0	100.0

* Others : Widow+Divorced+Separated.

Some Economic Characteristics of Women Interviewed in Selected Electronics and Food Processing Units April, 1992

Table 4 Percentage Distribution of Different Income-Groups of Women Interviewed in Selected Electronics and Food Processing Units, 1992

S. No.	*Average Monthly Income (Rs.)*	*% of Women Employees Interviewed*	
		Maharashtra	*Himachal Pradesh*
1.	300-600	32.8	2.5
2.	600-1000	35.4	65.8
3.	1000-1500	14.0	20.3
4.	1500-2000	8.1	5.7
5.	2000 & +	1.6	5.7
6.	Commission	1.1	-
7.	Piece-rate	7.0	-
	Total	100.0	100.0

Table 5 Percentage Distribution of Skill Levels of Women Interviewed in Selected Electronics and Food Processing Units, 1992

S. No.	*Skill Level*	*% of Women Employees Interviewed*		
		Maharashtra	*Karnataka*	*Himachal Pradesh*
1.	Professional*	-	-	1.9
2.	Clerical*		-	-
8.2				
3.	Supervisory*	-	-	10.1
4.	Skilled	10.8	43.7	55.1
5.	Semi-skilled	48.9	24.3	1.9
6.	Unskilled	40.3	32.0	22.8
	Total	100.0	100.0	100.0

Reference

* The field study for Maharashtra was co-ordinated by Aalochana, Pune and data collected by Nirmala Sathe and Lata P.M.; for Karnataka investigation was done by Sita Shekhar, and for Himachal by Vandana Rao and Sulochana Nanta.

8

Reproduction and Rural Women's Educational Underdevelopment: an Empirical Exploration

*Sandeep Parmar and S.B. Singh Parmar**

This paper purports to examine the tenability of the thesis that rural women's educational attainment and, consequently, their career are marred by the special role they have to play in the process of reproduction or procreation. It is contended that the childbearing and rearing roles are possibly the root cause of the subordination of women in society.

Inequality in the educational attainment between the sexes is viewed here as the result of women's reproductive activities and the prevailing social, economic and political milieu in which they are enmeshed. Since women generally fail to get adequate education, professional training and skill due to their involvement in the reproductive process since an early age, they are kept off from the public sphere and pushed mainly into the private sphere of life. The deprivation from education, blockade of career combined with various social handicaps force women to specialise in domestic activities. Since men's education and career opportunities are better, this perpetuates the division of labour that goes against the interest of women;

* The former author is Research Scholar in Agriculture Extension, Kanpur University, Kanpur and the latter is Lecturer and Head, Dept. of Sociology, Atarra Post-graduate College, Atarra (Banda), UP.

it places them in at the subordinate position. In what follows, an attempt has been made to examine the tenability of these assumptions with the help of some empirical evidence.

Theories about the Origin of Subordinate Position of Women

There are two prominent ideologies that explain the origin of subordination of women in society: the biology-is-destiny ideology and social-historical ideology. According to the biology-is-destiny ideology, basic biological and psychological differences exist between the sexes. These differences require each sex to play a separate role in social life. Women are the weaker sex, both physically and emotionally. Thus, they are naturally suited much more so than men to the performance of domestic duties. A woman's place, it is believed under normal circumstances, is within the protective environment of the home. Nature has decreed that women play the roles of the nurturant and caretaker as wife and mother. And, what is seen as biologically pre-determined is considered beyond the scope of social change.

The socio-historical approach to the origin of the unequal relationship between the sexes rejects biological pre-determinism. It sees the unequal, hierarchical and exploitative relationship between men and women caused by socio-historical factors.

As regards the origin of the position of women in society there are two prominent explanations: the Marxist and the feminist. Within the Marxist traditions, Engels traced the origin of the position of women in society and viewed the division of labour by sex as determined by the women's role in child-rearing and the separation of social from economic reproduction.

However, Engels considered this role as tied to the development of private property and class society. This ideology did not consider gender as the basis of its origin. However, Marx's analysis for an understanding of women's position in domestic and non-domestic activities seems to be inadequate on the ground that instead of going into the origin of women's oppression, Marx does not question the nature of division of labour between the sexes beyond suggesting that it is consequence of their respective different roles in the rearing of children.[1]

For him, women's emancipation lies not only in terms of their participation in social production, but also in terms of the elimination of private property and class society. In other words, Marxists paid little attention to the significance of the gender-related division of labour at all levels and to its origin.

In contrast with the assumption that the division of labour by sex is natural or a given due to women's physiology and their role in reproduction, feminists argue that sexual inequalities result from a variety of factors susceptible to change. More specifically, it is suggested that the change must proceed in two directions:

(a) sharing of tasks related to family responsibilities between the sexes and

(b) the full participation of women in non-domestic production and appropriation of society's output under conditions of equality between the sexes.[2] The World Plan of Action of the world conference of the International Women's Year (1975) has incorporated this objective in clear terms:

"The achievement of equality between men and women implies that they should have equal rights, opportunities and responsibilities to enable them to develop their talents and capabilities for their own personal fulfilment and the benefit of society. To that end, revaluation and allocation of roles traditionally allotted to each sex within the family and the community at large is essential. The necessity of change in the traditional role of men as well as of women must be recognised. In order to allow for women's equal participation in all society's activities, men must accept shared responsibility for home and children."[3]

However, the question as to how the change must proceed is a more complex one to deal with than to state a principle. As a starting point in this direction, we intend to study the structures that have supported them from generation to generation. This task calls for detailed studies specific to the great range of concrete situations. It is to this effort that this paper is addressed.

Conceptualising Reproduction

Sex-related differentiation is one of the most pervasive forms of human exploitation rooted in the personal interaction between the sexes and in basic social institutions such as the family and supported by socio-economic and political structures. Its manifestations are manifold, extend into all levels of society, and have a variety of forms and different degrees of intensity.[4] The male domination develops around the need to control reproduction[5].

Reproduction refers to a dynamic process of change linked with the perpetuation of the social system. Edholm, Harris and Young have made a useful distinction between three aspects of reproduction which correspond to different levels of theoretical abstraction: social reproduction, reproduction of the labour force, and human or biological reproduction. Social reproduction refers to reproduction of the conditions sustaining social system. The fundamental question in this case becomes the specification of what structures have to be reproduced in order that social reproduction as a whole can take place. Other aspects of social reproduction can be isolated as a part of the same process. Biological reproduction or procreation refers essentially to child-bearing. The reproduction of labour force is not only the maintenance of workers and potential labour, but also, "the allocation of agents to position within the labour process". That is, while biological reproduction refers strictly to the physical development of human beings, the reproduction of the labour force refers to the process by which they become workers.

The differentiation between these three levels of reproduction facilitates the analysis of how women in general and the division of labour in particular are affected by reproduction. Fertility analysis in dealing strictly with reproduction rates ignores the whole question of social reproduction and its implications for women's role.

Human fertility is basically a biological process. Nevertheless, it is not determined solely by the biological factors. But unfortunately, in all explanations, whether they stem from an evolutionist, a positivist-functionalist, or even a Marxist approach, inequal relationships between the sexes is seen as biologically determined and, hence, beyond the scope of social change. Consequently, all the labour that goes into the reproduction of life is usually defined as a function of their biology or 'nature', it is not seen as the conscious interaction of a human being with nature, i.e., a truly human activity.[6] However, we are beholden to the feminist's approach that the socio-historical-cultural factors play a role of singularly special significance in the determination of reproduction.

Education of the couple, particularly of the woman, is one of the significant socio-cultural factors affecting the reproduction. Education opens new vistas of professions, makes people more aware of the modern methods of contraceptives, and conscientises with the far-reaching implications of large family. The present paper intends to examine empirically how far the reproductive role of women hinders their educational opportunities and, thus, arrests the proper development of their personality.

Past Studies

As per the 1981 census, country's population crossed 680 million mark. The literacy rate has improved from about 8 to 25 percent between 1951 and 1981. But the data on education indicates a widening gender gap. The number of female illiterates show a faster rate of increase from 162 million in 1951, to 185 million in 1961, to 215 million in 1971, to 242 million in 1981 (figures are inclusive of 0-4 age group). During this period the number of male illiterates also increased from 137 million to 198 million. What is disturbing is that this gender gap is on a gradual increase. Till 1931, for every 1000 illiterate men there were 1058 illiterate women which jumped to 1138 in 1951, to 1250 in 1961, to 1248 in 1971, to 1322 in 1981 (figures inclusive of 0-4 age group). As many as 72 percent of the Indian women are illiterate excluding 0-4 age group. Of the total population literate males constituted about 47 percent and literate females constituted barely 25 percent. If the education of women is any indicator of development, it can be argued that they occupy a much inferior position of males. Their reproductive role of the women can be regarded as one of the causes of their backwardness.

Objective

The main objective of the present enquiry is to find out the impact of reproduction of women on their education. The specific hypothesis we propose to test is that the women's reproductive role tends to arrest their educational growth and the illiterate women tend to bear a greater number of children due to socio-economic compulsions than the better-educated women.

Research Design and Data Base

The study follows an exploratory-cum-descriptive research design. The data were collected from the maternity centre of the State Ayurvedic College and Hospital, Atarra in Banda District (Uttar Pradesh). In all, 300 women receiving maternity services during March-August, 1983 were interviewed. The interviews were conducted on the second day after delivery in the maternity ward.

The hospital is located in a semi-urban area. Here the mostly women of nearby villages receive medical care and services. The patients interviewed belong to different socio-economic strata. Among them 72 percent were illiterate or barely literate 22 percent had primary education and barely six percent claimed secondary and higher education (see Table 1).

Table 1: Characteristics of Women by Education, Husband's Occupation and Age.

Social Characteristics	*Percent*
Education of women	
Illiterate	72
Primary	22
Secondary and higher education	06
N=300	100
Occupation of husbands	
Agriculture	69
Others	31
N=300	100
Age group	
15-24	66
25-34	27
35-44	07
N=300	100

The majority of the respondent's husbands (69 percent) were engaged in agriculture and the rest of them were either in the Government services or were self-employed. Coming to the age composition of the women, 66 percent of them were in the age-group of 15-24 years and another 27 percent in the age-group 25-34 years. Against this, the remaining seven percent were in the age-group 35-44 years. The average age of the women was 23.4 years.

Analysis and Discussion

Education and stable employment outside the home delay the age of entering into a marital union. Delay in the age of the first birth results in a smaller family size. This smaller family size actually springs from the women's self-interest as a consequence of new expanded opportunities.

People tend to control their fertility, but they may control it at a higher rather than lower level. Poor people believe that having large families are not the cause of their poverty: indeed, many children could be a solution to their poverty.[7] Children can be economically useful in many ways for poor families.[8] Women get status from having a larger family—perhaps their only source of status in a generally sexist culture.[9] If women cease to be an economic asset to the family and become liabilities instead and at the same time are not social assets through education and adaptive ability to their new social circumstances, the only way to maintain their value within the family would appear to be through bearing more children.[10]

Keeping the above in view, let us scan our own data. It is obvious from the data that prevalence of the low age of marriage disrupts the education of girls. Besides, it is also responsible for child-bearing at an early age followed by more and more reproduction of children. The data are presented below.

Women's Age at Marriage

Table 2 presents women's age at marriage where it is apparent that there is a practice of marriage at an early age among women.

Table 2: Distribution of Women by Age at Marriage

Age at marriage (in years)	*Percentage of women*
10-14	42
15-19	55
20-24	03
N=(300)	100

According to the Child Marriage Restraint Act of 1929, a male under 18 years of age or a female under 14 years of age was considered a child. The Sarda Act laid down the minimum legal age of marriage at 18 and 14 years for boys and girls, respectively. The Hindu Marriage Act of 1955 had accepted 15 years as the minimum age of marriage for girls which was revised to 18 years in 1978.

The present study indicated that 97 percent of the respondents were married at the age of 19 years or below, with as many as 42 percent being married in the 10-14 years age group. On the other hand, only three percent were married at the age of 19 and in fact this is the age which can sufficiently affect the birth rate. The average age of marriage was as low as 15.1 years.

Women's Age at First Child-Birth

Data presented as above make it obvious that most of the women were married much before the minimum age prescribed by legislation. This resulted in early child birth. Table 3 provides information about the women's age at first birth.

Table 3: Distribution of Women by Age at First Birth

Age of first birth (in years)	*Percentage of women*
15-17	55
17-19	42
19-21	02
21-23	01
N=(300)	100

Table 3 indicates that more than half (55 percent) of the women interviewed gave birth to their first child in the age group 15-17 years. Besides, 42 percent women's age at first birth was between 17 and 19 years. On the other hand, only three percent women reproduced their first child in between 19 and 23 years.

Thus, it may be noted that early marriage and early child birth are the two important factors which determine the fact of women particularly by disrupting their education and thus their career too.

Education of Women

Education is a direct and powerful index of a woman's status, her propensity to be in the labour market, her specific position in the occupational hierarchy and her attitude towards family size. But education of women, as indicated earlier, is disrupted by their low age at marriage as well as early child birth. This has been reflected in Table 4.

Table 4: Distribution of Women by Education

Education of women	*Percentage of women*
Illiterate	72
Primary education	22
Secondary and higher education	06
Number of cases (300)	100

It is obvious from Table 4 that the most women (72 percent) are illiterate who cannot read and write and are forced to use their thumb impression wherever required. Besides, 22 percent of the women got primary education and the percentage of women having secondary and higher education was only six. This indicates the poor level of education prevalent among the women which ultimately affects their overall fertility behaviour.

Level of Education and Fertility

Our analysis shows that there is a negative association between education of women and their fertility.

Table 5: Distribution of Women by Education and Number of Live Births

Education of women	*Percentage of women and the no. of children ever born*			*Average children*	*No.of cases*
	1-5	5-9	9-13		
Illiterate	72	23	05	4.3	214
Primary	84	15	01	3.7	68
Secondary and higher Education	100	—	—	3.0	18
N=	-	-	-	-	300

Significant at .05 level of confidence

(Chi-Square Test)

It is obvious from the table that where the women were totally illiterate, there was procreation of the largest number of offsprings, the average being 4.3. As we proceed from the uneducated group to low and higher educated groups, it was found that women beget lesser number of children. The women who had education upto the primary level gave birth to a lesser number of children with an average of 3.7. However, the average of 3.0 births had been the lowest in the case of women who got a higher level of education. This also revealed the fact that the higher level of education, the lower the number of live births and viçe-versa.

The Chi-square test was employed to study the association between literacy and fertility. The calculated value of X^2 at 0.05 was 10.3 at d.f. 4, which is higher than the table value 9.49, and indicates association between education and fertility performance.

Conclusion

It may be concluded that the prevalence of low age at marriage among rural women results in early child-birth and greater reproduction of children which becomes a constraint in their development. Employment after education provides social security for old age and, hence, less value is attributed to children. In a society where women are illiterate and people are poor and ignorant, they are likely to depend more on human hands for their survival and security. Furthermore, there is very little work opportunity outside the home for illiterate women so they have no alternative but to attend to household chores and upbringing of the children.

Reproduction plays a significant role in arresting the rapid rise in education of woman which, in turn, leads to population increase and underdevelopment of women. The following vicious circle may help in analysing and explaining the aforesaid problem.

Implications of Early Age at Marriage

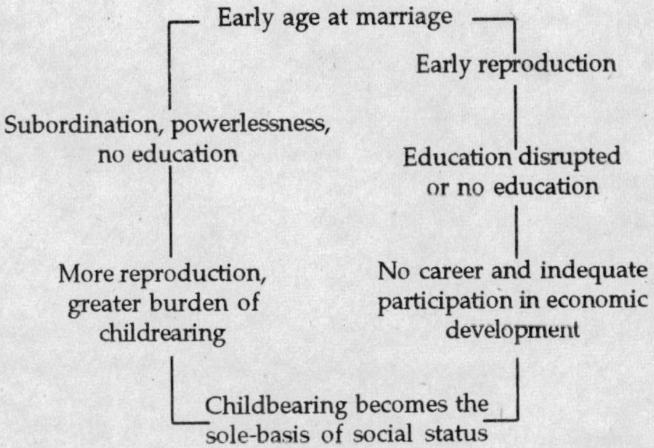

References

1. (a) F. Engels, *The Origins of the Family, Private Property and the State*, New York: International Publishers, 1975.

   (b) Karl Marx, *Capital*, Vol. 1, New York: International Publishers, 1967.
2. (a) R. Reiter (ed.), *Towards an Anthropology of Woman*, New York: Monthly Review Press, 1975.

   (b) M. Rosaldo and L. Lamphere, *Woman Culture and Society*, Standford: Standford University Press, 1974.
3. United Nations, *World Plan of Action of the International Women's Year's* Conference in Maxico City, New York: United Nations, 1975, 3-6.
4. E. Boserup, *Women's Role in Economic Development*, London; George Allen and Uniwin, 1970.
5. Lourdes Beneria, 'Reproduction, Production and the Sexual Division of Labour; *Cambridge Journal of Economics*, 1979, Vol. 3: 203-225.
6. Maria Mies, The Social Origins of the Sexual Division of Labour, *ISS Occasional Paper No. 85*, The Hague: Institute of Social Studies, January 1981.
7. Mahmood Mamdani, *The Myth of Population Control*: Family, Caste and *Class in an Indian Village*, New York: Monthly Review Press, 1972.

8. Rae Lesser Blumberg, 'Fairy Tales and Facts: Economy, Family, Fertility and the Female', in Women and World Development (ed.) lreve Tinker and Michele Bo Bramsen, Washington, D.C.: Overseas Development Council, 1976.
9. E.J. Michaelson and W. Goldschmidt, 'Female Roles and Male Dominance among Peasants', Southwestern Journal of Anthropology, 1971, Vol. 237: 330-352.
10. Vina Majumdar, 'Fertility Policy in India', in Perspectives on Population: An Introduction to Concepts and Issues (ed.) S.W. Menerd and E.W. Moen, New York: Oxford University Press, 1987.

9

Women's Movement in India and an Anti-Rape Campaign

*Vibhuti Patel**

Women's rights movement in India gained a national character with an anti-rape movement in 1980. Its genesis is linked with the excesses committed by the state repressive machinery during the Emergency in India from 1975 to 1977.

In the post-emergency period, civil liberties organisations also highlighted rape of women in police custody, mass rape of the poor untouchable and Muslim women during caste and communal riots, and sexual molestation of tribal women by Central Reserve Police Force (CRPF), State Reserve Police Force (SRPF) and other paramilitary forces. The print media gave enormous coverage to the testimonies of women victims of sexual violence. Many began to question the powers given to the police and state authorities in the control of people's lives. In 1980, when the Supreme Court of India gave its verdict on the Mathura Rape Case, there was a national outcry.[1]

Mathura, a teenaged tribal girl, was raped by two policemen in the police station at the dead of night, while her relatives were weeping and wailing outside the police station. The legal battle began when a woman lawyer took up her case immediately after the event in 1972. The Sessions Court blamed Mathura for being a woman of 'easy virtue', and the two policemen were released. In the High Court judgement, the accused were given seven and a half-year imprisonment which was reverted by the judgement of the highest legal

* The author is Visiting Fellow, at the London School of Economics and Political Science, London.

authority—the Supreme Court of India. It held that Mathura had given a wilful consent as she did not raise any alarm.[2]

The resulting nationwide anti-rape campaign in 1980 demanded the reopening of the Mathura Rape Case and effecting of amendments in the Rape Law.[3] Prominent lawyers took up the issue, as did the national and regional language Press. New groups of women were formed around this campaign. They organised public meetings and poster-campaigns, performed skits and street-plays, collected thousands of signatures in support of their demands, staged rallies and demonstrations, submitted petitions to MLAs and the Prime Minister, and generally alerted the public to the treatment meted out to rape victims. The initiative came from the middle-class, educated and urban women. Later on, political parties and mass organisations also joined the bandwagon.[4]

Debates on Reforms in the Rape Laws

The demand for amendments in the existing Rape Law touched a wide variety of issues concerning the social construction of sexuality that reflected in the assumptions in the law and in the civil society about women, past sexual history of the rape victim, procedures of the criminal justice system—First Investigation Report (FIR), inquest, medical examination and rights of women in custody in India.

Two booklets represented the debates and discussions amongst the feminists and the democratic rights activists on gang-rape, custodial rape, rape in the family, burden of proof, etc.[5] When the National Conference on 'Perspective for Women's Liberation Movement in India' was held in Bombay in November 1980, the proposed Rape Bill was the most controversial issue.

As a result of rigorous debate amongst the feminists, it was resolved that demands of the women's organisations should be as follows:

1. A woman should be interrogated only at her dwelling place.
2. During interrogation by police officer, a woman should be allowed to have a male relative or friend or women social workers present with her.
3. Women who are detained in custody should be kept in a separate lock-up meant for women only. If there is no such lock-up available then the women should be kept in a children's or women's home meant for the protection and welfare of women.
4. The medical report of a rape victim should state the reasons for arriving at the conclusions and should be forwarded without delay to

the magistrate to avoid possibility of tampering.

5. During the trial for rape, the past sexual history of the rape victim should be excluded from the evidence.

6. A police officer who refuses to record a complaint should be held guilty of an offence.

7. Section 375 of the Indian Penal Code which clarifies that the consent of the woman, in order to be considered as consent, must be absolutely free and voluntary, must be amended in view of the Mathura Case.

8. The provision about 'burden of proof' in Section 111a of the Indian Evidence Act must be changed, and it should be added that in cases where the accused in a rape trial is a public servant, police officer, superintendent or manager of a jail or hospital or remand home, where sexual intercourse is proved and the woman makes a statement on oath that she did not consent to the sexual intercourse, then the court shall presume that she did not consent.[6]

The last point raised a major controversy as many feminists felt that in all cases of rape the burden of proof should be on the accused and not on the victim, given the nature of the offence, the dominant position of men over women, and the impossibility of proving lack of consent in any other way except by stating that she did not consent. Women activists from the mass movement background felt that such a provision could be abused to victimise the male members of the trade-unions by the management and the male activists of the *dalit,* tribal and peasant organisations by local vested interests.

Criminal Law Amendment Act (1983)

After three years of heated debates in the women's groups, media and the Law Commission of India, the Parliament passed the Criminal Law Amendment Act (1983). This Act amended the Indian Penal Code, the Code of Criminal Procedure and the Indian Evidence Act with respect to the law relating to rape. As per this Act, revealing the identity of a rape-victim is an offence. Though this Act maintains more or less the same definition of rape, it introduces many new categories of offence of sexual intercourse by persons in custodial situations, such as superintendents of hospitals, remand homes, prison and police officials, with women in their custody.

In cases of custodial rape, the burden of proof lies with men and if a woman victim makes a statement that she did not consent, the court would believe that she did not consent. Feminists had demanded that marital rape should also be considered a punishable offence, but this demand was rejected, and thus, the Government supported the popular social belief that a married man has the right to have sexual intercourse with his wife, with or without consent. The rejection certainly meant that the Act did not fully meet the aspirations of the women's movement. In spite of this limitation, popular debate on the subject enhanced self-confidence and the sense of solidarity within the women's movement.[7]

Definition of Rape

The Act defines rape as being sexual intercourse with a woman under either of the following descriptions:

A. Against her will.

B. Without her consent.

C. When her consent is obtained by putting her or any person in whom she is interested in fear of death or of being hurt.

D. With her consent, when the man knows that he is not her husband and her consent is given because she is under an impression that he is her husband.

E. With her consent when she is incapable of giving consent because of unsoundness of mind or intoxication.

F. With or without her consent when she is under 16 years of age.

The Act makes it clear that "Penetration is sufficient to constitute the sexual intercourse necessary to the offence of rape."[8] The only change made by the amended Act, is in provision that sexual intercourse with consent, when it is obtained by putting any person in whom she is interested in fear of death or being hurt is rape.

Punishment for Rape

As per section 376 of the Act, the minimum punishment for rape is seven years and the maximum, life imprisonment. If the judge finds valid reasons he/she can impose a sentence of less than seven years. In the cases of 'custodial rape' or 'gang rape' the minimum sentence is of ten years and the offence is cognisable and non-bailable. Sexual intercourse by a man with his wife who is living separately from him under a decree of separation or under any custom or usage, without her consent is punishable with imprisonment which may extend to two years. This offence is cognizable and bailable. This definition of rape makes it clear that the husband has a right to have sexual intercourse with his wife with or without her consent. The underlying notion in this provision that does not see a man as guilty of raping his wife is that a woman is the private property of her husband and he can use/abuse her the way he wants.

Many women's rights organisations had demanded that forcible sexual intercourse by a man with his wife should also be defined as an offence of rape. But the Law Commission of India refused this demand. At the same time it introduced a new section, which makes forcible intercourse by a man with his judicially separated wife an offence. Commenting on this, a progressive legal activists' organisation, Lawyers' Collective, commented: "This new section is a small step forward in the direction of recognising the rights of the wife not to be raped by her husband."[9]

Rape Victim and the State Enforcement Machinery

According to the criminal justice system in India, rape is an offence against the state not a crime against an individual. The matter has to be reported by the rape-victim to the police and the First Investigation Report (FIR) prepared by the police, inquest and identification parade conducted by the police and medical examination report prepared by the recognised government hospital. These have a major bearing on the judgement. After the police files a chargesheet, the trial is conducted in a Sessions Court. During the trial the victim has no choice to select a lawyer to defend her case. The state appointed public prosecutor represents her. The rape-victim is merely the prosecution witness. Hence, during investigation and rape trial she is completely at the mercy of the state.

How does a Woman Experience the System of Law?

In a book by a retired Inspector General of Police, Mr. S.K. Ghosh, there is an admission to the fact of police involvement and connivance in the cases of rape as a generalised phenomenon.[10] In cases of custodial rape such as rape of prisoners by the jailer and other staff of the prison, or of a patient by her doctor, or of a woman employee by her employer or of women hostelites or inmates of remand homes by the members of the management the state apparatus in most of the cases chooses either to maintain a conspiracy of silence or to hush up the case.[11] In many parts of the country where remand homes for minor girls do not exist, minor victims of rape are kept either in police custody or in prison, sometimes for 8 to 12 years without any legal redress. In such cases the rapists lead free, 'respectable' life and the victims stay confined in institutions. In West Bengal, the Association for Protection of Democratic Rights has taken up the cases of such victims.[12]

When an individual woman accompanied by her relatives or neighbours approaches the police stations she is faced with either a hostile or indifferent attitude of the custodians of law and order. Lewd remarks, jokes, innuendoes, weird smiles and cynical laughter are used by police force to generate fear and uneasiness in the minds of the victim seeking legal redress. Comments on her dress, hair style, looks, figure, sex-appeal and overall physical attributes are considered to be a part of normal behaviour by the police. The National Conference of Rape in 1990 declared, "A woman victim of rape is raped twice—first by the culprit and then by the criminal justice system."[13]

Experiences of Women Activists

As a member of the Forum Against Oppression of Women (FAOW) since 1980 one has been experiencing the biases and misogyny of the criminal justice system that sees the rape-victim herself as an offender.

In response to a news item about the rape of a teenage construction worker by three policemen and a bootlegger in 1980, FAOW (at that time known as Forum Against Rape) decided to follow up the case. To get the FIR filed we had to organise a demonstration in front of the police station. The police, charged the women activists and the local social workers with 'riot, trespass and dacoity'.[14] This event took place before the amendments in the Rape Laws were made and the situation has not changed even after it.

In 1983, when a six year-old girl was raped by her neighbour, her uterus was ruptured and she had to be hospitalised. In spite of repeated pleas by the victim's mother, the police refused to register a case because there was no penis penetration. In this case, as the rapist could not succeed in penetration, he had inserted an iron rod and his fingers.[15] However, penis penetration remained the only and exclusive concern of the authorities while deciding the rape case.

Police Attitude

"Do you know the definition of Rape?"

Last year, as a member of an investigation team working on the gang-rape of a middle-aged woman worker living in one of the slums of Bombay, we had several meetings with the police officer-in-charge of the case. We had found out from the victim and the community that the police had not helped them in any way. The rape victim accompanied by her neighbour and social workers, approached the policemen to file an FIR. The police were not only indifferent but also very hostile. It was past midnight. The police station was busy making accounts of drugs they had confiscated during a raid. Initially, the police did not believe that a rape had taken place. When the victim kept repeating that she was raped and other witnesses also supported her statement, the police officers and constables had a hearty laugh. Then they cynically asked the victim, "Do you know the definition of rape?".

The victim was totally dazed. She showed her injuries on the forehead, head, neck, hand, chest, etc. Without doing any paper-work, they just told the victim and her friends to go to the government hospital without any note or accompanying constable. In the hospital she was just given first aid, a tablet of diazepam and some pain-killer. In the morning she approached a woman activist. Once again they went to the police station and after a great deal of verbal exchanges between middle class women activists and the police officer, finally the FIR was filed but in the meantime all important evidence was lost.

"If you pursue this case, no one will marry your daughter."

Every police officer has an obsession with the crime record in his area. He has to see to it that it does not exceed certain 'limits' or else his chances of promotion will be jeopardised. Hence, many a time he shows a reluctance to file cases of crimes against women. In 1982, we were involved in a case of a minor girl who was raped by a teenaged boy. The victim's mother was in deep anguish and a state of shock and wanted that the culprit be punished.

In their slum, comprising all communities, the victim's community had migrated from Haryana. They faced the great discrimination since they were sweepers, hence, untouchable. The police officer who conducted the inquiry was humane while dealing with the victim and her mother. But he kept on insisting that the case should not be filed as it would involve a long-drawn, tiring and humiliating legal battle. Moreover, he pointed out, the girl would get defamed, that no one would marry her, etc. The victim would be kept in the government remand home, as she was a minor, till the case ended. But the mother wanted us to take up the case as it would teach all other miscreants in the slum a lesson. We argued endlessly with the police to convince him of the necessity to file a case. Finally, he confided to us that if the crime record in his jurisdiction increased, it would reflect on his career.

"After all she is a petty thief".

A 16-year old poor girl was taken into custody, unlawfully confined and repeatedly gang-raped by the Bombay Suburban Railway Police. She became pregnant. The policemen quietly arranged an abortion for her in the government hospital. When this girl managed to reach her home after some weeks she was bleeding profusely. Her relatives appoached a feminist group. While conducting an inquiry we had verbal exchanges with the bosses of the rapist policemen. When we alleged the higher authorities of collusion with the rapists, they retorted, "why are you so worried about this girl? After all she is a petty thief, a pick-pocket. It is good that our men taught her a lesson."

"There cannot be smoke without a fire."

In urban as well as rural India a lumpanisation of socio-cultural life has taken place. In college and school campuses, on lonely roads, in buses and trains, in middle class neighbourhoods and in slums, incidents of eve-teasing have increased. Earlier, the law enforcement machinery did not take any cognisance of it. Women's groups in Delhi played a very important role in making this issue officially recognised. Eve-teasing and ragging during certain festivals (like Holi, the kite-flying festival of Gujarat or balloon throwing during the month of *Shravan*) have provoked many individual women as well as women's groups to protest against the law enforcement machinery.

Eve-teasing of women by bus conductors and bus drivers, railway police, traffic police etc., are still not paid attention to, in spite of legal provisions against them. Most often women or girls do not report incidents of harassment such as obscene phone calls or lewd remarks by miscreants for fear of getting into trouble. When the protectors of 'law and order' have a reputation of themselves being eve-teasers in the public eye, how can a woman approach them without 'fear or favour'? Class, caste and communal bias along with the gender bias of the police and other bodies of the state are responsible for the apathy, inertia, indifference and hostility faced by women when they seek support against eve-teasing.

Molestation of Madhushree Dutta

Two years ago, a noted film and stage director, Madhushree Dutta, was badly molested by two railway policemen who were in plain clothes at the railway station at midnight. At the time of molestation she was not alone. Ms. Flavia, a feminist lawyer, was with her. Both of them being involved in the women's rights movement for over a decade and fully aware of the legal provisions, immediately prepared a notice against the molesters. When they went to submit their application at the appropriate police station, the officer-in-charge refused to co-operate.

Madhushree was well-known in media circles and so, the news of the incident appeared the very next day on the front page of the leading newspapers of the country. In support of the news reports, a strong protest demonstration was organised by women's groups to demand suspension of the police officer as well as the molesters. To make her withdraw the case, the policemen kept on making anonymous and threatening phone calls to her lawyer's office.

The court trial was an extremely humiliating experience for Madhushree, as the defence counsel hired by the policemen kept on shooting question after question implying that for a budding artiste like Madhushree it was a cheap publicity gimmick to get her into the limelight. If a woman, so articulate, visible and well-connected with the media world, aided by an equally strong and articulate feminist lawyer, was forced to face such terror-tactics by the police, one can imagine what must be happening to ordinary and helpless victims of sexual violence. This incident happened in Bombay where anti-rape campaigns have been consistently taken up since 1978. In spite of the wide media coverage on the issue of sexual violence, the attitude of both the state as well as the civil society, as reflected in the readers' reaction in the newspapers, was amazingly, unsympathetic to the victim. The one question that many asked was, why was Madhushree there at such a late hour?

An analysis of the judgements of the Sessions Courts, the High Courts and the Supreme Courts since 1980 done by Madhushree's advocate, Flavia, reveals the extremely negative view taken by the judiciary of women's sexuality. She gives several examples of rape-cases were stereotypical arguments and victim-baiting were used liberally to have the punishment of the culprits reduced. Supposedly pro-women judgements, in cases of rape of minors were also found to be coloured by a conservative concern for 'chastity' and 'purity'. Flavia states, "The positive judgments which are reported involve rape of minor girls resulting in multiple injury where the question of consent does not arise. But even these judgments have a conservative reasoning for the conviction. Here is an example of how the judiciary looks at the issue. Virginity is the most prized possession of an unmarried girl. She would never willingly part with this proud and precious possession."[16]

Mass Rape During Caste and Communal Riots

Human rights organisations and women's groups have provided detailed testimonies of mass rape of *Dalit* women during caste riots in Marathawada (1978), Ahmedabad (1983), Bhojpur (1985), Nagpur (1988) and communal riots in Delhi and Bombay (1984), and Bhopal and Surat (1993) to the government.

In most of the above-mentioned cases the state enforcement machinery was either indifferent to the plight of the victim or directly involved in perpetrating violence against them in collaboration with anti-social elements. But, in none of the above mentioned cases has the criminal justice system brought the culprits to book.

Efforts to Activise State the Apparatus

During the eighties the women's movement in India was concerned mainly with fighting against the sexist behaviour of the state enforcement machinery, but now its efforts have been directed at creating of a pro-women environment so that the victims of sexual violence can get legal redress and societal attitude towards women's sexuality can change. Articulate women journalists, researchers, academicians, independent consultants and activists attend government-sponsored training programmes and act as resource-persons for 'gender-sensitisation' of police officers, administrators, judges, etc. Initially, women activists were reluctant to have a dialogue with them, as, while dealing with day-to-day practical issues, bureaucrats, forest officals and police officials were not found helpful to women's cause.

In the beginning of the anti-rape movement, many women's groups had put forward the demand to the state that it should increase its number of women judges to ensure gender-justice and more police-women to ensure sympathetic treatment to women victims. But the last one decade has given ample evidence that just by virtue of being women, they are not going to be more sensitive or judicious about women's issues. Women judges and women police being representatives of the state do not behave differently from the male judges when it comes to taking sides. After all Maya Tyagi was inhumanly tortured by a woman police constable who also encouraged her male colleagues to parade her unclothed in a public place. Women officials in jails and remand-homes behave as inhumanly with women in their custody as their male counterparts.

The government had set up several judicial inquiries to contain the public fury after an individual case of rape or cases of mass rape were reported. Reports of the inquiry commissions gather dust in government offices, and are not circulated or discussed widely. None of their recommendations are implemented. To the goverment, this exercise is a safety valve tactics to contain public fury.

Public Interest Litigation (PIL) by Women's Groups

Women's groups have filed PILs to activise the state enforcement machinery and to sensitise the masses. Manushi, a women's magazine filed a PIL in the Supreme Court of India after the Delhi riots in 1984 in which Sikh women were raped and who are still languishing in the refugee camps. So far, none of the culprits have been charged.

When a tribal woman, Guntaben, was raped by eight policemen, brutally beaten and verbally abused and paraded unclothed, the concerned police station, district magistrate and the hospital staff got together to hush up the matter. Atmosphere of terror prevailed in the community. In this situation two women's groups and democratic rights organisations filed a public interest litigation and launched a campaign for justice. The government responded by setting up a tribunal which declared that the rapists must be punished. Amnesty International also took up this case. Finally, the culprits were punished.

Role of Media in Activating State Apparatus

Media publicity has proved to be the most effective tool in activating the state apparatus. In the post-emergency period, investigative journalism got pride of place in the mainstream media. On the one hand, a plethora of sensational articles trivialised the issue, but on the other hand, several sensitive portrayals of related issues were also given space in the media. Many protest agitations by women's groups and mass organisations against rape of poor, *dalit,* tribal or minority women would have been ruthlessly crushed without media coverage. Thus, media publicity can be double-edged. Gender sensitisation programmes for journalists and other mass communication personnels are viewed as a necessity by the women's groups.

Conclusion

The existing rape laws do not recognise the unequal power-relations between the rape victim and the rapist. The victim is not given a choice in most cases to get her voice heard by her own lawyer. She faces sexist biases and hostility at every step inside her own family, within the community, at the police station, at the time of medical examination in a government hospital and in the court-rooms. The criminal justice system expects the victim not only to get over the trauma and be calm and composed at the time of prosecution but also shed all her inhibitions and give a vivid description of the event in the court-room. After the act of rape, if the victim washes herself (but, naturally), an important evidence will be lost. In this situation, the woman's movement and the concerned authorities need to direct their energies to amend the procedures so that the case can be handled speedily and the victim does not face humiliation at the hands of the administration that is known for its inertia, indifference and antipathy towards women.

The attitude of the judges in cases of rape is another deplorable area. Some feminist lawyers have put forward a demand of special courts for rape trials to ensure speedy dispensing of justice. A majority of judgements in rape cases are coloured by the preoccupation of the judges with the 'past sexual history' of the victim and their notions of 'virginity', 'purity' and 'chastity' of women. Gender-sensitisation programmes for judges must be given top priority by the state.

About re-definition of rape there is a consensus among the women's rights groups that 'rape', 'attempt to rape' and 'violating a woman's modesty' as they are defined at present must be clubbed together under the heading of 'sexual offence'. It is also suggested that the re-definition of rape must be brought out of the patriarchal confines where 'penetration of the penis' only is taken into consideration while defining rape.[17]

The most controversial issues for which there is no consensus amongst the women's groups are marital rape, punishment for rape and demand of monetary compensation to the victim. Women's groups providing support to women in distress have found that sexual assault by the husband is the most common and blatant form of rape. But those who refuse to recognise the existence of rape within marriage put forth the argument that when a woman enters into matrimony she knows that it is her duty to fulfil the desire of her husband. Many experienced lawyers have expressed their concern over the fact that stringent punishment codified in the law has resulted in fewer convictions. While the women's groups have always demanded higher punishment in rape-cases. Some women's groups have asked for a compulsory monetary compensation either from the state or the culprit taking into consideration the fact that rape victims face tremendous social stigma, employers shun them and in most of the cases even their own family disown them. After a decade and a half year of struggle against rape, most of the women activists feel that they have reached a square one position so far as changing the situation of rape victims or prevention of rape is concerned.

An international campaign initiated by the Centre for

Global Issues and Women's Leadership to include' 'violence against women as violation of human rights' in the UN Charter on Human Rights has become a rallying point for women's rights organisations in India. This campaign focuses on the issue of 'rape as a war-crime'.

References

1. Vibhuti Patel, "Women's Liberation in India", *New Left Review*, No. 153, 1985.
2. Tukaram and Ganpat versus State of Maharashtra, 1979, *Supreme Court of India*, Delhi.
3. Neera Desai and Vibhuti Patel, *Indian Women—Change and Challenge in the International Decade*, 1975-85, Sangam Publications, 1990.
4. See Vibhuti, Sujata, Padma (Forum Against Rape), The Anti- Rape Movement and Issues Facing Autonomous Women's Organisations in India" in Miranda Davies (ed)., *Third World-Second Sex*, Zed Press, 4th Impression, 1987.
5. See, Lawyers' Collective, *"Rape and the Law"*, Bombay, 1980 and Sudesh Vaid, Amia Rao and Monica Juneja, *"Rape, Society and State"*, People's Union for Democratic Rights, New Delhi, 1980.
6. Vibhuti Patel, "Needs and Rights: Experiences of Women's Movement in India", *United Nations University*, 1984.
7. Susie Tharu, "Slow Pan Left: Feminism and the Problematic of Rights", Paper presented at National Seminar on *"Indian Women—Myth and Reality"* on March 9, 10, 11, 1989 at School of Women's Studies, Jadavpur University, Calcutta. Also see, Neera Desai and Vibhuti Patel, 1990.
8. Flavia, *Journey* to *Justice Procedures to be Followed in a Rape Case*, Majlis, Bombay, 1990.
9. A Lawyers' Collective Publication, *Recent Changes in Laws Relating to Women*, Bombay, 1985.
10. S.K. Ghosh, *Women in Policing*, Light and Life Publication, Delhi, 1981.
11. Maithreyi Krishnaraj (ed.), *Women and Violence—A Country Report*, A Study sponsored by UNESCO, Research Centre for Women's Studies, SNDT Women's University, Bombay, 1991.
12. *Ibid.*, See the section on Women's Action Groups and the State Machinery.
13. Report of National Conference on Rape, Forum Against Oppression of Women, Kali for Women, Delhi, 1990.
14. See an evaluation report of one decade (1980-1990) of Forum Against Oppression of Women, *Moving...But Not Quite There*, Bombay, 1990.
15. *Ibid.*, p. 7.
16. Flavia, "A Critical Review of Enactments on Violence Against Women During the Decade 1980-1989", *Economic and Political Weekly*, April 25, 1992, ws 19-33.
17. Report, *op. cit.*, 1990.

10

Women, Technology and Development: Some Observations

*Raj Mohini Sethi**

Issues relating to the woman and technology gained importance when the issues affecting women's lives became prominent in the developed world. Technological developments throughout the world were seen to have affected women's expectations, opportunities and behaviour. The experience of the developing societies shows not only the economic marginalisation of women (especially rural women) as a result of development but also a shrinkage of their resource-base and opportunities of women's well-being as persons. These developmental experiences call into question the rationale behind development, that is, development for whom? A related issue is whether we should go on treating women as end products in our development experience or should we treat them as agents of change. Lastly, what kind of development is needed to integrate women with the overall development process? The present paper tries to highlight some of these issues by first developing a historical connection between technology and the status of women and there after elaborating upon the imbalances arising out of a misplaced emphasis on certain aspects of technology, and, then, pinpointing the factors responsible for these imbalances.

---

* The author is Professor of Sociology, Punjab University, Chandigarh-160014

Woman and Technology

Ideas concerning the relationship between property, production and women's status, historically speaking, have been related to different types of social structures. The first materialistic conception of the role of women was developed by Engels.[1] In his book *Origins of the Family, Private Property and the State*, Engels has stated that the determining factor in history has been the production and reproduction of immediate life. Production involves a double process. One process of production relates to the generation of means of subsistence such as food, clothing and shelter, and also the requisite tools and technology for the purpose; while the other involves the reproduction of human beings through which the propagation of the human species takes place. He has further observed that the social institutions of all human societies are conditioned by both types of production, that is, the stage of technological development (or of labour) and the stage of the family. A lower level of technological development allows for limited wealth. In all such social systems gender relations assume greater importance. However, when productivity of labour increases in these systems, it lays the foundation for the emergence of the institution of private property and its exchange by creating differences in wealth because of the increased productivity of labour. This leads to the basis for a new type of social order based on social classes which are territorially organised.[2]

While questioning the dichotomy between production and reproduction enunciated by Engels, feminist anthropologists contend that there exists a direct relation between mothering and cultural subordination[3]. However, with regard to the relationship between the nature or level of production, property and women's status in agricultural societies, there exists some broad agreement among most social anthropologists.[4] Describing the hunting and gathering societies these experts have pointed out that the small bands of hunters had simple but ingeneous technologies consisting of bows, arrows, spears, needles, skin-clothing and leaf or wood shelters. They also engaged themselves in fishing. Social life was more or less egalitarian and the division of labour was based on sex and age. Property was communally owned and personal possessions were freely exchanged. The unit of economic cooperation was the household and division of labour was among men, women and children in the household. While the men were engaged in hunting and fishing, the women engaged themselves in gathering of wild plants, fruits and nuts. The women also did most of the cooking, processing and storage of food. Household crafts such as basket-making, leather work, and designing clothes were mostly done by women. It has also been pointed out that women played an important role in the cultural development of these societies, through their overall position was more or less subordinate to that of men.[5] In this regard, social anthropologists make a distinction between two types of roles—one that of food procurers and the other that of food processors. In those societies where women play a vital role in food procurement they enjoy a relatively high social status than those where women merely process food. However, all of these tribes and bands were devoid of institutions emphasising male possessiveness and exclusiveness. On the contrary, they exhibit reciprocity as against domination or exploitation.[6]

In the context of agricultural societies a distinction is drawn on the basis of shifting (hoe culture) or plough cultivation.[7] Shifting cultivation is confined to sparsely populated regions and utilizes mostly the labour of women. In all such societies, the hoeing is done by women while hunting, fishing and cattle grazing are undertaken by men. Since women in these societies play a vital role in "food procurement" they derive only limited support from their husbands but enjoy considerable freedom and economic independence. The institutions of polygamy and bride-price are commonly encountered in these communities. Plough cultivation, on the other hand, is associated with densely populated regions and is carried on largely by the labour of men. Most of these societies are by the large monogamous and the practice of dowry is quite common among them. In all such societies, the wife is entirely dependent on the husband for economic support. The regional spread of these two technologies is said to be wide spread. Hoe culture is widely practised in Africa (the South of the Sahara) and South-East Asia, while plough culture is found to be dominant in the regions of the Arab, Chinese and Hindu cultures.[8]

The traditional Indian society seems to have escaped the notion of being called a savage society. The various archaeological finds indicate that it developed a neolithic culture. Among the semi-nomadic pastoral *Aryan* tribes, the concept of private property emerged with permanent settlement and the change to agriculture. Plough agriculture necessitated a greater division of labour through the multiplication of occupations such as trade and handicrafts. Among the *Aryan* tribes practising plough agriculture, the institution of patriarchy was prevalent and the eldest male was considered the head of the family. Women among the *Aryans* enjoyed relatively greater freedom and early marriages were quite uncommon. Women also exercised a fair amount of choice in the selection of mates, and both dowry and bride-price were practised. Monogamy was the accepted pattern of life though polygamy was also practised.[9] With the increased dependence on plough agriculture in subsequent epochs the status of women, however, shows a considerable decline. The increased sedentariness of agriculture also created greater demands on women's work because of two reasons: one, an increase in population and second, because of increased housework in terms of food processing. The subsequent categorisation of persons in terms of '*varna*' or '*jati*' created class differentials among them based on economic inter-dependence. The existence of such internal social relationships helped Indian society to remain completely indifferent to the exogenous political systems to which it was subjugated for a long period of time. This stability of the system has been extensively demonstrated historically.

The self-sufficiency of the peasant economy later made way for the accumulation of capital when trade with adjoining areas (countries) developed. The new mercantile economy did not, however, bring about a fundamental change in the form of subsistence production. Subsistence producers now consisted of tenants, sharecroppers, artisans and small traders. These subsistence producers were barely able to meet their survival needs and were unable to meet most of their reproduction costs.[10]

Whereas the broad framework of social relationships remained the same in India for a long period of time, the status of women underwent a perceptible change from around 600 B.C. onwards. Over the centuries various cultural and political influences led to the prevalence of child marriages and women could avail of only limited education or occupational skills. Married women were supposed to perform *sati* on being widowed. A widow was regarded as inauspicious and widow remarriage was unthinkable. The seclusion of women gained popularity during the period of exogenous political rule.[11] The strengthening of the institution of patriarchy by tradition and cultural practices resulted in giving preferential treatment to sons and the existence of differential set of norms for sons and daughters. A heightened emphasis on segregation and seclusion of women took away their limited right of choice in the selection of a mate and the quantum of dowry became a prerequisite to a stable marriage. Most of these cultural norms are being practised even today in various forms and in large parts of the country.

Industrialisation signified a break with traditional technology. It not only introduced new technology for the production of industrial goods but also helped in the improvement of agricultural technology. One of the most enduring consequences of industrialisation is the separation between the home and work. In the process the economic function of the family gets carried over to the factory which uses largely the labour of men. The detachment of the household from the place of work creates a clear-cut division between housework and productive work, and the expressive role of woman as a home-maker and nurturer gets highlighted because her economic dependence increases. This process of "housewifisation" connotes a further decline in the position of women. Improved agricultural technology also heightens the productivity gap between men and women. In mechanised farming, men monopolise the use of new technology even though it requires less muscular power. Increased use of mechanised farming relegates the role of women to simple manned operations. An immediate consequence of technological modernisation is the straight displacement of women's labour through the elimination of various traditional activities. Under these circumstances, men cultivate cash crops through the use of new technology while women are left with the cultivation of subsistence food crops with the help of traditional cultivation methods. An obvious consequence of this is that the labour productivity of men increases manifold while that of women remains stable or declines. This loss of women's productivity further contributes towards a decline in women's position. Women's production both inside and outside the home gets derecognised and is termed as "non-work" and is associated with their natural biological makeup and termed as reproduction. This process renders the productive role of women to a state of "invisibility" and insensibility". Thus, the natural corollary of the market-oriented production is the definition of women's work as non-work.[12]

Those women who enter the productive labour market get unevenly distributed along the occupational hierarchy which is viewed as an outcome of gender-free market processes because of the pre-market differences between male and female labour. The concentration of women in the lower rungs of the occupational hierarchy is seen as an effect of their natural endowments and preferences. Gender segregation is thus considered as an incidental aspect of the market mechanism and division of labour. The fact that pure economic forces get modified by ideological and political pressures is consistently ignored in the explanation of such gender segregation.[13]

Non-access to Appropriate Technology for Women

Another important aspect of modern industrial technology is the reduction of the drudgery of housework. An extensive use of household technology in the developed world has benefited the women in the management of the household. It allows for the availability of greater leisure time to women which could be utilised for the formation of skills necessary for the new productive roles required by the labour market. The United Nations Conference on the Decade for Women (1980) was the first to highlight the necessity of reducing the daily burden of women. It advocated the development of intermediate technology which required a low level of skill formation and yet could be utilised for the reduction of a women's daily burden of housework. The National Perspective Plan for Women (1988-2000 A.D.)[14] specifically mentioned that one of the reasons for the large-scale displacement of women from the labour force was their incessant child-bearing coupled with their hard domestic work. The two together are a hindrance in acquiring their formal education and training and the acquisition of new skills. This also explains why women's employment is confined to the unorganized sector. While chalking out the strategies for the development of women, the Sixth Five-Year Plan (1980-85) document on Women and Development[15] ignores the dimension of domestic work and emphasises only the threefold strategy of education, employment and health. It adopts the family as a unit of development only for the purpose of reducing the burden of child-bearing through health education and by limiting the size of the family. The economic emancipation of the family was to be achieved by securing a fair share of salaried, self and wage-employment opportunities for women. However, no strategy was adopted to reduce the burden of household chores for women. This situation was later remedied in the Seventh Five-Year Plan (1985-90)[16]. The chapter on Socio-Economic Programmes for Women specifically observes that "inputs of science and technology are required in housing, cooking and the performance of other household work which can lead to a considerable reduction in drudgery. Time and energy thus saved could be used by women for the improvement of their knowledge, skill and aptitude levels". In the light of these observations, the Seventh Plan document lays stress on evolving scientific and technological devices to reduce the drudgery of women so that the time saved thus is utilised for development activities.

Research material on the adoption of household technology and its impact on various social strata is scarce, rather non-existent. Whereas some research material is available on the adoption of household technology by rural women, there is a paucity of systematic studies in its adoption and impact in the urban areas where women of the middle and upper income groups seems to have adopted work-saving household devices in a big way. In the rural areas, research studies[17] point out that modern household technology is available to a very small proportion of the elite women. Knowledge and awareness of household technology among rural women is very poor. The burden of housework and productive work on elite women is much less as compared to the lower socio-economic strata of the village society because of the availability of hired household help and their non-participation in productive work. Intermediate technology designed in a way that simplifies and reduces labour time spent in household activities has not been introduced in the rural areas in a big way. The provision of basic technology such as accessible water points, electricity, bio-gas, smokeless *chulhas*, (stoves) and solar cookers to the rural women can, on the one hand, considerably reduce their burden of house work and, on the other, help them acquire knowledge and skills through a non-formal approach. The introduction of such technology would also create new opportunities for employment and further independence of women.[18] Some governmental and non-governmental agencies have been working in this direction but experience tells us that like all other governmental projects they fail to make an impact because of their half-hearted, piecemeal approach which contributes more towards the apathy, hostility, non-resilience or unsympathetic attitude of the recipients as opposed to becoming a part of their life. In this context the role of voluntary agencies and *Mahila Mandals* assumes a new importance.

Development of a Scientific Temper

Apart from the fact that our earlier plan priorities failed to look into the dimension of intermediate technology affecting the status of women, such as household technology (until the Seventh Five-Year Plan), we have also failed in the development of a scientific temper. The fact that science can be a dynamic force for social change has been well recognised by Indian society at large, but the fact that diverse social structures have diverse consequences for science has been overlooked. The development of a scientific temper in a democratic social order would mean the inclusion of universalistic criteria of scientific validation and scientific worth or utility. In such a social system, it is the people's capacities and achivements that matter rather than their ascribed status or origin. An important aspect of a scientific ethos is that knowledge must be made available to all the people, men as well as women, and the society must identify the areas where scientific innovations can change the life of different people by making the best possible use of it. Thus, there exists a close connection between science and society. A truly scientific temper or ethos can only develop and sustain itself if the socio-political institutions uphold the value of science.

Gender Imbalances

The reasons for the non-acquisition of modern occupational skills and knowledge by women are not far to seek. The last four decades of our planning process has relegated the needs of women to a secondary position. In the very framework of our developmental plans lies a strong ideological bias in favour of men. The situation gets compounded by the operation of our socio-political institutions at the kinship and territorial levels. Social research[19] on the subject indicates that women were consistently deprived of the teaching of modern farming techniques and the acquisition of industrial skills because of which the labour productivity gap between women and men increases. This widening gulf between the roles of men and women puts men at more progressive end of the continuum, while women remain at the traditional end. A few demographic figures produced below highlight the nature of this gap.

One of the first instances of gender imbalance is the sex ratio. The 1981 census[20] figures show that the overall sex ratio stands at 933 females to 1000 males and the rural-urban disparities are wider; 951 in rural as against 878 in urban areas. In the 1991 census, the overall sex ratio has further declined to 929 females as against 1000 males, but the rural-urban disparities seem to be narrowing down to 941 in rural as against 893 in urban areas.[21] A notable feature of our developmental process is that the overall sex ratio has declined from 941 in 1961 to 929 1991. The rural and urban data show that whereas the urban sex ratio has improved during this period the rural has considerably declined. The literacy rate for women is 24.9 as compared to 46.3 for men according to the 1981 census and the figures for the 1991 census are 32.4 for women as against 52.6 for men and the gap has widened between 1901 and 1981. The process of narrowing this gender gap seems to have begun with the 1991 census. The gap further widens while going up the ladder of education from the level of primary to secondary and higher education. The gender disparities are still more pronounced in technical and scientific education and in the case of the scheduled castes and the scheduled tribes. The rate of employment for women in rural areas is 16 percent as compared to 52.6 per cent for men in 1981, and the rates of urban employment stands at 48.5 for men and 7.3 for women. The 1991 census figures for employment show an increase in the work participation rates of women. Whereas the total rate of employment for men in the rural areas remained almost the same, the total rate of employment for women rose to 27.1 per cent as against 16.0 percent in 1981. The rates of urban employment also show a marginal increase in the employment of women, that is, the figures have increased to 9.7 in 1991 from 7.3 in 1981. Women's share of employment is confined largely to agriculture and allied activities where their role is that of paid or unpaid unskilled agricultural labour. The Integrated Rural Development Programme (1978-79) recognised the need for the creation of women's employment as a crucial breakthrough in bringing women in the mainstream of society.[22]

However, there is also a positive side to the impact of science and technology. The development of a rational ethos among the elite gave rise to a woman's movement in the nineteenth century which not only showed a sensitivity to women's problems such as child marriages, enforced widowhood and the right to property under the patriarchial Hindu joint family but was ultimately able to guarantee at least constitutional equality, justice and a right to adult franchise to the women. Various legislative measures which have tended to translate these Constitutional commitments have helped in the improvement of the legal status of women. On the quantitative side, the average age at marriage for girls has risen to 18.3 years in 1981 [23] as against 16.6 years in 1961, and the life expectancy has improved from 44.7 years in 1961 to 52.9 years in 1981 and 55.9 between 1981-88 [24]. The sex ratio also marginally increased from 930 in 1971 to 933 in 1981.

An explanation of gender imbalances, therefore, has to be sought within the socio-political framework. The continuing subordination of women in our society is a manifestation of gender ideology. Whereas science and technology have been increasingly used for raising the productivity of men, the productivity of women was relegated to the backseat and has gone down because of the interplay of various socio-cultural practices such as differential socialisation, segregation and seclusion of women and also because of a tight societal control over traditional male bastions such as the institution of patriarchy.

Conclusion

The above analysis helps us conclude that the development of a scientific temper such as the inculcation of modern occupational skills will help women become independent and self-reliant and also pave the way for the removal of poverty and ignorance in the country. However, in the propagation of the scientific temper, a balance has to be struck between the positive and the negative effects of science and technology. An unchecked use of science and technology could bring forth far more destruction than development as is evident from the indiscriminate adoption and propagation of the technologies of the developed world by the underdeveloped world. The use of technology has to be in tune with the socio-cultural milieu and its introduction has to be evaluated on the criteria of availability, practicality and profitability. Various forms of agricultural and reproductive technologies that are being transplanted in place of the indigenous technologies of the developing countries have not only reduced the diversity of their eco-systems but have also contributed to the marginalisation of their women. The marginalisation of women relates to the loss of control over their work, time and health and also their inability to handle new technology. The goal of science and technology, therefore, should not be the exploitation of human kind but the attainment of sustainable development. A controlled or regulated use of science and technology must become an integral part of all developmental approaches and all such checks and balances have to be harmonised at the global level.

In the end, it may be stated that a complete understanding of the processes of production would entail a proper understanding of the way in which they affect the lives of men and women and the extent to which are controlled by each sex. Thus, it calls for a complete restructuring of our planning process and a redefinition of our developmental goals and means which show not only a sensitivity to issues concerning women and the poorer sections of the society but also how it involves them in our programmes for development.

References

1. Frederick Engels, *The Origin of the Family, Private Property and the State*, Moscow: Foreign Languages Publishing House, 1891 or Eleanor Leacock (Ed.), New York: International Publishers, 1972.
2. Kathleen Gough, *"The Origin of the Family"* in Rayna R. Reiter (Ed.), *Toward an Anthropology of Women*, New York: Monthly Review Press, 1975.
3. Rayna R. Reiter, *Toward an Anthropology of Women*, New York: Monthly Review Press, 1975.
4. Kathleen Gough, *op.cit.*, pp. 62-64, Also see (i) Ester Boserup, *Women's Role in Economic Development*, London: George Allen and Unwin Ltd. 1970; (ii) Jack Goody, *Production and Reproduction: Comparative Study of Domestic Domain*, London: Cambridge University Press, 1976.
5. Ester Boserup, *op. cit.*, pp. 15-51.
6. Kathleen Gough, *op. cit.*, pp. 63.
7. Easter Boserup, *op. cit.*, pp. 15-27.
8. Easter Boserup, *op. cit.*, pp. 20-25; and Jack Goody, op. cit., pp. 31-33.
9. Romila Thapar, *Ancient Indian Social History*, Delhi: Orient Longman, 1978.
10. Sir Malcolm Darling, *Punjab Peasants in Prosperity and Debt*, Oxford University Press, 1947. Also see Maria Mies, *Indian Women in Subsistence and Agricultural Labour*, New Delhi: Vistaar Publications, 1987.
11. Saroj Gulati, *Women and Society: Northern India in 11th and 12th Centuries*, Delhi: Chanakya Publications, 1985. Also see:A.S. Altekr, *The Position of Women in Hindu Civilisation: From Pre-historic Times to Present Day*, Delhi: Moti Lal Banarsidass, 1959.

12. Easter Boserup, *op. cit.*, pp. 15-17 and 212-214. Also see.

    (i) Maria Mies, *op. cit.*, pp. 5-7.

    (ii) Raj Mohini Sethi, *Female Labour in Agriculture*, Chandigarh: Department of Sociology, Punjab University, 1982; and, "Women and Development: a Profile of Active Agricultural Producers", Sociological Bulletin,1989 Vol. 38: 2; 217-233.

13. John Finley Scott, "The Role of Collegiate Sororities in Maintaining Class and Ethnic Endogamy", *American Sociological Review* 1965, 30; No. 4, 415-26.
14. *National Perspective Plan for Women 1988-2000 A.D.*, Government of India, Ministry of Human Resources Development, 1988.
15. *Sixth Five-Year Plan 1980-85*: "Women and Development" Chapter 27, New Delhi: Planning Commission, Government of India.
16. *Seventh Five-Year Plan 1985-90*: "Socio-Economic Programmes for Women" Chapter 17, New Delhi: Planning Commission, Government of India.
17. Malkiat Kaur, *Rural Women and Technological Advancement*, Delhi: Discovery Publishing House, 1988; and Anita Kumari, *Adoption and Development of House hold Technology and its Impact on the Status of Women.* Chandigarh: Punjab University, (Unpublished M.A. Dissertation) 1983.
18. Raj Mohini Sethi, "Role of Non-formal: Education in the Empowerment of Women", *Guru Nanak Journal of Sociology*,1989, Vol. 10: 1-2 147-154.
19. *Women in Developing Agriculture*, No.4, Rome, Food and Agriculture Organisation of the United Nations, 1985. Also see:

    i) Geeta Somjee, *Narrowing the Gender Gap*, Macmillan, 1989.

    ii) Ester Boserup, *op. cit.*, pp. 212-213.

    iii) Raj Mohini Sethi, *Women in Agriculture*, Jaipur: Rawat, 1991.

20. Census of India, 1981, Series-I, Paper 2 of 1981, *Rural-Urban Distribution*, New Delhi: Registrar General.
21. Census of India, 1991, Series-1 Paper 2, pp. 99-153, *Rural-Urban Distribution*, New Delhi:Registrar General, and Census of India, 1991 and, *Provisional Population Total Workers and their Distribution*, Paper 3 of 1991, New Delhi: Registrar General p. 323. Also see: *Year Book 1988-89*, Ministry of Health and Family Welfare, New Delhi: Government of India, 1990.
22. Integrated Rural Development Programme (1978-79) was a strategy adopted by the Planning Commission which became an integral part of the Sixth and subsequent Five-Year Plans. It dealt with individual rural families below the poverty line and started schemes for the Training of Rural Unemployed Youth for Employment (TRYSEM) and opened a separate department for the Development of Women and Children in Rural Areas (DWCRA).
23. Year Book 1988-89, *op. cit.*, p.1. Also see:
24. (i) *National Perspective Plan for Women 1988-2000 A.D.*, *op.cit.*, pp.ix-xvi.

    (ii) Census of India, 1981, *Occasional Paper*, No. 2 of 1988, p. 20 New Delhi: Registrar General.

PART II

HISTORICAL AND LITERARY PROFILE

11

Changing Role and Status of the Indian Woman through the Ages

*N.V. Jagannatha Rao and Godavari D. Patil**

Introduction

One way to judge the state of a nation is to study the status of its women. In reality the status of women represents the standard of culture of any age. The social status of the women of a country symbolises the social spirit of the age.[1] However, to draw a conclusion about the position of women is a difficult and complicated problem. It is, therefore, necessary to trace this position in the historical perspective. In the course of Indian history from prehistoric to modern times there were distinct stages of the rise and fall in the status and role of women.

The recorded evidence found in the same period and in the same province have expressed opposite views about the worth, nature and importance of women. According to one school, a woman is the best gift of God to man. She brings prosperity when she is properly treated and respected and is called *Lakshmi*, the goddess of wealth and prosperity. The second school of thought holds the view that the best way to reach God is to avoid women.[2] Sage Agastya says, "Women combine the fickleness of the lightning, the sharpness of a weapon and the swiftness of the eagle."[3] Altekar says that to ascertain the position of women in Hindu society, one

*N.V. Jagannatha Rao is Associate Professor and Head, Dept. of Rural Sociology, University of Agricultural Sciences, Dharwad (Karnataka) and Godavari D. Patil is Assistant Professor of Sociology, University of Agricultural Sciences, Dharwad.

should study their position under different circumstances, like normal (in peace-time) and abnormal (in war time). During wars, the attitude of the society towards women was very unsympathetic, particularly if the women had the misfortune of falling into the hands of the enemies. They found it impossible to get re-admitted into their family and society. A study of ancient literature reveals that even during peace-time the position of women was not very satisfactory. The status of women was considered to be equal to that of the Sudras and killing of women was also not considered as a disgraceful act. The information on the traditional status and role of women is derived from historical accounts and classic texts.[4] For the purpose of depicting a brief history of the changing position and role of women in India five broad categories are considered:

(a) 2500 B.C. to 1500 B.C. Vedic Period

(b) 1500 B.C. to 500 B.C. Post-Vedic Period

(c) 500 B.C. to 500 A.D. Smriti Period/Pre-Islamic Period

(d) 500 A.D. to 1800 A.D. Islamic Period

(e) 1880 A.D. to 1947 A.D. British Period (Christian Period)

(f) from 1947 A.D. onwards contemporary Period.

The term 'role' is defined as a prescription for interpersonal behaviour which is associated with particular socially recognised categories of persons. Such categories are referred to as position[5].

The literature on Indian history abounds with contradictory and conflicting views on the status of women. It can properly be understood within the socio-cultural condition of the society. As Majumdar has rightly said, "The status of women in India can be more understood in the Indian ethnology than in that of religion or Brahmanism..."[6] The contradictory views about women's status is because of the emergence of the ideals of womanhood at different times. It appears that originally Hindu society had a flexible social structure. The concept of *ardhangini* suggests that there was equality between men and women; neither of the two being superior to the other.[7] Later on, barbarous practices developed and women were relegated to a subordinate status.[8]

The status enjoyed by the Indian woman cannot easily be assessed. While the 'ideal' was worshipped, the 'real' was neglected. Cormack asserts, "Traditional India has always accorded woman a high place and indeed equality."[9] Gorwaney also observes that, "Ideally, women were accepted as a living force in society, the embodiment of *'Shakti'* and a symbol of purity, religiousness, spirituality and sacrifice."[10] In practice, however, they were subjected to suppression, many deprivations and were exploited by men. They were denied equal rights in marital,familial, social, educational, economic and political fields. They were assigned a sub-ordinate status.

According to Mehta, there is recorded evidence to show that woman was not always without rights nor was she constantly in subjection. There is, however, greater evidence to show that the contrary was equally true; for many centuries her position continued to be one in which she did not have either legal or social rights to make her independent of the family into which she was born or married.[11] She further remarks that the status of women is a complex question and has to be studied as an integral part of the socio-economic structure in which women live. It cannot be dissociated from it. The changes that have taken place in their position are a part of the process of transformation of a traditional society. The various stages of this transformation may be briefly dwelt upon in the following pages.

The Vedic Period

Altekar argues that the position which women occupied in Hindu society at the dawn of civilisation during the *Vedic* age is much better than what we ordinarily expect it to have been. He further says that even before the Aryans came to India in about 2000 B.C., there is evidence to believe that Indian women shared a responsible position with men and played an important role in evolving a definite culture and tradition. Their status excelled that of the contemporary civilisations of ancient Greece, Rome and even early Christianity.[12] There is almost a consensus of opinion among great scholars of classical literature that during the age of *Vedas* (2500-1500 B.C.) a woman's status was equivalent to that of man.

Position of the Daughter

The position of women in *Vedic* period can be judged by the way in which the birth of a girl was received. None of the hymns of *Rigveda* considered the birth of a daughter as inauspicious. But we find prayers for the birth of a son in *Atharva Veda* which says, "The birth of a girl, grant it elsewhere; here grant a boy".[13] We do find a frequent longing for a male child in the *Rigveda*, while during the *Vedic* Age, there were some parents who would perform *Kanyasraddhas* on the second day of the moon; for the blessing of getting learned and capable daughters. The *Rigveda* praises the father of many daughters. Besides, it was recommended that "Matrika-puja" should take place first; the '*kumari puja*' was to be performed at the end of all Vedic rituals.[14]

Initiation of girls was common. Girls were educated like boys. Like their brothers, the girls wore the sacred thread (*Upavita-Dharana*) and used to pass through a period of Brahmacharya. After this *Upavita* ceremony, the *Vedic* women carried on the study of the Vedas, recited *Vedic mantras*, performed *Vedic* rites and rituals; undertook *Vedic* vows and did whatever was necessary for the proper performance of *yagayajna*, just like a son. According to *Sarvanukramanika* there were as many as twenty women who are credited with having composed the hymns of the *Rigveda*. Many of them became distinguished poetesses and were honoured by having their poems included in *Vedic* literature. Some of the high-class women were highly educated and they actively participated in intellectual and philosophical discussions. One comes across references to lady sages like Gosha, Apala, Lopamudra, Indrani, Maitreyi and Gargi. Gargi was one of the greatest *Vedic* scholars of her time. She challenged Yagnavalkya and put many subtle and intricate questions to him. Apart from a literary career women entered fields of teaching, medicine, business, military and administration.[15]

The marriages of girls used to take place at the age of understanding i.e., between 14 to 17 years and that, too, with their consent. The educated girls had naturally an effective voice in the selection of their life partners. Pre-puberty marriages were unknown as there were *Swayamvara* marriages where women were given the chance of selecting their partners. There were also many instances of love marriages. It can be concluded that both men and women had considerable freedom in selecting their partners though parents often arranged a suitable match.[16]

If for any reason a daughter remained unmarried, she was expected to live under the protection of her father, and after her father's death under the control and protection of her brother. Otherwise, she was on her own. Perpetual tutelage of women is of a later origin.[17]

The position of a daughter during the *Vedic* period did not suffer much from authoritative interference. She was socialised with a high degree of modesty.[18] She was expected to have tolerance, patience, submission to and an identification of her personality with her husband's. She, in turn, received affection, consideration and regard. Though marriage was of great social and religious significance it was not mandatory as there were some reference to girls who remained unmarried.[19]

Ordinarily, a daughter did not have any right to hold, acquire or dispose of property. This means that she did not enjoy any legal status in the *Rigvedic* times. But the unmarried daughter who stayed on in her father's house and got a share of his property. She could not claim a share in her brothers' property as it is clearly laid down in the Rigvedec that, "a son born of the body does not transfer wealth to sister."[20] Married daughters could inherit their father's property only in the absence of brothers.[21] The social or famiiial status of the daughter was fairly satisfactory in the *Rigvedic* period.

Position of the Wife

The *Vedic* society also was patriarchal and male-dominated. The household was ruled by a houselord, who wielded almost absolute control over all other members of the family and to him his wife or wives were bound by a strict tie of life-long duty and obedience.[22] Marriage, in fact, was a religious necessity for both men and women; but neither could reach heaven without being accompanied by his or her duly married spouse. The *Vedic* woman being *Sahadharmini* or *Patni* had the fullest right to participate in all the religious ceremonies with her husband. She could also perform sacrifices independently and was not regarded as an impediment in religious pursuits. Her position was an honoured one in the family. She was the joint-owner of the household with her husband though in actual practice she was the subordinate partner. This was because of the prevalence of a patriarchal family system as it is today. Her social status was not only of a loving wife but also of a loving mother. She was described by the *Vedic* sages as an ornament of the home. Her social status was of an absolute equality with man in the eyes of religion.[23]

The *Dharmashastra* has raised a chaste wife to the rank of a Goddess. Out of love and veneration, she has been placed above the father and teacher. The *Panchatantra* mentions that the maintenance of a home is known by the culture of the wife; without her, a home is like a dreary forest. *Rigveda* accords a high position to woman. As a mother the *Vedic* woman held a far more venerable position than a man as the father.

During this period asceticism was not of great prominence. Women had the right of free movement. Polygamy prevailed to some extent among the rich and royal families but ordinarily monogomy was the rule. The main disadvantage from which the wife suffered in the *Vedic* age was that she could neither hold nor inherit property. It appears that under certain Aryan customs the property rights in some kind of properties which women slowly acquired were assimilated with their rights in their portion of bride-price probably as being the only existing type of woman's property.[24] The recognition of women's property with absolute rights *(Stridhana)* was slow.

In the post-*Vedic* period, women were known to take up teaching career. She was accepted as an *Acharya*. Some of the lady teachers were specialists in theology and philosophy, the most obstruse and difficult subjects. Women had the privilege of adoption, e.g., Vadharimati adopting Haranyashasta and Loppada adopting Santha, the daughter of Dasaratha.[25]

The position of women during the *Vedic* age is clearly manifest from *Suktas* of revered Nari Risi or women seers in the *Rigveda*. Women as daughters, sisters, wives and mother had equally honoured places in the family, society and state alike. Thus, in all aspects they had equal rights with men and were their equal partners, friends, and helpers all through.

Position of the Widow

Though the Hindus of the Vedic period had a patriarchal society, the women in general did not suffer from disabilities which are characteristic of later periods. This is particularly true of widows. Widows of this age were permitted to remarry. This practice seems to have been accepted as normal from the *Vedic* period onwards. A number of references are found in the *Vedas* to show that widow remarriage was common, though the re-married widow could not aspire for the status of *'Grihini* (wife), where she could become the mistress of the house. The use of the word *'Parapurva'*, a woman who has had a second husband, proves that widows were re-married. The word *'Didhishu'* used in the *Rigveda* means the second husband of a woman. *Atharva Veda* refers to a *'Punarbha'*, that is, re-married widow. This shows that marriage of widows was not opposed. The custom of a widow marrying the brother of her deceased husband seemed to be common. Hence, the word *'Devara'* which means a woman's brother-in-law, literally 'the second husband'.

The institution of *Niyoga* (Levirate) came into Aryan society from some non-Aryan source. Under the system of *Niyoga,* a widow or a woman whose husband was not virile was allowed to have conjugal relations with her brother-in-law, who was regarded as the most eligible person for this duty, or some other near relation, till she gave birth to an offspring. A widow was allowed to have two sons through *Niyoga*. A son by levirate was always preferred to a son by adoption.[26]

We do not find any reference to *sati* or burning of widows in *Rigveda*. On the other hand, Vedic hymns refer to re-marriage of widows rather than their self-immolation. The burning of the widow on the funeral pyre of her husband might have been practised by the early Aryans. But, in reality in the *Rigvedic* period the widow was made to lie by the side of her dead husband. She was, however, asked to come down and a prayer was offered that she be granted a prosperous life enjoying the bliss of children and wealth.[27]

Attachment of importance to the birth of a male-child became responsible for the gradual decline in the status of women. The widow was given an inferior position as she was unfortunate enough to lose the all-powerful protecting male partner.

The custom of widow remarriage as we understand the term today did not exist. But even then we have some references to widow remarriage with the younger brother or with the next kinsman of her deceased husband. It can only be said that her life was not bound by so many restrictions and austerities as it was in the later days. She had not to ascend her husband's funeral pyre.[28] In other words, *Sati* system was not in practice. The right of *'Niyoga'* shows how a widow was very liberally treated in those days. The legal status of the widow was the same as that of the wife. The widow, however, did not have the right to hold property. But then, even a married wife did not possess that right.

Post-Vedic Period

The Age of the Later Samhitas, Brahmanas, and Upanishads (c. 1500 B.C. to c. 500 B.C.).

From about 1500 B.C. there were perceptible changes in the women's status due to various reasons, among which the most important was the denial of education. Traces of deterioration are found in all periods following 1500 B.C., but it became much more marked after the beginning of the Christian era and reached its peak after the Mongol invasion in the tenth century.[29]

With the lapse of time the position of the daughter also changed. During this period there was a gradual decline in women's education. Girls were not allowed to go to the houses of the preceptor or centres of education but were taught only by near relatives like father, brother or the uncle. Therefore, only the girls of rich and cultured families received religious and other training. As a result, there appeared a tendency to curtail the religious rights and privileges of women in general.

The desire to get a son to provide for the future, become quite intense and daughters came to be looked upon as encumbrances and the marriage age of the girls continued to be at around 16. They had some voice in the selection of their life partners. Love marriages were also common. Among the Kshatriyas, *Swayamvara* was fairly common in practice. The social and familial status of the daughter deteriorated in the post-*Vedic* period. Her proprietory right was also the same as it was in the *Vedic* age. Even so far as her right in the separate property of the father was concerned, she was not altogether ignored.[30] The following line aptly depicts the position of the daughter: 'A wife is a comrade, a daughter is a misery and a son a light in the highest heaven."[31]

According to the *Gautama Samhita,* a girl should be given in marriage before she attains puberty. He who neglects it, commits sin. Some declare that a girl should be given in marriage before she wears clothes.[32] *Vasistha Samhita* also says the same thing.[33]

There was a slight improvement with respect to her property right in her father's separate property. As these *slokas* make it clear, e.g.,

Manu said, 'As if self, son, and a daughter is equal to a son, how they, when one's self is living in the form of one's daughter, can anyone else take the wealth.'[34] Brahaspati said, 'The wife is declared to be the inheritor of the husband's wealth and, in default of her, the daughter; the daughter, like a son springs from the limb of a man; how can any other man inherit her father's property while she lives?'[35]

The daughters could only succeed that property if she were a widow or in default of the son, grandson, great-grandson. But in the normal circumstances, she could get one-fourth share of the property. As Manu said, 'but to the maiden (sister) the brothers shall severally give (portions) out of their share, one-fourth part, those who refuse to give (it) will become outcastes'.[36]

Yajnavalkya also said, 'but sisters should be disposed of in marriage giving them as an allotment the fourth share'.[37]

The intention of the *Smriti* writers was not to make her a shareholder in the son's property but just to reserve some wealth necessary for her marriage. But the daughter's right of succession in her father's property cannot be said to be satisfactory.

Position of the Wife

There were gradual changes in the position of women in this period. Women were not allowed to participate in the performance of sacrificial ceremonies. They eventually began to lose touch with the *Vedas* and were pushed back to domestic duties. The study of Vedas became the monopoly of men. Women also ceased to attend public meetings. Having lost their importance as comrades of men in public activities, they came to be honoured merely as mothers.

The reason for the deterioration of her status was the inter-marriages between the Aryans and the Dravidians. The non-Aryan wife, with her ignorance of the Sanskrit language and Hindu religion, obviously could not enjoy the same religious privileges as the Aryan consort.[38] The black non-Aryan wife could be her husband's associate in pleasure but not in religious rituals, say several authorities.

The discontinuance of *Upanayana,* the neglect of education and lowering of the marriage age produced disastrous consequences regarding the position and status of women. Early marriage became a hindrance in the education of girls. Women came to be regarded as being of the same status the *Sudra.* During this period on the one hand woman was being-idealised and on the other she was given a very degraded status.[39]

Over the property of her husband it was generally considered that a woman had no right during his lifetime beyond the right of maintenance and residence. According to the *Mitakshara* law, in the matter of partition, a wife was allowed to get an equal share with her own son or sons when the division took place in the lifetime of her husband. But she could not herself demand a partition. She could get a share only if the husband himself separated from his sons during his lifetime or if the sons claimed partition during the father's lifetime.[40] Though a woman had her own property called *Stridhana,* she was given only limited ownership. It seems the spirit of the Hindu law was not to allow women independence as regards the disposing of property, but had the right of possession and right of enjoyment.[41] It can be said that the social status of the wife was not satisfactory. However, her status was improved in the sphere of proprietary right.

Position of the Widow

The deterioration in the status of widows commenced from the epic period. Widowhood was considered both undesirable as well as inauspicious. The position of widows became more pitiable because the *Sutras* ordered a widow to avoid, for the duration of a year, the use of honey, meat, spirits and liquor as well as salt and to sleep on the ground. At the expiry of six months, she could, with the permission of her *Guru,* bear a son by her brother-in-law in case she had no son. The custom of *Niyoga* came into existence during this period. Remarriages are not found among the Aryan widows but there are instances of non-Aryan widows marrying Aryans. The *Mahabharat* says, 'a child widow can remarry, and her sons by the second marriage can offer oblations to the manes.'[42] The children by the second marriage of a widow were given a social as well as religious status. Child widows, therefore, married without fear of social ostracism. During this period *Niyoga* was preferred to widow re-marriage.

The custom of widow burning came into existence around 400 A.D. Though there are instances of widows surviving their husbands and offering them funeral oblations, on the whole the position of widows was not so honourable before this period.

The rise of Brahmanism during the Smriti period became detrimental to the status of woman. The Hindu law-givers of this period imposed certain duties on widows, who did not ascend the funeral pyre and chose instead to survive the husband. All the sages, prescribed a life of strict discipline and penance on such widows or their whole life.

The custom of *Niyoga* was condemned by *Smriti* writers when chastity became the main qualification of marriage. Manu disapproved of the custom of *'Niyoga'* and declared that it was fit for cattle only. Although it is still practised in some communities in India, the custom appears very strange and unacceptable to the modern mind.[43]

Widow marriage was prohibited. The practice of *'sati'* was recommended by many of the later authorities and was well-established by the end of 6th century A.D. The practice prevailed as early as Alexander's invasion about 325 B.C. Travellers like Strabo, Megasthenes, and Diodarus who accompanied Alexander, allude to this practice. The law-givers forced the widows to lead a life of austerities, fasting and abstinence from pleasure. Manu, the Hindu law-giver, says:

1. Until her death, let her be patient of hardships, self-controlled, and chaste and strive to fulfil that most excellent duty which is prescribed for wives who have one husband only.

2. At her pleasure let her emaciate her body by living on pure flowers, roots and fruits but she must never mention the name of another man after the husband has died.

3. A virtuous wife, Manu says again, is one, 'who after death of her husband constantly remains chaste, reaches heaven though she has no son, just like those chaste men'.[44]

The codes of the Hindu Law commended that a widow should lead a chaste life. Loss of chastity of the widow affected not only her social status but also her proprietary position. But the injunctions to emaciate her body and to live on a frugal and abstemious diet, were in the nature of a religious or moral injunction.

Unjust, archaic social customs like child marriage, *'sati'* and polygamy reduced the status of women to the level of mere goods or a chattel. They were regarded as *'nari-sudras'*. The status of widows was still more inferior.

Smriti Period/Pre-Islamic Period

The Age of Later Smritis, Commentators and Digest Writers (c. 500 A.D. to c. 1800 A.D)

Altekar says that the period between 500 A.D. to 1800 A.D. was one of progressive deterioration in the position of women. In the history of India, these dark and depressing days of total injustice, intolerance and inequality will remain as the darkest spot for ever. There were varied and many reasons for the deterioration or fall in the position of women. The only good thing that developed during this period was the recognition of certain proprietary rights for women.[45]

Chaudhury has stated that, women of India rose to the heights of knowledge and realisation, worked with men in all spheres of life and even surpassed them in many respects, and were entitled to the fullest freedom as well as to untrammelled self-dependence and self-determination. Such bold and blessed, self-confident and independent women found themselves suddenly confined within four walls of dark and dreary homes, with their minds desolate and depressing, with almost all their fundamental birthrights totally or almost cut off. They were deprived of any rights to justice, freedom, education, equality, and were degraded domestically, socially, legally, economically, politically and in every other way. They came to be called *Abala* (the powerless) or *'Griha-pinjarakokila'* (cuckoo of the cage of the house) and subject to the most derogatory maxim: *'Putrartha kriyate bharya'* (women has to be taken in marriage for procreation only).[46]

There are contradictory views regarding the position and status of women. While some of the earlier authorities have described women as abodes of more evil than good, the progressive and liberal thinkers are in favour of women. They have gone to the length of worshipping her as a living image of the Divine Mother. In *Manu Smriti* we find two contradictory statements:

1. Where women are honoured, there gods dwell.

2. A woman is to be protected and sheltered all through her life by her male relatives—by the father during her childhood, the husband when a housewife and the son during her widowhood.[47]

The position of women in all other spheres, except the proprietary rights continued to deteriorate in this period. Most of the causes responsible for the degradation of women during the last period continued to operate in this age also.

The age of marriage was fixed at eight. The *Upanayana* ceremony of girls was completely discontinued. The commentators were of the opinion that the parents would be committing sin, if the girl's age exceeded eight years. Only in Kshatriya families girls were married at the age of 14 or 15. Girls of rich families, however, still received education and a few of them distinguished themselves as poetesses and critics. The ignorance of most girls created a tendency among men to treat them lightly and pass cynical remarks about their weakness and worthlessness.[48]

Unjust and stupid social customs like child marriage, *Sati* and polygamy reduced the status of women to the level of mere goods or chattel. They were regarded as *Nari-sudras.*

Gradually, the practice of marriage of child-widows was stopped. Permission to the child-widows to remarry was withdrawn during this period. In the beginning of 1000 A.D. only widows from the higher strata of society were not allowed to marry, but in course of time the custom got extended to the lower sections also in the hope of attaining respectability. Widows were ordained to lead a strict ascetic life. An ascetic generally removes the hair on the head. The custom of disfiguring the Hindu widow appears to have originated from this. During 11th century the cruel custom of *'sati'* was widely practised. Most of the widows voluntarily ascended the funeral pyres of their husbands because of the cruel and tiresome life they would be required to lead as widows. Sometimes, the cruel relatives of the widows burnt them forcibly, because they were either afraid that the widows might misbehave and bring disgrace to the family or wanted to misappropriate their share in the family property.[49] Consequently, the practice of *'Sati'* or *Jauhar* became quite common and popular particularly in North India.[50]

By 1200 A.D. the widow's right to inherit the share of her husband's property came to be recognised all over the country. The recognition of the right of inheritance was thus a blessing to the poor widows. The daughter comes as the next heir to the widow. Even Manu placed the daughter in the fifth position.

Islamic Period

In the Muslim period, i.e. in the 11th century onwards, the position of women further deteriorated. Women faced a number of hardships and cruelty due to evil practices like child marriage, the *purdah* system, *sati*, widowhood, prostitution and the *devadasi* system. As Hate mentions, the advent of the Muslims arrested the progress of Hindu civilisation and an era of blind faith and perpetuation of old customs followed.[51]

Hindu women, like their Muslim counterparts, adopted the *purdah*. In Northern Indian this practice was very rigourously enforced. As Sridevi has stated, 'Most women, being subject to *purdah*, had no opportunity for education. They remained somewhere in between the two portals, with no education, no special privileges but simplicity, patience, perseverance, endurance, understanding, immense love for home and children and intense religious (inclinations) adorned them.[52]

During this period the role of women conformed to the dictum laid down by Manu, the great law giver of second century that, 'a woman does not deserve freedom' and that her life should throughout be one of dependence on man. Another similar dictum laid down by him was that a woman should be subservient in all stages of her life-'in childhood to the father, in youth to the husband and his elderly kins and to the sons when widowed.'[53] Among the traditional Hindu families the fate of a woman, especially of the daughter-in-law, was always of subordination to all other members.[54]

The position of the daughter in Hindu society reached its nadir. As child marriage was a popular practice of the social life of the Mughal period. Hindu daughters, too, were married before the age of nine or ten and in some cases were married even before they had learnt to talk.[55] The legal position of Hindu women with regard to inheritance was again unsatisfactory. Women were excluded from succession to property and made them dependent on men.[56] Due to early marriage girls were deprived of education. All these social circumstances led to the further deterioration in the position of daughters.

Along with the insecurity and uncertainty which prevailed in the Mughal period, the practice of *purdah* became rigid and women were forbidden even to visit the holy shrines. Both Hindu and Muslim women lost all their liberal activities and became the property of their male masters. The practice of *purdah*, invented to protect women, had a restrictive effect. As a result, the soical life of women narrowed down.[57]

Widow re-marriage was prohibited in general. Altekar says that the prohibition of widow re-marriage began to be imposed from about 1000 A.D., even on the child-widows. It was totally prohibited in Hindu society from about 1100 A.D. Initially, society upper caste widows were prohibited from re-marrying whereas lower caste widows were allowed to do so.[58] Since the last century the lower castes, due to Sanskritisation and the desire to increase their respectability, began to impose upon themselves the prohibition of widow re-marrriage.

The practice of tonsuring of widows was prevalent among many high castes until recently. It is believed to have come into vogue in about the 8th century A.D. This system of tonsuring of widows is believed to have been adopted by the Brahmins under the influence of Buddhism where the Buddhist nuns underwent tonsure in imitation of the monks.[59] However, Kane suggests that a widow was tonsured just as the sons of a deceased man underwent tonsure as a matter of purification and as a symbol of bereavement.[60] From 12th century A.D. onwards the tonsure of widows became prevalent all over India. It was commoner more in the South than in the North of the country. Though the cruel practice is dying out, it is still practised by some orthodox sects of Brahmins in Southern India.

Once widow marriage was prohibited, society desired to make the widow as unattractive as possible so that no man could ever want to marry her. With this idea in mind, the widow was tonsured and made to wear white clothes only. The idea might probably have been borrowed form the Buddhist or Jain nuns who wore white clothes, when they renounced the worldly life, since the widow too was supposed to have renounced the world. She was forbidden too wear any jewel. She had to sleep on the bare floor and partake a frugal meal cooked by herself only once a day. This deprived her of good health and good looks, so that even if she wanted to remarry no man came forward to do so. Even Vedvyasa opines, 'if a widow does not become a *sati*, she should shave her head.[61]

Widows had to follow strict rules and restrictions. So, they frequently preferred *'Sati'* to the tiresome life prescribed for them. Most widows voluntarily ascended the funeral pyres of their husbands. This cruel custom of *sati* was widely practised during this period.

Henry Maine opines that superstitious belief, coupled with the Brahmanical dislike of the enjoyment of property by women, had led to the practice of *'sati'* and was intended to fight the ancient rule of civil law, which made her a tenant for life in respect of her husband's property[62]. It is also believed that the custom came into practice due to frequent wars and foreign invasions which left behind widows who preferred to commit *'sati'* to leading a life of disgrace or dishonour. However, though it started as a voluntary gesture, as time went on, many cases were reported where widows were forcibly cast into the flames of the pyre much against their will.[63]

'Sati' became more frequent among the royal families in northern India, and quite common in Kashmir during the period 1500 to 1800 A.D. The practice of *'sati'* or *'Jauhar'* was also quite common as well as pupular particularly among the Rajputs and Marathas of Central India.[64] The incentive that were dangled before a *'sati'* were, as Sankha and Angirasa say, that she who follows her husband in death, dwells in heaven for 3.5 crores of years.[65]

Several Muslim emperors discouraged *'sati'* and adopted measures to prevent it as far as possible, but didn't succeed. This era led not only to the degeneration of women's physical, mental and social life, but her rights in educational, social, religious and economic fields were also lowered gradually.

The legal position of Hindu women with regard to inheritance rights was also unsatisfactory. Under the doctrine of *Stridhana* they were generally excluded from succession to property and this led to their dependence on men.[66]

Denial of education produced far-reaching effects on the status and role of women. The subordinate position of women became an accepted cultural norm for the majority section of society until the beginning of the nineteenth century.

From time to time, protestant movements like Buddhism, Jainism, Vaishnavism, Veerashaivism and Sikhism made sincere efforts to improve the status of women. They too regarded women as mothers and wives but necessarily inferior to men. Buddhism considered male monks as superior to the nuns. In Jainism though women were given a respectable position in congregational life, they were condemned severly. In the 12th century Veerashaivism permitted their women the right to divorce and re-marriage. The Bhakti movement also played an important role in raising the status of women by allowing them to seek spiritual solace independently. The little but powerful orthodox forces in the society erased the good effects brought about by these revolutions.

In the history of India, the 18th century was a period of all-round decline. It was the darkest period so far as women were concerned. Political decay following the disruption of the Mughal empire and disorder due to the advent of various European powers, combined with fossilised customs, tradition, superstition and irrational bigotry, ruined the nation. Under the new conditions, women lost their independent identity. They did not enjoy a separate world of their own. Until quite recently their very existence was almost merely a bare necessity and taken to be an indispensable appendage to the male population. They were totally and forcefully subjugated to male superiority physically and intellectually.[67]

British Period (Christian Period)

In the latter half of the 18th century, when the British came to India, women's status had dropped to the lowest level. It was the worst period in the history of the country because of child-marriages and sati system, etc. A.L. De'Souza says, 'Women were denied equal rights in marital, familial, social, educational, economic and political fields. They were assigned a subordinate status. The marriage ideals, power and authority exercised by the joint-family and caste system, combined with illiteracy, age-old traditions, seclusion within the four walls of the house, made it difficult for them to seek fuller personality development. They had scant personal identity and few rights".[68]

Cousin, referring to the status of women at the end of the 19th century, states that the condition of woman was at its lowest point of literacy, of individuality, of health, of social status, of freedom of movement, or initiative of economic status of power.[69]

According to Dube, this deterioration in the status of women brought about a number of consequences. To quote his own words, with these changes in the status of women, it was inevitable that their character and personalities should also be affected. The uneducated were considered on a level with *shudras*, married before their characters were fully developed, transferred from the loving and sympathetic atmosphere of the parent's house to the house of the parents-in-law. Where an atmosphere of awe prevailed apprehensive of suppression, frequently forced to drag on a miserable existence in an interminable widowhood, their character suffered from forced repression in some directions and unnatural stimulation in others. They had no status in society, none in their own estimation. They were more like puppets which move when someone else pulls the strings than individual human beings with minds of their own."[70]

The reasons that are responsible for the deterioration of the status of women in India were - (1) patriarchal joint family system, (2) polygamy and the *sati* system, (3) enforcement widowhood, denial of the right to divorce and right to remarry after widowhood, (4) child marriage and the *purdah* system. Because of child marriages to much older men there was an increase in the number of widows. Both child marriage and the *purdah* custom led to low literacy rate among women. Their entry to social, political, and religious functions was prohibited. They were depressed to such an extent that they could not comprehend their own freedom and independent personality. During this period one finds exceptional women like Chand Bibi, Jhansi Laxmibai, Kittur Rani Channamma and Rani Abbakka who made their remarkable impact in the field of administration.[71]

The British were the first rulers who unified the country as a whole and were liberal in their thinking. They believed that rational thinking had to be the basis for all customs and institutions and all customs and institutions not so based on reason had to be done away with. Hence, during the British rule Indian society faced significant modifications. The British government worked slowly and succeeded in providing an alternative way of life for those who wanted change, by introducing a new type of economy, state structure, educational system and also by passing new social legislations.

For the upliftment of women in India several factors are responsible. The first one was the direct influence of the British noted for their courtesy towards women; the general awakening of Asians in the twentieth century and the political struggle for Indian's independence also gave considerable force to the feminist movement in india.[72]

The position of girls, women and widows improved the during British period. They introduced female education in India. But the system of child-marriage came in the way of the spread of female education. Hence in 1929 they passed the Child-Marriage Restraint Act. (This Act was also amended by the Acts VIII and XIX 1938, and in 1978). This Act restricted the evils of early marriage andincrease in the number of girl widows. The Act not only prohibited the solemnisation of child-marriages but also raised the minimum age for marriage of girls to 14. Under Section 5 of the 1929 Act, the marriage of girls below 14 years and boys below 18 years of age was to be penalised. This 1929 Child Marriage Restraint Act was also known as the Sarda Act. Besides removing the evils of child marriage, it promoted female education. This led to the improvement in the position of the daughter.

The familial social status of the wife also improved during the British period because of rise in female education and the rise in the age of marriage. The Hindu Women's Right of Separate Residence and Maintenance Act of 1946 enabled Hindu wives to claim maintenance even without having judicial separation under certain circumstances. Women acquired a new social status because of new social legislation called the Civil Indian Marriage Act III of 1872.

In spite the cruel practice of *'sati'* its incidence was on increase throughtout the 1`7th and 18th centuries, because at this time religion had become corrupt and people were governed by the priests. Hindus at this time were unenlightened and had become strict followers of customs and conventions. People firmly believed that man's sins were completely washed out if his widow was burnt alive with his dead body.

The pitiful and pitiable plight of the widows who were forced to commit *'sati'* attracted the attention of a good number of enlightened Indians and the British under the leadership of Raja Ram Mohan Roy and Lord William Bentinck. In spite of the strong opposition, a historic resolution of great importance was passed on December, 14, 1829, by which *Sati* was made "a crime of culpable homicide punishable with fine, imprisonment or both."

The widow was ill-treated by her in-laws and kinsmen as the virtual destroyer of her husband. She was never allowed to appear cheerful or wear bright clother or ornaments. She had to drudge along day and night and was the victim of all kinds of insolence by other women of the household including servants. The tragedy became all the more poingnant if the widow happened to be a child. Therefore, in order to improve her lot, the British passed the Hindu Widows Remarriage Act, 1856. This Act was enacted to remove all the legal barriers to re-marriage of Hindu widows.

Later, the British realised that they could stop *'sati'* by police force but that theycould not arrange the remarriage of widows. These widows had to suffer because they had no property of their own. To improve the economic condition of the women the Hindu Women's Right to Property Act of 1937 was passed. According to Section 3 of the Act, on the death of a Hindu male, not only his son would succeed but also his widow and the widow of the pre-deceased son. By this Act a widow got the right to claim partition and a right of enjoyment of that property during her life-time. Though she was made a limited owner of her husband's property, she was freed from depending on other members of her husband's family for food and other necessary requirements.

Besides these governmental activities, in 1917, Mrs. Annie Besant tried to promote women's education through the Indian

Association. In 1920 the Federation of University of Women was established and in 1925 the National Council of Women started. Great personalities like Raja Ram Mohan Roy, the founder of Brahmo Samaj, Ishwarchandra Vidyasagar, as the founder of Arya Samaj, Dayananda Saraswati, Keshub Chandra Sen, Gopal Krishna Gokhale, Ramakrishna Paramahansa, Swami Vivekanand, Byramji Malabari, Pandita Ramabai and others tried to bring about unprecedented awakening among women, who were down-trodden and had been oppressed for centuries.

The familial, social and legal position of the Hindu women was greatly improved during the British period, as compared to the Muslim period. Although a small section of women took advantage of these measures and privileges given, their initiation was indeed significant. During India's struggle for independence, thousands of women took part under the leadership of Mahatma Gandhi sarojini Naidu, Vijayalaxmi Pandit and Kasturba Gandhi were some of the unique women personalities. Gill has rightly observed about the achievements with regard to the status of women during the British period: 'If a person who died a hundred years ago comes to life today, the first and most important change that would strike him is the revolution in the position of women.'[73]

Contemporary Modern Period

Due to the principles of democracy based on liberty, a woman's role began to change toward greater emancipation from man's domination. The role of wife-mother was affected by this new freedom. In India, due to efforts of social reformers and social legislations, women were brought out of the confines of their home.[74] The process of industrialisation and urbanisation had their share in the changes which followed.[75] It was the 20th century that brought about dynamic changes and new concepts which affected the status of women giving them fresh dignity and importance.

The Constitution of the Indian Republic has incorporated in tis objectives the principle of equality and has ushered the Indian womenfolk into a new era. It has also proclaimed the equality of men and women in all domains of life.[76] In Article 15 of the Constitution it is mentioned that, 'the state shall not discriminate against any citizen only on the ground of religion, caste, sex, place of birth or any of them. An Article 16 expressly provides, 'there shall be equality of opportunity for all citizens in matters relating to employment or appointment to any office under the State.' Under Articles 325 and 326 women are only given voting rights but also the right to stand for elections. They can take part in the political life of the country and hold any office from the highest to the lowest. Even the Directive Principles of State Policy enumerate certain directives towards the emancipation of women. Article 39 provides 'equal pay for equal work irrespective of sex'. The modern Indian legislations have stabilised the position of the woman by offering her the same rights, opportunities, and openings which men have.

The Hindu Succession Act, 1956 has statutorily recognised the right to property of the Hindu daughter. This Act has placed the daughter on a par with the son. Now she can succeed to the undivided interest of her father in the joint property and to the separate property of the father along with other heirs specified in clause I of the schedule. Dowry system, an abominable social evil, which makes young women's life miserable, has been curbed by the enactment of the Dowry prohibition Act of 1961. Education is also made free and compulsory for all the children of 5-14 age group. Accessibility to education and availability of incressing opportunities for acquiring education has brought about tremendous changes in the role of women.

At present, the wife enjoys a respectable position. She can even live separately under Section 18 of the Hindu Adoption and Maintenance Act, 1956, and can claim maintenance under certain circumstances. The husband cannot adopt a son or a daughter under Section 7 of the Hindu Adoption and Maintenance Act 1956, without the consent of his wife. The wife under sect. 8 can adopt a son or daughter when her husband has completely and finally renounced the world or has ceased to be a Hindu or has been declared by a court of competent jurisdiction to be of unsound mind. Under the Hindu Marriage Act 1955 both husband and wife can claim divorce. Further, the Act has provided the wife with more grounds, viz. sodomy or bestiality under Section 13(2) to divorce her husband.

Widow remarriage is legalised. Section 14 of the Hindu Succession Act 1956 has made her the absolute owner of the property. She is not divested of the property which she has inherited from her first husband even after her remarriage. Under Section 6 of the Act she inherits the coparcenary interest of her husband along with the son and daughter. Section 8 of the Hindu Adoption and Maintenance Act, 1956 empowers her to adopt a son or daughter to herself. Section 6 of the Hndu minority and Guardianship Act, 1956, recognises her as the natural and legal guardian of her minor childern after their father.

These legislations have promoted emancipation of women to a very large extent. Besides these legislations, under the provision of the Directive Principles of State Policy each state has undertaken women's welfare programmes. The Central and State Governments have evinced keen interest in betterment of the legal, social, educational and cultural status of women. These is hardly any field today wherein women have not entered. According to the Indian Census of 1971, there were 31 million working women out of whom 28 million were in rural areas and 3 million in urban areas. Now in urban areas a working wife is considered economically advantageous.

The United Nations by declaring 1975 as Women's Year and the next decade as Women's Decade called upon its member states to develop new measures for emancipation of women and to ensure equal opportunities and equal respect and recognition in all fields. These steps have also influenced the status of women in India.

In a nutshell, it can be said that education and women's participation in all fields of economy, science and culture will help them in achieving the real equality. The future will help women to emerge as socially and economically independent beings.

Conclusion

It appears that the Ancient Hindu society had a flexible social structure. There was equality between men and women. Women were given freedom to move about in society and to take part in public life. This gives us an idea as to how they had realised the truth that women too have their own contribution to make to the society's development and progress.

Later on, many barbarous practices developed and women were confined to a subordinate status. The *shastras* directed women to be in the state of dependence and submission. The deterioration of the status of women started with Manu, who equated women with slaves and said, 'a woman should never be independent.' He led society to consider a woman to be a perpetual minor and as such should always be looked after by others. Education was denied to her and she was consigned to the shadows of ignorance. She used to be behind *purdah* and living in the seclusion. Woman was known as *abala*, a weak, helpless and powerless person, incapable of managing and preserving the family property. A wife was treated as a property of her husband. She was made to immolate herself on her husband's funeral pyre. The subordinate position of women was deep rooted in the Indian society of that period.

Women's role began to change towards greater emancipation from the domination of man with the advent of the British rule, democracy and liberalism all over the world in the eighteenth century. This new freedom brought about new changes in the role of women. In additon to this the processes of industrialisation and urbanisation also brought forth a lot of changes in the life of the people. With the efforts of a number of social reformers of the 19th century and the legislations passed after Independence, women were brought out of their homes and helped in achieving equality with men. These changes have caused profound influence on different dimensions of the family system and women's status.

References

1. K. Gill, *Hindu Women's Right to Property in India*, New Delhi: Deep and Deep Publications, 1986, p. 17.
2. K. Gill, *Ibid.*, p. 17.
3. Quoted by Altekar, A.S., *The Position of Women in Hindu Civilization*, Delhi: Motilal Banarsidass, 2nd Edn., 1983, p. 319.
4. Altekar, A.S., *op..cit.*, pp. 305 and 317.
5. J. Hess, *Family Roles and Interaction*, Chicago, Rand McNally, 1968, p. 1.
6. P.N. Majumdar, *Races and Cultures of India*, New Delhi: Asia Publishing House, p. 206.
7. P. Prabhu, *Hindu Social Organisation*, Bombay: Popular Book Depot, 1958, p. 22.
8. Y.B. Singh, *Social Life in Ancient India*, New Delhi: Life and Light Publishers, 1981, p.75.
9. M. Cormack, *She Who Rides a Peacock—Indian Students and Social Change* Bombay: Asia Publishing House, 1961, p. 104.
10. N. Gorwaney, *Self Image and Social Change—A Study of Female Students*, New Delhi: Sterling Publishers. p. 2.
11. R. Mehta, *The Western Educated Hindu Women*, Bombay: Asia Publishing House, 1970, p. 16 and 113.
12. Sudha, G., 'Changing Status of Women in Society' in Sarojini Shintri (Ed.). *Women: Her Problems and Her Achievements*, Dharwad: Karnatak University, 1977, p. 91.
13. *Atharva Veda*, VI. 2-3.
14. Upadhyaya, B.S., *Women in Rigveda*, New Delhi's S. Chand & Co. Pvt. Ltd., 1974, p.43.
15. B.S. Upadhyaya, *op.cit.*, pp. 44-46.
16. A.S. Altekar, *op.cit.*, p.338.
17. Radha Binod Pal, *The History of Hindu law*, Calcutta: University of Calcutta, 1958, p. 302.
18. M.N. Banerjee, 'Hindu Family and Freudian Theory', *Indian Journal of Social Work*, 1944-45, pp. 180-186.

19. Shakuntala Rao Shastri, *Women in the Vedic Age* (3rd edn.), Bombay: Bharatiya Vidya Bhavan, 1960, pp. 4-5.
20. *Rigveda*, II. 17.
21. *Rigveda*, III. 31-32, quoted by S.R. Shastri, *op. cit.*, p. 4-5.
22. Radha Binod Pal. *op.cit.*, p. 45.
23. A.S. Altekar, *op.cit.*, pp. 338-39.
24. K. Gill, *op.cit.*, p. 23.
25. Venkatarayappa, *Feminine Roles*, Bombay: Popular Prakashan, 1966, pp. 36-37.
26. A.S. Altekar, *op.cit.*, pp. 144-145.
27. *Ibid.*, p. 118.
28. Shakuntala Rao, Shastri, *op.cit.*, pp. 23-24.
29. V.V. Prakash Rao and Nandini Rao.
30. A.S. Altekar, *op.cit.*, p. 340.
31. K. Gill, *op.cit.*, p. 26.
32. *Gautama Samhita* 11. 9. 24.
33. *Vasistha Samhita*, XVII-70-71, quoted by K. Gill, *op.cit.*, pp. 24-25.
34. Manu, IX. 100.
35. *Brihaspati*, XXV. 56.
36. *Manu Smriti*, IX. 118.
37. *Yajnavalkya Smriti*, 11, 124, quoted by K.Gill, *op.cit.*, pp. 24.25.
38. A.S. Altekar, *op.cit.*, p. 345.
39. *Ibid.*, p. 348.
40. *Yajnavalkya Smriti*, 11.115.
41. *Ibid.*, 11.148, quoted by K. Gill, *op.cit*, pp. 29-30.
42. *Mahabharat*, XIII. 55.7.
43. A.S. Altekar, *op.cit.*, pp. 146-149.
44. Manu V. 157, 158, 160 quoted by R.M. Das, *Women in Manu and His seven Commentators*, Varanasi: Kanchan Publications 1962, pp. 221-227.
45. A.S. Altekar, *op.cit.*, p. 353.
46. R. Chaudhary, 'Status and Role of Women: Great Indian Women Through the Ages' in, *Role and Status of Women in Indian Society*, Calcutta: Firma KLM Pvt. Ltd., 1978. p. 31.
47. Susheela Kaddipudi, *Exploitation of Women*, in Sarojini Shintri (Ed.), *op.cit.*, p. 80.
48. Chandrakala, Hate, *Changing Status of Women*, Bombay: Allied Publishers, 1969, p. 173.
49. Abbe, J.A., Dubois, *Hindu Manners, Customs and Ceremonies*, (Translated by H. Beauchamp), O.U.P. (III Edn.) 1906, p. 357.
50. Ila, Mukherjee, *Social Status of North Indian Women*, Agra: Shivalal Aggarwal and Co., 1972, pp. 114-135.
51. C. Hate, *op.cit.*, p. 175.

52. S. Sridevi, *Century of Indian Womenhood,* Mysore: Rao and Raghavan Co., 1965, p. 75.
53. Banerjee, *op.cit.,* p. 184.
54. Brabara Ward, *Women in the New Asia,* New York: UNESCO, 1963, p. 102.
55. Misra Rekha, *Women in Mughal India,* Delhi: Oriental Publishers, 1957, p. 132.
56. Tara Ali Baig, *Women of India,* Delhi: Govt, of India Publications, 1958, p. 12.
57. K. Gill, *op.cit.,* p. 34.
58. A.S. Altekar, *op.cit.,* p. 156.
59. I.B. Horner, *Women Under Primitive Buddhism,* Varanasi: Motilal Banarsidass, 1975, p. 73.
60. P.V. Kane, *History of Dharmashastras* II, Poona: Bhandarkar Oriental Research Institute, 1955, p. 587.
61. Vedavyasa I, 53, quoted by A.S. Altekar, *op.cit.,* p. 160.
62. Henry Maine, *Early History of Institutions,* London: John Murray, 1934 p. 335.
63. J.A. Abbe, Dubois, *op.cit.,* pp. 357-8.
64. A.S. Altekar, *op.cit.,* p. 130.
65. P.V. Kane, *op.cit,* p. 635.
66. Tara Ali Baig, *op.cit.,* p. 12.
67. Basu Krishna, 'Movement for Emancipation of Woman in the 19th Century' in, *Role and Status of Women in Indian Society,* Calcutta: Firma KLM Pvt. Ltd., 1978, p. 38.
68. A. De'Souza *Women in Contemporary India,* Delhi: Manohar Publications 1975, pp. 79-81.
69. Cousin Margret E., *Indian Womanhood Today,* Allahabad: Kitabistan, 1947, p. 13.
70. S.C. Dube, 'Mah's and Women's Role in India: A Sociological Review' in Barbara Ward (Ed.), *Women in the New Asia,* New York: UNESCO, 1963, p. 196.
71. G. Sudha, *op.cit.,* p. 90.
72. K. Gill, *op. cit.,* p. 35.
73. K. Gill, *op. cit.,* p. 38.
74. B. Kuppuswamy, *Social Change in India,* Delhi: Vikas Publishing House, 1972, p. 84.
75. Ailen D. Ross, *The Hindu Family in its Urban Setting,* London: Oxford University Press, 1961, p. 17.
76. Tara Ali Baig, *op. cit.,* p. 32.

12

Matriliny and Mother Right in the Early South Indian Society

*R. N. Nandi**

Studies on Dravidian ethnic survivals suggest that the family in the preliterate society of South India was both matrilocal and matrilineal. A perusal of historical data would, however, indicate that the matriarchal character of the old Dravidian family was substantially compromised under the influence of a Brahmin dominated patriarchal culture. Instances of this social metamorphosis begin to suface in the literary and epigraphic records from the early centuries of the Christian era. The present study draws on this valuable information to assess the effects of this interaction on the overall position of female folk in the peninsular region.

Sangam literature which witnessed this process of cultural interaction points towards certain practices which would emphasize the survival of matriarchal traditions in a predominantly patriarchal order. The custom of bride-price, mentioned in several sangam texts is, for example, alien to brahminical ideas regarding marriage. The *Tolkappiyam* evidence relating to the substitution of earlier *kalavu* marriages by the brahminical ritualistic marriages seems to be equally meaningful in this context. The Padirruppattu references to the practice of matrilineal inheritance similarly point towards a period when the family was set up on the basis of a matrilineal descent system. The *basavi* and *devadasi* practices are in fact attempts to revert to the *marumakkatthayam* law either temporarily or on a permanent basis. The Kaikkolan weavers, for example, are a caste from which a large

* The author is Professor of History, Patna College (P.U.), Patna 800 005.

number of *devadasis* were recruited during the medieval period. Even in the present day the daughter of a sonless Kaikkolan father is dedicated as a *dasi* which signifies her marriage with the local deity. The dedication entitles her to work at the loom just as male member of the family does. At the time of her dedication to the temple, which also entitles her to receive favours from brahmin suitors, it is the maternal uncle or his representative who ties a gold band on the forehead of the girl. As for the actual nuptial a rich brahmin or in his absence, a lowly brahmin is invited to the family[1]. Both the temporary reversion to the *marumakkatthayam* law and the importance attached to the maternal uncle are characteristic survivals of an old matrilineal ordering of Dravidian families. Among the Malabar Nayars the familiy continues to be nucleated round the mother's house and maternal ancestors.

The Importance of Mother's Ancestry

The historical records of early South Indian people show the popularity of metronyms among literate families which were patrilocal in constitution and followed a patrilineal descent. This may refer to a lingering influence of the old Dravidian mother right in an otherwise patrilineal ordering of society. A few early instances of this practice may be of interest here. The Satavahana family, which was at once patrilocal and patrilineal, publicised in their official records their maternal descent. The tribal or non-brahminical origin of the family also seems to be confirmed by the ceremonial brahminisation of a Satavahana king. Metronymics were also used by the Iksvaku rulers of eastern Deccan who were among the earliest dynasties of the peninsular region and who proclaimed in their records that they were Ksatriyas descendants from the prestigious solar race[2], which once again smacks of a suspect origin.

Epigraphic records refer to important feudal houses, families of high officers and even lay brahmin families as giving publicity to their mother's ancestry in obvious preference to paternal descent. For example, an inscription engraved on a pillar of the gateway at Bharhut refers to someone as Vatsiputra Dhanabhuti who was the son of Gosiputa Agaraju and grandson of king *(rajan)* Gargiputra Visvadeva as having constructed the said gateway.[3] On the evidence of brahminical *gotra* names the persons would appear to be high brahmins for whom a description of the paternal ancestry would have been more appropriate.

Another interesting example of a brahmin family publicising its maternal descent in preference to paternal ancestry refers to a brahmin, Asvibhuti, who was the son of a woman whose *gotra* was *Varaha* and from whom Saka king Usavadata purchased a field by paying 4000 *karsapanas*[4]. The term *Varahi* is more relevant as a totemic clan-name than as a brahminical *gotra*-name. Other examples of men publicising the mother's ancestry in preference to the father's pedigree include a Maharathi who was a Kosikiputra,[5] a Mahabhoja who was a Kautsiputra,[6] a royal physician who was a Vatsiputra,[7] and another Maharathi who was a Gotiputra.[8]

The frequent use of certain recognised brahmin *gotras* such as Kautsa, Vatsa and Kausika might give the impression that these families were genuine brahmin families. However, the practice of publicising the mother's ancestry as well as the presence of certain tribal clan names unknown to the accepted brahminical lists of *gotra* and *pravara* seems to suggest that the families were unbrahminical in origin and that, in the course of their association with brahmin patriarchal groups, they were lured by the prospects of a higher brahminical status to employ a brahmin chaplain for whom it was customary to lend his clan-name to his valued clients.[9] The tribal matrilocal origin of various literate families becomes clear from a few examples. An Amaravati inscription refers to a Buddhist Upasaka who is described as Gomdiputa[10] or the son of a Gond woman. Gund or Gonda does not figure in any of the brahminical *gotra* catalogues, it is fairly likely that the family originated from some matrilocal tribe and in keeping with tribal practice traced its descent from the mother in marked preference to the father who remains obscure in such examples. This is further substantiated by another record which mentions a Buddhist missionary, who was the teacher of all the Hinayana countries, as Kotiputa and Kasapagota. The patronym Kasapagota shows that the Buddhist monk was the son of a brahmin father who had married a woman of the tribal Kota family. The Allahabad pillar inscription refers to a Kota chieftain who was captured by Samudragupta.[11] That the Kota family was a petty ruling house is evident from the coins of this family found round about Delhi and eastern Punjab.[12]

The foregoing would suggest that during the early centuries of the Christian era and also a little earlier, it was common practice to trace the descent of a family in the maternal line. The examples would further illustrate that the practice, which constitutes a dominant feature of the matrilineal descent system, was fairly popular with all sections of population of both brahminical and non-brahminical origin.

The inscriptions of the early medieval period testify to the eagerness of tribal families and petty bureaucrats, who lived in intimate contact with the Sanskrit-educated patriarchal families to adopt paternal brahmin *gotra* and follow brahminical rituals and observances in an attempt to find a suitable place in the status-system of brahminical society.[13]

The ancestral data of different ruling houses would also confirm the process of cultural interaction between the Dravidian matriarchy and brahmin patriachy. For example, the Salankayana, and the Visnukundin, both of which were important brahmin dynasties, publicise in their records their paternal clan-name only, but the Satavahnas, the Kadambas, and the Calukyas, all of whom were of tribal descent, mention in their records both their paternal clan-name and maternal ancestry. Some of the later Pallavas also occasionally mentioned their mother's descent though the paternal clan-name Bharadvaja is uniformly recorded in all their inscriptions. The Valayur and Velurpalaiyam grants of the family refer to a Pallava ruler as Cutu-Pallava, meaning thereby that the donor king was born of the marriage of a Cutu girl with a Pallava prince.[14] Similarly, the Ganga king Anantavarman, who described himself as a *Codaganga*, was publicising the fact that he was born of the union of Ganga king Devendravarman and Cola princess Rajasundari.[15]

The Basavi System

A few early instances of the dedication of daughters as *basavi* may be considered in this connection.

In 800 AD, one Aridara Polayamma of the village Mayile dedicated a virgin to a local temple along with eight *matters* of land, 1000 coins and a swing for the use of the deity.[16] In 974 AD, the blacksmith Bidi dedicated two girls to another temple in Hulgund taluk of the Shimoga district.[17] While the donation of property emphasizes the donor's desire to obtain religious merit and social recognition, the dedication of daughters might reflect the urge to prevent transfer of family property by way of dowry which the parents would have to give along with the daughter without any chance to recompense in the absence of a male heir in the family. The desire to prevent the family property from going to an outsider often induced a couple to ritually dedicate their daughter to a divine husband, the purpose being to convert her into a *basavi,* who will then be entitled to inherit the family property and stay with her parents even though married to an `outsider'.

Sometimes, the absence of a male heir in the family prompted the couple to convert daughters into *basavis* and procure through her a male heir for the family. Since the daughter is already a *basavi* by virtue of her dedication to a temple, her marriage to a 'real outsider' would not in any way compel her to leave her parents' house and go over to her husband's family. This seems to be very well illustrated by a Karnataka inscription of the ninth century. According to this record, Kadacci, who had been dedicated as *basavi* by her father, took a mate of her own selection and tried to procure a male issue for the family of her father.[18] Unfortunately, she had a daughter named Ayacabbe. Ayacabbe, in her turn, renewed the attempt but gave birth to a daughter, Kalingabbe. Kalingabbe's marriage to one, Pallaraki, again resulted in the birth of a daughter, also named Kalingabbe. The second Kalingabbe ultimately gave birth to a son whose name was Parakayya. The inscription which stops with Parakayya is meaningful inasmuch as it suggests that Mayadamarasa's lineage was continued by temporarily reverting to the *marumakkhatthayyam* system which resulted in the birth of Parakayya. The inscription does not name any of the husbands or mates of the women who are named. This is in keeping with the present insignificance of a male partner in the *basavi* system. Kalingabbe I's husband is mentioned as a token of gratitude, because it was his daughter who succeeded in procuring a male issue and thereby helped the family to revert back to the system of descent-through-son *(makkathayyam)*.

The record, which describes Parakayya as one belonging to lawful descent (*dharma santati*), also anticipates the present position of the children of a *basavi,* who do not suffer from any social stigma. The practice of dedicating a girl to some deity in the absence of a male heir is very much prevalent among certain castes in the peninsula. Hutton observes that in Bellary and its neighbourhood, in the absence of a male heir, a daughter is offered to the temple.[19] After her dedication she becomes by established custom the heir of her parents' property and can perform funeral rites as if she were a son. She takes to herself a man of her own choice, of any equal or higher caste, but continues to live in her father's house and her children take his (mother's father) name and belong to his family and not to their father's.[20] If she has a son, he inherits the property and the question of dedicating a daughter as *basavi* does not arise. But, if she has a daughter then again this daughter becomes a *basavi* and renews the attempt to procure a son for the family.[21] The women of the Madiga caste are often made *basavis* or dedicated as *devadasis*. In the case of the left hand Kaikkolan caste, which observes temporary reversion to the *marumakkathayam*, the women often belong to the right hand faction.

But, while the lack of a male heir led some families to temporarily revert to the descent-through-daughter system, there were many others which practised it although male issues were not wanting. A record of the eighth century mentions a woman who after saluting her preceptor, her elder brother and blessing her son, announced that "if the inheritor be without a husband, or having a husband, has all daughters,—if they obtain husbands and marry, it is not a violation of this agreement.[22] Even if the daughter, after her marriage gave birth to only daughters, the property which she inherited from her mother was to remain hers. In other words, absence of a male heir would not deprive her of her right to property. On the other hand, her female issues were entitled, in their turn, to inherit their mother's property, even if they obtained husbands. Much more direct evidence comes from a few south Karnataka inscriptions of the twelfth-thirteenth centuries. A Virasaiva document of 1251 from the Maddur *taluk* refers to the distribution of as many as 34 shares of cultivable land among the peasant and lay followers *(bhaktas)* of the sect who included several women. The concluding part of the inscription states that these 34 *vrttis* will descend from the holders to their daughters *(hemnu)*, wives (*hemdiru)* and children of maid servants *(tottina makkalu)* who are followers of the sect *(bhaktas)*[23]. Significantly, many of the shares were received by male *bhaktas* but in this case inheritance was also to follow the female line of descent. The mention of maidservants and children is also meaningful inasmuch as it seeks to forestall any likelihood of inheritance reverting to a male line in the absence of a female incumbent in the women's family.

The Coorg inscription of 1297, which is a re-issue of an earlier regulation promulgated by a feudal lord of the *mahamandalesvara* rank, furnishes an almost identical instance.[24] The record states that in Kundur the property of females will belong to a female *(hemninge)*, to female children *(hemnu makkalinge)* and children of the female slaves *(totina makkalinge)*.[25] The chartered promulgation of the *marumakkatayam* law seems to have been necessary to protect those families which practised the matrilineal descent but were threatened by the possibility of male members claiming entitlement to ancestral property in the fashion of dominant patrilineal families around them.

Aliya Santana Rule

The practice of the *aliya santana* law or descent through the sister's son, which is reminiscent of the maternal uncle's influence in a matriarchal family, is also illustrated by the inscriptions of the early medieval period. Earlier, the prevalence of the custom is confirmed by the southern law-givers. Baudhayana mentions that a southerner is delighted to take the hand of maternal cousin[26]. Marriage with the *mutula-kanya* is also mentioned by the early Tamil classic, the *Manimekhalai*.[27] Inscriptions show that the *aliya santana* was fairly popular even among the brahmin families of Karnataka and Andhra. The grants of land or village by persons, who themselves received such charity from some king, to their sister's son would illustrate that the *aliya santana* law which was a survival of the Dravidian matriliny and was practised by members of the literate society including some high brahmins. Gandanarayana, who was a feudatory of the eastern Calukya king Badapa and who received a village from the king, regranted it to Candana, the son of his own sister.[28] Two brahmin brothers Svamiyasas and Visnuyasas, who received a village from Jayasimhavallabha, also of the eastern Calukya house, donated a ninth portion to their own sister's son Visnusarman; Visnusarman belonged to the Gavisni *gotra* and was a student of Bahvrca *sakha*, and his maternal uncles belonged to the Vatsa *gotra* and were students of the Chandogya *carana*.[29] The law of *aliya santana* became more popular among certain castes in later medieval times.

Cross-Cousin Marriage

The transformation of the Dravidian social order from a matrilocal to a patrilocal descent-system was characterised by the persistence of the matrifocal marriage and marital traditions. Marriage between cross-cousins and the practice of *aliya-santana*, both of which continued into the historical period, illustrate the process fairly well.

Baudhayana, who wrote about the fourth century B.C. and who is considered to be a South Indian legal writer includes in his list of typically South Indian practices both the types of cross-cousin marriage.[30] Marriage with *matula-kanya* is also mentioned in the *Manimekalai*, an early Tamil work.[31] But Manu holds a different view. He states that the daughter of maternal uncle, or maternal aunt or paternal aunt is a *sapinda* or having the same blood or the same physical origin.[32] Marriage with any one of them is a sin which can be expiated only by performing the *candrayana* rite. Haradatta, commenting on *Apastamba*, gives a similar opinion[33]. Some other medieval commentators also denounced the custom, but others held it to be legal. Medhatithi, commenting on Manu, states that the practice obtained in some parts of the country.[34] Apararka also criticises it.[35] All this would suggest that the cross-cousin marriage was widely practised in different parts of South India despite its condemnation in the traditional legal writings which represent brahminical theories of patriarchal dominance. Some later authors, however, tried to justify the practice by quoting from Vedic literature. The *Smrticandrika* and the *Parasaramadhaviya*, for example, argue that although Manu and other legal authors condemned the practice, it could be justified on the strength of a passage in the *Satapatha Brahmana* which refers to marriage with the daughter of maternal uncle or paternal aunt.[36]

Literary evidence of a secular nature also bears out that cross-cousin marriage was fairly popular in different parts of South India from very early times. The *Manimekhalai* mentions a secret affair between Dharmadatta, a wealthy merchant and his meternal uncle's daughter Visakai. Both proposed to marry each other in the *gandharva* style (love marriage).[37] The *Varangacarita* shows that cross-cousin marriages, particularly marriage with the maternal uncle's daughter, was a popular custom in the lower Deccan. It refers to the minister Anantasena, who in the course of deliberations regarding Varanga's marriage suggested that marriage should be settled with Sunanda, the daughter of king Devasena who was the prince's maternal uncle. The minister argued that marriage with the daughter of maternal uncle was a well accepted practice.[38] Although Varanga's marriage was settled with another princess, the prince wedded his maternal uncle's daughter during his sojourn in his maternal uncle's kingdom.[39] This marriage was not an accident because Varanga, who accepted Sunanda's hand in marriage, knew well his mother's brother. The maternal uncle himself disclosed later that he knew the real identity of his sister's son from the very beginning. Probably, such marriages were considered to be a privilege by either party. For

Devasena, who had already married one of his daughters to Varanga, was eager to give his other daughters as well to his son-in-law in marriage.[40] When Varanga replied that he was quite happy with Sunanda, the maternal uncle pressed him to accept at least one more of his daughters as wife; the prince ultimately agreed to the proposal. The second wife of Varanga was princess Manorama who, from the day she saw Varanga, fell in deep love with him. She even sent her companion to Varanga to convey to him her feelings. Falling in love or a secret affair with the son of paternal aunt was not immodest behaviour and could materialise in a happy marriage.[41] Marriage with the *matula kanya* has been mentioned approvingly in the Adipurana, a Jain text brought out in the eighth century by a Digambara monk of Karnataka.[42]

Even today certain castes consider it a privilege to marry the daughter of a maternal uncle with the son of a paternal aunt. In some cases such marriages are compulsory. Some castes like the Baiga, Agariya, etc., consider the marriage of a daughter with her mother's brother's son as "giving back the milk".[43]

Kumarilabhatta, the great philosopher who lived in Andhra Pradesh and who was a contemporary of Sankaracharya, corroborates the custom of cross-cousin marriages. In his *Tantravarttika,* Kumarila states that a southerner is generally pleased in taking the daughter of his maternal uncle in wedlock.[44]

Some Negarjunakonda inscriptions of the third century refer to marriage of Siri Virapurisadata with his paternal aunt's daughter.[45] Several Rastrakuta inscriptions indicate the popularity of cross-cousin marriages. One of the records of the dynasty mentions, for instance, the marriage of Jagadrudra, son of Rastrakuta king Krsna, with the two daughters of his mother's brother, king Sankaragana of the Kalacuri dynasty.[46] Amoghavarsa, who was the great grandson of Kalacuri king Kokkala I thorough his mother Govindamba, married princess Kandakadevi, daughter of the Cedi king Yuvaraja[47]. The Rastrakuta king Indra married Divijamba, the great-grand-daughter of Kokkala I.[48]

Inscriptions which speak of special favours bestowed upon a maternal aunt's son or sister also indicate the popularity of the custom. Gandanarayana was the son of Nayamamba and Nayamamba's uterine younger sister was Samakamba. Gandanarayana, who received a village from the eastern Calukya king Badapa, re-granted it as a freehold to Candana who was the son of his mother's sister.[49] Similarly Bhima I, who drank the milk of his mother Nagipoti together with Gamakamba, who was Nagipoti's own daughter, was the maternal uncle of Mahakala the son of Gamakamba. Bhima I not only appointed his sister's son as a general in his army but also granted to him a village as a freehold.[50] Another inscription of 659 refers to the grant of a village to two brahmin brothers who are reported to have apportioned a ninth portion of the donated village for the benefit of their sister's son.[51] The grant of villages or portions of villages by kings and private individuals to the sister's son or the son of a maternal aunt indicates that the donees happened to be the sons-in-law of their maternal uncle or maternal aunt.

Even today the sister's son enjoys a privileged position vis-a-vis the maternal uncle's daughter. Among the Komatis brother's daughter is claimed by the sister as a matter of right[52]. When a man has no daughter to give in marriage, he has to procure one for his sister's son.[53] Among the Koracas, it is a binding custom that the first two daughters of a woman must be given at a reduced bride price to her brother either to be married to himself or to his son.[54] The Todas of Nilgiris and the Kodagu aristocrats of the Coorg region[55] practise both the forms of cross-cousin marriage while the Kallars of Tamil Nadu, certain Reddis of Andhra Pradesh, the Kathi, the Ahir, the Gadhave Chara and the Garasia castes marry their maternal uncle's daughter.[56] This very unbrahminical custom of cross-cousin marriage crept even into certain sections of the Brahmins. Thus the Rigvedi Desastha Brahmins and the Havig Brahmins of Karnataka accept the daughter of maternal uncle in marriage. The Ayyar Brahmins of Tamil Nadu also deserve mention in this connection.

Women in Political Life

The dislike shown by Brahmin theorists in respect of female participation in political life can be judged from the *Nitivakyamrta* of Somadeva, a tenth century writer on polity and a distinguished member of the Rastrakuta court at Manyakheta. The text states that the son, the brother, the step-brother, and the uncle of a deceased king can succeed to the throne in order of preference.[57] If none of them is available, then any male member of the dead king's family or, in his absence, the son of the daughter of the king is entitled to succeed.[58] But if these heirs are wanting then either a suitable person can be elected to the royal office, or a person who usurps the throne can be acknowledged as a legitimate successor[59]. Notable omissions in this list of successors include all female kin of the deceased king which indicates that they had no right to sit on the royal throne under any circumstances. The list of preferences is clearly dictated by the norms of political behaviour in a regimented patrifocal society.

Notwithstanding, however, the prescriptions of Somadeva which was more attuned to tradition than to reality, at least in respect of South Indian women of princely families ruled with full authority during the minority of their sons and also when a male successor was not available. Sovereignty of these women rulers is apparent from the fact that they freely disposed of crown property, landed or otherwise. The Satvahana queen, Naganika, ruled during the minority of her son Vedisri.[60] Prabhavatigupta of the Vakataka family wielded sovereign power during the minority of her son Divakarasena.[61] The Poona charter issued during her reign compares with another charter issued 100 years later; the former was issued by the queen without any reference to her minor son, but in the latter inscription the queen-mother made certain grants after specific reference to her son who had assumed power.[62]

In the seventh century, Vijayamahadevi, the widow of Candraditya of the eastern Calukya dynasty, succeeded to the throne following the death of her husband.[63] Vijayamahadevi, who was the crowned queen *(mahisi)* of the deceased Candraditya, is described as Vijayabhattarika; the suffix *bhattarika* probably indicates rulership of the kingdom, just as *bhattaraka* does in the case of sovereign kings. In the fifth year of her reign she issued in her own right a charter registering the grant of certain fields to a brahmin; the donation was made for obtaining religious merit. Divabbarasi, a Kadamba princess, dedicated village as an *agrahara* in the sacred memory of her husband.[64] She had succeeded to the throne on the death of her husband and continued to rule the kingdom as a sovereign till her minor son came of age and assumed regal power. The record adds that the queen mother looked forward to the day when her minor son would get the throne. During her reign she also granted Yelanagar as a freehold estate to the temple of Siva which she had caused to be built; to this temple she gave a `sin-destroying bell'.

The practice of elevating the widow of a deceased king to the position of a sovereign ruler is noticed in later inscriptional records also. For example, Tribhuvana Mahadevi of the Kara dyansty of Orissa is stated to have been requested by the feudatories to accept the sovereignty which had come to her by way of succession upon the death of her husband.[65] To persuade her into accepting rulership of the kingdom, they cited the example of Devi Gosvamini of the same Kara dynasty who had agreed to administer the kingdom under similar circumstances. Thereupon, the widowed queen 'ascended the throne like Katyayani.' Dandi Mahadevi[66] and her step-mother Vakula Mahadevi[67], both of the Kara family, exercised sovereignty on different occasions; the latter granted a village to one Mihadhica. The imperial Kakatiya dynasty of Andhra Pradesh also produced women rulers of note.

The widowed queens came to power mostly in emergent situations and prevented the throne from being usurped. In other regions where women were excluded from the line of succession, the throne was usurped giving rise to political instability.

Women also shared the responsibility of administration with their husbands. An early grant indicates joint rulership of Gautamiputra Satkarni and his queen, who jointly issued an order regarding gift of a plot of land to some Buddhist monks.[68] In the early medieval period joint rulership assumed two forms. In one type, the wives of the feudal lords ruled over the entire principality together with their husbands. In the other type, wives or relatives of the feudal chiefs were appointed governors of varying territorial units. The first type included the Kadamba chieftain Harikesaridеva, who was a feudatory of the Calukya king Somesvara I and who ruled over the Banavasi 12000 province together with his wife Lacchaladevi.[69] Under the second category came Kancikabbe, the queen of the Ganga king Sripurusa. According to a record of 767 Sripurusa himself ruled over the kingdom, and his queen governed Agali.[70] A Challakere taluk inscription of 815 shows that Paramesvara Pallavadi ruled Nolambalige 1000 and Nirggundanad 300, and his wife Gavaganabbe ruled Madarikal.[71] In a grant of 975 Bhujjabbarasi, mother of Butayya, the reigning Ganga king, is described as ruling the village Perbal or modern Kebbal.[72] Akkadevi, the sister of the Calukya king Vikramaditya V, is spoken of in a record of 1010 as the governor of Kisukad 70.[73] Similarly, Ankabbarasi, the wife of Ganga king Marasimha II, is referred to in a charter of 971 as administering Pullungur or modern Hulgur.[74] In 900 a Sira taluk inscription tells us of the four women of a royal family as ruling over four different principalities.[75]

Women, who were called upon to administer territories of varying size appear to have been already familiar with the tasks of territorial administration. The training might have been a part of formal education although works on polity prescribe such training for male heirs only. Kadambamahadevi, the queen consort of Pulakesi II is depicted as a woman versed in political wisdom, *naya*.[76] Lacchaladevi, who is described as adept in all the arts, possessed, in addition to text-book knowledge, certain qualifications for rulership. Eloquent and discerning, the lady is described as delighting the whole court.[77] Obviously she took a prominent part in discussions with the courtiers. An inscription tells us that Jakkiyabbe, who was in charge of the Nagarakhanda 70 sub-division, was skilled in the art of good government and gave adequate protection to the people of her district.[78]

Some women, who appear to have been powerful feudatories, administered large territories almost independently of the king. They granted state lands to priests and temples, making a nominal reference to the overlord. Akkadevi who acted as the governor of Kisukad 70 granted in 1058 a charter to god Akkesvara and the 1000 members of his temple.[79] Kancikabbe, another feudatory of the western Calukya kings, granted 5000 kammas for the supply of food to the ascetics of the temple of Suvarnaksi.[80] Similarly, the four women who were administering four different areas, made grants of land in their respective territories for the benefit of a Jaina temple.[81] One of the four women was Bijjamadevi, the governor of Baragur, who gave 12 *kandugas*; similarly, Paramamahadevi, who was ruling over Dharmmavolal, gave 12 *kandugas;* Akkabbe, who was ruling over Siyavur, gave 8 *kandugas;* and Dombabbe who was administering Tailokvolal, gave 6 *kandugas* of land.

Women made their mark in the sphere of local administration too. Inscriptions refer to them as holding the offices of the district headman and village headman. Some even functioned as secretaries in the state departments while others served as advisers to the local officers. A record of 902 refers to the wife of one Bittayya who held the office of the headman of the village Bharangiyur.[82] Another record of 1055 mentions Candiyabbe as *gavundi*, and Jakkiyabbe as her *mantraki*, counsellor.[83] A charter issued by Shri Ranaka Jayavarmadeva refers to Trikalingamahadevi, probably the wife of the king, as registering the deed of donation.[84] Since the composer and the engraver of the charter are separately mentioned, the queen probably served as the secretary of the state department, and as such entered the deed of donation in the records of the government.

Proprietary Rights of Women

Though the male-dominated brahminical society discouraged matriachal institutions it could not altogether eliminate these. This might help us to explain large degree of difference which existed between a northern woman whose right to property and spheres of social participation were constantly circumscribed in favour of men and a southern woman who inherited, administered and bequethed property and public offices alike, notwithstanding the consistent denial of any such rights by the brahmana law-givers.

The earliest legal opinions, as expressed by Gautama, Vasistha and Baudhayana, denied proprietary rights to women, and regarded them as dependent upon the father in childhood, upon the husband in youth, and upon the son in old age.[85] Manu and Narada also hold similar views.[86] Sabara, who was of a later date than Narada, however, remarks in his commentary on the *Purva Mimamsa Sutra* of Jaimini, that a woman who desires to perform a vedic sacrifice should set aside the injunctions of the *Smrti* and possess herself of wealth.[87] The commentator who wanted to ameliorate the condition of women, prescribed that the wife is the rightful owner of *parinaya* or the property received by her at the time of marriage.[88] She is also stated to be the owner of what is acquired by the husband.[89] Sabara's views partly conform to the early juridical thinking on the subject. For, Vishnu, Yajnavalkya and Brhaspati, the three early *smrti* writers recognise the right of a sonless widow to inherit the property of her deceased husband.[90] Later, on the attitude seems to have become much more rigid. For example, Medhatithi, a ninth-century commentator of the *Manusmrti* takes a hard look at woman when he states commenting on a passage that whatever the wife acquires belongs to the husband[91]. He also adds that the wife is not to inherit the property of her dead husband.[92] By comparison, some of the southern law-givers show a much more liberal attitude in allowing property rights to widows. The *Mitaksara*, an eleventh century commentary on the *Yajnavalkyasmrti* by a distinguished South Indian law-giver Vijnanesvara states that a virtuous widow is entitled to inherit the property of her sonless husband.[93] Notwithstanding small variations the consensus of legal writers was not in favour of allowing any substantive property-rights either to the wife or to the widow.

Judging from the evidence of inscriptions, which we have already discussed, it would appear that the restrictive rulings of legal writers, most of whom were North Indian brahmins, did not find any slavish acceptance among South Indian people. On the contrary, the permissiveness allowed to women in matters of property rights influenced the thinking of several writers who cared to take particular notice of the South Indian customs. As early as the fifth century B.C., Yaska commenting on the *Nirukta,* states that in the southern countries the widow of a sonless husband was entitled to inherit the entire property of her husband.[94] In the sixth century, AD Varahmihira advocates the possession of wealth by women.[95] What is more important, inscriptions speak of women who owned property and freely disposed of it.

Women of the princely families owned and managed property in their own right as is evident from the example of the Satavahana queen Naganika, who spent royal resources on the performance of vedic rituals.[96] Similarly Queen Vijayamahadevi of the eastern Calukya dynasty gave away a few plots of land to a brahmin.[97] Gifts of villages as freehold estates to priests and temple also indicate the right of princely women to property.[98] Examples of priestly women receiving landed property in donation, either jointly or singly, also point in the same direction. In 688 the village Navatula in the Ganjam district of Orissa was granted jointly to a brahmin woman Pillikasvamini and her brother Pillasarma as a freehold estate.[99] Similarly, the 12 *nivartanas* of land granted to a brahmin woman for the performance of the *prajapatya* rite, was as much the property of the priestess as the 25 *nivartanas* of land donated to priest Aditya of the Kamika *gotra* for the same purpose.[100]

Cases are also on record to show that public offices and personal estates could be inherited and administered by the wife and the daughter in succession. An inscription of the Shikarpur taluk of Karnataka refers to the wife of a district headman *(nadgavunda)* who succeeded to the office of her deceased husband, and enjoyed privileges and emoluments which the office carried with it.[101] The incumbent also inherited the estate of her late husband. Later, the daughter of the widow succeeded both to the office and the estate which her mother had inherited earlier. Another woman who had lost both her husband and son and was living with the four sons of her widowed younger sister, must have inherited the entire property of her deceased husband, a man of some influence in the government, so as to be able to spend profusely on works of public welfare and religious merit.[102]

The Jain community of the lower Deccan also treated its nuns and priestesses at par with the monks and priests. Nuns served as preceptresses of householders, both men and women; they were also acknowledged as preceptresses by monks. Priestesses managed the property of the temples or the monasteries. The widow of the priest Srutakirtti was appointed the manager of the estate of a Jain temple at Halsi and a village was granted to her as a freehold. She was entrusted with the arrangement of important festivals of god Jinendra as also the feeding of Jain monks.[103] Huliyabbajjike of the Surastha Gana monastic order was yet another Jain nun who served as the priestess of a Jain temple. She received the gift of a village in 1071 from Baladevayya, the *herisandhivigrahika* for the upkeep of the temple of which she was the superintending priestess.[104]

At present, the matrilocal and matrilineal family is found among certain tribes and among the sudras, who live in peripheral contact with brahminical society but are seldom recognised as party of it. The present tension between the brahmins and sudra communities of Tamil Nadu, where status displacement following the introduction of patriarchal instiutions was greater than in other parts of the peninsula, can perhaps be related to this historical phenomenon. However, with the progressive alienation of landed property, administrative authority and trade rights to the brahminical classes the roots of brahmin patriliny struck ever deeper.

Abbreviations

ASWI - *Archaeological Survey of Western India.*
BK - *Book.*
EC - *Epigraphia Carnatica.*
EI - *Epigraphia Indica.*
IA - *Indian Antiquary.*
IC - *India Culture.*
IHQ - *Indian Historical Quarterly.*
JBORS - *Journal of Bihar and Orissa Research Society.*
JRASB - *Journal of the Royal Asiatic Society of Bengal.*

References

1. Edgar Thurston, *The Castes and Tribes of Southern India, Volume III.*
2. *EI*, 22, cf. Iksvaku inscriptions.
3. Luder's list of Brahmi inscriptions, no. 687 cited in *EI*, 22, no. 8, p. 35
4. *Archaeological Survey of Western India* (henceforth *ASWI*) Vol. II, p. 9 a, *Brahmanasya Varahiputrasya Asvibhutisu.*
5. *ASWI*, vol. 4, p. 8, Kautsi is derived from Kutsa *gotra.*
6. *Ibid*, p. 83.
7. *Ibid*, p. 84; the relevant passage has *rajavejasa Vacctuputasa Magila danam.* Magila was a royal physician.
8. *Ibid*, p. 90.
9. The process has been illustrated in two different essays titled "Gotra and Social Mobility in the Deccan", and "Clan-name and Social Mobility in the Deccan", *infra.*
10. *Luders' List of Brahmi Inscriptions*, Inscription No. 1271.
11. Luders' List of Brahmi Inscriptions, Inscription No. 158.
12. *EI*, 22, no. 8, p. 35
13. See R. N. Nandi, "Gotra and Social Mobility in the Deccan", *Proceedings of the Indian History Congress*, (32nd session Jabalpur), Delhi, 1972; also "Clan-name and Social Mobility in the Deccan", *Proceedings of the Indian History Congress*, (33rd Session, Muzaffarpur), Delhi, 1973, pp.111-118. The boasts of genuine noble ancestry are also more frequent in southern epigraphic recods.
14. *JRASB*, 8. p. 3
15. *Ibid*, 12, p. 112.
16. *EC*. 8, Sb. 9.
17. *EC*, 7, Hl. 64.
18. *EC*, 11, Dg. 17.
19. J.H. Hutton, *Caste in India*, p. 162 f.
20. *Ibid.*
21. *Ibid.*
22. *EC*, 11, Dawangere 17.
23. *Annual Report of the Mysore Archaeological Department* (for the year 1933), no. 40, p. 47 ff.
24. *EC*, IX, Coorg 59, AD 1297.
25. *Ibid.*
26. *Baudhayana Dharma Sutra*, I, 19-26 cited in P.V. Kane, *Dharmasastra Ka Itihasa*, vol. 1, p. 28.
27. *Manimekhalai*, bk. XXII.
28. *EI*, 19. no. 24, p. 137 f.
29. *EI*, 31, no. 20 B, p. 133 ff.

30. *Baudhayana Dharma Sutra,* 1.19-26, cited in Kane, *op.cit.,* vol. 1, p. 280.
31. *Manimekhalai,* BK. XXII, p. 169.
32. *Manusmriti,* 11. 172-173, cited in Kane, *op. cit.,* vol. 1, p. 280.
33. *Haradatta on Apastamba Dharma Sutra,* 2.5.11.6, cited in Kane, *op. cit.*
34. Medhatithi on *Manusmrti,* 2.18, cited in Kane, *op. cit.*
35. Aparacka, pp. 82-84, cited in Kane, *op. cit.*
36. *Smrticandrika,* pt. 1, pp. 70-74 and *Parasaramadhaviya,* 1.2, p. 63 ff, cited in Kane, *op. cit.,* vol. 1, p. 280.
37. Manimekhalai, 22.169.
38. *Vaivahiki nah kulasantatih sa sthira ca maitri nanu matulatvat tasmadaham bhogyataya tayasu sunandayecchami vivahakama, Varangacarita,* ch. 2, v. 20.
39. *Varangacarita,* ch. 19, vv. 9-13.
40. *Ibid,* ch. 20, v. 39.
41. In the early medieval period cross-cousin marriage was prevalent in western India as is evident from the *Upamitibhavaprapuncakaha,* pp. 242, 253, 281, 568 (of the Bombay edition) cited in B. N. Sharma, *Social Life in Northern India,* p.11.
42. *Adipurana* (ed. Pannalal Jain).
43. Hutton, *op. cit.,* p. 62.
44. IC, 5, p. 6.
45. Cf. Genealogical Table of the Iksvakus in D.C. Sircar, *The Successors of the Satavahanas,* p. 16.
46. Cf. B. Sheshgiri Rao, *Studies in South Indian Jainism,* p. 83 (1922).
47. *Ibid.*
48. *Ibid.*
49. *EI,* 19, no. 24, p. 137, ff.
50. *EI,* 5, p. 131 ff.
51. *EI,* 31, no. 20B, p. 133 ff.
52. *Mysore Gazetteer,* 1, (Descriptive), p. 182.
53. *Ibid.*
54. *Ibid.*
55. Iravati Karve, *Kinship Organization in India,* p. 249.
56. *Ibid,* pp. 191, 194
57. P.V. Kane, *Dharmasastra Ka Itihasa* (in Hindi) vol. 2, p. 596.
58. *Ibid.*
59. *Ibid.*
60. *BC* Law Volume, pt. 1, p. 159 (1945)
61. *EI,* 15, p.41 cited in *EI,* 22, no. 17, p. 98 ff.

62. *JRASB*, vol. 20, p. 58
63. *IA*, no. 53, p. 163 ff.
64. EC, 10, Mulbagal 38, p. 78, A.D. 890.
65. *EI*, 22, no. 17, p. 98 ff.
66. *JBORS*, vol, 2, p. 422 f.
67. *EI*, 36, no. 38, p. 307 ff.
68. *EI*, 22, no. 17, p. 98 ff.
69. *EI*, 13, no. 14, p. 168 ff., AD. 1055.
70. EC, 10, Mulbagal 80, p. 97.
71. EC, 11, CL. 33, p. 100.
72. *EI*, 4, no. 50, p. 350 ff., AD, 975.
73. *EI*, 15, no. 6, p. 76.
74. *EI*. 24, no. 12, p. 59 ff., AD. 971.
75. EC, 12, Sira 24.
76. *A.P. Government Museum Copper Plate Inscriptions*, vol. 1, p. 11 ff.
77. *EI*, 13, no. 14, ll. 20-23.
78. EC, 7, Sk. 219, p. 130 f.
79. Cf. EI, 15, no. 6, p. 76, AD. 1010 & , *EI* 15, no. 6(2), p. 83 AD. 1058.
80. *EI*, 16, no. 1, ll. 43-46.
81. EC, 12, *Sira* 24.
82. *Mysore Archaeological Report*, p. 38 (1911).
83. EC, 11, Cg. 30, 31, pp. 172-73.
84. *EI*, 23, no, 42 D, pp, 267-69.
85. P. V. Kane, *op. cit.*
86. *Manusmrti*, p. 185; 9.217; *Naradasmrti*, 24-26, cited in Kane, *op.cit.*, pp. 900-07.
87. *B.C. Law vol.*, *op.cit.*, p. 160.
88. *Ibid.*
89. *Ibid.*
90. Kane, *op.cit.*, p. 329.
91. *Ibid*, p. 906 ff.
92. *Ibid*, p. 908.
93. *Ibid.*
94. Kane, *op.cit.*, *vol.* 1, p. 329.
95. *Ibid*, p. 327.
96. *B.C. Law Volume*, *op.cit.*, p. 159.
97. *IA*, 7, no. 53, p. 163 ff.
98. *EI*, 4, no. 50, p. 350 ff.

99. *IHQ*, 20, p. 332, AD. 668
100. *IA*, 6, p. 88
101. *EC*, 7, *Sk*. 219, p. 130 f.
102. *EC*, 8, *Nr*. 35.
103. *IA*, 6, no. 22, i. 16, p. 12.
104. *Bombay Karnataka Inscriptions*, vol. 1. pt. 1, no. 111.

13

The Devadasi System in South India

*Awadh Kishore Prasad**

The practice of employing girls in temples is an old social evil. In some degree or other the practice was prevalent in almost all ancient and medieval societies. In India, the development of the practice in an institutional form is noticeable from the seventh century of the Christian era, by which time, the temple itself had emerged as a big employer and landlord.

Development of the *devadasi* system in South India may be understood in the background of the early medieval social and economic formation. This is necessary in view of the fact that the institution of *devadasis* was an integral part of the religious services in any temple, and that the temple itself was an essential part of the early medieval society and economy.

The period fifth-sixth centuries A.D. is said to mark the end of the ancient and beginning of the medieval phase in Indian history.[1] From this period, certain economic factors came in to play a decisive role in paving the way for a new social and political structure, based essentially on the land distribution system. During the early medieval period we notice the emergence of a feudal economic order, the most important feature of which was the system of large-scale land grants to persons of political, military and religious standing who were earlier paid salaries in cash.

* The author is Reader, Dept. of History, Patna University, Patna 800 005.

In South India the practice of land grants started during the period of the Satavahanas and gained currency under the Pallavas. It is from a Pallava inscription of the third-fourth centuries from Andhra Pradesh that we get the first instance of share croppers being transferred along with the land to the beneficiaries who were Brahmins.[2] By the fifth-sixth centuries land grants had become quite common.

Larger-scale transfer of lands to Brahmins, religious institutions and officers of the state, coincide with some other developments, such as the decline of trade and commerce, the disappearance of coins and the decay of urban centres.[3] All these ultimately led to the closed economy of the villages.[4] The situation proved favourable to the expansion of the temple system. Owing to the closed economy of villages, large-scale conversion of agricultural surplus into money was difficult. The surplus had, therefore, to be spent within the village or group of villages, and preferably on public works, e.g., irrigation channels, wells, tanks and places of public worship[5].

In the matter of building temples there arose a sense of competition among aristocrats and royal families for building large and magnificent structures.[6] The king or chieftain wanted to surpass his ancestors and other contemporary rulers in building temples. The Pallava king Mahendravarman I records his achievement in an inscription which says that he made the *ayatana* (home) for Brahma, Isvara and Visnu without the use of traditional material like bricks, timber, metal or mortar, and calls himself *Vicitracitta* (of a curious or inventive mind.)[7]

In Oriya sources it is recorded that Ganga king Narsimhadeva I, who built the majestic temple of Konark, aimed at building a temple which would outdo the great temple at Puri.[8] Numerous land-owning *samantas*, princes and kings of the period wanted to acquire *punya* (virtue) and fame by building temples and donating land and villages for their maintenance.[9] Inscriptions show that in villages and mofussil towns temple constructions were entirely financed by land revenue in kind.[10]

Another development, which coincides with large-scale land transfers, was the growth of the *Bhakti* cult, which ultimately led to further popularity of temple building activities. The *Bhakti* movement provided the opportunity to worshippers of all castes—whether he was a *vellala*,[11] *pulaiya*,[12] washerman,[13] or a *panar*,[14] to serve God and aspire for liberation. Service to gods could be rendered by constructing and renovating temples, cleaning their premises, making garlands of flowers, lighting temple lamps, singing praises of the deity and dancing for their entertainment[15]. All this presupposed the existence of temples and provided a natural impetus to the construction of temples on a large-scale.

The preachings of *nayanar* saints were also popularising the temple system to a large extent. Tirumular was a great champion of the temple cult. But advising people to follow right conduct *(carya)*[16] he encouraged them to build new temples; for *carya* consisted, besides other things, in the construction of temples and cleaning their premises.[17] Thus, all these factors combined to create a favourable atmosphere for the spread of temple-building activities on a large-scale.

Large-scale transfer of *devadana* lands to temples, supplemented by recurring levies in cash and kind, together with the periodic interests charged on fixed sums of money deposited with the temple, added to their wealth and magnificence.[18] The temple grew to become one of the wealthiest institutions of the time. On it depended a large number of persons belonging to different professions. Like a landlord, the temple engaged labour to cultivate its lands, and true to the nature of a landlord, it required a large body of attendants, from priests to dancing girls.[19] And accordingly, the abode of god now came to be called *Koyil,* which previously denoted kings's palace.[20] The term *koyil* referring to temple occurs for the first time in the Pallava inscription of Sirrambakkam belonging to the first year of Paramesvaravarman I (670-700) A.D.[21]

The growth in the economic resources of the temple led to a corresponding increase in the rituals and festivals of the temple.[22] The temple naturally required a large number of servants to manage its vast property and observe its rituals. The number of priests increased with the multiplication of rituals. In the Pallava period, when gifts in cash and kind were made to the temple on a limited scale, it was not possible for it to engage many persons for its maintenance. Nor was it necessary owing to the comparatively less complex routine and mode of worship of the deity.[23] During the reign of the Pallava king, Paramesvaravarman I the Siva temple at Kuram was managed by only four persons who offered daily worship to the deity, watered the *mandapam* every day and recited passages from the *Mahabharata.* But the number of the functionaries in the temple rapidly increased during the next century.[24] The *Muktesvara* temple at *Kanci* which was built by the Queen of

Nandivarman Pallavamalla (A.D. 731-96), had 54 employees, of whom as many as 32 were dancing girls.[25]

By the ninth century the process of worship and offerings had become more complex. The worship offered was sumptuous; scented water for bathing the deity, costly clothes and rich *naivedya* were provided for the god. Besides, some other items were included under the term *angabhoga*[26] and *rangabhoga*[27] of the deity for which provisions were made in several Rastrakuta and Cola records. Both these terms, *angabhoga* and *rangabhoga,* refer to dance and drama performed by the dancing women in the *range-mandapa* or *natya-mandapa* of the temple (which were built for that purpose) for the amusement and enjoyment of the deity.

Besides *angabhoga* and *rangabhoga,* the number of new items relating to the worship and celebrations in the temple went on increasing during tenth-eleventh centuries. The process can be illustrated by reference to the Pidariyar temple of Kolar. Between 966 and 1071 A.D. this temple received seven endowments from the Cola kings.[28] Villages were granted to it in 966, 1006, 1027, 1019, 1033, 1054 and 1071 A.D. The growing income was utilised to meet the expenses of the new cults and ritual services instituted in the temple.

It is interesting to observe that in 966 A.D. when the earliest grant to the temple was registered, no provision was made for dance services by dancing girls. But a hundred years later, in 1071 to be exact, donations were recorded for the provision of those services in the same Pidariyar temple. The inscription states that temple employed 24 dancing girls to perform dances in honour of the gods. A dancing master was also appointed for the proper training of these dancing girls. An inscription of the time of the Rastrakuta king Krsna III shows that temple dancing had become a hereditary occupation favouring thereby the formation of a *devadasi* caste in the future. The inscription also shows that by this time it had also become customary for dancing girls to dance in front of the deity during festive processions.

The number of priestly and non-priestly functionaries also increased with the multiplication of rituals. The earlier donations merely provided for the offerings of *naivedya* to the deity, without specifying the hours when these offerings were to be repeated. Sacrificial rites or other rites do not figure in these records.[29] All these appear later in the grants of the tenth-eleventh centuries. A charter of 1071 refers to such elaborate rituals as the *ardhayama*, the *navahoma*, the *madapattiyam* the *matirusandi*, the seven days festival of the god *Astradeva*, and the blood rites performed in honour of the goddess.[30] All categories of temple servants, including the twenty-four dancing girls and a dancing master, were allotted their allowance in rice and money in the year 1071.[31]

A secondary development which encouraged the *devadasi* system, is known as *a basavi*[32] system. In the absence of a male heir in the family some women temporarily reverted to the system of descent through daughter (the *marumakkathayyam* system). The daughter was dedicated to the temple as a *basavi* among whom descent was always in the female line. After dedication, she became the heir of her parent's property, and could perform their funeral rites as if she were a son. She could select a man of her own choice of any equal or higher caste.[33] And her son inherited the property of her father. But if she had a daughter, only the daughter would become *basavi* and renew the attempts procure a son for the family.

The process may be explained on the basis of epigraphic evidence. Thus, in 977, the blacksmith Bidi dedicated two young girls to a temple of the Shimoga district.[34] An inscription of 889 refers to the prostitute (*sule*) Kadacchi and her husband Mayadamarasa, who had only a daughter and no son. They dedicated their daughter Kadabbe to some god. Kadabbe, in her turn, took a mate of her choice and tried to procure a male issue for the family of her father. Unfortunately, she too had a daughter whose name was Kalingabbe. Kalingabbe accepted one Pallaraki as her mate and she too gave birth to a daughter who was also named Kalingabbe. The second Kalingabbe ultimately gave birth to a son, whose name was Parakayya. The inscription, which tops with Parakayya, is meaningful in asmuchas it suggests that Mayadamarasa's line age was continued by temporarily reverting to *marumakkathayyam* system, which resulted in the birth of Parakkayya. The inscription does not mention any of the husbands or mates of the several women who are named. This is in keeping with the insignificant position of a male partner in the *basavi* system.[35]

"Among the Holeyas" M.N. Srinivas reports, "if a girl remained unmarried from the absence of suitors, she was married to some tree and then dedicated to shrines (like those of Biligiriranga and Siddappaji). Then she could live with any man of her choice without loss of status, and was known as `*Kula maga*' son of the family, inherited the rights and privileges of a son, and discharged the son's duties by performing funeral ceremonies."[36]

The above evidence illustrates the tendency of certain families to temporarily reverting to the system of descent through daughters in the absence of a male heir in the family. And such families,[37] in their own way, and for their own purpose, gave succour to the development of the *devadasi* system.

A study of the epigraphic records shows that by the ninth-tenth centuries the practice of employing *devadasis* in temples had struck deep roots in different parts of India. The Tejpur copper plate inscription dated back to the ninth century, records the dedication of the dancing girls to a Siva temple there.[38] In the Surya temple of Multan Huen-tsang (seventh century) had watched several dancing girls in action.[39] The account of the Arab traveller Abu-Zeid al Hasan, who came to India in 867, states that *devadasis* earnings from prostitution went into the hands of the priests, and was used for defraying the expenses of the temple.[40] Alberuni, however, records (in the 11th century) that income from prostitution in temples used to be taken by the king for meeting the expenditure of the army.[41] It is well known that the famous temple of Somanatha, which Mahmud of Ghazni destroyed in the year 1026, had five hundred *devadasis,* who provided music before the deity all the day and night.[42]

The Rajarajesvara temple of Thanjavur, built by the Cola king Rajaraja I, in the first decade of 11th century had four hundred dancing girls, who were transferred to the great temple from different temple establishments of the Cola kingdom.[43] All the four hundred *devadasis* were provided with a separate house in the street running round the temple. The name of each *devadasi,* the house number allotted to her, and the street in which the house was situated, were all carefully engraved on the walls of the temple. In 930, a *devadasi* of the Jayabhimatali temple at Thanjavur made a gift of a piece of land to the Mahadeva temple at Tirukkarugavur.[44] A copper plate charter of 812, found at Kadba in the Tumkur district, speaks about the Kannaresvara temple, where the minds of citizens were enchanted by the dances of moon faced girls.[45] A Vatteluttu record of the second year of Pandya Maranjadaiyan (acc. A.D. 862) registers a gift on behalf of a *devaradiyal* (*devadasi*) of Tirunelveli.[46] The period between eleventh to thirteenth centuries is the climax of the *devadasi* system. During this period, inscriptions relating to *devadasis* are in sufficient number. Going by the number of inscriptions the decline of *devadasi* system is noticed from the fourteenth century. But the system was not completely wiped out of the peninsula. It became a part of the South Indian society and religion. During the Vijaynagar period also the *devadasis* continued to be patronised, which had been noticed and discussed by the Portugese travellers. With the decline of the Vijaynagar Empire the patronage given to the *devadasis* by the Vijaynagar rulers came to an end. However, the custom became integrated with the social and religious life of the people to such an extent that even without royal support it continued to flourish.

Provision was made for the regular training of dancing women in the temple. A number of epigraphs mention the dancing masters in the temple. The Thanjavur inscription of Rajaraja I shows that as many as 12 dancing masters were employed to keep the four hundred dancing women in proper training. Eight of these twelve received an annual salary of 200 *kalams* of paddy each, and the remaining four were given 150 *kalams* each. It is to be mentioned here that the *devadasis* were given 100 *kalams* of paddy each. This shows that the dancing masters enjoyed considerable respect. Dancing masters served in other temples also. A record of 1055, which mentions dancing girls of a temple, refers to a dancing master for whom 5 *mattars* of land was apportioned.[47] Another record of 1071 mentions that in the temple of Pidariyar in the Kolar district were 24 dancing girls and the dancing master.[48] While each dancing girl of the Pidariyar temple got 22.5 *kalams* paddy as their emoluments, the dancing master was allotted 37 *kalams*, I *tuni* and 1 *padakku* of paddy per year.

Some inscriptions from Andhra Pradesh and Tamil Nadu throw light on the corporate activities of the *devadasis*. It seems that the *devadasis* had formed their own associations and commanded considerable influence and confidence among the people. They had some say in the management of temple affairs. It is interesting to note that in Andhra Pradesh there were large settlements of *devadasis*. These settlements, which included 300 or even 500 *devadasis*, were centred at important temple towns such as Draksharama, Bhimavaram, Palakol, Srikakulam, Chebrolu and Velpur.[49] In several records these associations of *devadasis* are found to be administering the different temple endowments. They were entrusted with the responsibilities of the proper utilization of the endowments in accordance with the conditions and purposes specified by the donors. Thus, in 1119, an endowment of 6 *uttamagandamadas* was entrusted to three hundred *sanis (devadasis)* of Kommuru for maintaining perpetual lamp in the temple of *Agastivara*.[50] A Vaisya, named Kota Komisetti, entrusted 10 *rajaraja-madas* to the three hundred *sanis* of Ghantasala in the Krishna district. Here too the purpose was the same for maintaining a perpetual lamp in the Jaladhisvara temple of the place.[51]

In the course of time the *devadasis* grew in strength and status, and we find them constituting an integral part of the temple management. This is indicated by a number of inscriptions in which they were associated with the *sthanapatis* (local trustees of the temples) in managing the temple affairs. In 1141, dancing girl Proli-pava of the temple of Vasukiravi Somesvara at Duttika made a gift of 50 *inupayedlu* (sheep) for a perpetual lamp. The *sthanapati*, the three hundred *sanis* and the *nibandhakartas* (officers responsible) were enjoined to see that the gift was properly administered.[52] At Juttiga in the Tenali taluka of the Krishna district, one Annapasari obtained a *vritti* with the consent of the temple accountant, saiva brahmanas and the *sanist*.[53] In the year 1075 an agreement was reached between the *devaradiyar* and *niyayattar* (a high officer of the central government) of the temple that they would continue to conduct the celebration in the temple of the festival in honour of the *nayanar* Terualvar-Ulavar, whose image, with those of the other *nayanars*, had been removed to the Pillaiyar temple at Iruvidaikkali owing to bad times. They also agreed that they would reconstruct the gateway, the north wall and the carstand which had fallen down in cyclone.[54] A 13th century record from Kottamangalam in the Tiruchirapalli district registers a gift of some house site by the *tanattar* and the *devaradiyar* to one Aditta Devan, who had set up the images of the deities.[55]

Since *devadasis* were married to gods, theoretically they were gods' wives, and their intercourse with the mortals should have been forbidden. But, in actual practice there was no restriction on *devadasis* having affair with their human lovers. Very often these affairs appear to have gone unnoticed. Sometimes they got married and led settled family lives. Sometimes they married respectable persons including the princes and entered the palace as the kings's consort.

The *Rajatarangini* contains an interesting information.[56] Sahaja, a temple dancing girl of Kashmir, was the sweetheart of prince Harsadeva. Later, she started friendship with his brother, prince Utkarsa, whom she married and entered the palace. After twenty years of his rule, being dethroned by his brother Harsa, Utkarsa killed himself in the palace. At this stage prince Harsa, again tried to win her (Sahaja) back but she refused his offer and became a *sati*, for which she was highly praised.[57] Another such example the *Rajatarangini* mentions is that of Durlabhak Pratapaditya who married the girl of his choice when she was offered to a temple as a *devadasi*.[58] We have a similar story in the *Kathasritsagar*. Devasena, the king of Sravasti fell in love with Unmadini, the beautiful and charming wife of his General. When the trusted General came to know of it, he proposed that he would offer his wife to the temple as a *devadasi*, and the king would take her up from there without incurring any social stigma.[59] In Assam too, we learn, the two cousin sisters—*Phulesvari* and *Draupadit who happened to be devadasis* in the temple of Joydal— were taken in marriage by the king.[60]

In addition to the above references to *devadasis'* love affairs leading to their marriage with mortals, there is evidence to suggest that *devadasis* were no better than the ordinary courtesans doing their profession in streets. There is a story in the *Kuttanjmatam*. In the course of his visit to the Visvanatha temple at Kasi, the king of Devarastra had an occasion to witness the drama, *Ratnawali* in the temple in which the main role was played by Manjari, a dancing girl, attached to the Gambhiresvara temple. As was expected and planned, pleased with the performance, the king issued a charter containing the grant of a village. And in the night, he enjoyed the company of the *devadasi* in his bed chamber.[61]

There is a similar story in the *Rajatarangini*. Prince Jayapida of Kashmir, once went on a visit to the city of Pundravardhana in the territory of the Gauda king in modern Bengal. He went to witness a dance recital in the Kartikeya temple. When the recital was over, people went home, the dancing girl Kamala, who was an surpassed beauty, whose conversation was refined and wit subtle, taking the king by the hand, entered the bed chamber.[62]

The adulterous and amorous life of *devadasis* is depicted by foreign travellers also. Abu-Zaid states, 'She takes an apartment in this public place and spreads a curtain before her door and awaits the arrival of strangers, she prostitutes herself at a certain rate and delivers her gains into the hands of the priest to be disposed off for the use and support of the temple.[63]

Alberuni also confirms this, but he differs on the point of the disposal of the earnings. He records that the income from prostitution in temples used to be taken by the kings.[64] The fact that *devadasis'* earnings were collected by the state is also referred to by Abdullah Wassaf who wrote in the beginning of the fourteenth century.[65] Abbe

Dubois, who worked in the former Madras Presidency in 1892, make the following comment: "They are called *devadasis* (servants or slaves of the gods), but the public call them by the more vulgar name of prostitutes. And in fact they are bound by their profession to grant their favours, if such they be, to anybody demanding them in return for ready money. It appears that at first they were reserved exclusively for the enjoyment of the Brahmins."[66]

It is noteworthy that with the prevalance of the system of *devadasis* on a wide scale, opposition to the custom is also sometimes noticed. Alberuni took note of its prevalance and opposition to the custom. He reports that the Brahmins and priests were deadly opposed to the presence of dancing girls in the temple, but they could not succeed because of the kings who were bent upon perpetuating the practice.[67] Two inscriptions of identical nature from Soddadi and Nadol in Rajaputana lay down the order of the king Jojalladeva (11th century) with regard to the management of the festivals in the local temples. According to the order, when the festivals of any temple commenced, *devadasis* attached to all the temples of the place would come to attend the function with their *sulapalas* (keeper of the dancing girls). The king had envisaged some opposition to the arrangement, and so, enjoined upon the succeeding princes to see to it that the arrangement was not disturbed. The king had particularly instructed his successors to prevent ascetics, old persons and learned men from working against the arrangement.[68] On the basis of above evidence it has been remarked that the princes alone were responsible for the spread and continuation of the evil practice. To quote Altekar, "It is therefore clear that the opposition of the majority of the Brahmanas and puritan thinkers to the association of dancing girls with temples was so strong down to the tenth century that even kings were afraid that their arrangements might fail owing to the success of the puritanical crusade.[69] Dasgupta holds a similar opinion[70]. However, the above observations do not seem to be impartial. There are evidences that lead us to form different opinion.

The *Prabandhacintamani* narrates a story that the king Mulraja of Gujarat who was desirous of appointing a learned ascetic named Kanthadi as the Chief Priest of the Tripurusa temple built by him at Anhilwad Patan, his capital. The ascetic refused his requests. But one of his disciples could be persuaded to accept the priesthood provided the king everyday supplied him with eight *palas* of genuine saffron, four *palas* of musk and one *pala* of camphor for the rubbing and massaging of his body. Besides, thirty women or *varangana* with a white umbrella and a grant of land were also demanded.[71] The king agreed to fulfill all his conditions. The story in the *Kuttani-matam* narrated above itself reveals that the priests had planned to placate the king of Devarastra by showing him the sensuous dance drama the *Ratnawali* in which the main role would be played by the charming and beautiful dancing girl Manjari, and then he would enjoy her at night. They were successful in the mission, and got the grant of a village in return.[72]

In addition to these there are references that the *devadasi* system was supported and patronised by the Brahmins in purely Brahmin villages. An inscription[73] of 1112 from the Ittagi *agrahara* in the Dharwar district mentions that a Brahmin General of Chalukya Vikramaditya VI constructed a number of temples in his native home Ittagi and collected and brought *devadasis* who were 'very descen-dents of mind-born *(Kama)* and Rati and Rambha'. They were also provided with free accommodation. In this connection it is to be mentioned that the *agrahara* Ittagi consisted of the four hundred houses of learned Brahmins who are said to have been "skilled in scripture of the *Vedas*, the *Vedangas*, and the ancilliary sciences, in the six modes of logic and so on and so forth." General Mahadeva, who was also a Brahmin and belonged to the same village, was highly praised for his so-called pious deeds. There are several such examples.[74]

Going by the above, it is evident that the Brahmins, both priestly, and non-priestly sections, supported and encouraged the practice, and in no way were they less responsible for perpetuating it. In fact the ruling class and the priestly class depended on each other's support; and the vices connected with the institution of *devadasis* continued.

A significant aspect of the *devadasi* system was the permanent and hereditary nature of their work in the temple. Land or some times cash was set apart from different functions to be performed by them. Once a *devadasi* was appointed for a particular chore, such as dancing before God in the temple during the procession, festivals of waving fly-whisks, etc. not only did her post became permanent, but also the right to do the particular work assigned to her and the endowments set apart for that went to her permanently and hereditarily.

To illustrate the above point we may refer to the following epigraphs. An inscription from Tiruppulivanam in the Chingleput district mentions that the right of holding *camara* (fly-whisk) before a deity during the procession was presented to a *devadasi* and her descendants.[75] Similarly, a dancing girl from Simhachalam was conferred on a hereditary basis the right to wave *camara* before God during the car processions.[76] The record clearly specifies that the privilege will be enjoyed by her descendants also. In 1119, *devadasi* Nemmaluri Suray donated 6 *uttamandamadas*[77] for maintaining a perpetual lamp in the Agastivara temple of Kommuru. The work was entrusted to the 300 *sanis (devadasis)* of the place 'for ever and for ever'.[78] In 1171, Rajendra Coda Gonka made similar gifts of lands to dancing girls and *sthanapati* (local trustee) of the temple of Ramalingesvara at Sripuram in the Guntur district. The land was gifted to them 'till the sun and moon' (exist).[79] Each of the eight *devadasis* in the temple of Codesvara Mahadeva at Moparru was granted a piece of land measuring 1 *kha* and 10 *ma*, for the maintenance of perpetual lamp. The record clearly mentions that the donees would enjoy the land till the sun and moon.[80] In 1153, one Muppa Naga Nayaka endowed lands for the dancing girls and priests in lieu of their services in the temple of Ramisvara at Chunumuru. Here also the period of the land to be enjoyed by the donees is till the sun and moon.[81] There are several other examples of provision of the period 'till sun and moon' in the inscriptions.[82]

But the most significant record throwing light on the nature of appointment, functions and remuneration of *devadasi* is that described in the Thanjavur inscription. By the order of the Cola king Rajaraja I (A.D. 985-1014) *devadasis* from different temple establishments of the Cola kingdom were transferred to the Rajarajesvara temple at Thanjavur. Each of them was given house, free of cost, in the *tirumadaivilagam* (temple street), and by way of remuneration, was given one *veli* of land, the produce of which was calculated equal to 100 *kalams* of paddy[83].

Regarding appointments against casual vacancies, the following instruction of the king was engraved on the wall of the temple: "....Instead of those among these share-holders, who would die or emigrate, the nearest relations of such persons were to receive that allowance (*kani*) and to do the work. If the nearest relations were not qualified themselves, (they) were to select (other) qualified persons, to let these do the work, and to receive (the allowance). If there were no near relations the other incumbents of such appointments were to select qualified persons from those fit for such appointments, and the person selected was to receive the allowance".[84] The above passage makes it clear that the *devadasis* were appointed on a permanent and hereditary basis. Once appointed, they could not be disturbed or interferred with by the temple authorities. The above evidence suggests that land, in lieu of her services, was permanently made over to the *devadasi*, and the particular work, for which the land was given to her, had to be continued by her and her descendants. It was her responsibility and prerogative both. In the event of death or retirement from active service, her daughter, or any close female relative was entitled to do the particular work and receive the allowance set apart for that. So, it was natural that each *devadasi* would like to be associated with that function which fetched more income. The epigraphs suggest that *devadasis* made efforts to be associated with the work of dancing before God in the temple or during the procession festivals, singing or holding *camara*, etc.[85]

A natural corollary of the instruction contained in the Thanjavur inscription was that once a *devadasi* became associated with the temple, she would never part with it. She was bound to make all efforts to perpetuate the practice. As a result of this there began a process which was not to end. According to the inscription, the responsibility to fill up the vacancies first fell on the nearest relations of *devadasis*. If they, from among themselves, could not select one, capable of performing that work, then other *devadasis* would select qualified ones from those fit for such appointments and the person selected was to receive the allowance.[86] In any case there was no scope for interference by the pontiff, priests, or the local trustees, etc. This instruction made the status of *devadasis* in the temple autonomous. And it is natural that in the event of any interference in this autonomy they became organised and opposed it. And gradually, they established their monopoly not only on casual vacancies, but also on fresh appointments of *devadasis*. It became customary for a new dancing girl seeking admission to the temple to represent her case to the senior *devadasis* first and obtain their approval.[87] These applications were then recommended by the *devadasis* to the *dharmakartas*[88] for final approval. If the temple authorities tried to by pass the *devadasis'* consent, there arose serious dispute; the *devadasis* resisted it. We find some examples in the latter half of the nineteenth century. In one case,[89] when the *dharmakarta* of a temple dedicated two dancing girls to the service of the temple without the consent of the existing body of dancing girls, the latter protested, and challenged in the law court the validity of the appointment and the authority of the *dharmakarta* to hold that office. In another case, a dancing girl of Sri Virargavaswami temple at Trivellur, refused to approve the admission by the *dharmakarta* of new dancing girls into the temple service of which she claimed the monopoly for herself and the then existing families of dancing girls.[90]

Hence, permanent land grant to *devadasis* permanently fettered them to the temple service. And the vices connected with them also became a permanent feature. Consequently, the attempts made in the 19th century and 20th century to weed out the evil practice largely failed, because the *devadasis* had developed permanent vested interests which they would not give up so easily.

In modern India the agitation to weed out the evil practice started as far back as the second half of the 19th century. And in 1861, with the coming into force of the Indian Penal Code the recruitment of girls for employing them as *devadasis* was made an offence punishable under section 372 of the I.P.C. It appears from the evidence relating to the cases involving them that the judiciary did not accept the rationale of the existence of the institution of *devadasis*. In fact, it regarded this institution as prostitution under religious cover. The judges denounced it in strong terms. However, in several cases of a civil nature it was with much constraint that the court had to recognise and defend the temple dancing girls. In one case, when the dancing girls of a temple sought that they should be declared to have by custom a veto upon the induction of any new *devadasi*, the High Court of Madras (consisting of Justice Innes and Justice Karnak) observed, "We cannot shut our eyes to what is the main purpose of this profession as it is perfectly notorious that it is prostitution ..... If the religious services which the *devadasis* have to attend, or in which they are required to join, be anything more than mere veil to cover the real and substantial occupation of their lives, it is still impossible to regard their religious services as disconnected from the other inevitable pursuit of their profession as *devadasis*".[91]

In another case the High Court of Bombay observed, "The rules by which such an association endeavours to make itself and its mischievous influence perpetual would be directly opposed to the "laws of God", and the usage itself, therefore; not as valid and coercive like a law, but as essentially invalid on account of its contradiction of law."[92]

The main obstacles in weeding out the *devadasi* system were the endowments and perquisites which these women received from the temples. The temples had allotted land to *devadasis* which they had been enjoying from time immemoirial as a hereditary right in lieu of their services in the temples. They could not afford to shun the practice even if they wished to do so. For, saying good bye to their traditional profession also meant saying good bye to all the emoluments and perquisites. It is evident therefore that under no circumstances would a *devadasi* have liked to forgo the perquisites and income which she received from the temple. It was normal practice for an ageing *devadasi* to induct her daughter into the temple service and thereby retain the benefits in the form of perquisites and income. In the absence of a daughter, a *devadasi* would go to the extent of securing an heiress, either by way of adoption or purchase.[93]

Another obstacle was the prevalence of superstition among the *devadasis* that the god would visit them with some punishment if they did not continue the practice.[94] For example, the *Harijan* families of Bijapur, among whom the practice is fairly widespread, consider it their sacred duty to present their best possession to the family deity. Being very poor, the best thing they have in the family is a beautiful daughter. In traditional parlance of the *Harijans*, the practice of sending a girl to a temple for dedication is in no way different from the sending of a son by the local high caste Hindu family to a village school.[95]

When a newly-wed couple has no child within a few years of their marriage, or when somebody in the family keeps suffering from a disease, or meets with an accident or suffers any natural calamity, the immediate thing that strikes a *Harijan* mind is that something has gone wrong with their conduct towards the family god or goddess and has aroused the deity's wrath. Nothing less than the dedication of a girl under such circumstances is supposed to mitigate the anger of the deity.[96] Thus, in most cases, it was the ignorance combined with poverty which were the impediments in the way of abolishing the age-old custom.

The first effective step for abolishing the system was undertaken by the Princely Family of Mysore in the first decade of the present century. The *inams* and *miras* lands which the *devadasis* enjoyed from time immemorial bound them to be in regular duty in the temple. As a consequence of it, when a *devadasi* desired to dissociate from the traditional profession, she had to make an alternative arrangement for her livelihood. The Raja of Mysore was aware of these implication, which is reflected from the way he took steps to abolish the custom. The *devadasis* were excluded from any kind of service in the temples. The lands and *inams* which were held by them for their service in the temples were ordered to be confirmed in their names, under Rule VIII, clause F of the *inam* rules, to the holders, as permanent, subject to the payment of quit rent. The quit rent thus imposed had to be credited to the Government (of Mysore) Treasury and an equivalent amount had to be granted as cash *inam* to the temple concerned.[97]

In the autumn of 1927, when the Sarada Bill was first debated in the Madras Assembly, the Council of State discussed the motion of a Madras member for the prevention of the practice of dedicating girls as *devadasis* to the Hindu temples, since it inevitably entailed a life of prostitution for the girls so dedicated.[98] The motion was opposed by the then Law Member on the ground that the alleged consequence of such dedication was not inevitable, and also that the case was covered by Act XVIII of 1924, which amended the sections 372 and 375 of the Indian Penal Code, extending their scope to cover the cases of girls dedicated to the temples. Hence, the motion was withdrawn. However, an undertaking was given by the Government of India that before a Bill was introduced it should be circulated for opinion.[99]

In November of the same year, a resolution was moved in the Madras Legislative Council, demanding a complete ban on the dedication of girls to temples. Speaking on the resolution, a lady member of the House, Muthulakshmi Reddy, suggested that the lands which were given to the families of the dancing girls in lieu of their services in the temples, which they had been enjoying from time immemorial as a hereditary right, be permanently settled upon without any expectation of service in return, which would automatically force them to give up their service. Others who spoke for the resolution were S.N. Dorai Raja, Basheer Ahmad, P Anjaneyulu, C.V. Venkataramana Ayyangar, A.B. Shetty, K.R. Karant, C.N. Muthuranga Mudaliar, V.I. Muniswami Pillai and Syed Ibrahim. The following was the resolution: "This Council recommends to the Government to undertake legislation or to recommend to the Government of India, to undertake legislation at a very early date to put a stop to the practice of dedicating young girls and young women to Hindu temples which generally resulted in exposing them to an immoral life under the pretext of caste, custom of religion."[100]

Speaking on the resolution, C.P. Ramaswamy Ayyar, who was representing the Government, cited the incidence of temple dancing in the ancient world to justify the continuation of the *devadasi* system in India. He also pleaded the government's inability to give effect to the resolution in view of the religious nature of *miras* and *inam* lands.[101] In spite of this, the above amended resolution was unanimously passed by the House.[102]

In 1930, Dr. Muthulakshmi Reddy brought a Bill in the Madras Council, prohibiting the performance of the dedicatory ceremony in any Hindu temple and enabling the dedicated women to contract a legal marriage.[103] In 1934, the Bombay *Devadasis*-Protection Act was passed.[104] Thus, by the close of the third decade of this century, preventive legislation covered almost the whole of the area where the *devadasi* system was prevalent.

In spite of these prohibitory Acts and Regulations every year three to four thousand girls in the bordering districts of Maharashtra and Karnataka are recruited as *devadasis* who ultimately reach the red-light areas of Bombay, Pune and other towns, and live by prostitution. The *Devadasis*-Protection Act (1934)[105] prohibits the marriage of girls with idols. But it is a law honoured more in the breach than in the observance. Most of the *jogtis*[106] have not even heard of this law. Till now there has not been any conviction under the Act. Pointing out the apathy of the Maharashtra government to this problem, Dr. Baba Adha, Chief of the Mahatma Phule Pratisthan, said that not a single case had been filed against anybody under the Bombay *Devadasis* Protection Act of 1934.[107]

Mrs. Suniti Pungliya of Pune, the President of the *'Devadasi Mukti Vahini'*, alleged that on an average 5,000 young girls were dedicated to goddess Yellamma on *Magha Poornima* day, and later sold to brothels in Bombay and elsewhere.[108] Surveys conducted in the red-light areas of the major towns of Maharashtra have shown that almost 80 percent of the prostitutes were former *devadasis*.[109] There has been a regular chain of some agents, priests and *akkas* (madames) for bringing *devadasis* to the brothels. Besides, there are some *devadasis* who have relatives among the prostitutes.[110] The price of a *jogti* bought for the whole life is as low as Rs. 50.[111]

The custom of high caste married women in rural and urban Karnataka, worshipping Yellamma, has gone a long way in keeping the *devadasi* system alive.[112] On this occasion (usually the full moon day in the month of *Magh*) a group of five to ten *devadasis* are invited to assist in worshipping the goddess. This is because the *devadasi* is supposed to have direct communion with the deity. The high caste women who invite them bestow gifts which include personal items such as blouse, sarees, and some cash. This yearly income to a poor *harijan* family, which has a *devadasi* among them, becomes a great asset. The acceptance of such gifts is a kind of birthright for a *devadasi*, who is, in a way, supported throughout the year by such gifts and presents from high caste families on secular and religious festivals celebrated by them.

The importance of such gifts can be understood in the sense that most *Harijan* families in a village usually get full labour employment only for three months in a year during the harvest season. During the drought period even this is not possible. They are at the point of starvation. As reported in a field study, it was found that quite a large number of *Harijan* families did not get full meals for all the days in a week. Under such acute circumstances they look for different sources of income. Particularly when even their religious begging, *jogva*, does not bring enough to make both ends meet,[113] then the easiest means of supporting themselves remain to induct their daughters or young women into prostitution. "A beautiful girl is equivalent to three acres of land," they say with an eye on prostitution. There is little stigma attached to this way of earning a livelihood[114].

The regional branch of the *All-India Harijan Sevak Sangh* at Bijapur ran an *ashram* school for boys and girls ever since 1935 until 1972. One of the peculiar problems faced by the boarding house authorities was to decide under whose guardianship to register the names of an inmate—whether in the name of the mother or the father. For, if they recorded the ward under a mother's name as the students' only guardian, then technically, it amounted to their being involved in sanctioning the *devadasis* existence.[115] In order to avoid this embarrassing situation, a mother was requested to change her name from the feminine to the masculine gender—by adding to it *'appa'*(man) instead of *'avva'*(woman). There have been cases in which the children of *devadasis* changed their names to sound like Muslim names under the pretext that they were the worshippers of a Muslim saint. Moreover, the *devadasis* living in the *ashram* school never gave any guarantee of not re-entering into that life later on. In fact, some of these girls were improving their qualifications in order to have an edge over an uneducated *devadasi* prostitute. Their parents were aware of these additional benefits and encouraged them to stay there in the boarding house which was free of cost.

Recently, a study conducted by Asha Ramesh and H.P. Philomena of the Joint Women's Programme, reveals that the system has not been weeded out and the recruitment of the girls for the dedication takes place clandestinely[116]. The recruitment is made not in the temple, but, in the homes of the parents with the connivance of the priests of the Yellamma temple at Saundatti. However, the management of the Yellamma temple at Saundatti and the Karnataka Government have emphatically denied the report, made by sociologists and others that the custom flourishes there. The Karnataka Chief Minister denied the report regarding the recruitment of girls as *devadasis* and proposed to depute a team of lawyers to the temple to investigate into the affairs of the temple.[117] The Assistant Commissioner and the executive officer of the temple, Mr. T.S. Hosamatt, had also reacted sharply and challenged that either the sociologists should prove the existence of the custom or tender an apology.[118]

Recently, the problem has drawn the attention of the Parliament. On August 4, 1980 the matter was discussed in the Lok Sabha. Replying to Mr. K.C. Haldar who wanted to know what steps the Government proposed to take to stop the *devadasi* system, Mr. B. Sankaranand, Union Minister of Education and Social Welfare, said that it was a matter of shame that such system was still prevalent in the country.[119]

The Mahatma Phule Pratisthan organised a convention of *devadasis* at Nipani on the Maharashtra-Karnataka border which was attended by 500 *devadasis*. The convention was chaired by *devadasi* Gaurabai Satware. Addressing the conference Gaurabai posed some startling questions: "Why does Yellamma not demand girls from other communities like Brahmins, Marathas, Lingayats and Gujars? When caste Hindus also worship Yellamma, why don't they dedicate their girls to her? Why should we be asked to dedicate our daughters and not our sons?"[120] Gaurabai appealed to the members of her sect not only to educate their daughters, but also to take their consent before offering them to Yellamma."[121] This caused a flutter at the convention. A *devadasi,* believed to be under trance, got up and declared that Yellamma did not approve of what was being spoken about her. Gaurabai, pacified her and alleyed her fear that the goddess would not be angry if she loved our children.[122]

But the ignorance and superstition of these *devadasis* are not the only hurdles in the way. There are some agents who have developed vested interests in the continuation of the flesh trade. This is evident from the fact that when Gaurabai became the President of the 'Devadasi-Conference', she was harassed, and even assaulted by the agents.[123] Unfortunately, she was not given any protection by the police.[124] The convention resolved that since it was a socio-economic problem, the Governments of Maharashtra and Karnataka, where the system was largely prevalent, should set up rehabilitation boards. They could, the convention felt, extend financial help to those *devadasis* who were prepared to give up their profession and educate their children. The convention also urged social organisations like Rotary and Lions Clubs to extend help in the rehabilitation of these children and provide free education and free hostel accommodation for some years. But they are yet to get any positive response.

Abbreviations

ARIE	=	Annual Report of Indian Epigraphy.
ARSIE	=	Annual Report on South Indian Epigraphy.
EC	=	Epigraphia Carnatica.
EI	=	Epigraphia Indica.
I.H.R	=	The Indian Historical Review.
I.L.R.	=	Indian Law Reports.
JASB	=	Journal of the Asiatic Society of Bengal.
JAHRS	=	Journal of the Andhra Historical Research Society.
JASB	=	Journal of the Asiatic Society of Bengal.
PIHC	=	Procedings of the Indian History Congress.

References

1. Nihar Ranjan Roy, 'The Medieval Factor in Indian History', *PIHC*, 29th Session, Patiala, 1967; R.S. Sharma, 'Problem of Transition from Ancient to Medieval in Indian History', *IHR*, Vol. I, No. 1, Delhi, 1974.
2. R.S. Sharma, *Bhartiya Samantvad* (Hindi), Tr. by Aditya Narayan, Delhi, 1973, p. 2.

3. R.N. Nandi, *Religious Institutions and Cults in the Deccan*, A.D. 600-1000, Delhi, 1973, p. 13.
4. *Ibid.*
5. *Ibid.*
6. Devangana Desai, *Erotic Sculpture of India (A Socio-Cultural Study)*, New Delhi, 1975, p. 154.
7. T.V. Mahalingam, *Kancipuram in Early South Indian History*, Bombay, 1969, p. 17.
8. Desai, *Erotic Sculpture*, p. 154.
9. *Ibid.*, p. 11.
10. Nandi, *op.cit.*, p. 14.
11. C.V.N. Ayyar, *Origin and Early History of Saivism in South India*, Madras, 1936, pp. 166-7.
12. *Ibid.*, pp. 169-70.
13. *Ibid.*, p. 171.
14. *Ibid.*, pp. 147-8.
15. *Ibid.*, p. 153 & 315.
16. R. N. Nandi, *Religious Institutions and Cults in the Deccan*, p. 10.
17. Ayyar, *Origin and Early History of Saivism in South India*, p. 253.
18. Nandi, *op. cit.*, pp. 168-69.
19. A.L. Basham. *The Wonder that was India*, New York, The Crave Press, 1954, p. 285.
20. Hardy, "Ideology and Cultural Contexts of the Srivaisnava Temples". *The Indian Economic and Social History Review*, Vol.14, No.1 (Jan.-March 77) p. 132.
21. *EI*, 32, p. 290; Cited by K.R Srinivasan, *Some Aspects of Religion as Revealed by Early Monuments and Literature of the South Madras* : University of Madras, 1960,. p. 15.
22. Nandi, *op.cit.*, p. 24.
23. D.N. Jha, "Temples as Landed Managers in Early Medieval South India (C.A.D. 700-1300)", R.S. Sharma (ed.), *Indian Society: Historical Probings*, New Delhi, 1974, p. 204.
24. *Ibid.*
25. Minakshi, *Administration and Social Life Under the Pallavas*, Madras, 1939, p. 178.
26. The term *bhoga* means pleasing enjoyment, the hire of dancing girls or courtesans, food offered to an idol, etc. Pandit Kulapati Jibanada Vidyasagara, *Shabdasagara*, Calcutta, 1900, p. 538. The term *anga* means the act of play or ornament, decoration etc. *Shabdasagar*, p. 8.
27. The term *ranga* refers to a dancing place, a place of public amusement or for dramatic exhibition, theatre, play house, etc. M. Williams, *Sanskrit English Dictionary*, Delhi, 1976 (first published from Oxford, 1899), p. 862.
28. Nandi, *op.cit.*, p. 24.

29. *Ibid.*
30. *Ibid.*
31. *EC.* 10 Kolar 106.
32. The *basavis* are non-Brahmin women dedicated to the gods. The word *basavi* is the feminine of *basava* the bull of siva." According to C. Hayavadan Rao the term literally meaning the bull" carries with it the import of 'procreator'. This name has been given because she raises the progeny for the family". M.N. Srinivas, *Marriage and Family in Mysore,* Bombay, 1942, p. 176.
33. J.H. Hutton, *Caste in India,* London: Oxford University Press, 1967, p. 162.
34. *EC.* VII, Hl. 64, cited in R.N. Nandi, *"Family and Inheritance in Early South India",* PIHC, 1974, p. 73.
35. *EC,* XI, Dindigul 17, *Ibid.,*
36. M.N. Srinivas, *op.cit.,* p. 184
37. The custom was common among the Mediga, Holeya, Bedar and other castes of South India.
38. J.A.S.B., 9, pp. 766 f, cited in B.N. Sharma, *Social and Cultural History of Northern India: c 100-1200,* New Delhi, 172, p. 75.
39. P. Thomas, *Indian Woman Through the Ages,* Bombay, 1964, p. 237.
40. B.P. Mazumdar, *Socio-Economic History of Northern India: 1030-1194 A.D.,* Calcutta, 1960, p. 371.
41. *Ibid.,* p. 372.
42. P.Thomas, *op.cit.,* 239.
43. *SII,* Vol. 2, Part III, No. 66.
44. *SII,* 3, pt. III. No. 102.
45. *EI,* 4, No. 49, p. 437.
46. *SII,* 14, No. 19.
47. *EI,* 13, No. 3.
48. *Ec.* 10, Kolar 106.
49. V. Yesoda Devi, "History of the Andhra Country," *JAHRS,* 26 p. 61.
50. *SII,* 10, No. 80.
51. *SII,* 10, No. 115.
52. *SII,* No. 110.
53. *ARSIE,* 1921, B. 729.
54. *ARSIE,* 1925, B. 171.
55. *ARIE,* 1962-63, No. 638.
56. *RT,* VII, 850-60
57. *Ibid.*
58. *RT,* IV, 17-32.
59. *Kathasaritsagara,* Ch. III, Tarang I, pp. 247-49.

60. R.N. Das Gupta, "*Institution of Devadais in Assam*" *op.cit.*, pp. 8-19
61. *Kuttamimatam*, Vs. 747-49.
62. *RT*, IV. 421-24, 433-34.
63. B.P. Mazumdar, *Socio-Economic History of Northern India*, Calcutta, 1960, p. 371.
64. *Alberuni's India*, Edward C. Sachau, (ed. & Tr.) New Delhi, 1964, Vol. II, p. 157.
65. Abdullah Wassaf, Tarikh-e-Wassaf, Elliot and Dowson, *Bharat ka Itihas* (Hindi), Vol. III, Agra, 1974,. p. 22.
66. Abbe J.A. Dubois, Hindu Manners Customs and Ceremonies, London, (3rd Ed.) 1959, p. 587.
67. *Alberuni's* India, *op.cit.*, p. 157.
68. *EI*, XI pp. 26-28.
69. Altekar, *The Position of Women*, p. 184.
70. R.N. Das Gupta, *op.cit.*, p. 569.
71. Merutunga, the *Prabandhacintamani* (Eng.) tr. by C.H. Tiwney, Calcutta, 1901, p. 26.
72. *Kuttanimatam*, Vs. 747-49.
73. *EI*, III, No. 4.
74. *EC*, V, Arasikere 134, EC, VIII, p. 150, etc.
75. *ARSIE*, 1923, C 210.
76. V. Yasoda Devi, "*A History of the Andhra Country*" *JAHRS*, XXVII, p. 14.
77. *Madai* was standard gold coin under the Colas issued by different kings under their names., e.g. *Madai* of Rajaraja, *Madai* of Rajendrasolan, *Madhurantakadevamadai* etc. From the reign of Kulottunga I several other types of madais were issued by local rulers. KAN Sastri, *The Colas*, (reprint of 2nd edn). Madras, 1975, pp. 614-15
78. *SII* X, No. 80.
79. *Ibid.*, No. 177.
80. *Ibid.*, No. 171.
81. *Ibid.*, No. 130.
82. *Ibid.*, No. 115, 110 etc.
83. SII, II, pt, III, No. 66.
84. *Ibid.*
85. There are several proofs mentioning valuable presents made by *devadasis* to the temple for being assoicated with these functions. *ARSIE*, 1940-41, nos. B.161, 144, 149 etc.
86. *SII*, II, pt. 3, no. 66
87. E. Thurston, *Castes and Tribes of Southern India*. Vol. II. Delhi, 1975, p. 143.
88. *Ibid.*
89. "*Chinna Umayi Vs. Tegarai Chetti*," *ILR*, Madras, Vol. 1, 168 (1876-78).
90. "*Kammalan Vs Ramasami Chetti*", *ILR*, Madras, Vol. 1, 356 (1876-78) .

91. *"Chinna Umayi Vs. Tegarai Chetti"*. *ILR*, Madras, Vol. I, 168, (1876-78).
92. *"Mathura Naikin Vs. Esu Naikin*, *ILR*, Vol. 454 (1980).
93. Roy, Sripati, *Customs and Customary Law in British India*, Calcutta, 1911, p. 145.
94. Nadkarni, Vithal C., *"Devadasis-Married to God and Mammon"*, *the Illustrated Weekly of India* (14-20 December) 1975, p. 9.
95. Trivedi, H.R. *Scheduled Caste Women: Studies in Exploitation*, Delhi, 1977, p. 82.
96. *Ibid.*, p. 83
97. *Procd, Mad, Leg, Coun.*, p. 514
98. Chatterjee S. *Devadasi*, p. 70
99. *Ibid.*
100. *Procd. Mad. Leg. Counl.*, p. 524.
101. *Ibid.*, pp. 523-24
102. *Ibid.*, p. 524.
103. Chatterji, Davadasi, p. 70
104. Nadkarni, *op.cit.*, p. 11.
105. *Ibid.*
106. *Devadasis* dedicated to goddess Yellama are also called *Jogtis*, as they live by ceremonial begging called *jogwa*. The brass mask of Yellamma is called jag. Jag also means the brass pitcher that is carried by *jogtis*, when they go out to beg. Nadkarni, *op.cit.*, pp. 8-11.
107. *The Times of India* (Delhi), June 30, 1980.
108. *Ibid.*, July 27, 1981.
109. Nadkarni, *op.cit.*, p. 13.
110. *Ibid.*
111. *Ibid.*
112. Trivedi, *Scheduled Caste Women*, p. 83 ff.
113. Trivedi, *op.cit.*, p. 84 ff.
114. *Ibid.*
115. *Ibid.*, p. 63 ff.
116. *The Times of India*, July 27, 1981.
117. *The Indian Nation* (Patna), January 7, 1981.
118. *Ibid.*
119. *The Times of India*, August 5, 1981.
120. *Ibid.*, June 30, 1980.
121. *Ibid.*
122. *The Times of India*, June 30, 1980.
123. Dubey, Satyanarayan, *"Devadasiyon ki Kahani Devadasiyon ki Jubani"*, *Manorama* (Hindi fortnightly), Allahabad, February 1, 1981 p. 44
124. *Ibid.*

14

Gender Relationships in Guru Nanak's Adi Granth

*J.S. Grewal**

Guru Nanak's emphasis on the unity of God is well-known. Many a scholar has underlined also the transcendence and the immanence of his God. What is generally not appreciated is that these two aspects are not opposed to each other. They are the reverse and the obverse of the same conceptual coin. Guru Nanak's God is *nirgun* and *sagun* at one and the same time. Before the creation of the universe and the beginning of time, God exists in a void (*sunn mandal*), and nothing can be attributed to him. In this state, he is without any sign (*niranjan*); he is neither female (*nār*) nor male (*purkh*).[1]

However, God manifested himself through his creation, acquired attributes in his *sagun* state, and he can be known to the extent that he has revealed himself . As in every thing in the universe, he is in all living beings.[2] Guru Nanak underlines God's immanence as much as his transcendence in several ways. For example, he who created the vessels (*bhānday*) placed the same light (*jot*) in all of them.[3] His light is in every heart (*Ghat*).[4] The light that shines in all is his light.[5] Guru Nanak is quite explicit that God created both 'man and woman'.[6] His light is in both 'man and woman'.[7] The human body is the abode (*mahal, mandar, ghar*) of God (Har), and in this body is placed the light.[8] When this light mingles with the primal light, one attains emancipation, or liberation. No distinction is made by Guru Nanak between the male and the female body in this context.

* The author is Professor of History, Guru Nanak Dev University, Amritsar.

Quite explicitly, God has female *sevaks* as well as male *sevaks.*[9] He bestows his best gifts on all, irrespective of their sex.[10] Since liberation from the chain of re-birth and death was the highest purpose of human life in the eyes of Guru Nanak, the path to liberation was meant to be open to women as much as to men.

Guru Nanak's conception of *māyā* like his conception of God, is relevant for our present purpose. The whole universe is God's *māyā*.[11] In contrast with the eternal existence of God, the universe he created is impermanent. What is eternal is true; what is impermanent is false. The opposition between truth and falsehood, between God and his *māyā*, is basic to the thought of Guru Nanak. This opposition is always assumed, and it is clearly posed at many places in his compositions. For example:[12]

False is the king, false are the subjects; false indeed is the whole universe. False is the palace, false is the mansion, and false are they who dwell in them. False is gold, false is silver, and false are they who wear them. False is the body, false are the garments, and false is the beauty of the highest order. False is the husband and false is the wife; they are was ted away at last. The false love the false; they forget the creator. With whom should one seek friendship when all are bound to depart ? False are sweets and false is honey: through falsehood has drowned the whole boatload. There is nothing but falsehood without you, O Lord, says Nanak.

Anything other than God is *māyā*: it is the other play (*daja khel*).[13] It is 'deceit '(*dhoh*), but its pleasures are intoxicating to the point of making one oblivious of death.[14] *Maya*, thus, becomes poison (*bikh*).[15] Affiliation to *maya* keeps one attached to falsehood, and attachment keeps one chained to the cycle to death-and-rebirth.[16] *Maya* is comparable to the attendant in a temple; any one who remains attached to the attendant never reaches the Lord.[17] This world is the abode of falsehood; one should seek the true abode by adoring the 'true one' and thereby appropriating 'the truth'.[18]

Ordinarily, however, man and women remain attached to things which belong to the realm of *māyā*. There is pleasure in gold, pleasure in silver, pleasure in women, pleasure in scents, pleasure in horses, pleasure in the conjugal bed, pleasure in sweets pleasure in the flesh —there are so many pleasures of the body that there is no room for the name.[19] Among the things which induce men to forget God are pearls, diamonds, thrones, armies, power, and beautiful women.[20] Another way of referring to the objects of attachment is to refer to things which are left behind after death: forts, palaces, mansions, elephants, caparisoned horses, large armies, gold, silver, sons, conjugal bed, scents, garments, beauty, ornaments and social status.[21] Among the objects attachment in these verses are 'women', 'beautiful women' and 'conjugal bed'. Obviously, they are the source of attraction for males and quite logically, the woman becomes a part of *māyā*.

Indeed, there are several other verses in which the woman is the object of attraction for males as a part of *māyā*. The 'housewife' is bracketed with sons, relations, wealth and youth. Like avarice, greed and pride, they keep men attached to *māyā* which is compared with the herb which the thugs use to induce unconsciousness in their victims.[22] The beautiful women are bracketed with clarified butter (ghee), sugar and fruits.[23] Elsewhere Guru Nanak brackets the woman with sons, gold, horses and elephants as the objects of attachment.[24] The more popular pair of 'gold and women' also figures in a verse in which the wife too is mentioned together with the son, the daughter, the mother and the father.[25] The five patent thugs are power (*rāj*), wealth (*māl*), caste (*jāt*), youth (*joban*) and beauty (*rūp*), and there is a close link between beauty and sexual desire.[26] The fascination of beautiful women is mentioned also in a verse in which the great importance of remembering the name of the Lord is emphasised.[27]

There are some other verses, however, in which the woman figures as the dupe of *māyā* rather than as its part. There is the woman of the ruling class, for instance, in one of the Babur-Bani verses, who suffers because of her indulgence in a life of luxury, including the enjoyment of her conjugal bed, to the point of forgetting God. Some Hindu women too suffer because of their indifference to God.[28] It is interesting to note that they are the counterpart of men who suffer a similar fate for the same reason, including the enjoyment of beautiful women 'whose sight banished sleep'.[29] The son is an object of attachment for the mother as much as for the father.[30] The husband too is an object of attachment for the woman.[31] The woman longs to look beautiful's to enjoy sensual pleasure, and to collect gold and silver.[32] The unregenerate woman appears in these verses to be the counterpart of the male *manmukh*. Indeed, Guru Nanak uses the term *manmukh* for the woman too. Such a woman finds no place any where. Without the instruction of the *guru*, she remains blind. She has been duped by *māyā*. 'Lost in delusion, she is the *dohāgan* who never unites with beloved spouse.'[33]

Nevertheless, Guru Nanak defends the female sex in some of his verses against what he regards as Brahmanical superstition. The best of these verses is the one in which he underlines the indispensability of the woman for continuing the human race:[34]

We are conceived in the woman's womb and we grow in it. We are engaged to women and we wed them. Through the woman's cooperation new generations are born. If one woman dies, we seek another; without the woman there can be no bond. Why call her bad who gives birth to rājas? The woman herself is born of the woman, and none comes into this world without the woman; Nanak, the true one alone is independent of the woman.

The longish stanza on the pandit's prejudice against the use of flesh (*mās*) can be taken in a light favourable to woman.[35] There is no ambiguity about Guru Nanak's sympathy with the woman in the verses which relate to *sūtak*, the notion of impurity attached to the woman who delivers a child. Strictly speaking, there is 'impurity' in the cow-dung, in fire-wood, in grains, and in water itself. How can we observe ritual purity in such a situation ? Actually, the impurity of the mind is greed; the impurity of the tongue is false speech; the impurity of the eye is to look at another's woman with lust; the impurity of the ear is to listen to slander. The notion of impurity is a delusion: it amounts to believing in something other than God. Through his order are we born and through his order do we die. Whatever is bestowed by him is pure. They who understand this do not observe *sūtak*.[36] It is not surprising that Guru Nanak feels deeply anguished over the rape of women in one of the Babur-Bani verses in which the army of Babur is referred to as the marriage-party of sin (*pāp*) and the 'ceremony of marriage', that is rape, is performed not by the Brahman or the Qazi but by Satan.[37]

The total absence of misogyny in the compositions of Guru Nanak appears to be due in part to his acceptance and advocacy of social commitment which precludes renunciation and asceticism. He denounces the *jogis* more frequently than any other set of people. Among many other things, he disapproves of the *jogi's* renunciation and his preoccupation with celibacy involving the ideal of subduing sexual desire.[38] In one of his verses Guru Nanak makes his preference for the house-holding devotee (*grihi sevak*) abundantly clear over the *jogī*, the *bhogī*, the *kāparī*, the *pandit*, the *pādhā*, the *josī*, the *tapsī*, and the *jatī*.[39] The path of emancipation does not lie in asceticism and renunciation, or in ritual of any kind; it lies in loving devotion as conceived by Guru Nanak. Thus the opportunity to follow this path is created in the home itself as much for woman as for man.

II

The purpose of life for the woman, as for the man, is to attain liberation from the cycle of death and re-birth, to enjoy the bliss of union with the eternal Lord. The woman with spotless white garments, sweet speech, sharp nose and beautiful black eyes is asked if she has ever seen the master.[40] Seeing the Lord is what matters. The woman with fascinating eyes, who has adorned herself with all the sixteen items of *singār,* and who is extremely attractive, is told that she is bound to be jilted everyday if she does not devote herself to the Lord (Jagdis)[41]. The spouse (*sauh*) is in the heart of every woman as he is in the heart of every man: the *sohāgans* are they who see the spouse by turning to the guru.[42] Thus, there are male and female *gurmukhs* just as there are male and female *manmukhs*. The joyous Lord enjoys the *sohāgans* everyday, and sad is the plight of those who are not enjoyed by him.[43] They who accept the Lord's will, the word (*sabd*) is lodged in their hearts. They who love the spouse are *sohāgans.* He looks at them with grace and unites them with himself. And who are *dohāgans*? They who are separated from the spouse (*khasm*) and wander in a helpless state, dirty are their garments, and they pass the night in pain.[44]

The state of separation resulting from forgetfulness of the Lord is painful : 'If forget my Lord I die of pain'. This is why the woman should remember him with every morsel and every breath she takes; she should search for him; on seeing him through the name, she would become a *bairāgan* for ever.[45] If a woman adorns herself without the beloved spouse (*piria*), her body becomes hot and it cannot bear even the dress. She cannot live without her love even for a moment, and she cannot sleep without meeting him. He is near, but she does not know; the true *guru* shows him to her. She attains peace in *sahaj* and the word quenches her thirst.[46] As the arena of union and separation, human life is an opportunity for men and women to attain liberation. Therefore, they who are not enjoyed by the spouse (*kant*) remain regretful: dejection and dismay is visible on their faces when the night is past. No women should miss the opportunity, so that she does not experience regret. Otherwise, she will have to wait for her turn to meet her love in another life.[47]

The opportunity for union is not un-related to merit. The *sohāgans* who have reached the spouse are superior to the woman who does not possess merit; she has no one but herself to blame for this. If she were to go to the *sohāgans* and implore them to tell her how to reach the spouse, they would tell her that she should recognize his will (*hukam*), adorn herself with the fear (*bhau*) of the Lord, and cultivate virtue as the charm to gain access to him.[48] Every woman, like every man, receives the same precious thing (*vath*) from the Lord (*sauhray*), but differences arise in their lives on the earth (*piukaray*). She who is ill- cultured (*kuchajji*) does not know how to preserve the gift. The good wife knows how to embroider the cloth for her skirt and she knows how to manage the house: she does not indulge in superfluities, and she is loved by the spouse.[49] The metaphor of God as the spouse creates the possibility of his having innumerable brides. There are verses of Guru Nanak in which one woman invites others to come together and cultivate those virtues which please the spouse so that he may enjoy them all.[50] The contextual references to the abundance of wives and women in an affluent house indicate the prevalence of polygamy in contemporary society, and Gudu Nanak was obviously aware of this situation.[51] The metaphor remains close to the social reality in which a number of female were attached, institutionally as well as emotionally, to a single male.

However, the metaphor is seldom sustained. To illustrate this point we may turn to a longish stanza which opens with the idea that all women are the brides of the same spouse and adorn themselves to please him. It is useless to flaunt the red dress if the bride lacks dedication. Love is not enjoyed by fraud; the imposter is exposed. When the spouse is kind of a woman, he enables her to adorn herself with virtue and then he enjoys her. She is adorned with the *guru's* word, and her body and mind are dedicated to the spouse. She offers sincere prayers in utter humility. She is imbued with the love of the Lord and the fear of the Lord, and she is imbued with truth. She recognizes the Lord's name, and she becomes his slave. True love never ceases and the true one unites such a woman with himself. The woman who is united by the true *guru* is never widowed. Enjoyed by the beloved spouse, her body remains fresh and she never dies. Through his grace he enjoys the *sohagān* everyday. Her capital is the truth, and her *singār* is love; the fragrance she uses is the Lord lodged in her mind, and the temple in which she worships is the highest state of consciousness (*daswa duār*). With the name of the Lord lodged within her, she blossoms with the light of the word. Her inside is beautiful and the jewel of love adorns her forehead. She loves the true one and her consciousness is made beautiful by the praises she sings. She does not know anyone other than the true one, and cherishes loving devotion for the *guru*. The ignorant woman who is indifferent to the beloved spouse finds it hard to pass the night. Her body, her mind, her limbs and her riches and singed; her youth is wasted if the spouse has not enjoyed her. She is in the bridal bed with spouse, but she does not know. She is asleep while the spouse is wide a wake. She who is united by the true *guru* subsists in fear and enjoys the peace of love.[52]

Most of the images and similes used in this stanza relate to situations connected with domestic life. In another verse, the father-in-law and the mother-in-law symbolize manual labour and consciousness; the wife herself is compared to life devoted to good works; the auspicious time of marriage (*sāhā*) is union (*sanjog*); the marriage itself becomes detachment from the world; the progeny from such a union is truth. This is presented as the true path[53]. The house of the in-laws is generally a metaphor for the life hereafter (*parlok*) while the natal home is life on the earth (*lok*). That is why if the young woman is imbued with the word in her natal home she is loved by the spouse inher marital home.[54] In another situation, the young woman is so intoxicated with the wine of youth as to forget that she is no more than a guest in the home of her parents.[55] Occasionally, Guru Nanak can refer to the situation in which the husband feels estranged from the wife; the sons become the means of their reconciliation.[56] Procreation is so vital to domesticity that Guru Nanak can ask at one place 'what is a home to a eunuch'?[57]

Metaphorically, the death of a woman becomes her 'marriage'. The implication is that she can meet the eternal spouse now. The suspicious time (*sāhā*) is fixed, and she can ask her friends to come and perform the ceremony of putting oil on her head and sing their good wishes so that she is united with her master. She is not alone, for the message from the master comes to every home, and one should look forward to the message.[58] Indeed, one's whole life should be a preparation for death. To attach oneself to God, to discern the path that leads to him, to realize that he who gives life can take it away, to understand that whatever happens is due to his will, to accept what he decrees, to appropriate the true name — this is the way to prepare for death.[59] There is no point in wailing for 'the colourful friend who has gone to the wilderness to sleep for ever'. The woman who does this does not know that she herself will not stay for ever in the 'parental home'; she has to leave for her 'in-laws' sooner or later. She should use her life as a rare opportunity to earn merit.[60]

Guru Nanak refers to woman in some other situations too. For example, there is the mother whose children attain liberation; she is a blessed woman.[61] The state of widowhood, by contrast, is a curse. Thirst is not quenched without the beloved spouse; the widow feels helpless against sexual urge, or she is in need of money; she gives her body to a stranger.[62] This is hardly complimentary to the widow, but it is a contextual statement. In another contextual statement, the falsehood of the false comes to them as naturally as the menses to a woman.[63] Guru Nanak also refers to men as 'wailing like women' with the obvious implication that it does not behave them.[64] However, such statements are rather rare. We have to scan the compositions of Guru Nanak word by word to detect a few. The deserted woman is compared in one verse to a corpse, with the implication that the husband is comparable to the soul. At the same time,looking at another's woman with lust is condemned.[65] Elsewhere, to lust for another's woman is to eat poison.[66] What is appreciated by Guru Nanak is fidelity on the part of man and dedication on the part of woman. The smiles used for the latter are those of the female deer, the nightingale, the fish and the female snake. Above all, the dedicated woman is 'the *banjāran* of Ram'; she trades in the Lord's name and here capital too is the name.[67] There is one situation outside the sphere of domesticity which is highly commendable in the eyes of Guru Nanak. It is the position of a *bairagān*. She discards all *haumai* and turns towards God. She is no immersed in truth that she is not bothered about what people think of her. In her own consciousness she is above all social taboos.

III

Much more frequently, however, Guru Nanak addresses himself to the unregenerate woman, the young innocent maiden with a potential for pleasing the spouse, or the spouse to be. She is told that the beloved spouse is the source of happiness. She can meet him through his kindness. His bed is glorious. She would be in bloom to see him . She should dedicate her mind and body to him. Imbued with his love, she would find peace in the name. She has to cultivate virtue and merit; she has to thirst for him.[68] It is useful to address the young woman because many of the ideas related to liberation can be brought in. We may cite another stanza to see how these ideas are expressed.[69]

Intoxicated with the wine of youth in the home of her parents the woman has forgotten that she is but a guest here. Dirty with demerit, she can not acquire virtue with out the guru. Alien to virtue, she has wasted her youth in delusion. The spouse is at the door of her home but she is not awareof the beloved spouse. She does not go to the true guru to follow the right path, and she has wasted the night in sleep. Nanak, she has become a widow in girlhood, and her boy is withering.

Find for me the divine spouse whom I like; I am a sacrifice to him. He pervades the four yugas and all the three worlds obey his word (bānī). The spouse enjoys the sohāgans in the three worlds, but the meritless one remains at a distance from him. One finds as one aspires; the Lord fulfils all wishes. The woman of the Lord remains sohagan for ever, and the widow never tastes the union. Nanak, I cherish the true spouse, the beloved friend who remains the same throughout the ages.

Find out the auspicious time so that I may go to the in-laws. The auspicious time is determined by the Lord and it cannot be postponed. One does what is decreed by him; what is written by him cannot be effacted. He is the bridegroom who does not need a marriage-party; he pervades the three worlds. I am indistress and I wail in separation, like a young woman who pines for her young lover. Nanak, through the word one attains the peace of his abode, and one gets attached to the Lord's feet.

The father has sent her far away; she does not come home. She is pleased in the presence of the beloved spouse and he enjoys her; she adorns the house. Sought out by the true and beloved spouse, she is united with beloved friend; she has acquired perfect wisdom and she has become distinguished. Through understanding imparted by the guru, the woman of merit has attained happy union in the abode of peace. She is in possession of truth and contentment; the true speech is what the beloved spouse likes. Nanak, she does not suffer the pain of separation. She becomes one with the Lord through the guru's instruction.

The basic theme of the passage, as of many others, is the pursuit of *sahaj*, to become a *sohāhan*. This depends ultimately on the Lord's pleasure or grace. But one can prepare oneself for the possibility by listening to the *guru's* instruction, reflection the word, acceptance of the *hukam*, discarding sensual pleasures, and by acquiring virtue. The metaphors of the natal home, the marital home, the state of widowhood, the bridegroom, and the guest are brought into deliver the essential message.

In another longish passage the young innocent girl is told not to be proud of her youth for she is a stranger of the husband-god within. Why foolish woman are you looking for him out side when he is near, within yourself ? The young woman is told to adorn herself with the fear of the Lord (*bhai*) and devotion to him (*bhav*) to receive the love of the spouse to becomes *sohāgan*. What can the young one do if her husband (*kant*) does not desire her? She implores but finds no access tohis palace. Nothing avails without good deeds, howsoever hard she may try. Sheis immersed in *māyā* due to her avarice, greed and pride. These are not the ways of meeting the spouse (*sauh*), but the simpleton of a woman does not know. She should ask the *sohāgans* how to get to the Lord. They would tell her that whatever he does should be welcome, and his command should be obeyed. Only he whose love enables her to receive the bliss should be the object of her devotion. She should do what he says and dedicate her body and mind to him—this is the 'scent' the attracts him. This is what *sohagāns* say should be done. Sacrifice your 'self' to obtain the Lord, for there is nothing else that works. Auspicious is the day when he chooses her for his grace, when she obtains the bliss. She becomes respectable in her family too when she becomes *sohāgans* by receiving her husband's lov. Drenched in love and intoxicated with *sahaj*, she is dyed in his colour. She is the woman who is beautiful and wise.[70] But for the idea of the fear of the Lord, the ideas and metaphors used in this passage are close to what we found in the earlier passage.

Guru Nanak is seldom so immersed in femaleness as to lose his discrete identity for long. It is easy to paraphrase his metaphors. The following is a rather literal translation of one verse:[71]

The bride is bewitched by her Lord and sleep in his embrace. She attuned to the truth and moves in the will of guru. She is attuned to the truth and sleeps in the Lord's embrace, in the company of her women-friend. The name is enshrined in their minds and in single-minded dovotion they are united with the Lord through the true guru. They do not leave their Lord for a single moment; within them shines the light of the word, and all their fears are removed.

This verse has been actually paraphrased as follows :[72]

The soul-women (jiv-istri) who lives her life according to the guru's instruction and who is devoted to the eternal God, remains attached to the feet of the creator of māyā. In the company of her companions she remain constant in her devotion to the everlasting God, and the name takes root in her heart. She begins to trust the guru and she does not forget God even for a moment, remembering him with every breath. With the light of the guru's words she is able to put an end to all kinds of fear.

The diction used by Guru Nanak appears to work simultaneously at two levels even when the women expresses her pangs of separation. For example, 'how can I live without Har, my mother's is followed by 'Hail to the master of the world (Jagdis), praise be to him, I cannot live without Har. The thirsty women thirsts for him all the night. The master of Lakshmi has captured my heart: only the Prabh knows the pain of others. The body is much in pain without Har: I have found Har through the *guru's sabd*. Be gracious O'Har, grant that my mind remains attached to your feet. Manohar has shown his grace to me; by singinghis praises I have attained to fearless *sahaj*.[73] The use of the epithets Har, Jagdis, Prabh and

Manohar in these lines does not allow the reader, or the listener, to be completely immersed in the female metaphor.

Here it does not seem so necessary to cite many passages in support of the points made. However, we may refer to a few more to illustrate variation on the theme. In one verse ,'the woman of merit communicates merit and the woman without merit carries her distress within herself. She who seeks the spouse should now that he cannot be met through falsehood. Without the boat it is impossible toreach the beloved spouse who is far away: The *guru* povides the boat to ferry across and he provides the ladder to ascend the citadel of the Lord.[74] In another verse, 'the friend has come home', it is an occasion for rejoicing. "The 'true one' has made this union possible. The purpose of life is attained. The women can sing the song of joy. The Prabh likes the praise of the true one. The *sabd* set things right. The collyrium of *gian* shows all the three worlds. The body and mind are imbued with nectar, and the treasure of love is found within.[75] The woman who is indifferent to the spouse suffers the pain of separation. Immersed in *kām*, *krodh* and *ahankār*, she remains attached to *haumai*. Without the true name, she remains in delusion and regrets in the end. No one desires anything else but her spouse. Without the pleasure of *nām* and *sabd* there is nothing in one's life. Without *nām* one keeps on coming-and-going. The path is hard but there is no other way to reach the beloved spouse. It is only through the *sabd* of the true *guru* that the woman separated from him meets him. There is great pleasure in such meeting. You are being called to his abode, do not delay matters any more; prepare yourself to meet him. Discard pride, for the *manmukh* keeps on coming-and-going. Smash your pitcher and dance with abandon without the veil on your face. When you reflect on the matter by turning to the *guru*, you know that the Lord recognizes himself in you.[76]

In yet another passage, men and women of the world are compared with the crow that eats filth. This is false attachment. The deadly poison of *Kām* and *krodh* finds its antidote only in *nām*. Human life is comparable to the whirlwind of sand in one sense and to the bubble of water in another. It is also like the potter's wheel. The light of *nām* the *guru*, loving devotion and the *sabd* lead to the Lord's abode'.[77] Even the verses of the Baramaha, in which we may expect greater authorial immersion in femaleness, are no different. We come upon the same ideas, the same images and the same metaphors. The essential concern is the same. Blessed are all seasons, months, day and hours if one meets the Lord to attain *sahaj*.[78] Even in a verse in which Guru Nanak makes use of the Krishna Gopis lore, the young woman dicards all sensual pleasures on Hari's arrival in the *goil;* adorning herself with the *sabd* she prays to the *guru* in all humility that he may enables her to meet the lover-god; considering her devotion, he makes her free of *kām* and *krodh*: he leaves hehind a young woman who is adorned with beauty.[79] Finally, we may notice a passage in which God's beauty is depicted in terms which are supposed to be appealing to women: his beautiful eyes and sparkling teeth, his sharp nose and luxurious hair, his lustrous body as if cast in gold, his necklace like Krishna's, his pleasing gait, his sweet voice, his alluring youthfulness, his rhythmic movements and his majestic appearance." She who is intoxicated with devotion to him becomes pure like the flowing water of the Ganges.' In this passage there are references also to *nām* and *bānī* the rule of the Lord, *sahaj* through his service, the true Murar, the grace of the *guru,* the ineffable master, and the truth.[80] Though the Lord is clearly male and the devotee female, the metaphor is not sustained.

IV

There has been a tendency among the historians of medieval India to equate devotional theism with 'Bhakti Movement'. However, the idea of loving devotion to a personal God was common to Vaishnava *bhakti,* the Sant tradition, and Sufism. Nevertheless, even within Vaishnava *bhakti* the phenomenon of differentiation was noticed by R. G. Bhadarkar more than half a century ago.[81] Though a clear distinction is made by scholars now between Vaishnava *bhakti* and the Sant tradition, the latter is treated as a single undifferentiated whole. It may be relevant, therefore, to bring in Kabir, who is belived to be the most important exponent of the Sant tradition, for a comparison with Guru Nanak from our present viewpoint. Fortunately, a good analysis of Kabir's position on the subject of patriarchy has been published recently and we can safely turn to this analysis for the purpose of comparison.[82]

In Kabir, according to Kumkum Sangari, the egalitarian concepts of body, of soul, of knowledge, of *māyā* and creation, and of *nirgum* god contest caste, sectarian differences, and orthodox rithul, but not patriarchal value structure. The moment his god becomes *sagun,* he acquires male attributes and it is possible to enter into relationship of love with this personal God. Kabir dwells on all the emotions of love: longing, intoxication, the pain of separation, delirium, and suffering. At the same time, he constructs a patriarchal typology of woman for ascetic transcendence. The woman is an obstacle to salvation. Her sexuality should be subjected to usual regulation.

The idea is elaborated further. Kabir has two notions of *māyā.* At one level, *māyā* is a pervasive cosmic illusion: it is everything that is false. Therefore, it is a levelling, a democratizing and an egalitarian concept which can be used to attack caste, sectarian differences and Brahmanical institutions. This *māyā* is ungendered: it is neither male nor female. At another level, *māyā* is conceived as a removable obstacle to salvation. Here, women and *māyā* become indistinguishable, if not virtually interchangeable. Kabir appears to postulate three sorts of femaleness : the *strisbhav*, the *stridharma*, and the 'higher femaleness' the *bhakti*. The first is to be totally subdued, and of commendable traits of the second are to be etherialized into spirituality for transmutation into the femaleness of *bhakti*. The women of the *stribhava* is the mistress ofthe senses; the use of patriarchal metaphors in relation of her evokes the typology of *dohāgin.* By contrast, the *sohāgin* is the model of *stridharma*, a model in which sexual desires are well channelled; she is all fidelity, without the slightest trace of promiscuity. She surrenders her heart, body and mind to her husband; her *shringārā* is to please him alone. It is of no use without devotion; it is worthless if he does not desire her. She is rewarded with fidelity when she discards all other hopes and desires. Thus, in Kabir, patriarchal values centre on the family as an institution which guarantees licit, righteous progeny, restrains female sexuality, and reproduce a normative notion of marriage.

In many of his verses, Kabir uses female voice with differing degrees of immersion in femaleness, ranging from analogy with *bhakti*, in which the *bhakt* retains his discrete identity, to an authorial immesion in metaphor. The woman of this voice is one among many who are devoted to a single lord. Their objective is *sohāg*, that is union with the lord. The ideology guarantees wifely fidelity and indissoluble marriage as much as metaphoric recognition of god who leads to *mukti*. The use of female devotional voice gives access to divine love. However, the saint masters *māyā* inorder to enslave himself to god. Kabir poses an active opposition between sexual desire *(kām)* and spiritual desire (*prem*). The female devotional voice tends to become an abstraction, and the union of wife with the the husband becomes unity in duality. The soul-wife may sometimes desire reciprocity, but much more often she guarantees only her own strict fidelity. The invocation is monogamous in its intensity and the associated structure of values. The *bhaki-ātmā* is in effect the *patīvratā* and the *sohāgin* rolled into one. For self-transformation to become a saint, negotiation of the lower female desire becomes necessary to incorporate higher forms of female duty into male transcendence. Somewhere on this path patriarchal values are re-ligitimized, and the choice of renunciation begins to appear as an option open to men alone. Thus in a circumlocutory fashion women continue to get salvation through their husbands.

Sangari finds in Kabir a sustained and complex adjustment with patriarchal values in uneasy companionship with an egalitarian *bhakti* which offers direct access to God, claims a single origin for all human beings, and describes the body, the heart, the soul, and true knowledge as ungendered. Patriarchal values are not incidental; they actively compose Kabir's *bhakti*. The *pativrita* rejects but also regulates worldiness. Disorder in marriage and in the faculties of the soul are analogues for each other. Their inter-relation in ultimately to be located not inthe figural realm of devotional poetry but in existing, or desired, patriarchal relations. Coherence is sought and guaranteed in both the social and the transcendent realm. One institutional base is retained to facilitate attack on other institution. Patriarchal values and 'belief' interlock. The paraphraseability of analogies and 'low risk metaphors' suggest a process by which religious bonding can occur on a patriarchal consensual ground.

A few other aspects of Kabir's position are noted by Sangari in a section on patriarchal values and the use of female devotional voice in other *bhaktas*. She makes it clear that 'Kabir is not alone in his contradictions'. For our present purpose, we may concentrate on him alone. He poses opposition between natal family (*nahar*) and marital family (*sasural*) as metaphors for this world (*lok*) and the other (*parlok*), the first symbolizing falsehood and ignorance and the second, truth and knowledge. In the figure of the *virahini*, which is common to all devotional theists, the female voice becomes the embodiment of an exquisite suffering. Since *maya* separate the devotee from god, all life becomes yearning. There is a movement first from the actual to the metaphor, and then to metaphysic of the human soul, love is experienced as suffering. In Kabir, there is a slide from *virah* to widowhood. Since the beloved is 'within', oneself, immolation of the 'self' leads to union with husband -god. In the figure of *satā*, thus, come together the virtue of the *Pativrata*, the burning pain of the *virahini*, and the idealism of the *virah*. What she represents becomes an ideal model for the *bhakt*.

As a social definition and as a metaphor, femaleness for Kabir begins to prop a metaphysic which underpins patriarchal social practice. Logically, just as it is possible to become *jivan-mukta*, it is possible to become *sati*-in-llife. The relevant question is posed; why not immolate 'self' while the husband is alive, why wait for his death? This position contradicts the practice of immolation, but nonetheless it uphold sati metaphgorically, ideologically and inspirationally.

V

Turning again to Guru Nanak, we may notice first that the female of the *strisbhav* is virtually absent in his verses. In spite of this use of a common diction, the import changes. The counterpart of the 'fallen' female is the woman attached to *maya*. She is a victim of the same five adversaries (*kam, krodh, lobh, moh, ahankar*) as keep man in bondage. She is very much the counterpart of Guru Nanak's *manmukh*, the self-willed man. The good woman is devoted to her spouse, but much more important is her appropriation of the truth, the name and the word. She needs the mediacy of the *guru* and the grace of God as much as the man who turns to the *guru* (*gurmukh*). If no man can 'achieve' or 'earn' emancipation, for in the last analysis it depends on God's grace, it is for the 'spouse' of the good woman too to decide whether or not to make her *sohagan*. The ultimate objective for woman as for man is *sahaj*, the state of eternal bliss in union with God, the mingling of light with light. The metaphors used in the case of the woman can obviously be different, but the import remains the same because the metaphors are seldom sustained. The female voice appears to bring the woman within the orbit of emancipatory venture, so much so that even the widow can become a *bairagan*.

To pursue the argument further, to covet the wife of another person, or an unwedded woman, is immoral in Guru Nanak's system of values. However, the advocacy of mutual fidelity does not necessarily ensure monogamy. Furthermore, the ideal wife is squarely placed in the patriarchal structure as a *sohagan*. Guru Nanak appears to create a larger space for women than what we find in Kabir or perhaps in the whole range of Indian literature spiringing from devotional theism. Total equality of woman with man in the spiritual realm was a radical idea in Indian history, especially because it embraced all women; it was not confined to female *bhikhus* or *bhaktas*. Guru Nanak's symbolic attack on discrimination against women due to physiological differences carried the idea of equality a long step forward. If he does not carry it into the home, giving a share to the daughter in ancest ral property, he does not say anything which can be used to support inequality of any kind. However, much of the space he creates for women is created within the patriarchal framework.

References

1. *Adi Granth, Rag Dhanasari (Ashtpadian)*, 685. The printed *Adi Sri Guru Granth Sahib*, abbreviated hereafter as A.G., has a standard Pagination.
2. A.G. *Rag Gauri*, 228.
3. A.G. *Sri Rag*, 62. The idea of God's light being every where is expressed at several other places too, as in A.G. *Rag Ramkali*, 876.
4. A.G. *Sri Rag*, 19.
5. A.G. *Rag Dhanasari*, 663.
6. A.G. *Rag Vadhans Dakhani*, 580.
7. A.G. *Rag Gauri*, 223.
8. A.G. *Rag Malar*, 1255.
9. A.G. *Rag Ramkali*, 879.
10. A.G. *Jap*, 2.
11. A.G. *Rag Asa*, 351.
12. A.G. *Rag Asa* (Slok), 468.
13. A.G. *Sri Rag*, 72.
14. A.G. *Sri Rag*, 15.
15. A.G. *Rag Suhi (Chaupaday)*, 728.
16. A.G. *Rag Majh (Ashtpadian)*, 109.
17. A.G. *Rag Gauri (Ashtpadian)*, 229.
18. A.G. *Rag Vadhans*, 581.
19. A.G. *Sri Rag*, 15.
20. A.G. *Sri Rag*, 14.
21. A.G. *Sri Rag*, 14.
22. A.G. *Sri Rag*, 51.
23. A.G. *Sri Rag (Slok)*, 142.
24. A.G. *Rag Gauri Guareri*, 222.
25. A.G. *Rag Asa*, 416.
26. A.G. *Rag Sarag* (*Slok*), 1288.
27. A.G. *Sri Rag*, 14.
28. A.G. *Rag Asa* (*Ashtpadian*), 417. Also Appendix, Extract VII.
29. Appendix, Extract VIII.
30. A.G. *Rag Sorath* (*Chautukay*), 596.
31. A.G. *Sri Rag*, 23.
32. A.G. *Rag Basant* (*Ashtapadian Dotukian*), 1187; *Rag Gauri Cheti*, 155
33. A.G. *Sri Rag* (*Ashtpadian*), 60.
34. A.G. *Rag Asa*, 473.
35. A.G. *Rag Malar* (Slok), 472.

36. A.G. *Rag Asa* (Slok), 472.
37. A.G. *Rag Tilang*, 722.
38. A.G. *Rag Suhi*, 730; *Rag Parbhati*, 1329 & 1332.
39. A.G. *Rag Asa*, 418.
40. A.G. *Rag Malar*, 1257.
41. A.G. *Rag Gauri*, 225.
42. A.G. *Slok Vāran te Vadhik*, 1412.
43. A.G. *Sri Rag*, 23.
44. A.G. *Sri Rag* (*Ashtpadian*), 73.
45. A.G. *Rag Bilawal*, 796.
46. A.G. *Rag Tilang*, 724.
47. A.G. *Rag Tilang*, 724.
48. A.G. *Rag Tilang*, 725.
49. A.G. *Rag Basant*, 1171.
50. A.G. *Rag Basant*, 1170.
51. A.G. *Slok, Vāran te Vadhik*, 1412.
52. A.G. *Sri Rag* (*Ashtpadian*), 54-55.
53. A.G. *Rag Gauri*, 151-52.
54. A.G. *Rag Tukhari*, 1111.
55. A.G. *Rag Suhi* (*Chhant*), 763-64.
56. Gopal Singh, tr., *Guru Granth Sahib, vols.* 1-4, Delhi: Guru Das Kapur and Sons, 1960-62, 134.
57. Gopal Singh, 134.
58. A.G. *Rag Gauri*, 157.
59. A.G. *Rag Vadhans*, 579.
60. A.G. *Sri Rag*, 23.
61. A.G. *Rag Malar*, 1257.
62. A.G. *Rag Gauri*, 225-26.
63. Gopal Singh, 466.
64. Gopal Singh, 577.
65. A.G. *Rag Gauri Cheti*, 154-55.
66. A.G. *Rag Malar*, 1255.
67. A.G. *Rag Gauri Bairagan*, 147.
68. A.G. *Rag Asa* (*Chhant*), 435

69. A.G. *Rag Suhi* (*Chhant*), 763.

70. A.G. *Rag Tilang*, 772.

71. A.G. *Rag Bilawal* (*Chhant Dakhani*), 843.

72. Sahib Singh, *Sri Guru Granth Sahib Darpan.*

73. A.G. *Rag Sarag* (*Ashtpadian*), 1232.

74. A.G. *Sri Rag*, 17.

75. A.G. *Rag Suhi* (*Chhant*), 764.

76. A.G. *Rag Tukhari* (*Chhant*), 1064.

77. A.G. *Rag Basant* (*Ashtpadian Dotukian*), 1187.

78. A.G. *Rag Tukhari* (*Chhant*), 1107-10. Also, Appendix, Extract XXI.

79. A.G. *Rag Bilawal*, 843.

80. A.G. *Rag Vadhans*, 566.

81. R.G. Bhandarkar, *Vaishnavism, Shaivism and Minor Religious Systems*, Bhandarkar Oriental Research Institute, Poona, 1929.

82. Kumkum Sangari, 'Mirabai and Spiritual Economy of Bhakti' *Economic and Political Weekly*, July 7, 1990, 1464-75; July 14, 1990, 1537-51.

15

The Metaphors of Womanhood in Indian Literature

*Mridula Garg**

An analysis of the making of literature leads one to the exploration of the social reality, which in turn takes one on a search for the genealogy cf metaphor in literature. The relationship between the reality of any cultural entity and its literature is two-fold. Literature draws the basic premise of its metaphors from the social reality but transmutes it in a manner that changes the image people have of themselves. It takes times but is powerful enough to bring about a gradual change in reality itself. Hence it is important to study the relationship between the reality and the metaphor of, as controversial and explosive a concept as womanhood, in a country as little understood as India.

The Reality

There are, broadly speaking, three kinds of women in India. First, there are the women of the "Third World," who are no better than beasts of burden. They are burdened with a higher and higher load of work with less and less to eat with each act of development, inasmuch as these acts lead to the denuding of the forest and the destruction of other natural produce.

Then there are the women who belong to the middle class with a certain degree of education. They are increasingly being

* She author is a distinguished literary personality and columnist (E-118 Masjid Moth, New Delhi).

pushed to work outside the home for payment, out of economic necessity rather than a need to develop and utilise their talent and time. They have a certain degree of political awareness. It is out of this section that both rebels and die-hard conservatives among women emerge. These can be called the women of the "second world."

Third, we have women who are highly educated, well-placed, articulate, adventurous, holding important and socially powerful jobs. These, along with those women who are merely objects of decoration, engaged largely in the pursuit of the accumulation of consumer goods, compose the "First World" within the "Third World" country of India.

With regard to the aspirations of these women, the women of the Second World largely perceive the women of the First World as their ideal. They usually aspire to possess the same degree of affluence, leisure and above all consumer goods, some also to the same degree of education and opportunity. They are the most mobile among the classes and manage sometimes to cross over to the First World through sheer determination, hard work and grit. These are the women most seen and heard. They often give a picture of a highly volatile and rebellious women's movement in India. Properly seen in the context of the total number of women in the country and their situation, such an impression would seem to be highly exaggerated.

The Third World women perceive themselves to be different and do not think they can ever become the equal of the Second or First World women. All their energies are devoted to earning a livelihood. In the villages and the city slums, they perform the functions, which in developed countries as well as the First and Second World of India, are performed by the welfare state: that is, the provision of basic amenities of life like water and energy. Their natural aspiration is to have a normal year of harvest with normal rainfall so their routine of life is not disrupted and they are not displaced from their homes. Their highest aspiration in life is to give a modicum of education to their children so that they may move to a world, unknown to them, but brought within the realm of their consciousness through developments in communications.

This is the reality of women in India.

The Metaphor

I propose to see how the reality outlined above is changed into a metaphor of womanhood by literature, particularly that written by women. This I shall do with reference to the metaphor handed down to us by the literature of the past, both oral and written. I shall try to point out both the persistence of the inherited image of woman and the changes that have occurred in it.

Heritage of Oral Literature

We can discern three distinct images to woman in the oral literature of India: Goddess, beloved, and householder. Although these are common to the literature sung and enacted in all the languages of the country, I will deal specifically with Hindi, my own language.

1. The Goddess is perceived as *Devi*[1] or as a being who is incorruptible, pure, all-merciful and for giving as in the presentation of Sita[2] in the *Ramayana* or Savitri[3] in the tale of *Satyavan Savitri*. The same is true of Damyanti in *Nal Damyanti*[4] and *Ahilya*[5] in *Ramayana*. The Goddess is seen as *Shakti*[6] or the embodiment of power. This is manifest in stories dealing with Durga and Kali, the destroyers of evil.

2. As a beloved, the woman is often perceived as a tragic heroine as in the folk love tales of *Heer Ranjha, Shirin Farhad, Laila Majnu*, and the beloved aspects of Sita and other *devi* embodiments. The highest and most complex form of this lover-beloved image is enshrined in the *Radha-Kishnana* love tale. If not a tragic heroine, pure and incorruptible in her love, she is portrayed as a scheming "other" woman. This is best seen in the stories of *Tota Maina*, where the perfidy of woman and man is related in turn by the male *Tota* (Parrot) and famale *Maina* (Nightingale). It can also be seen in the stories of *Panchatantra* and other tales.

3. The householder and the housewife are quite distinct as far as the picture of women in Indian oral literature is concerned. The woman is never alone with her husband in the household. She is part of the larger family in which her predicament emerges not only from her relations with her husband or lack of them, but also from her relations with a wide host of other females and males of the household.

The folk songs which sing of the predicament of woman as a member of the joint family have humour and satire as their hallmark. The high flown piety or righteous anger of the Goddess as well as the intense overtones of the beloved are exchanged for an earthy humour and a wry sense of resignation. The scheming "other" woman is not only the possible *Saut* or beloved of the husband but also the sister and mother-in-law. The husband becomes the lover, as privacy with him is hindered by the other members of the family. Sex is openly flaunted, with no holds barred. Vulgarity is taken in its stride. Risque banter is made. At the same time, the folk songs stress the changing of the seasons with the accompanying chores that women have to perform. This is significant as it means that woman, in the folk form, was seen both as a sensual and a work-burdened being.

A part from these principal divisions, women were portrayed some times as warriors, other than the divine *shakti* embodiments, as patriot queens or helpers of men. They were depicted sparingly as scholars such as Vidyottama, the wife of poet Kalidasa and, of course, the legendary Gargi and Maitraiye of the Vedic period, so often dug up to prove that women held wonderful positions in the golden Vedic age.

It is interesting to note that women were hardly ever shown as economic beings, whether as landlords, traders, farmers or members of other professions. It is true that even in case of men the hero was always a warrior king or a mendicant but oral literature as well as the written *Panchtantra* is full of traders, travellers, inn-keepers, farmers and craftsmen. The exclusion of women as economic beings is especially significant, as her image of householder included a host of tasks, relating not only to a housewifely nature but also to sowing, harvesting and other farming operations. The thread that inter-linked the *shakti-Devi* and the householder concept was the concept of woman as mother. The mother figure embraced within itself not only the concept of the dutiful wife or the Sita-Savitri image but also the image of woman as the provider of food and comfort in the family. This Annapoorna image is, perhaps, the single most significant aspect of womanhood in India, celebrated through the ages. Like other figures, it has its beneficent and exploitative repercussions. But it remains the most significant aspect of the metaphor of womanhood in India.

This is true, I suspect, in all societies subsisting at low levels of affluence or what the affluent call the "Third World." The whole idea is that woman, in her role as householder, has the responsibility of providing the basic needs of life such as food, fuel, water, fodder, medical, and childcare; this she is expected to do despite the rigors of penury of *Abhava* as it is called in Hindi.

Significantly, in the *Mahabharata*, when the Pandavas are cast out in the forest and forced to face the rigors of *Abhava*, it is Draupadi, the wife, who feels responsible. She expresses her grief to

Lord Krishna and is given an *Akshaya Patra* which has the quality of regenerating the food put into it. It becomes empty only after Draupadi has eaten. What is important here is not only that it assumes that Draupadi would eat last, so dear to the heart of feminists, but that it is the reponsibility of Draupadi to provide food, even though she is not the bread winner.

Today 80 per cent of the women of the Third World are the providers of essentials like fuel, water, fodder and food. They spend more than a normal working day collecting these every day. Yet their perception of themselves as well as the perception of the society and its literature is that they are primarily engaged in household work. We can say then that the dominant metaphor of woman handed down to us from ancient and oral literature is that of Sati-Ma-Annapoorna i.e. Dutiful Wife-Mother-cum-Provider. This is celebrated, not only as the ideal or utopia, but is the normal aspiration of every woman.

Modern Literature

The image of Durga or the warrior woman, derived from the concept of *Shakti*, though invoked now and then did not have the popular currency of Sita image for the obvious reason that it was hardly something that could be copied by the large majority of women. Quite simply, Durga was not a housewife or a householder, while the majority of the Indian women were. Durga became the utopian image, to be invoked in times of emergency or invasion, unfortunately, at the convenience of the leader rather than the inner or felt need of the woman. For example, during the Independence Movement, Gandhiji placed great emphasis on the role of women; they responded with fervour, producing not only freedom fighters but a number of writers who protrayed militant woman patriots.

Of particular interest is the fact that women revolutionaries, when portrayed by male writers such as Rabindra Nath Tagore, or Sarat Chandra Chatterji, the great Bengali writers, were cast not as thinking leaders but fighters under their leadership of men.

Jaishankar Prasad was the only significant male Hindi writer, who cast his women in the Durga image. He chose a period in history when dying and killing for the honour of the family was the name of the game. His women took up the mantle of heroic avengers in the absence of males, against male transgressors. In the process, they suffered tremendous mental agony as they had to perform against their natures. Often enough, they, like Madhulika in *Akashdeep* fell in love with the enemy. That has been a pet ploy of writers all over the world. A woman caught between love and family honour. Naturally, honour or virtue is the winner.

Jaishankar Prasad was a contemporary of Premchand but his choice of subject and character was so totally different that it is important to underline his particular brand of women. The women here, as everywhere else, took the accepted value of heroism as given. They neither questioned the rationale behind the norms nor evolved a rationale of their own. That is not to say that the ordinary men did, or that the male characters in literature always worked out a new set of norms. The period of history chosen by Prasad precluded any individual line of thought or choice.

In fact, much before Prasad came on the scene, Bankim Chandra Chatterjee had written *Anand Math* with the famous revolutionary song, "*Vandematram*," as early as in 1885. But his chief protagonists were men. His women were aggressive enough but they depended more on divine powers.

It was left to a woman to immortalise the rebel queen of Jhansi, one of the leaders of the 1857 revolt against the British in her poem, "*Jhansi ke Rani*" (1923). The writer was Subhadra Kumari Chauhan, and her poem became a rallying cry for the freedom fighters in the 1920s and 30s. There were others who wrote patriotic poems but none is as vividly remembered for a single poem. In any case, the period of the 1920s and 1930 saw the *Durga* image of woman gain the greatest currency ever in modern India.

Other than this literary manifestation of the *Durga* image, the representation of woman underwent a reverse transformation in the direction of subservience during the period of colonial subjugation. It seems to me a perfectly logical result of a situation where a large body of the population was subjugated and resigned to it. But there was also a sustained and country-wide revolt against the political masters. The image of woman increasingly became that of one subservient and secondary to man, both in her manifestation as the mother-wife-provider and as the beloved. The seeds were there in the image proclaimed by the epics and the oral literature. With increased insecurity and penury, she came to be relegated to the position of an inadequate provider and a weak being in need of masculine protection.

She did retain her participatory character as a representative of her class, suffering class exploitation in the same manner as men, in Premchand's writing from 1910 to 1930. She was not the chief protagonist in novels like *Godan* and *Premashram* or *Rangbhoomi*, in which he dealt with the ramifications of economic, social, and political exploitation in the rural-urban society. She was secondary to the chief protagonist, who was a man, but she was not insignificant as a representative of her class and as a victim of the exploitative system. Nor was she portrayed as a being suffering more from sexual than socio-economic-political exploitation. That came later. But even in Premchand, women became the chief protagonists, only when he was particularly concerned with the family and the specific exploitation of woman as a sexual and oppressed being. Then she was usually shown to be caught in the mire of false values imputed to her by the social value system; e.g. she inflicted her sufferings on herself by an excessive love of ornaments in *Gaban*. In the story *"Beton ki Maa,"* she was shown to suffer from unjust laws and social values. Yet she retained her character as a woman of her class rather than a woman with a capital W. Later, ironically as men and women became more and more consicious of the exploitation of woman as woman, her individuality was wrested from her and she became the representative of a sex rather than a class.

The first development took place in the 1930s, with a depending of the mystique around woman and the consequent over-emphasis on the beloved image. Jainendra and Agyaye were the doyens in this field, but women writers soon took over and internalised the image. Woman in the hands of Jainendra and Agyaye became a beautiful if non-rational being, whose irrational and intuitive nature made her a natural object to be coveted and pursued by men. She did not become the sex object of the Western world, because after all the pursuing and winning were done, she was still, in essence, a mother; hence, an object of worship. This was not quite as illogical as it may seem to the Western mind. The duality was the logical outcome of the superimposition of Freudian psychological insight on to the inherited image of woman as a tragic beloved who could always find salvation in the mother image, if all else filed her. The never-ending refrain said that woman was, in her very essence, different from man. She was the giver, man the taker. She was beneficent, man was aggressive. She was intuitive, man was coldly rational. She was physical, man was cerebral.

Jainendra was the least hypocritical and the most explicit in painting a self-sacrificing, other self-negating image of woman who was, at the same time, so totally unpredictable, mercurial and passionate that it was quite impossible for a staightforward, selfish, rational man to understand her. Others who came after him ostensibly rebelled against the Jainendrian picture but actually did very little to demolish it. The major change was that women's sexulaity received more emphasis as a way of disowning the self-negating postures of Jainendra in heroine. Among women writers, Amrita Pritam and

Krishna Sobti were inheritors of this image of a mysterious, sensual, yet, self-sacrificing metaphor of womanhood, with the emphasis shifting from negation to sensuality. The mystique, however, remained intact.

A new aspect of the woman as beloved which emerged in the 1930s under the influence of the quasi-liberal attitudes of a semi enlightened, educated elite was that of the *patita* or the fallen woman. Fallen from where? Not a position of influence or power but from the image of the Sati Savitri (the chaste woman wholly devoted to her husband) or the purity of the body, of course. Because, all said and done, was woman not a physical being, however beautiful in form? The liberal man did not ever cosider denying that; all his liberality allowed him was a show of compassion for the fallen woman. The archetype was naturally the prostitute. Men, naturally or unnaturally, acquired a monopoly on portraying her. They were, after all, the buyers, and it was the age of the buyer's market. The net result was that their compassion made them see sings of *devatva* (godliness) in the *patita* (fallen woman).

After all the tears had been shed and the circumstances of her fall dissected, she was found to be, at heart, even more self-negating, and intense in her aspirations for a home, husband and brood of children than an ordinary woman. Sharat Chandra Chatterjee, Ila Chandra Joshi, and the later writers, Kamleshwar, Jagdamba Prasad Dixit, Manohar Shyam Joshi all tried their hand at it. Others like Rajendra Yadav and Mohan Rakesh chose women from the ostensibly respectable Second World, treating them with pity, sympathy, compassion, even humility. But the picture remained that of a woman with a capital W, a creature wronged surely because of the wickedness of men but also easily led astray because of her own supercharged sensuality and erratic behaviour.

This picture, largely unchanged until today, had important repercussions on writing by women. The preoccupation with the fallen woman led logically to resentment against men as the perpetrators of crimes against women, which brought about their fall. Later came in the 30s, most devastatingly from the pen of Mahadevi Verma, a celebrated Hindi poet. Although she did not deal with the prostitute, which continues to be the natural or unnatural preserve of men, she dealt with the outcaste among poor women in the villages as well as small towns. They were cast out of their homes and deprived of the little they possessed because of the tyranny of men. She wrote of women who were poor, unlettered and ignorant but had a fund of love and good humor. And she wrote of them in such an earthy and natural manner that one felt the portraits were drawn by someone who had chanced upon them at the village well or in a women's gathering. This is all the more surprising, considering that Mahadevi's poetry, for which she won far greater renown in her time, is full of mystic romanticism and the pain of eternal separation from the lover. She wove a mystique around men and women in her poetry but rejected it in favour of the earth and the earthbound in her prose. As was to be expected, this no-nonsense attitude toward women did not find many successors among the women writers who came after her. It was the resentment against men that took root and later found expression, more widely and effectively, under the influence of feminism.

Effect of Feminism

Here I would like to point out that feminism has come to India, not so much as an ideology or body of thought representing a world view of women, distinct from the accepted world view of men, but in the form of a movement emphasising the need for freeing women from the tyranny of men. More pragmatic than theoretical in approach, it focuses on the emancipation of woman rather than the development of a philosophy of political thought. This may have something to do with the fact that woman's sexuality was never in doubt in our traditional literature or folklore. Nor was woman merely a sex object, because of the enthroned mother ideal that invoked the mother-goddess image of women whenever difficulty arose. This led to the exploitation of women in its own way, in the imposition of a self-sacrificting and self-negating ideal, but at the same time it prevented them from being reduced to passive sex objects in need of asserting their sexuality. Sexuality was not something to be hidden and ashamed of, a point made amply clear by the eroticism permitted in all art, architecture, poetry, fiction and oral literature of ancient India.

The open outlook toward sex got lost with the advent of colonialism and Western cultural influences. The mother and *Annapoorna* not only gained precedence over the wife and the beloved, but sexuality became someting to be ashamed of in a woman. The new breed of women writers, schooled alike in the tyranny of men by earlier writers like Premchand and Madhadevi Verma, and in the inescapable mystique surrounding women by writers like Jainendra and Ila Chandra Joshi, responded in two ways to the advent of feminism.

The earliest response came as an assertion of woman's unabashed sexuality as a force in itself, not subservient to love for the male. Krishna Sobti deals with it in her *Mitro Marjani,* as does Kamla Das in her autobiography, poems and stories. It is worth noting that even when women writers celebrated women's sexuality, they did not give up the celebration of motherhood. More often than not, they surrendred the erotic to the maternal in the conclusion. This seems to have been an effect of the earlier search for the Sati in the *patita* syndrome; that is, trying to find an underlying chastity in the fallen woman. The other response to the increased awareness of woman's sexuality was the heightened perception of her as an exploited sex and, more important, the perception of her exploitation as mainly sexual.

The second was especially significant, with both beneficient and maleficent repercussions. In a country like India, where 80 percent of the women belong to a class subject to inhuman lengths of exploitation, economic social and political sexual exploitation is not of prime concern. The women of weaker sections of society are, undoubtedly, subject to horrendous sexual exploitation, ranging from outright rape and physical violence, to discriminatory illiteracy and malnutrition. But the fact remains that this sexual exploitation is largely a function of the socio-political and economic exploitation. When all women are bracketed together as the exploited sex, their essential class difference is glossed over. Since most women writers come from the Second World women of India, their concentration focuses on rebellion against men and the ultimate aim of attaining equality with them which again dilutes the class difference. It focuses attention on the exploitation of women by men of their own class, and only as a fallout, by men of a more privileged class. Even here, the perception of exploitation being largely sexual, the exploitation of women as producers, farmers, artisans, bonded labourers, service caterers, and so on, gets portrayed as mainly sexual rather than socio-economic and political. It was only natural for feminist politics to concentrate on seeking redress mainly from inequality with men rather than inequality between men including women, or between women including men. Marriage came to be regarded as the hotbed of women's exploitation, a fetter rather than a source of fulfillment. This was expressed, in turn, in three different forms.

First, there was an increased and franker depiction of extra marital affairs, sexually more gratifying but ending more often than not in tragedy. This was as much a harking back to the tragic image of the beloved enshrined in tradition as a primary concern with men rather than for a total redefinition of identity. The parameters were defined by male-female relationships, rather than a search for an independent identity in the wider and more complex socio-political milieu. Second, there was increased depiction of the torments suffered by women within marriage from physical abuse to the strangulation of talents and sexual frustration. A recent novel by one of the younger women writers, Simi Harshita, dealing with marriage and subsequent living in a joint family, in succinctly called *Yatna Shivir* or *Torture Chamber*. Third, sometimes the woman was shown to turn against marriage altogether, but the point of reference remained men. The refusal to marry was an act of defiance, an aberration which required explanation and formed the theme of a story and did not occur as a matter of course in its development on a wider canvas. For example, in Raji Seth's story, *Mere Liye Nahin*, the heroine says, "I'm made differently...I don't have the capacity to adjust to that extent... I tell you! They are great... these wives... know how to kill themselves silently for others... real martyrs!" That is her reason for not marrying.

This is not an insignificant development, considering that marriage is regarded as essential for women in India; so essential indeed that it gives rise to social evils like dowry (money given to the bridegrooms's parents as an essential part of the marriage contract), female infanticide and foeticide to escape the payment of it, femicide in the form of killing for dowry and *Sati* (burning a woman on her husband's funeral pyre). Generally speaking, the birth of a female child is an economic loss.

Interestingly, marriage is considered necessary not only for women but also for men too. I feel this is a part of the security syndrome. The reason could be twofold: a culture so old that is has by now come to recognise the need for security above adventure, and the general atmosphere of economic insecurity fed by large-scale unemployment. Marriage insures all kinds of security: economic, sexual and emotional, both for men and women. Yes, economic too. For, even when women do not go outside the home to work, which increasingly they do, they perform the essential function of family provider or the *Annapoorna* battling with *Abhav* (scaracity) as a part of their upbringing.

With the advent of feminism in the 1950's the aspiration of woman in literature shifted from being man's support to being his equal. Her mood changed from resignation and forgiveness to disillusionment and rebelliousness. But this rebelliousness was aimed only at her exploitation at the hands of men, not at the politico-economic system or the socio-ethical values which shackled women and a massive percentage of men as well. That was the limiting factor in women's writing on women and on men.

Concomitant with the advent of feminism came the entry of a far greater number of women into literature, especially in the field of fiction, both short story and novel, thought sparingly in drama. But it was in the field of jounalism that feminism emerged as an uncompromising critical procedure and political platform. Literature takes longer to change and jell and is cast in more timeless a form. So, the change is slower, more tentative, probing, doubting, but finally, more definite than anything else. It changes the image of woman almost without seeming to do so.

Curiously, women who are quite uncompromising in their attitudes as feminists or at least independent, thinking individuals in seminars and conferences, proceed in an indeterminate, vacillating and even paradoxical manner when delivering a creative work. Or they go to the other extreme and create a utopian world of free women, untrammelled by the trivial or the commonplace. This is a part of the creative process. The parallel world of fiction has to run alongside and be born of experienced life and sensibility, or shall we say *Samskara* and not simply of a logically thought out theory of change. In this indeterminate situation of half-change where the majority of women, along with their men, were no more than beasts of burden, while minority reached out for equality with men in education, opportunity, freedom for sex-typing of roles and self-expressions, a limited kind of rebellion took place.

Almost all the portrayals of women which show her as dissatisfied by her wife-sex object image continue to cast her as a sexual or at best a family being. She is almost always portrayed with reference to men: supportive of men or rebellious to them; supported by men or exploited by them.

This brings us to the single most important and ironic development in writing by women in India today. When the women writers want to portray the complexities, intricacies, inequities and incongruities of the socio-economic or the value system, they choose men as their protagonists.[7] They choose women protagonists only when they want to portray the complexities, inequities or intricacies of personal relationships, family life or sexual exploitation, both within and outside marriage. Innumerable examples can be given.

When Mannu Bhandari delves into the making of a broken home and its effect on the psyche of the child, as in Aapka Banti (translated in English as **Banti**), she chooses a woman as her protagonist. When she deals with political corruption, caste exploitation and nascent rebellion in *Mahabhoj* (translated as the *Great Feast*), she choose men as her protagonists. When Krishna Sobti talks of the positive sexuality of woman (*Mitro Marjani*), the unending sexual exploitation of a woman cut off from her home ("*Dar se Bichuri*") the dream of love of woman suffering from a contagious disease (*Badlon ke Ghere*") or the permanent scars left by rape (*Surajmukhi Andhere ke*), she chooses women protagonists. But when she portrays the corrupt manipulations of the bureaucracy through clearks in an office ("*Yaron ke Yar*"), she chooses male protagonists. Not only that, women appear as nothing more than commodities in it.

I have done it myself. When I deal with a woman's search for identitiy outside the orbit of men, I first take her through love for two men and enough disillusionment to last a lifetime. Only then do I hand her the realisation that she has to find fulfillment within herself and with her own effort and talent (*Uske Hisse ki Dhoop*, translated as *A Touch of Sun*). Of course, the protagonist is a woman. But when I deal with the broader canvas of the Independence Movement, its paradoxes and incongruities, the dilemma ending in compromise and the ideal degenerating into resignation and stagnation, I choose men as my protagonists *Anitya*, translated as *Halfway House*. The only saving grace is the woman Kajal Bannerji in it. She is not the chief protagonist, but she is certainly not insignificant. Nor does she function with reference to men within their orbit. She is courageous and discerning. Her involvement with the movement is more honest and passionate, and she makes a far greater impact on the next generation than any other character. She is a social, not a sexual being, a representative of a class of people, not of a sex. She could have been the chief protagonist but she is not.

A somewhat similar example can be taken from Nasira Sharma's novel *Sat Nadian Ek Samandar*. This novel is in the nature of all collage of the happenings during the revolution and the counter revolution in Iran, during and after the overthrow of the Shah. Both men and women of the middle class had got involved caught in it. An important woman character drawn by Sharma is that of Tayyaba. She grows with the progress of the revolution both in depth and stature. From a slightly non-conformist but fundamentally rational girl, she grows into a courageous and strong revolutionary, who suffers the grue- some horrors and the unspeakable torture of the jail without flinching or compromising. She is unique in that the other women in the novel remain largely suffering wives, mothers and housekeepers, though caught in the throes of the violence of the revolution. Tayyaba, like Kajal Banerjee of *Anitya* remains the 'almost' chief protagonist. The revolution is not of her making, but she refuses to be a mere cog in the wheel. She is a thinking participant and she leaves a deep impress upon the others.

This portrayal of women, who could have been the chief protagonists but are not, is of crucial importance in understanding the process by which the metaphors of womanhood are created in literature. A writer does not choose her or his protagonists deliberately after cool calculation and reference to the fund of knowledge and the political ideology she possesses. She cannot. That is not how literature is made. The protagonist chooses the writer in a manner of speaking. He or she is born in her sphere of sensibility formed over a lifetime of experienced reality, its re-creation into fantasy and reality again. The knowledge accumulated by the writer plays a part, but not separately from the experience of the lifetime. The two together form the sensibility in which the memory of culture gone by and its inherited traits play equally important roles. We come back to the hold of the *Samskara*. This *Samskara* is a terrible thing. It encompasses tradition, sensibility, civilisation, ideology, a way of life, a code of conduct, what-you-will. Its hold is tighter than that of the old man on Sinbad, the Sailor. Most of what literature does and fails to do in India can be explained by the invisible, insidious working of *Samskara*. This has to be remembered always, when dealing with writing now and then, with the change in thought, new movements and ideologies and all that they change and all that they fail to. Feminism is no exception.

There is nothing esoteric in this process. I am not creating mysteries or trying to impute a mystique to writing that it does not possess. The mystique is there in every art. However rational the explanation, however analytical the instruments of criticism, the element of mystique has to be there for writing to be something more than a logical exercise.

This brings me to the question of women characters in women's novels or stories, whose chief protagonists are men. I have given an example of Kajal Bannerji in my novel *Anitya*. She is the exception rather than the rule. Generally, the women play a secondary role in male-oriented novels. They may be educated, enlightened, independent, even aggressive, but they appear only in relationship to men. They need not necessarily be the traditional wives and lovers. They need not be sex objects at all. They may even escape being mothers, though that is rare; the craving at least is there. They can be advisers, companions, even conscience keepers, but to whom? To men, of course. Their terms of reference are always men, and they are brought in to fill the natural need for personal relationship in a novel. Their concern may be humanist but their concerns in the novel are those pertaining to men.[8]

The question is, can the novels written by women in India really be called feminist or are they merely novels written by writers who happen to be women? If by feminist writing, we mean texts which project a unique world view, different from the historically accepted world view of men, then most writing by women in India cannot be called feminist. It is definitely a step in the direction of feminist writing inasmuch as it looks at woman as a unique class. It also considers the world from the point of view of the writer who is a woman committed to recognising womanhood as a class and an exploited one at that. It is, however, only the first step as it excludes women whose world view feminism is supposed to project from the making of that world.

One interesting exception is a novel, *Patrangpur Puran* by Mrinal Pandey. I do not think it would please feminists to call this a feminist novel. But it does give a woman's world view. The only thing is that the women are not rebels or thinkers or even independent individuals conscious of their identity. They are women who are fully engrossed in their domestic concerns. They look at the world from inside the home, somewhat like one looking out of a window at the outside world. The outside world is in a turbulent period of history. The women see history in the making and record it from their own traditionally accepted point of view, even if they do not make it. It is an interesting experiment. It is also a comment on the image women have of themselves. Above all, it proves my point. Mrinal is a crusader for women's rights as a journalist and activist. Yet, when she sets out to write a novel with women protagonists, she selects middle class women and imbues them with every possible accepted attribute of womanhood.

The emphasis on the sexual or familial nature of women persists despite the fact that 80 percent of the women of India are basically producers, workers and providers. Of the remaining 20 percent a large percentage, belonging to India's Second World, are engaged in economic and political participation. But the decision making remains in the hands of men, both in real life and in women's writing. That is why, perhaps, women are relegated to the sphere of interpersonal relationships in novels dominated alike by men and women. The social reality has an insidious and subtle effect on writing, but because it is a fractured and vitiated reality, the effect, too, is fractured and only half the truth. We must remember that in India, as indeed in most Third World countries, we live not in one but two

Indias. One is scientifically conscious, technologically ambitious, rich, well-equipped annd ostentatious. The other is poor, devoid of basic amenities of life and constantly being pushed to the margin. The emancipation of women is essentially a variable of the well-being or non-well-being of the other India. Literature recognises it but vaguely. Even while it seeks to portary the predicament of the Third World, it ends up imputing to it the aims and aspirations of the Second, if not the First World. It is hardly surprising then for women writers to take the half-feminist stance that they do, coming as they are almost wholly from the Second World.

The greatest losers in this portrayal are the Third World women. They are portrayed often enough; it has become increasingly the t rend to do so. The concern of women and men writers of the Second World is humanist. The humanist concern requires that the Third World women be the protagonists. They are thus chosen, sometimes deliberately, sometimes automatically. It is in the weaving of the fabric of thier lives that Second World concerns take over. The experienced reality and the wide gap in the reality of the two worlds forces the hand of the writer until she or he does one of two things.

She may fix her attention more often on the women living in the slums of cities and towns than on those who continue to live in the villages. With an uncanny command over dialect and manners, Chitra Mudgal, for example, focuses her stories on the women of Bombay slums. Her Third World women are quite often portrayed as social beings. In many of her stories, like "*Bhookh*" and "*Lane,*" her women protagonists from the slums are engaged primarily in an unequal economic struggle. I hope she soon writes a novel and treats this subject on a larger canvas. Interestingly, her Second World stories deal with male protagonists "*Anubandh*" and "*Pesha*".

The woman writer may perceive the exploitation of women, who are not only working in highly exploitative conditions but are overburdened with all kinds of work as mainly sexual. This applies equally to those who continue to live in the decaying villages, those pushed to the periphery in the more prosperous ones, and those who come to the cities as ecological and developmental refugees. I do not say that they are not subject to sexual exploitation, only that it is a direct consequence of the social situation, where all the members of the family, children included, spend all their time in earning a livelihood, which turns out to be below the minimum necessary for healthy survival. It is this which is largely ignored in the development of the metaphor.

A notable exception is Manjul Bhagat's novel *Anaro*. It portrays a working woman from the slums without subjecting her to sexual harassment or assault in the course of her work. She has problems with her husband, of course, but the story deals independently with her struggle as a worker and a wife, without creating any sexually exploitative situations in her working life. She is a full-blooded character, full of lust for life, but quite the despair of feminists because she escapes from other restraints and constraints. She is equally the despair of social reformers because she insists on giving a dowry to her daughter and takes a loan to celebrate the marriage feast even though there is no social pressure to do so. Is the writer then laughing at them all? Or perhaps Anaro is. Or may be it is all the fault of our *Samskara*! Be that as it may, you can feel frustrated with Anaro but cannot pity her. Nor can you dispute the fact that her story is a faithful account of the reality of a Third World woman of the city slum. For the rest, literature, along with sociology and the feminist movement has conspired to limit portrayals of women to sexual beings and projected ther aspirations and agitations to the exclusion of their roles as social and economic beings.

In real life, the most glaring example of this has been the perception of the *Chipko* Movement, a movement of the poor forest dwellers and farmers of *Uttarkhand* in the Himalayas against the indiscriminate cutting of forests. Just because women have taken a lead in this, it has been portrayed as a feminist rather than a peasant movement against a faulty national policy, despite the fact that *Uttarkhand* has seen a large-scale migration of men to this cities or the Army in search of livelihood. This again is a manifestation of the effects of an ill-conceived national economic policy, which centralises the opportunities for employment in a few cities, to the neglect of the vast hinterland. The women are the only representatives of the villagers left in *Uttarkhand* and are, thus, leading a peasant movement against national policies, rather than a woman's movement against men. This remains true even when there is a conflict of interest between the women and the men, because the conflict is between men who are city-based and women who are village-based. The conflict thus is a city-village conflict and not a male-female conflict. But that is how it gets in the media.

It is important to note some changes have appeared in the writing of women about women in the last decade. Though as yet marginal in nature to the main body of literature, they are portents hat raise hopes of seeing women portrayed as social beings in the future.

The first interesting characteristic, shared by Indian literature with the literature of all emergent countries as well as Black America, is the emergence of woman as a teacher. Not woman with teaching as a career but teacher in the wider sense of someone who changes people's perception of history and politics. Particularly significant is the characterisation of woman as a history teacher. In fact, the writer herself emerges as a history teacher in that she under takes to rewrite the history of her country in general, and the female race in particular. Our history has suffered from a twofold distortion as it has been conceived and analysed according to the perception of the male coloniser. A rewriting of history is, thus, of crucial importance to the Third World countries from both gender and race-class point of view. In India, while most novels written in 1970's, like Mannu Bhandari's *Aapka Banti* or Usha Priyamvada's *Pachpan Khambe Lal Deewar* contented themselves with portraying the woman as a professional teacher and, hence, a thinking individual, some of the recent novels assign a more important role to her. In Nasira Sharma's *Theekre ki Mangni* the woman teacher influences the struggle of the deprived youth of the village for a better life. In my *Anitya* the teacher sets out to rewrite the Indian history from a non-British point of view and in the process, influences the thinking of an entire generation.

From the standpoint of feminists, another vitally, important character which needs to be explored is that of the daughter of a prostitute. Inasmuch as she has no maternal role model and has to struggle not only for acceptance in society but the formulation of her own sense of identity, she is the ideal other voice. The prostitute, as I pointed out earlier, has held sway over theliterature of the world for centuries, as the archetype of the fallen woman. But no one bothered to look at her daughter as anything more than a victim of her mother's sin. Certainly not as woman with a brain and a body together with a desire to set right the wrong done to her mother. In this context it is illuminating to see the role of the daughter of a prostitute in two novels; Krishna Sobti's *Mitro Marjani* and my *Anitya*.

Mitro of *Mitro Marjani* is the daughter of a prostitute but married into a landowning family in Punjab. She continues to hold her mother as a role model and is explicit in the expression of her sexual desires. The frank depiction of her sexuality is quite in the tradition of Sanskrit literature. But Sobti succumbs to the pressure of the fallen woman syndrome when in the end, she makes Mitro turn back from a sexual encounter arranged by her mother. And this, after she had gleefully drugged her not-potent-enough husband and reached the door of the room of her paramour. The mother joins her in bewailing the lot of the fallen woman and encourages her to return unmolested to her husband and home, quite in the Victorian tradition.

Sangeeta of *Anitya* loves her prostitute mother and is an accomplished musician like her. But she is not willing to stop at that. She aspires to become a doctor and becomes one with the financial help of an older man. In the process, her search for a father figure makes her accept him as a lover. After being humiliated by him, she embarks on a crusade of revenge on all men, more to avenge her mother than herself. Hate has its disasterous consequences and destroys both Sangeeta and the older man. But in the process, she emerges as strong character with a catastrophic impact on the lives of all the other characters. She succeeds in breaking away from the constraints imposed by her birth without ever denouncing her mother.

The third notable development of recent times has been the toning down of the revolt against marriage and finding refuge in the age-old Indian wisdom: for the most part ignore your husband. Live your life as if he was not there. Do not take the trouble of getting rid of him because you will end up with another just as cumbersome. An interesting statement occurs in Nasira Sharma's Shalmali. Where she says that her husband lives in her house as a guest, a mediocre person in need of help but otherwise not of much consequence. The significant point is that it is the wife's house and not the husband's. She is the bread winner, a successful administrative officer and brilliant in every way. When I wrote a review of the novel,[9] I pointed out that actually the husband was more of an experiment than a guest of Shalmali's. She did not want to turn him out or divorce him because that would leave her with nothing to experiment with in her dreams of reforming mediocre men into sensitive creatures.

A few women writers have produced novels which deal with the preoccupations of women, other than the suffocation of marriage. Chitra Mudgal deals with a woman in the advertising world in her novel *Ek Zameen Apni,* Chandrakanta with the gradual decay of a neighbourhood in a town in Kashmir in *Eilan Gali,* Manjul Bhagat with the agony of a woman refuges and exile, yearning to be back in her land of birth to fight in the war raging there, in *Khatul.* These are some recent examples of novels written by women in Hindi which deal with women as social beings and not merely sexual appendages.

By far the most significant literary event of the last decade has been the publication of *dalit* literature or the works of low caste, neoliterates in Marathi and in translation. First, the men wrote. Then came the women, demystifying the male reformers yet remaining faithful to the reality of the *dalits* at large, embracing both men and women. The recently published autobiographical tales of *dalit* women like *Pan on Fire* by the Indian Social Institute and *Truth Tales by* Kali for Women, have the women hitting out at the sexual harassment by the male revolutionaries along with the other aspects of their lives. An analogy can be drawn with the black women's writing in the USA. Writers like Toni Morrison and Alice Walker and others see black women as both black and women rather than just members of one female race. So do the *dalit* women. Everything, the language, the ethos, the idiom and the form is different from middle class, white writing. The message that comes through is that, despite the sexual harassment, perversity and violence against women, the ultimate solution lies not in the *dalit* women revolting against this or that *dalit* man but in all men and women rising out of the mire of a social system that forces them to be *dalits*. I will not call the *dalit* literature the only or even, definitely the authentic account of *dalit* life because the illiterates may again find the literates only partly participant in their lives. But despite the fact that there will always be a difference in the viewpoint of the articulate and the silenced, it remains the most authentic chronicle available of the texture of the life and psyche of the deprived world within India.

A question often asked in the West is about the place of lesbians in the writing of women in India. Agian, this has not occurred in the nature of a compaign or as part of the feminist philosophy here. the earliest story on lesbians, *Lihaf* (*The Quilt*) was written by Ismat Chugtai in the 1950's. But it could hardly be called a story on Lesbianism as it portrayed it as a pervert act. Since then a few more novels and stories have been written, including Shubha Verma's novel *Anam Rishton Ke Nam*. But it portrays love between women just as another form of love story without raising any fundamental questions about female identity or rebellion. It remains an aberration and is dealt with, in literature, as other aberrations are. There is no taboo on it as such, at least, it is no more taboo than other frank depictions of sexual activity. Sisterhood or affinity between women rather than between men and women has always been a part of the ethos of India. It continues to be dealt with on that level in literature. Women in war and peace with other women, in all kinds of relationships, ranging from the other woman, colleague, competitor in career, to mother and mother-in-law were always portrayed more often in Indian literature than in that of the West. They continue to figure in the modern writing as well. But lesbianism has not yet claimed in the modern writing as well. But lesbianism has not yet claimed the attention and concern of our writers.

Conclusion

There are three things I would like to say in conclusion. First, though there is much to be learned by looking at women as a separate class in certain economic and political context, this is not possible in a country like India where there are two if not three distinct classes of women. I have no quarrel with Engel's contention that the relegation of women to the four walls, leaving men free for hunting was the beginning of slavery. Women certainly formed a class at that moment.

It is similarly possible to think of women versus men as two clsses of have-nots and haves, in prosperous societies where the gaps between the economic well-being of different stratas of society are not so glaring. In a capitalist society, which has accepted free competition among the people for ownership of scarce resources is an essential part of the system, one can say classes have ceased to be important. The gap between them may be wide enough but if there is enough affluence to guarantee employment and a decent minimum standard of living for everyone, one can assume, for purposes of argument, that there is not much class conflict. Women, under these circumstances, would naturally emerge as a handicapped sex compred with men, and could be regarded as forming a separate and unique class. The exploitation would be seen along sex-dictated linesfor the simple reason that men and women are the only groups which remain unchanged in their social placement. All other classes, by virtue of equal opportunity, at least theoretically, are mobile and can flow from one to the other.

None of these apply to the economic and political set-up in India. As I said at the beginning, there are distinct classes among women, from the point of view not only of economic well-being but of availability of opportunity, welfare coverage and policy concerns. The largest section of society functions more or less along fedual lines, while the minority operates in a highly exploitative capitalist system without the safeguard of equal opportunity and mobility between classes. The state does step in to offer certain palliatives to the weak, but again the most vocal groups get them, others do not. It is sound policy, then, to project women as the weakest of the weak, which they are. But the whole thing backfires when women as a whole are portrayed as subject to similar exploitations, and the differences between classes among them forgotten. Only a very judicious admixture of Marxism and feminism can give us a framework that can be applied to the class-ridden female society of India. Can there be such a mixture? That is the question. Maybe yes, but so far it has not been worked out in the writing of women, whether in fiction, journalism or theoretical works in India.

Secondly, it is important to point out that literary criticism remains largely the domain of men in India, while women are the ones to watch as far as significant literary writing is concerned. Under these circumstances, it is natural, though unfortunate, that writing by women is deliberately kept out of the general assessment of literature and relegated to a separate category of female writing. The male critics have, in a manner of speaking, turned feminist, in treating women as a separate class, but their grasp of feminist theory or concepts ends there. So women writers do not get deserved or unbiased critical assessment. This is perhaps the greatest distortion that a feminist critique is being subjected to in this country.

Lastly, it is but in the fitness of things that when men turn mock-feminists, women should turn the tables on them and do their most powerful writing, not on women's issues, but on the vast arena of male-dominated social issues with men as the chief protagonists. The current breed of male critics many ignore it. But I feel confident that some day, not in a very distant future, the mock-feminists will have to bow out. A correct assessment of novels and stories of writers who are women will be done. May be by women and true feminists. Maybe, without qualification as literature. In any case, whether recognised by male critics or not, writing by women forms, at the present moment, the curx of modern writing. It fights shy neither of experimentation nor of contradictions. It grapples with both "women's issues" and larger social and political issues. It even dares to grope and probe its own psyche and half-successful attempt at breaking free of tradition and half-hearted acceptance of a feminist world view. It prossesses, despite its other shortcomings, the one thing necessary for survival and development. That is honesty. Ultimately, the only commitment a writer can have is honesty to herself. Women writers are thus committed and hence shall prevail. Perhaps the time is now ripe for the emergence of women critics who are as committed and perceptive as the women writers.

References

1. *Devi* is the Goddes as all merciful and forgiving woman. The term pertains to women as pure and good. Gods and Goddesses in Hindu mythology are divine beings or life-giving forces. Anything which sustains life, water, fire, wind, even trees and grains are portrayed as Gods or Goddesses. They are not to be confused with God *per se* of other religions or the Trinity composed of Brahma (creator), Vishnu (preserver), and Shiva (destroyer).
2. Sita is the wife of Rama and heroine of *Ramayana*, an epic written first in Sanskrit by Valmiki, then in various regional languages of India including *Ramcharit Manas* by Tulsidas in Avadhi, a dialect of old Hindi.

3. Savitri, wife of Satyavan, in an old tale of Savitri Satyavan, is famous for following the God of Death (*Yama*) when he came to fetch the soul of her husband, Satyavan, and successfully bargaining it back with wit and perseverence. But it is her faithfulness to the husband that is celebrated, not her shrewdness or wit. Incidentally, she had chosen her husband herself and married him in defiance of the parents and the prophesy of his death within a year.
4. Nal and Damyanti are husband and wife in the tale of the same name, where they undergo all kinds of travail through which Damyanti remains steadfast and faithful in her love for Nal.
5. Ahilya, a woman character in the epic *Ramayana*, is cursed by her husband to become a stone because she was seduced by another man under false pretences. She was restored to womanhood by Rama and reunited with her husband without demur. She is celebrated as the epitome of both the faithful and forgiving wife.
6. *Shakti* is an embodiment of power. Durga and Kali, female Goddesses celebrated as destroyers of evil, are manifestations of *Shakti*.
7. The following is a list of works (N designates novels) in which women authors employ male protagonists: Mannu Bhandari, *Mahabhoj* (N); Mridula Garg, *Anitya* (N), Vanshaj (N); **Urf Sam & Other Stories**; Mamta Kalia, *Beghar* (N); Kamal Kumar, *Aparth* (N) Krishna Sobti, *Yaron ke Yar* (long story); Raji Seth, **Yatra Mukt & Other Stories**; Manjul Bhagat, **Kitna Chhota Safar & Other Stories**; Namita Singh, **Woh Doosra Asdmi & Other Stories**: Pratima Verma, **Mukadma & Other Stories** Usha Priyamada, **Vapsi & Other Stories** Sudha Arora, **Damanchakra & Other Stories**; Shubda Misra, *Jansevak & Other Stories* Nirupama Sevti, *Bantta Hua Aadmi* (N); Chandrakanta, *Elin Gali* (N); Meera Mahadevan, *Apna Ghar* (N).
8. The following is a list of works by women in which the woman protagonist is portrayed as a socio-economic, political and sensate being, rather than primarily a sexual or domestic figure, and holds a primary not a secondary role in the work: Manjul Bhagat, *Anaro* (novel, 1977) Mridula Garg, *Agli Subah* (story, 1984), *Kharidar* (story 1977, *Antya* (N) 1980; Raji Seth, *Yog Deeksha* (Story, 1981) Chitra Mugal, *Bhookh* (story, 1986), *Lane* (story, 1987); Nirupama Sevto, "Ghat Parighat" (story, 1984); Chandrakanta, *Bhitri Safai* (story, 1984); Sudha Arora, *Mahanagar ki Maithili* (story, 1977), *Sat Nadian Ek Sama.ıdar* (N), 1980.
9. *Kaddawar Auraten*, Mridula Garg, Hans, October 1991.

   Dalit: belonging to the lower castes.

   Dalit writing: Writing by the first generation literates belonging to the lower castes.

   The following woman writers reflect a period of great literary activity after 1950: Krishna Sobti, Mannu Bhandari, Usha Primayamvada, Mamta Kalia, Meharunnissa Parvez, Deepti Khandelwal, Nirupama Sevti, Manjul Bhagat, Mridula Garg, Jyotsna Milan, Raji Seth, Mirnal Pandey, Simmi Harshita, Chitra Mudgel, Chandrakanta, Sunita Jain, Sudha Arora, Namita Singh, Pratima Verma, Achla Sharma, Shubda Mishra, Nasira Sharma, Kamal Kumar, Meera Mahadevan.

16

A Critique of the Portrayal of Women in Hindi Fiction

*Ravindra Rajhans**

This paper proposes to examine the portrayal of woman in Hindi fiction in the last one hundred year during which her image has been projected in different ways in Hindi fiction. As we know fiction is the best medium for mirroring social realism and we can safely depend upon the textual evidence that we gather from the novels portraying the plight of women in contemporary society. A doctoral dissertation of Vindu Agrawal of the 50's, now available in a book-form,[1] has made a critical survey of the portrayal of Indian women in Hindi novels of the first half of this century. A similar effort has also been made by Urmila Bhatnagar in her book on conjugal life.[2]

At the outset, I would like to make it clear that by an Indian woman we generally mean a Hindu woman as conceived in the Hindu scriptures. The term *devi* is invariably appended to the name of a Hindu woman. This custom largely reflects the basic conception of an Indian woman. She symbolises *Matri shakti* (the Mother Power) or *prakriti* (Nature) whose purpose is to perpetuate Brahma's *Sristi* (creation) in this world. Thus, there is a divine purpose behind her creation. There is a halo of divinity around her.

According to the traditional view, an Indian woman has been

* The author is Professor of English, College of Commerce (M.U.), Patna-800020.

identified with the following noble traits of personality, sacrifice (*utsurg*), kindness (*daya*), respect (*shraddha*), forgiveness (*kshma*), chastity (*sateetva or pativratya*), affection (*mamta*), obedience (*agyakarita*), slavery (*dasata*), etc. Thus, in theory, a woman occupies a very high position. She is almost a goddess. But, in practice, she is a helpless creature, too weak to uphold her dignity in a male-dominated society. She is tolerated as long as she does not appear as a threat to man's supremacy in the form of father, husband or a grown-up son. According to our scriptures, she always needs a regulator or guide and protector.

The early novelists of Hindi fictions, particularly of the 1890's, justified the Hindu view of a woman in their characterizations. The titles[3] of some of the novels of this period project the point of view of the novelists who were sentinels of Hindu heritage. They were critical of those ladies who came into direct contact of the anglicized ladies of the elite society, who were considered to be carriers of an infection of the decandent culture of the west. Naturally, they were not in favour of higher education for girls. Only primary education was recommended for young girls so that they could read scriptures, and story-books, write letters and maintain household accounts of day-to-day life. They were advised to be dedicated to their husbands only and emulate the pious women like *Sati Savitri, Ansuya, Rukmini, Subhadra, Dayamanti, Madalsa,* etc. Ishwari Sharma's *Vama Sikshak,* Chandika Prasad Mishra's *Suhagini,* Paras Nath Singh's *Manjhali Bahu,* Shaligram's *Adarsh Ramani,* Girija Kumar Ghosh's *Chhoti Bahu,* Priyamvada Devi's *Kaliyugi Parivar Ka Ek Drishya* deserve special mention, as they uphold the cause of the tradition-bound woman.

The Premchand Era

Munshi Premchand gave a major jolt to the earlier trend by portraying real female characters with all their human strengths and failings. His focus shifted to the socio-economic forces of the feudal set-up that debased a woman. He exposed the forces of exploitation that victimised a woman at every step in her life. He addressed himself to the following problems that plagued the life of an average Indian woman: child-marriage, widow re-marriage, illiteracy, the purdah system, menace of dowry, psychological problems of ill-matched couples, especially from the point of view of age, prostitution as a social institution and poverty. The woman in Premchnad's novel is not always at the receiving end. She stands up against injustice, oppression, exploitation and torture. The solutions that he found to the above mentioned problems were highiy idealistic, for example, change of heart or attitude of the oppressor due to the exemplary good behaviour of a woman belonging to the middle class family. But his treatment of rural woman was quite different. In the character of Sukhda of *Karmabhoomi,* Premchand portrays the upsurge of political consciousness among women during the freedom struggle. She boldly faces the police and openly incites her comrades, her fellow freedom-fighters not to be cowed down by police atrocities of the British regime. She cries out: "Brothers why are you running away?" this is not the time to escape, this is the time to stand up boldly".[4] Munni, a rural woman of *Karambhoomi* kills two Englishmen. Salonee, another illiterate woman of the same novel, violently protests against social injustice and bureaucratic harassment and spits on the face of an officer of the British Raj, and hurls abuses on being hit with a baton. Dhaniya of *Godan*[5] also protests against the slavish attitude of her docile and servile husband who borrows Rs. 30 to bribe a police officer to hush up a case against his brother. She exposes the agents of feudal exploitation by addressing them as killers and blood-suckers of the poor people.[6]

Post-Premchand Era

Higher education among women was no longer forward upon by Hindi novelists, as they had gradually developed a sympathy for the problems of educated ladies, who were facing an identity crisis. We notice the emergence of an educated section of women in the post-Premchand fiction, especially in the novels of Yashpal. Shail, an M.A. student of *Dada Comrade*, Geeta of *Party Comrade,* and again an M.A. student, Manorama of *Manushya Ke Roop* all belong to this new variety of female characters in Hindi fiction. Lavang, Leena, Indira and Rani of Rangaya Raghav's, *Gharaunda* are all college-going girls. Shashi of Agyenya's *Shekhar Ek Jeevani* is also an intellectual woman. Katyani of Jainendra's *Kalyani* is an England-returned lady doctor. Highly educated women slowly gained respectability in the society and due attention from their life-partners as they proved to be better companions for their educated husbands. Thus, the deep-seated prejudice against educated women gradually disappeared.

The problem of widows was no longer the central concern of these novelists, as widow re-marriage was no longer opposed by on humanitarian grounds. In this era, a widow could re-marry wihtout much family opposition. Raj of *Deshdrohi*, Seema of *Manushya Ke Roop* by Yashpal, Sunanda of *Muktipath* by Ila Chandra Joshi, Lavang of *Gharaunda* by Rangaya Raghav all testify to this fact.

Further, there was a qualitative change in the treatment of prostitutes by Hindi novelists of this period. Prostitutes were no longer considered as selfish creatures out to fleece their male customers in the flesh trade, but someone who deserved our sympathy. Unlike Pemchand, novelists of this period did not try to suggest reform of the prostitutes, but tried to expose the social forces that compelled helpless women to adopt this condemned profession for their livelihood.

Several new problems related to women were presented in the novels of this period, for example, free-love, inter-caste marriage, maladjustment of married couples, post-marital love-affairs, clash of egoes between husband and wife, divorce and disintegration of the joint family. Several new patterns of human relationships in family life also found expression, for example, the relationship between co-wives, two sisters or sisters-in-law *(Jethani Devrani)* or the husband's sister and brother's wife (*Nanad-Bhaujai*), elder brother's wife and husband's younger brother (*bhabhi-devar*), mothers-in-law and daughters-in-law, etc.

The following novels of this period present other dimensions of a woman's life: Usha Devi Mitra's *Piya*, Ram Vriksha Benipuri's *Qaidi Ki Patni* (1940), Pratap Narayan Shrivastava's *Vida*, Chandika Prasad Mishra's *Suhagini*, Raja Radhika Raman Prasad Singh's *Ram Raheem*, Upendra Nath Ashka's *Girti Deevaren* and Siya Ram Sharan Gupta's *God*.

The extra-marital relationship of a wife has been portrayed in Jainendra's *Suneeta*, Bhagwati Prasad Vajpayee's *Pipasa* (1937), Sarvadanand Varma's *Prashna* (1938), and *Narmedh* (1941), and Yashpal's *Deshdrohi* (1943). The extra-marital relatioinship of husbands has been portrayed in Yashpal's *Manushya Ke Roop*, Bhagwati Prasad Vajpayee's *Nimantran*, etc.

The pre-marital relationship of a wife gets greater attention than that of a husband. A girl often fails to get a boy of her choice. But the contrary is not true because a boy has greater chances of getting a girl of his choice. This happens because man enjoys more freedom than a woman in our patriarchal society. Besides this, women are more sentimental than men and they cannot easily forget the men they loved before marriage. Men go back to their first love when they feel frustrated in the company of their wives. Here, again, we find that women are the sufferers. Ila Chandra Joshi in his *Parde Ki Rani* shows how Indra Mohan kills his wife Sheela because he is still emotionally involved with his first lady-love, Niranjana. Sheela, like the traditional Indian wife, even sacrifices her life to please her husband. But Sheela's reaction cannot be generalised. The new woman of that period fails to conform to the old social norms and reacts like any other human being whose feelings have been hurt. She no longer treats her husband as *devta* or *parmeshwar* and herself as a maid-servant (*Charno Ki Dasi*). She feels embarrassed in addressing her husband as master (*'Swami'* or *'Sain'*) because she does not consider herself as a 'chattel'. This attitudinal change was brought about by exposure of women of the middle class to higher education. The impact of science education also cleared a number of cobwebs from the mind of orthodox people. Earlier, being issueless was a great curse as far as the wife was concerned. Nobody ever cared to find out as to who was actually responsible for her barrenness. A woman may fail to conceive beacuse the husband is impotent, frigid or has some organic defects. But, earlier this unpleasant fact was repressed by the conniving parents of the husband, daughter-in-law was made scapegoat for the son's physical defects. Gradually, the approach towards women became more rational and humane. The spread of education saved the contemporary women from a number of superstitions, customs and rituals that made their life hellish. The emergence of an educated class of woman produced ego clashes between husband and wife. Earlier, a husband never took into account the personality of his wife who was almost a non-entity in the house at the decision-making level. Later it got difficult for husbands to treat their wives as pets or domestic animals. In *Kalyani*, Jainendra portrays the ego-clash between Dr. Asrani and Mrs. Asrani who is also a highly educated woman. In Ila Chandra Joshi's *Sanyasi*, Jayanti committed suicide because she could not adjust with her suspicious husband.

Modern Fiction

Inspired by the 'Women lib' movement the faminist writers, particularly the women writers, stood openly against the exploitation of women by men in beauty-contests, modelling, sex magazines, blue-films, and commercial advertising, etc. Modern women have been clamouring for one more freedom in matters of sex and trying to catch up fast with men. Despite this new consciousness, women still love to be loved and respected in their sweet homes and prefer arranged marriages, of course, in a suitably modified form. They love to be counselled by their parents in matters of choosing their life-partners, but they still dislike the dictatorial attitrude of their parents and their complete indifference towards their emotional problems.

Andhere Band Kamre by Mohan Rakesh depicts the story of Harbans and Neelima. Harbans earnestly desires that his wife should become an eminent dancer after getting lessons in dancing, but at the same time he is apprehensive that her social importance might overshadow him. He grows jealous of her growing importance. As a result of that there is an obvious ego-clash between the couple. Neelima at times, revolts but finally surrenders before her husband. The surrender of Neelima is the surrender of the New Woman before the traditional values in which husbands have always an edge over their wives. The Indian woman, temperamentally, still prefers to lead a protected existence. Previously, she rarely exercised her right to protest, but now she often rises to whatever occasion confronts her in self-defence and asserts herself with confidence.

It may not be out of place here to refer to the decisive moment in the life of Usha of *Meri Teri Uski Bat*[7], a novel by Yashpal who is well-known for his progressive views regarding women. Usha, a widow, decides to enter into civil-marriage with her lover, Rudra, but just on the eve of marriage she falters and tells him, "Dear, excuse me, I am yours and will be yours in every respect, but without removing the *Kuntha* (complex) from my son's mind, I cannot get the satisfaction and pride of being your wife."

Usha's utterances in the novel shows how an Indian woman readily sacrifices her own aspirations at the altar of motherhood which is totally a selfless love. Usha's statement clearly stresses that it is very difficult for an Indian woman to be completely free from her cultural heritage in which motherhood overrides all other passions.

In case a woman decides to re-marry for her personal happiness, she invites immense mental trouble for her child or children from her former husband. Mannu Bhandari, in her famous novel '*Apaka Bunti*,'[8] presents the injured feelings of a small child who is, after all, a product of the same society. When somebody tells him "Hey Bunti! Now you have become Joshi—Bunti Joshi not Arun Joshi", back comes the reply from Bunti who burst out in anger: "Why should I be a Joshi. I am Arun Batra, Bunti Batra." Gradually, Bunti gets estranged from her loving mother and goes back to his father, refusing all the gifts brought by his mother. This refusal lacerates the consciousness of the mother, filling her with guilt. In a way, this portrayal suports the Indian value-system which Indian women have been cherishing for so long. Mannu Bhandari shows what happens when an Indian woman departs from her traditional role. Often, she becomes miserable. Towards the end of the novel, Shakun realises her mistake and feels that Indian traditional family life is based on a sounder footing. She feels that she has wasted her life. The fragmentation that started with the divorce lands her in a peculiar emptiness that torments her deeply. She holds herself responsible for the complete disintegration of her personal and family life.

Krishna Sobti in her novel, *Surajmukhi Andhere Ki,* portrays Ratti who adheres to and appreciates the western value system of family life. She behaves like a member of a permissive society where pre and post-marital reationship is a commonplace affair. Ratti has boy-friends, but not lovers. But Ratti is an exception, and represents only a microscopic minority of the Indian womanhood. Similar is the case with another of Sobti's heroine Mitro, of *Mitro Marjani. Lajja* (coyness) and *Sheel* (feminine graces) which are supposed to be the two ornaments of an Indian woman. Mitro does not possess either, Sardarilal feels disgusted in the company of such a woman who lementably lacks graciousness. In *Rukogi Nahi Radhika,* Usha Priyamvada depicts the inner conflict of an Indian woman who returns home from abroad and does not feel at home in India which has an alien setting for her now. She had earlier failed to conform to the western values either.

If we analyse the female characters of Hindi fiction, we immediately notice two attributes: they have changed but not completely and there is a clear ambivalence in their basic character. They are not prepared to lose their Indian identity completely. The basic core of their personality remains unchanged. Its outward manifestation can be seen in the dress of Indian woman. An Indian woman whether she is in India or abroad still prefers to wear the *Sari* and blouse *(choli),* she still prefers to be maintained by her husband and enjoys the status of a housewife (*Griha Lakshmi*). A section of ultra-modern women does not use vermilion (*Sindoor*) dot or line in-between their parted-hair. This is done out of a sheer sense of vengeance. If men can enjoy the right of confusing young girls regarding their marital status, why cannot they look like virgins who get greater attention from men whether married or bachelor? The motive behind not observing some social obligations is to be translated as symbolising the wish to compete with men in every walk of life. The signs of a married women (*Suhagan*) are gradually disappearing from our social life, possibly because there are no such restrictions for married men of Hindu society. Modern women are losing faith in such *pujas* and religious fasts which are performed and observed for the welfare of their husbands and sons, for examples, *Hartalika Vratam* (a special puja for the welfare of the husband), *Karva Chauth* (a similar puja), '*Jeetia*' (a fast for the welfare of the son, observed by mothers in parts of North India).

In the following novels we see different facets of the women of cosmopolitan cities. To mention only a few representative ones: Surya Kumar Joshi's *Digambari*, Krishna Sobti's *Soorajmukhi Andhere Ke*, Krishna Agnihotri's *Bauni Parchhainyan*, Pramod Sinha's *Uska Sahar*, Raghvendra Mishra's *Pani Ke Beech Meen Piyasi*, Shivani's *Krishnakali*, Shivsagar Mishra's *Andhere Ka Sooraj*, Vishwambhar Manav's *Kaveri*, Shailesh Matiyani's *Jaltarang*, etc. The following novels also present the pre-marital and post-marital experiences of the modern women for whom sex experience at their own sweet will is no longer a taboo: Rajkamal Chowdhury's *Machhali Mari Hui Hai* and *Ek Anar Sau Beemar*, Mohan Rakesh's *Antral*, Manhar Chauhan's *Kya Kya Roop*, Yadvendra Chandra's *Alag Alag Akritiyan*, Rajni Pannikar's *Mom Ki Moti*, Krishna Sobati's *Mitro Marjani*, Usha Priyamvada's *Machhaliyan*, Mridula Garg's *Chhat Par Dastak*, Nasira Sharma's *Sangsar*, Mrinal Pandey's *Apaka Bunti*, *Ek Neech Tragedy*, *Ek Thi Hansmukh De*, *Pariyon Ka Nach*, Raji Seth's *Undhe Mod Se Age*, Chandrakanta's *Noorabai*, Mehrunnisa Parvej's '*Ankhon Ki Dahleej*, *Ayodhya Se Vapasi*', Namita Singh's *Ungoothi*, Chitra Mudgal's *Lakarbaggha*, etc.

The women in the writings of contemporary novels and short stories by contemporary women writers of Hindi, particularly Mamta Kaliya, Pratima Verma, Sooryabala, Sashiprabha Shastri, Aruna Seetesh, Mehrunnisa Parvej and Mrinal Pandey have focussed more on the problems of about two percent women of our country belonging to the higher strata of society who are career-oriented, self-reliant, and economically independent. The rural women labour force and tribal women have yet to find their advocates among women writers.

From the portrayals of female characters in Hindi fiction, we easily infer that the exploitation of women by men is still continuing in different forms in Indian society, but it is no longer taken for granted. The voice of protest against such exploitations has also been recorded and registered by feminist writers as well as women writers. The mood of the contemporary women of the enlightened section of our society is defiant, non-conformist and aggressive. There is a vigorous search for self-identity among the upper middle class women of the contemprary Indian society.

References

1. Vindu Agrawal, *Hindi Upanyason Mein Nari Chitran*, 1870-1950, New Delhi, 1968.
2. Urmila Bhatnagar, *Hindi Upanyas Sahitya Mein Dampatya Chitran*, Jaipur: Archana Prakashan.
3. *Adarsh Hindu, Adarsh Grihastha, Adarsh Dampati.*
4. Premchand, *Karmabhoomi*, p. 209.
5. Premchand, *Godan*, p. 142.
6. *Ibid*, p. 143.
7. Yashpal, *Meri Teri Uski Bat*, p. 760.
8. Mannu Bhandari, *Apka Bunti*, p. 13.

17

The Woman in India and the West: a Comparative Conspectus

Shankar N. Prasad *

Let it be made clear at the outset that a comparative study of the woman in India and the West—obviously not a very simple task—would belong more properly to disciplines other than literature, mainly anthropology and sociology. Yet, the main purpose of the present research is happily confined to seeing in what may and to what extent the aforesaid conflict has been put to use in literature (or fiction, to be more specific) in India and the West.

I

In the recent reviews of world literature, one writer who seems to have caught the imagination is perhaps the great playwright from Norway, Ibsen. Obviously, this accretion of interests mainly in his female characters who appear to have been built up around a perception of the bare fact of being born a woman. To be female: just what does it imply?

This should, conceptually speaking, take us to a concentrated study of feminism so as to place in a proper perspective whatever is vital about woman in life and literature. Preferably, this should be apart from whatever the 'ism' stands for in the history of ideas—chiefly in the context of the rise of woman today, of her awakening

* The author is Professor and Head, Dept. of English, Manipur University, Canchipur, Imphal-795003.

as well as ripening consciousness and the consequent battle against a tradition-bound, male-dominated society. Yet the fact remains that feminism is essentially a movement, social in basics and socio-political in proliferated dimensions, and is primarily directed against the sufferings of women at the hands of heartless, soulless male villains. Perhaps this would provide an interesting starting point for Indian scholars approaching various literatures, ranging from British to Indo-Anglian and Indian. Also, perhaps this would require a first-hand understanding and appreciation of literary history and criticism of the concerned area, and, above all, of related life and culture. So, hopefully, this essay may well result in a significant approach to fiction—created literatures in different languages—in the larger perspective of life and literature. C.D. Narasimhaih's efforts, through his **Literary Criterion,** constitute one major example; yet, instead of enlisting examples, it may be more profitable to realise that there is always ample promise of another determined start in this direction and it should not by altogether impossible to say something of significance. (Admittedly, in this context, the advantages of a growing library of Indiana or Americana in India may well compare with the improving prospects of study grants and fellowships, and one only wishes the assistance extends to the whole gamut of Commonwealth Literature.) It seems reasonable to hope that the present review of an area, historically covered by the movement of feminism, should lead to a searching analysis of some basic points at issue.

Literature has always held up a faithful mirror to the society under investigation, and men and women are among the subjects of an extraordinary study in literature, whether as victors or victims, as protagonists or mere creatures of a plot. Yet, on a closer scrutiny, it would appear to the analyst that, in at least seven cases out of ten, men have been surpassed by women as centres of interest or occasions of experience, comprising more sorrows than joys. Also, let it be underlined that though the occasions for the analyses contained in the present study are works of literature or their authors, **the real subject is life itself**, life comprising the multitudinous aspects of society as revealed through the works of art, and primarily the complex, demanding, and diverse arrangements that women and men make (or unmake?) with one another. Frankly speaking, one would do well to keep in mind the fact that not only the women protagonists lie Nora, Hedda Gabler, Binodini, Daisy and Savitri, but also the women artists like the Bronte Sisters, Virginia Woolf and Sylvia Plath are cases in point. Honestly, one may also go on to include in the list the chancy accomplishments of 'amateurs' like Dorothy Wordsworth, Jane Carlyle and Zelda Fitzgerald, women whose literary or historical existence became inseparable from their respective roles in the lives of the great men they were related to.

Incidentally, one may well refer to the greatest example of creative motivation in fiction, one from a woman as evidenced in case of great American fiction—**the Image of Minny Temple,** Henry James's **Albany Cousin.** This Image, as will be amply borne out by the delineation of his immortal heroines, got deeply and richly embedded in his memory and consciousness as man and artist and provides (true till date) the primal clue to the understanding of his American women. Also, in the growth of this image is mirrored the inevitable evolution of the mind and aesthetics of Henry James. In consequence, it ranks as the greatest example (in the American novel) of the transmutation of a personal loss and pain into a value and theme of art. The women pecpling his novels with force and compassion provide a glowing testimony to the fact that, freed from the flux of time, the Albany Cousin lives in an eternal moment in the realm of art, her image reigning supreme in his mind and attaining to salvation in, for example, Isabel Archer or Milly Theale. They illustrate happily the Jamesian principle that what once was life is always life, irrespective of the diverse forms it takes, abandons or resumes.

Incidentally, the example of Minny Temple, like the examples of the created women characters in world fiction, chiefly the masterpieces, should also enable us to have a full look at the changing face of woman, as victor an victim both. Also, values have been changing fast. In the age of Fielding and Richardson, seduction was crime as well as sin, such that every human heart since then goes out to the battling Clarissa in the clutches of Lovelace, the sadist. But how would the contemporary scene look like? Is not the old plot almost dead, fallen into obsolescence? Today, it appears, innocence is hardly a value worth living or dying for such that seduction no longer matters. Now under such a drastically altered set-up, would sex (one wonders) continue to be the germ or seed of fiction? Perhaps, at most, it might help an episode assume dimensions eventually maturing into an irony of life. A systematic study of the cases of women in India and the West, taking a full note of the changing faces of woman in the changing social pattern must include a close scrutiny of this important aspect as well.

Simultaneously, it is noteworthy that feminism, destined to establish a new set of values in the fictive set-up, would boil down to a statement of protest, thus, making for a new literary kind-the novel of dissent. And the novels that are chosen as cases in point are, to quote Shantha Krishnaswamy, "a spectrum presentation of the ways of dealing with the binary opposition of male versus female dominance, of woman as subject versus woman as object."[1]

Yet, as will be borne out by an elaborate study of cases, these women, subject or object, are seen as demeaning themselves as beasts of burden, the burden of traditional Hindu values. Naturally, the question that is of values here and, must be faced squarely, is this : just who or what forces made woman, endowed with rare potentialities, the beast under reference? Through the ages, women's history reads like a grim saga of suffering and battle. There are old models and new models, but the paramount question of adjustment or rebellion in search of identify remains. That there are no simple solutions to the problem is the ultimate truth. Yet, perhaps the novels are not, necessarily, problem novels, and the triumph of art that they aim at or even attain has little to do with a triumphant answering of questions. Some women may be more unfortunate than others on one count or another, but that is another matter.

As is on record, there is a tremendous variety of delineation of women in diverse literatures including portrayals in Sanskrit literature to go to the very beginings. To take one example, it was said by a learned Sanskrit scholar:

"Even angles cannot decipher woman's character and man's destiny : where is man, poor man?"[2]

And to take another example, the great Vidyapati had to lament in these moving words :

"Let no one be born,

But if one must,

Let no one be a girl."[3]

From such bemoanigs rendered in the ancient past, in the days when writers were sages and seers to the present times when woman's liberation has been reduced to a bandwagon is a sensitive history of the origin and growth of feminism. Besides, the woman's issue in India is different from what it is in Western countries. If, in West, the issue is one of identity, equality of opportunities and sexual experiences, here the very survival of woman is the theme. This broad distinction is an aspect of the milieu, which is of vital significance in all its ramifications.

> "All talk of transcending biology", say Shantha Krishnaswamy, "of clonal reproduction, polymorphous perversity, cybernetics, ERA and burning the bra would be out of place and out of time in an Indian milieu."[4]

In fact, the distinguishing aspect of the milieu can be better appreciated in terms of the different priorities in East and West. But even in East, within the limits, the urban scene contrasts with the rural scene—the only common factor being that in both cases, for women, the odds are comparably inseparable. Of course, the urban women, thanks to education and opportunities that come with it, can have legitimate and viable aspirations. Not so their rural sisters, whose predicament has been summed up admirably in these words:

> "Her own situation is so inextricably intertwined with her husband's economic condition, that questions such as why she is being paid half of her husband's salary for the same amount of work on a construction site or why she has to manage all the housework alone after working outside all day, became semantic—only to be considered as finer points in living."[5]

These differences, however, are significant details of a general fact, which is that all over the world the cry of the peacock betrays the same agony—it is a common cry for emancipation. Everywhere the truncated self of the woman has come out in rebellion and aspire to emerge as a whole human being. It may be a Nora[6] in Norway or a Sunita[7] in India, but the desire is the same—to get out of the man-made cage and fly freely. Small wonder, writers and critics are veering round this highly inflammable material: all want to visualise the changing face of woman, both in life and in fiction. Seminal thinkers and artists, all over the world, are now more and more inclined to look upon woman as a very sensitive rendering of their own realisation of the collective compulsions of social life. Of course, the ancient law-giver, Manu, had chanced upon a strong sentence on the woman's dilemma. He would not allow woman to be independent at any stage:

> "In childhood a woman must be subject to her father, in youth husband, and when her lord is dead, to her sons.[8]"

Ironically, Manu's dictum can be seen as prevailing in many quarters even today, and women are seen as the helpless non-choosers. They are deprived of selfhood, which, in fact, form the very basis of the woman's story in the West.

Basing upon this, distinct feature of the different social milieu, Meenakshi Mukherjee seems to have found something specific and even unique about the context of Indo-Anglian fiction. It is so important a fact and has been so well put by Mrs. Mukherjee that a whole paragraph may be quoted in full:

> "Sometimes the conflict resolves itself neatly into two issues: duty to the family, and personal fulfilment. The fulfilment of oneself, however, desirable a goal according to the individualistic ideals of Western society, has always been alien to Indian tradition, especially when it is achieved at the cost of duty to the family. The Indo-anglian novelist thus faces a curious predicament. He is using the language and form of the English novelist, but he has to operate within a totally different frame of reference. Sexual love and personal happiness, those two prime concerns of the Western novelist, do not have such central importance in the Indian context. The classic ideals of the god-like hero and the patient heroine extol the virtues of the extinction of the ego whereas the novel in the Western world often focuses upon the achievement of selfhood or personality. One might argue that classical ideals no longer obtain in the Indian context. But in actual literary practice, numerous characters are found to adhere to classic prototypes—especially the women of fiction who persistently re-enact the suffering, sacrificing role of Sita or Savitri."[9]

Whatever the facts of the Indo-Anglian novelist's predicament, there is one very important reality which should be underlined at this point. It is that the flowering of the new genre—Indo-Anglian fiction—could not have happened more auspiciously: it almost coincided with the rise of the novel in the several regional languages of India. In this context, it seems easy to agree with Mrs. Mukherjee as she goes on to make another very significant observation:

> "If the social and literary conditions which gave rise to the novel in the Indian languages also brought forth the Indian novel in English, and if parallel trends can be observed in the Indo-Anglian novel as well as in the novels of the regional languages, then we must regard Indo-Anglian fiction as a branch of Indian fiction rather than British fiction. Furthermore, if the Indo-Anglian novel is firmly rooted in the social and cultural ethos of India, then Indo-Anglian fiction has claims to be considered independently of the great tradition of the English novel."[10]

Perhaps one would do well to be very clear about this special feature of the tradition of the Indo-Anglian novel, such that one cannot ignore or underestimate the current of change ushered in the Indian milieu by the major writers in the regional languages. This reflects the Pan-Indian situation relating to the changes in the sensibility of the Indian woman. Shantha Krishnaswamy is very perceptive in her remark :

"It is through the confines of a novel that we see what it means to be an Indian woman today."[11]

But, perhaps, women of the other countries also can be viewed equally clearly through the spectrum provided by the novels written in their respective languages. This, however, is not valuable because of its having any direct link with the dialectic of feminism: the value derives from the virtues of the fictive world that lay bare the inside story with the utmost sensitiveness and sincerity and also enable us to participate, of course, vicariously, in the experiences of the women in fiction as also of the women who have been great authors of fiction. The reference to the last-named group does not, however, suggest that it would be doing well at all to differentiate between the male author's and the female author's points of view. In fact, creative imagination in several cases transcended the level of sex, a fact which is conclusively attested to by creations like Ibsen's Nora, Flaubert's Emma Bovary, Richardson's Clarissa, Tagore's Binodini, Sharat Chandra's Kamal, Anand's Gauri and several others. Even Simone de Beauvoir's estimate is that the primary aspiration of writers should be "full membership in the human race"[12] without yielding to a prejudice that no **man** can truly unfold the inside story of the feminine experience with dependable objectivity. After all, the glorious battle for the woman's emancipation fought by Ibsen, Zola and Shaw cannot be overlooked. In this context, Shantha Krishnaswamy's another remark may be quoted:

> "There is no need to invalidate the imaginative art; fictive experience allows us a vicarious participation in the lives of the women in these novels. And we can live in fiction as another sex, in other skins, in other times. It is facile to transmute oneself into Captain Ahab or a meek Gouri. All that we need is a Shankespearean fellow feeling, a kind of faith in basic human nature, and the belief that in our ends lie our beginnings."[13]

Continuing the argument Krishnaswamy takes up the male-dominated culture as the true context and goes on to remark:

> "Our models are male whether in India or in Europe or in America—and we cannot escape the fact that a female point of view has never truly existed and may not ever exist. Is it not then all the more informative to take a close look at these fictional heroines, girls, wives, mothers and widows, all who had the courage to confront the male-created reality head on? They knew what it was to be a woman, and, true rebels in their individual ways, with a new sexual resonance, they paved patterns of revolt against similar exploitative systems in the fictive world. Fiction helps us see the abundant depths of a woman's heart—as a mother, a lover, a victim and always a heroine."[14]

Obviously, the advice contained in the aforesaid perception is an attempt to map out a complete graph of the general literary sensibility of the different periods and different countries towards women and see for oneself whether the implied gaps or differences encountered in a sweeping transition from the portraits of western women like Madame Bovary, Isabel Archer and Jane Eyre to their Indian counterparts, chiefly, Gouri, Monisha, Kironmayee, Suneeta and very many others of the tribes are bridgeable. At least, this is a major point at issue.

Small wonder, a feminist of the calibre of Simone de Beauvoir, apparently in full agreement with the relevance of a concentrated study of women created out of fact by fiction, devoted a whole chapter entitled as "The Myth of Women in Five Authors" in her famous book on the women theme, **The Second Sex.** Here, it may not be altogether out of place to clarify that the point of the fictive experience consists primarily in the significant task of searching for permanent values such that no author of fiction, worth the name, can afford to get bogged down by polemical dogmas or by any academic debate on the ontology of sexuality. The fictive world, rich, varied and highly imaginative, is deeply involved in revealing woman's nature and predicament (almost all experiences that the second sex is heir to) in literary terms. The global range of the status of woman provides a highly impressive vision. While Ibsen's supreme question remains: to be female, what does it mean? And Mao Tse-Tung observes that in sharp opposition to a Chinese man's destiny to carry on his back only three mountains, his unfortunate female counterpart has four on her slender shoulders:

"The colonial oppression from outside, the feudal oppression from within and his own backwardness. The fourth, for the woman, is the Chinese man,"[15] this existential concept had been perhaps kept in abeyance in/since the heyday of the classical period in India. Here, it would appear, she belongs to poetry, mystery and romance, and writers have indulged in rich metaphoric vocabulary to render their women. Even in the contemporary scene, the master visionary among Indo-Anglian novelists, Raja Rao, appears admirable for having attempted to render the ideal woman by comparing her with Mother Ganga. In his masterpiece, **The Serpent and the Rope,** Rao quotes copiously from Jagannath Bhatta's **Gangalahri**:

> Sole giver of pleasure to the young centre of holy waters
>
> Bright garland of the three worlds.[16]

In fact, from the classic of **Nayikabhed** to the world-famous sentence on woman passed by the law-giver Manu is a complete range of the Indian view of womanhood that relates vitally to the Indian fabric of living. It is necessary, therefore, for the impassioned polemicists on feminism to remember that India, through the ages, provides a very complex picture of womanhood. If in modern times we have luminaries like Kasturba Gandhi, Sarojini Naidu and Indira Gandhi, we had in the past the historic queens of the calibre of Tara Bai, Ahalya Bai, Rezia Begum, Rani Durgavati, and above all, Lakshmi Bai of Jhansi, and going further back to the ancient times, we would come across equally great names (or even greater!) examples of pristine Vedic reverence, chiefly the poetesses and philosophers, and above all, mathematicians like Gargi and Maitreyi. In fact, examples could be multiplied, but the point of the picture is to suggest that in the comparative picture of woman in the West and in India, it may not be very fair or accurate to insist on a view that the Indian sister has ever been a back-bencher in contrast to her western counterpart. At the same time, since the present essay is primarily concerned with a purely literary review, the digression to the historical perspective need not be stretched further.

II

As one begins with a survey of the Western horizon first, apart from women characters, some women creators deserve special mention. (But for sheer illustrative purposes, I would take up only three of the luminaries.). First, the Brontes, or to be more specific, Charlotte Bronte, who seems to be of immense symptomatic significance in the context of the slender public esteem women writers could command in the nineteenth century literary setting in England. One example is Southey's curt retort to Charlotte in response to her having posted a few poems to him, hopefully.

> "Literature", Southey gave out, "cannot be the business of woman's life, and it ought not to be. The more she is engaged in her proper duties, the less leisure will she have for it, even as an accomplishment and a recreation."[17]

One wonders if a remark, as illustrative of the nineteenth—century British mood as this, would not compare pretty well with whatever obtained in the contemporary Indian scene. Just what were the "proper duties" for the women and what could constitute their" accomplishment" and "recreation"—these were some of the questions raised by those whose opinion, (like Southey's) did matter at that time. The Bronte sisters were no doubt some of the most gifted creative talents. Of them, Emily Bronte, the author of **Wuthering Heights** is among the greatest in English fiction. But even she, like her sister Charlotte, did not escape the society's contempt for the prodigious efforts they made (to tell the truth) not so much for fame as for their very survival. Driven by absolute need, verging on poverty, they were not having what could by any standard be called a living. They were not beautiful either—another gross liability, and added to their natures and curious gifts including a marked intellectuality, it posed a real obstacle to marriage or settlement of any kind. Taken together, these artists symbolised a woman's real predicament; no wonder, the humiliations encountered and endured in their heroic efforts for existence affected considerably the raw material of their fiction. Only **Wuthering Heights** perhaps could emerge unscathed and rose to heights that are a record till date. Thinking seriously about this typical 'woman' case, one could easily see that writing was very much an escape from the drudgery and servitude they were battling against—in fact their writing was as heroic as their battle for survival. One is led to suspect that perhaps the crudity of the challenge and the perils of their future ingrained in them a remarkable professionalism. One brief but really telling account should help one see their actual position:

> "Necessity, dependence, discipline drove them hard; being a writer was a way of living, surviving, literally keeping alive. They worked to get their books published; they worried about contracts, knew the chagrins and misunderstandings of authorship. Emily was disappointed in the inane reception of **Wuthering Heights**: Charlotte's first novel, **The Professor**, was turned down everywhere. (In fact, the crossed-out publishers' addresses on the manuscript showed her perseverance even if they were somewhat dampening to the receiver)."[18]

But nothing like this or worse could prevent the gifted sisters from going high. If about Emily, her sister Charlotte in remarkably accurate as she says: "......indeed, I have never seen her parallel in anything",[19] Charlotte's own successes cannot be underestimated. **Jane Eyre,** a masterpiece in its own right, and the later one **Villette** rank till today as powerful images of nineteenth century "female feeling". There is indeed a marked identification at `several' points between the writer and her creations—Lucy Snow and Jane Eyre. As in her life so in her works, there is one conspicuous note the undertone of hysteria and threat. It seems that it had become her ambition to render as sensitively and truthfully as possible the plight of poor, high-minded young women of the day. Charlotte, a lot more than her more gifted sister, Emily, appears to be an example of the struggling female consciousness, a fact that is clearly reflected from the following note:

> "How to live without love, without security? Hardly

any other Victorian woman had thought as much about this as Charlotte Bronte. The large, gaping flaws in the construction of the stories—mad wives in the attic, strange apparitions in Belgium—are a representation of the life she could not face; these gothic subterfuges represent the mind at a breaking point, frantic to find any way out. If the flaws are not only to be attributed to the practice of popular fiction of the time, we cannot then explain the large amount of genuine feeling that goes into them. They stand for the hidden wishes of an intolerable life."[20]

To sum up, the Bronte sisters symbolise at once the despondency of their class and situation as well as the remarkably heroic battle waged by the great women talents of the times against the insufferable hostilities which were their destiny, to say the least.

As a victim of male-sponsored hostilities, Sylvia Plath is another great name in the context. She is important for our purposes because she also represents "a sense of combat and brute force, new in women writers."[21] Yet, by and large, her poems, great as they are, reveal a mind in a state of sensual distortion as also a peculiar vulnerability to her father and husband. **Daddy,** a celebrated poem by Plath may serve as a typical example:

"Every woman adores a Fascist,

The boot in the face, the brute

Brute heart of a brute like you."[22]

Yet, it would be futile to search for anything of the social revolutionary in her: she remains too much of an individual—a shattered one, indeed—to be linked up with any movement or "ism", as is surely true of one of the greatest woman novelists in English, who is also an avowed feminist, Virginia Woolf.

Virginia Woolf, daughter of Leslie Stephen and married to Leonard Woolf, belonged to the famous Bloomsbury group of geniuses: "the grand, isolated singularities, like Virginia Woolf, fortunately a feminist."[23] Regrettably, her marriage was, as apprehended, a failure, thanks to her famous frigidity and in spite of Leonard's exemplary endurance. Yet, more importantly, the failure had perhaps its roots in her feminism, in which she was really a revolutionary. Her great friend, Vita Sackville-West said of her:

"She dislikes the possessiveness and love of domination in men. In fact, she dislikes the quality of masculinity."[24]

Frankly, this is the picture of a radical anti-masculinists, and comes significantly from a woman belonging to Virginia Woolf's most intimate private circle. There are facts galore which leave one in no doubt about the fact of her ardent feminism, the fact that—

> "....She thought and wrote seriously not only about being a woman but about the defaults and defects of the world made by men. Some of her friends found our insistencies about all this a little sharp and tedious; Forster called her feminism 'old-fashioned' and felt, writing in the forties, it was also unnecessary, since 'by the 1930s she had much less to complain of, and seems to keep on grumbling from habit.' A new phrase that is used in this regard is 'androgynous vision', which relates to `the excessive, almost smothering "feminity", or the fiction of a feminist like Virginia Woolf."[25]

No wonder, in her novels, men pale into insignificance before women. Her women characters like Mrs. Dalloway and Mrs. Ramsay are memorable, while in contrast, the men exist, by and large, as foils to such superior women. It is impossible to find in her novels anything like Lydgate—Rosamond relationship, which is marked by a perfect realism embodying the destructive power of sex and marriage, simply because she cannot afford the "masculine knowledge', which George Eliot had easily acquired from her impressionable years in Warwickshire. On this Elizabeth Hardwick's remarks seem convincing and conclusive:

"The aestheticism of Bloomsbury, the 'androgyny' if you will, lies at the root of Virginia Woolf's narrowness. It imprisons her in femininity."[26]

The brief story of women artists should end here, as one turns to the significant women characters in western fiction. The very titles of the masterpieces by Zola, Flaubert and Tolstoy relate to the celebrated women they are done round. They are **Nana, Madame Bovary** and **Anna Karenina.** In all these novels, the inner life of the woman is all important and lends credibility and vitality to the stories. Each of these protagonists, perhaps like a later master creation, **Isabel Archer** by Henry James in his unforgettable 'Portrait' is shown as having been caught in the very nemesis of an experience. According to R.B. Blackmur, what dramatises the action in **Madame Bovary** (to take out one of them) is the frightfully close identification of the illicit with the romantic and the beautiful. This is at the centre of Nana's most engaging experiences, while Anna Karenina's story cuts still deeper. Today, of course, their struggle is valued more for the psychological dramatisation than for the moral, but this does not lessen the intensity of the experience or the depth of the realisation which the women protagonists are seen as undergoing. And above all, the force derives from the inevitableness of the doom, from the ultimate truth that once you are involved in an action, which may be illicit and irresistible. You cannot escape the consequences. The fate of these protagonists impresses everyone as defined by adulterous love, which is, in fact, the central and enduring theme, not only in these novels, but in most of fiction.

> "Love and power", writes Elizabeth Hardwick, while analysing the centrality of seduction and betrayal in fiction, "are the landscape in which imagined destiny is lived. Power as a consequence of conventional love is suitable for comedies and for the intense dramas of the well-to-do classes and their daughters. Love destroys power in the great tragic heroines, in Greek drama, in Anna Karenina, in Cleopatra. It is infinitely more complicated and mixed in the bourgeois novel. What is asked of the heroine is not always a grand passion, but a sense of reality, a curious sort of independence and honour, an acceptance of consequence that puts courage to the most searing test."[27]

In this context, one is tempted to refer to a very leader of women characters, Chaucer's **Wife of Bath**. Not that she is in any way a model of virtue. Far from it, her main attraction in the tale is the fact that while she is as coarse and lecherous as any man, she comes to tell one of the best tales in the narrative, a tale of immense psychological resonance. Her story, in brief, is about a young knight who on the verge of being banished from the court for rape, is ultimately saved by the intervention of the queen and her ladies, and this throws Chaucer's question in face of everyone's: everyone what is it women most desire? Significantly, Chaucer puts this question on women through a woman—**Wife of Bath.**

Samuel Richardson was a moralist par excellence, but his deepest morals came through the story of the seduction of women.

His heroine, Pamela, is so good that it is hoped that a daily look at this apostle of virtue should reform the worst among men. Yet it is Clarissa's story that illustrates Richardson's 'feminism' much more profoundly, and **Clarissa**, is frankly a novel about seduction. Volumes flow, one after another, from the avowed moralists pen only to show consummation threatened but delayed. Perhaps Richardson was planning a text book on precautions for the menaced eighteenth century damsels. Yet, the central drama in the novel is all-important, in which the opposed forces are fully matched as they appear poised against each other. Clarissa thinks the fort of her virginity is invincible, while Lovelace is a finished artist in seduction and will not be deterred by anything.

A point is reached when the novel looks intolerably grotesque, devoted unbelievably to a purely sexual conception of virtue and villainy. The point is intense because both Clarissa and the rake are so self-centred. Inevitably, the sordid end comes, and Lovelace, with no intention to marry her, ultimately destroys her virtue. The question that crops up here—which is apart from whatever the apostle woman, Clarissa, may think about the whole thing—is whether it is seduction or merely a case of adultery, achieved fraudulently. This is the uniqueness of the case in point—Clarissa, the symbol of purity, is virtually unseducible. Yet the vitality of the story derives from sex at a deeper level, which is that the model of virtue has been eventually drugged and raped. Richardson's point, however, must not be missed, which is that a woman of Clarissa's calibre could not be raped unless she had been drugged first. Everything said and done, Clarissa may appear to many to be the novelist's mouthpiece, an apostle used by the novelist for his preachings. Not so Moll Flander, the very first portrait of woman in English fiction, whose claims to immortality in art cannot be questioned. Moll's creator was no feminist, but he was a great realist, absolutely free from any inhibition. Small wonder Moll remains memorable for her courage and naturalness and, above all, a total freedom from any pretensions, whatsoever. She passes from one husband to another (all told, she marries five times) with an ease which is surprising, but viewed in the context of experiences, not unconvincing.

In fact, among English novelists, the best known for his women is Thomas Hardy. His women can be compared only to the best in the language—those created by Shakespeare. This is so in spite of the fact that Jane Austen, herself a woman, has done more women than men at the centre of her stories. In fact, her novels look like a sort of social hieroglyph, and this puts her characters in a different category. Hardy is closer to nature, to earth and poetry. His gallery of women is, therefore, more attractive and varied. While on the one hand there is Bathshelea, the very flower of womanliness at the centre of the story of love in **Far from the Madding Crowd**, the depth is touched in the tragedy of Tess. Superficially, the seduction of Tess may resemble another seduction story, that of Hetty Sorel in **Adam Bede**, written by George Eliot, but the resemblance does not go below the surface. Hetty does not belong to Tess's class: the former is a victim of her own errors and imperfections that, along with her false expectations, simply trivialise her. She is at most pathetic. Not so Tess, in whose case the very President of Immortals is referred to. To be fair, Tess's predicament and tragedy appear to have been conceived absolutely perfectly. She is not a slip of a farm girl—ignorant and easily entrappable: she is engagingly natural—indeed worthy of the predicament that befalls her. Her seduction is not very usual because she does not like Alec, yet it is seduction from the latter's point of view. What is more, it is the starting point of a series of entanglements and calamities. A child is born, and even though it does not survive, it causes her the biggest loss—the loss of her love—Angel Clare. Clare's rejection of Tess is the unkindest cut not only in Hardy's novel but in all fiction. Ultimately she kills the destroyer of her love, which redeems her in a great way, transmuting her from a mere theme or idea into a complete human being.' A pure woman faithfully presented', Tess emerges as one of the most original women in fiction. This is so in spite of the fact that at many points she appears to be a paradox in terms of the plot of sex and its destructive force for woman. She comes out as highly convincing because she has every plausible right to supersede the man who is the cause of her ruin.

The range of portraiture of women in Western fiction is vast and can well go beyond the Tragedy of Tess, but the map is convincingly complete as one starts from one model of naturalness, Moll Flander, and ends with another, perhaps greater and more poetically conceived—Tess.

III

As we proceed towards a few concrete examples from the Indian context, the first great Indian novel in English that stands out as a supreme masterpiece is **The Serpent and the Rope** by Raja

Rao. It is a masterpiece both as a novel and a treatise on womanhood. It is such that one may well open the examination of the novel with a typical exposition of the thesis that woman is:

> "Woman is the earth, air, ether, sound; woman is the microcosm of the mind, the articulation of space, the knowing in knowledge; the woman is fire, movement, clear and rapid as the mountain stream; the woman is that which seeks against that which is sought. To Mitra she is Varuna, to Indra she is Agni, to Rama she is Sita, to Krishna she is Radha. Woman is the meaning of the word, the breath, the touch, art; woman is that which reminds man of that which he is and reminds herself through him of that which she is. Woman is kingdom, solitude, time; woman is growth, the god's inherence; the woman is death, for it is through woman that one is born; woman rules, for it is she, the universe."[28]

This Vedic view of woman, coming strangely from a novelist who has spent decades in the West, reads like an exegesis of the *Shakti*-cult. Even Shiva, the type-figure of the supreme male manifestation of God, is just *Shava* (a corpse), when separated from the *Shakti*-half, that is grammatically embodies in the texture of the word. No wonder he is the only God who assumes the unique, dual personality of *Ardhanareeshwara.* But coming to the story of love, of a complex of human relationships embedded in the novel, the questions that stand out are as follows:

What is Madeleive to Rama?

What is Savitri to Rama?

Who does Saroja represent (to Rama)?

What is the significance of little mother?

If woman is 'the meaning of the word', just what is the peculiar meaning in each case? The novel, which, to take Rao's own words, relates "the sad and uneven chronicle of life, **my life**" (emphasis mine)[29], however, need not be explained away as an autobiography. What is a lot more significant is Rama's continuous quest for the meaning of life, as the meanings unfold themselves in diverse female forms.

Taking up the last-named woman first, let us try to understand the underlying significance of the portraiture. The little mother has been left nameless in the novel, but is intended by the novelist to be a very synonym of the mother-figure. Though quite different from the Western woman, Madeleive, and the Indian women, who have been exposed to cross-cultural patterns and conflicts, she is in her own right a supreme force in the novel. She is a pure giver, who is always seen giving away, radiating joy and confidence throughout, without having any notion about individuality, much less a bother like ego. Widowed at twenty-one, she puts up a brave fight, which in her case, is another word for dignity and all love for traditional values. She very naturally succeeds in proving to be a mother to Rama in the typical Hindu way, not only lavishing on the son (who is older than she herself) all motherly love, but also regarding him as head of the family, the *Karta* figure.

But Madeleive is a different case, made of different stuff. She is a good woman, a rich character in fiction, but very much an individual, who has loved Rama, her husband ungrudgingly, and yet would not hesitate to register her grievance as and when she realises it is genuine and must be given expression to. She writes to Rama a letter to say:

> "I bore him, your son, with such love, for he was a child of love; but you were more interested in his sonship than in his being my son. The feminine to the Indian must always be accessory, a side issue."[30]

In its abstract, this is unabashedly loud feminism, signifying, in the main, the basic East-West conflict, and yet it comes from a highly devoted wife, a very sincere woman, who gets out of her husband's way when she genuinely realises that they cannot walk together, step by step, in the journey of life. The shrewd Westerner in her must avoid false steps: she is simply grand in her genuineness and cannot bow down to any pretensions, even though they might have saved her married life. How different is Savithri, another Rao woman, from both little mother ad Madeleive? Not surprisingly, Savithri evokes a peculiar sense of disapproval in Rama in the first encounter as an ultra-modern type:

> "I could not understand these northerners going from strict **Purdah** to this extreme modernism with unholy haste. We in the South were more sober and very distant. We lived by tradition—shameful though it might look."[31]

But later on, as her emotionally-rooted womanhood assumes vital dimensions, she emerges as the ideal companion to Rama. As is clearly reflected in the ritual that follows, she seems to have won him over completely. But in essense Rao is simply demonstrating another triumph over man by another woman. In sheer exultation, Rama says: All women are perfect women for they have the feminine principle in them, the *Yin*, the *Prakriti*.[32] Similarly, he bows down to his sister, Saroja, as she also, in her own charming way, symbolises the growing woman form: "What a deep and reverential mystery womanhood is: I could bow before Saroja and call her queen."[33]

Yet, Savithri, to be fair, is shown as transcending the level of commonness with remarkable ease, and illustrates not only the feminine principle, abundant in her, but also the transcendental Radha-cult. "A Hindu woman", she says, "knows how to worship her Krishna, her Lord."[34]

Rama has become Krishna to her as she herself has metamorphosed into Radha. In effect, the human relationship rendered here becomes also a symbolic one, a mythical one, for the woman claims, in a fit of love and faith: "I have known my Lord for a thousand lives, from *Janam* to *Janam* have I known my Krishna....."[35]

All this is so charming as a rendering of love-relationship that one does not even mind whether the symbolisation or the use of myth is convincing also. Meenakshi Mukherjee also has raised the issue in these words: "It is arguable, therefore, that the fond description of these rituals has its birth in the sentimental longing of the writer himself, and expatriate Indian, who sees all traditionally Indian actions developed in a mist of nostalgia."[36]

Perhaps much more pertinent than such questions is the fact that Savithri is just another experiment with the "meaning of the word" as the journeyman Rama visualises in his quest for truth. It is, however, apparent that Raja Rao's primary interest is in propounding metaphysical truths and propositions: even personal relationships, which should have remained supreme in fiction, seem to have been made to fit in with some archetypal pattern. That is why, at some moments, some gaps are left in the dramatisation of a situation or in the development of character.

For example, while at one point, Rama is seen as highly enthused by the flowering of sublime womanhood in his sister, Saroja, he looks blank when grim realities raise their ugly face, and the same vivacious sister confronts him with her reactions (including her serious objections to an odious marriage proposal). Let us quote a part of the significant dialogue between them:

> "She wished she had been a European woman: it would have given her so much freedom, so much brightness."
> "What freedom?" I exclaimed, "The freedom of foolishness." "In what ways, Saroja, do you think Catherine or Madeleine is better off than you ?"
> "They knew how to love."
> "And you"
> "And we know how to bear children. We are just like a motor car or bank account. On better still, we are like a comfortable salary paid by a benign and eternal British government. Our joy is a treasury receipt." Later she adds with bitterness: "Like cotton, we women must have grown on trees" Rama finds no answer to give. On the eve of the wedding....she cried out: "Oh Brother.....I cannot marry him.....It is selfish of one to marry a man whom I detest....."[37]

All these protestations are loud but very moving: yet it is a pity that the same Saroja collapses soon into a passive mood, bordering on some vague idealism, which leaves us cold. In terms of fact, she pales into insignificance before her own younger sister, Sukumari, who, faced with a similar challenge, puts up a fight and refuses to give way.

Finally, as far as Rao's women are concerned, one is left in no doubt about the fact that he is too much of a traditionalist to allow for any radical departure in his perceptions. His women do not suffer from any want: most of them are fairly well off. But even then they fail to throw away the fetters of domestic and social injustice and also the tyranny of customs.

A markedly different note is struck in the portrayals of women by another luminary in the line, Bhabani Bhattacharya. His women vibrate with exuberance and remain pure, even though victimised. They are intended to grow full-length as highly redeeming prototypes. He says in **Shadow from Ladakh**,

> "Who could hold her back from her urge, a woman's primal urge, to be nothing but a woman?[38]

Whether it is Suruchi or her daughter Sumita in **Shadow from Ladakh** or Mohini in **Music for Mohini**, all are innocent, pure women, being persecuted by a villainous society. The basic concept is that the innocence of the women tempts the villains to tyrannise her, and this forms the vital centre in all his novels. What gives this theme an added verve is the fact that these pure women are not only noble: they are, in essence, close to nature and all in full harmony with their instinctive urges. Mohini is faced with the unkindest cut in her wedding night itself, when she discovers that she has married an idealist, Jayadev, who will not come down to her. Her femininity is crushed and this defiles her spiritual nature also. How long can she respect her husband who is callously insensitive to her needs as a woman? Why can she not be allowed to be nothing but a woman, a real, natural, full woman? "The sad thing for women", says Susan Lydon, "is that they have participated in the destruction of their own eroticism."[39]

In the context of the theme of purity and nobility, a very pertinent question has been raised by another western critic, Dorothy Spencer, who wonders whether these pure and good and noble women are not unreal in their very consistency.

> "As we observe", she says, "with the mind's eye this procession of devoted, submissive, faithfully, loyal, self-sacrificing women, the question arises, are these characters intended as realistic portrayals?"[40]

Her finding, based on her study of Premchand and Bankim Chandra Chatterjee, is that these novelists have really wanted their idealisation of characters to be taken as an aspect of realism. Yet, perhaps, some of the subtlest portrayals of women have come from Sharat Chandra (another novelist of the calibre of Bankim Chandra and Premchand) whose Kamal **(Shesh Prashana)** and Kironmayee **(Charitraheen)** can easily impress anyone, all over the world, by their revolutionary attitude to life, particularly in the area of human relationships. They impress the reader—common and uncommon alike—by their absolute freedom from inhibition: in fact, they very happliy illustrate the idea of a "natural" woman. One wonders whether Dorothy Spencer's sentence would hold true in case of these 'radical'women. (It is another matter that Sharat Chandra's novels also end as an attempt at a fusion of the real and the ideal. For example, very few readers would feel convinced by the ending of one of the most forceful masterpieces in fiction, **Charitraheen,** particularly by Upendra's second coming on the scene and tilting the balance of forces by taking away Savitri from Satish and finalising his marriage with Sarojini). So, by and large, the fact remains that the line of demarcation between realism and idealism is very thin in Hindi and Bengali novels, and the same is applicable in case of Indo-Anglian novels. Yet, as a generalised observation on this aspect, Meenakshi Mukherjee's comments do not appear to be very different from the sweeping remark of the "outsider" Dorothy Spencer. Mrs. Mukherjee remarks:

> "The man-woman relationship in which the man's role is dynamic and the woman's passive is a pattern that goes very deep into the Indian ethos. The ideal is so much a part of the Indian mind that an Indian reader never pauses to wonder whether the Indian novels that portary this relationship and present the woman as the symbol of purity and goodness draw their material from real life, or merely follow a literary convention."[41]

In fact, Ms. Mukherjee's own analysis of Mulk Raj Anand's novel, **The Old Woman and the Cow**, a novel done round a woman protagonist, Gouri, who cannot be dubbed a conventional prototype of the suffering, passive woman, would prove my point. True, at the beginning, she is shown as a Sita-type ideal woman, and several details of development confirm the continuance of the parallel. When her uncle sells her to a lecherous shopkeeper, she, like Sita, shows her mettle and proves too strong and virtuous for the purchaser as he proceeds to have his money's worth. But, as in Sita's case, her chastity remains suspect in public view and her husband also refuses to accept her. The parallel, however, does not go further. Here there is no *Agnipariksha* for the simple reason that our days are not Sita's days. Obviously, the myth cannot proceed further, and here the new Gauri emerges, which is something new in the Indo-Anglian fiction. The rise of the new woman out of the old one is a great event of immense historical significance.

> "...for a brief moment the thought that the earth must open up to rescue her as it had opened up to receive Sita, came as an echo from the memory of her race. But the ground was hard and solid under her feet and showed no sings of opening up to prove her innocence."[42]

And then follows the momentous division, denoting a definite discovery of her real self: "She waved her head to forget Sita, and thought of the road to the town."[43]

Suddenly, she is transformed form the gentle, submissive cow-figure to a real, full individual, with a personality of her own. The only other woman protagonist whom one remembers as a complete parallel is Ibsen's Nora. In her case, it is only at the end that the doll's house goes to pieces as she realises with awe and wonder what a heartless, soulless husband she had been doting on all the eight years. She opens the door with a resolute decision and walks out of her husband's house. No doubt the sparking off of dynamism in Nora and Gauri is an event of great significance in the entire context of world literature. But there are other examples worth attention and analysis.

The submissive woman, Savithri **(The Dark Room)** again a type-figure for quite some time, eventually yields place to the new woman, the liberated self, typified by Daisy **(The Painter of Signs)**, masterpieces by one of the greatest Indo-Anglian novelists, R.K. Narayan. From Savithri to Daisy is a complete story of woman's suffering, struggle and emancipation.

Savithri figures as a born victim, at the farthest end from the courageous Moll Flanders and not having the potential of Nora or Gauri either. When she is thrown out of her husband's house, one is brought face-to-face with a crude Indian setting. But the depths of an Indian wife's despair are demoralising, indeed. She is equally moving and convincing, even in her despair and dismay, as she mutter, unheroically:

> "No one who could not live by herself should be allowed exist.... What is the difference between a prostitute and a married woman? The prostitute changes her men but a married woman does not, that's all; both earn their food and shelter in the same manner."[44]

The villain of the piece is none else other than her husband, Ramani, who swears by the heroines of the epics and wants his wife to follow their footsteps and in that follow him "like the shadow following the substance."

Thus, he typifies the common male attitude of possessiveness. Yet, through his women, R.K. Narayan intends to draw a complete graph of womanhood, and proceeds from type to type. In fact, all the types are cases in one point, which is that, pitted against an insensitive age with males like Ramani at the helm, it is the women, who, either by submitting and suffering (Like Savithri) or by their dynamism (like Daisy) would establish and reserve the age-old human values.

One stage further, one meets in Narayan's galaxy, Bharathi of **Waiting for the Mahatma**. She initiates the active feminine principle, which, eventually, finds its apogee in Daisy. Narayan's idea is that in this can be seen the progression of feminism, as one passes from Savithri's passive feminism to the active feminism of Bharathi, touching the heights with the dynamic Daisy. Surely, the writer's sensibility is remarkably progressive, and it is his women protagonists who are very much at the points of growth. Professor Walsh has a positive view of these women, who, according to him, represent: "Custom and Reason' and 'know what is and what is not proper."[45]

A very important question arises here. Will woman ever be satisfied with the quantum of freedom she gets or snatches or is given? The fact of the matter is that once the feminine consciousness is provoked and the woman tastes freedom and power, there will be no stopping her. Naturally, she would proceed from indirect power to direct power. This is clear from the story of Daisy, who is more radical than Bharathi, a mere trend-setter by comparison. Bharathi's positive achievement, however, cannot be ignored: it is she, who, for the first time in Narayan's fictive world, broadens the woman's perception in the context of nationalism. She is, indeed, at the point of transition, demonstrating the fact that the new woman has come of age. Naturally, as she grows vibrant, the hero, Srinivas is reduced to a non-hero. Yet, when we proceed to another case, the case of Rosie of **The Guide**, says Shantha Krishnaswamy:

> "...the woman no longer forms part of a mutual imagination in wedded life. There is no music, no harmony in marriage. It is an invalid life where love is invalidated. Every relationship is, in Sartrian parlance, a contest for possession. One either possesses or gets possessed. What we have here is exclusivity, the feminine exclusivity. The female is the possessor, the aggressor, the male is possessed, bewitched and fooled."[46]

In Paul Verghese's opinion, Rosie is a typical Indian heroine. She is alive to the demands of *Dharma* and *Karma* both; naturally, she exhibits a remarkable duality, leading to an ambivalent attitude towards self-assertion which is demonstrated twice, once in running away from her impossible husband, and a second time from her dashing lover, Raju, because she detests being treated like a commodity, a plaything in the hands of an over-confident masterplayer. This, eventually, disillusions Raju as well, who confesses:

"Neither Marco nor I had any place in her life, which had its own sustaining vitality and which she herself had underestimated all along."[47]

Yet, compared with Rosie, Daisy is a sharper image of revolt. She aims at becoming a whole woman and for this she must get autonomy. It appears that she flees from the family to vanish into life in the Chekovian way. Readers and critics are impressed by her assets, which are dynamism, and a psychological and sexual satisfaction. According to Shantha Krishnaswamy, here is a case in which

"The existing cultural absolutes are transformed, the roles are reversed and we get a Huxlean picture of a new world where, without the aid of new biological weaponary like cybernetics and partheno-genesis, the female attains a titanic womanhood, disregarding all known bounds.[48]

At the same time, there is a very important authorial suggestion which must be underlined: it is that liberation of the woman may be a positive gain, but it must know a limit. If the limit is crossed, whether it is the woman's or the man's freedom in question, there would be disaster. Daisy's decision to get rid of the absurd male fetter, love, reminds one of Anna Karenina. Small wonder, in the face of dynamic and heroic women like Rosie and more so, Daisy, their men, Raju and Raman are rendered passive and weak. Yet the great question of consequences remains. As in the case of Savithri's dismay and humiliating return to a despotic husband, so here, one asks: where will this new-found Amazonian stance take the modern woman—where? Narayan's achievement consists in posing this important question imaginatively: but he does not have to give an answer. He only smilingly completes his graph of womanhood, dramatising the long journey of the feminine principle, from the likes of Savithri to those of Daisy. Clearly, one feels, one has travelled very far, not only from Narayan's Savithri, but also from Tagore's Binodini. In fact, this example of female chauvinism has raised many questions in many quarters. The main apprehension is that like male chauvinism, female chauvinism also may be counter productive. After all, equality is not sameness. Besides, in striving for equality, woman may lose womanliness. An unwomanly woman is undeniably as undesirable as an unmanly man. In either case, the certain casuality is human relationship, the warmth of it, in fact, humanity itself. To quote Susan Lydon:

> "Sexual liberation for women is wrongly understood to mean that woman will adopt all the forms of masculine sexuality. As in the whole issue of woman's liberation, that is really not the point."[49]

In a similar vein, Betty Friedan remarks that the feminist frontier in the 1980's is the family, an idea which is bound to irk much of the feminist movement. She is unhappy to find that the feminine mystique has been replaced by a feminist mystique, which is equally limiting as it freezes women in reaction against men and family life. Narayan's portrayal of so many types and cases in only to suggest that women's sexuality is very varied and delicate and that the healing touch can come mainly from literature. Narayan is neither a committed traditionalist nor a rebel against tradition: his novels, and more particularly, his women reveal his determination to evolve through all the cases a pattern of real, lasting, positive love. This is the true gospel of unfettered mutuality, which is love as well as relationship in the most human form.

Among other Indo-Anglian novelists who bring new dimensions in the delineation of man-woman relationship with a determination to reveal the woman's case to advantage, Anita Desai, Arun Joshi and Kamla Markandeya stand out. They are notable for bringing fresh insights to the sextist nature of the relationship, which naturally takes them deep into the inside story. Yet, it would be wrong to treat them as a group because each has a strikingly individual approach, a distinct point of view, a very personal perception of the problem.

Anita Desai's uniqueness consists in concentrating on the psychology of woman's realities, which are to her, principally a creation of the mind. It is through her total involvement in the consciousness of the woman that she enables her reader to see the Indian woman fully from the inside. Not that she does her main investigation like a formal psychologist: she is too much of an artist, a novelist, to commit herself or yoke her perception to any metaphysics of consciousness.

Her very first novel, **Cry the Peacock,** is a milestone in this direction. Completely representative in its essentials, it is a woman's story, woman is both story and theme; indeed, she is the vital centre. The story, here, is of Maya, a failed wife—a story of marital discord marked with a streak of neurotic fantasy on her part. As early as at page 9, one hears Maya grumbling: "But then he know nothing that concerned me. Giving me an opal ring to wear on my finger, he did not notice the trans-lucent skin beneath, the blue flashing veins that ran under and out of the bridge of gold....Telling me to go to sleep while he worked at this papers, he did not give another thought to me, to either the soft, willing body or the lonely, wanting mind, that waited near his bed."[50]

The woman novelist has minced no words in exposing the woman character's shattered inner world. The woman-complex here comprises two wanters—the body and the mind, but whose want is greater has been left delightfully vague, even though the 'drunken desire' of the hungry wife does not remain hidden. Later in the novel, when she finds the main utterly inert and lost in his useless world, she bursts out: "Oh, you know nothing, understand nothing!" I raised my voice, 'Now will you ever understand. You know nothing of me-and how I can love. How I want to love. How it is important to me."[51]

Not only here, but in her other novels also, Desai has made her point absolutely clear, which is that in the awful tangle that the failed man-woman relationship is reduced to, it is the woman, fatally sensitive as she is, who is aware of the malaise. Here is the tragedy of the unfulfilled, and it is as a truncated self that she occupies centre-stage. She is bundle of unanswerable questions; at least, her man will not answer them. Man-made myths matter little to her, and she is up against the whole facade. No wonder, a typical Desai woman is a longer, which results from a serious disparity in sensibilities, male and female. This also explains her dedication to the task of interiorising the woman's consciousness: the external world that may consist of the cruder issues of existence remains utterly immaterial. Like Maya, other woman protagonists also (in Desai's novels) turn romance upside down, thus making for an altogether new perception of feminist fiction where the woman is set on an unending quest that may lead to nowhere, but surely the purpose is to explore the true meaning of life. Maya is only the first among Desai's several cases of the isolated trapped psyche.

Yet the basic theme of her novels is not exactly of quest, as is true of the novels of Arun Joshi—particularly, **The Last Labyrinth** and **The True Case of Anil Biswas.**

Well, as in Desai's novels, so here also, the irressitable spell comes from a fascinating exploration of the inner world of an otherwise successful young urban Indian, Arun Bhaskar. (Like Bhaskar, Biswas also is another materially successful man). But in these cases, the central motif is quest in a manifest form.

Aftab, the occupant of a mysterious *Haveli* and husband of a still more mysterious woman, Anuradha, tells Bhaskar: "It is a great relief to know that there is no new thing under the sun. At least for me. For people like you, it must be different." "I am still running around looking for some new thing under the sun."[52]

In the complications and mysteriousness of the *Haveli,* the story's spiritual and sensuous dimensions are interwoven with a subtlety that distinguishes the novelist adequately. Here also, the vital centre is a unique woman, Anuradha, even though the protagonist is a man, Bhaskar, who unfolds the heart of the matter thus: "I never felt more alone than when locked in this, the most intimate of dialogues. I knew that others—Geeta, Leela—had perhaps sensed the aloneness and had left it undisturbed for fear of disturbing more than they could handle. Anuradha, on the other hand, was the daughter of disturbance. I could feel her pushing against this shroud of silence—with her hips, her mouth, her nails, her teeth, and finally, a prolonged, wild, hoarse crying that could have been the cry of the world's first lost lover or of all men, destined as they are to cry, unfulfilled, to the stars."[53] Anuradha's onslaught may be fully physical, on the face of things—but inwardly, she means a total conquest of Bhaskar's soul. Here, an important question arises. Of the two—who is the wanter, Bhaskar or Anuradha, man or woman, or both? In expressed terms, of course, it is Bhaskar—'a chronic wanter', but there are other terms as well—unexpressed, and they point towards the woman.

No wonder, Gargi, the knowing man understands both of them and advises the man to go to his woman, saying: "She is your *Shakti.*"[54]

In Joshi's world, all the terms of the quest are not physical: the physical blends with the spiritual, but throughout the gamut, man and woman will continue to want each other for a fuller realisation. This alone renders the basic quest meaningful.

The quest, in a way, continues in the novels of Kamla Markandaya also, but the terms are different, and so are the ends. Here the complex fabric of relationships, chiefly the man-woman relationship, centres round the East-West motif.

> "The definition of 'East', "says Meenakshi Mukherjee," as well as of 'West' varies from novel to novel, but each tries in its own way to grapple with the problem that has continued to concern the Indo-Anglian novelist for more than fifty years."[55]

In fact, it had concerned others also—the great Anglo-Indian novelists, Kipling, whose thesis is unforgettable: "The East is East and the West is West and the twain shall never meet," and E.M. Foster, who made the second notable attempt to explore the potentialities in inter-racial relationship, only to tell the truth on the last page of his masterpiece, **A Passage to India** in Kipling's own terms, adding that the time was not ripe yet.

In Markandaya's novels, the inter-cultural tension marks the man-woman relationships vitally and has been rendered wtih a competence and sensitiveness that the task requires.

Mira, who narrates the story in **Some Inner Fury** is an Indian girl, vibrating with gut and understanding, and thus, well-equipped to meet the challenges of life under a mixed hierarchy—Indian and English. What helps her is the fact of a fortunate upbringing: she has been used to Eastern and Western ways of living. But what endears her all the more is her dual vision. Much earlier in the novel, commenting on Kit and Premala, she notes:

> "There is a tradition perhaps not only in India, that women should not be worried, that the best way to ensure this, is to keep them as far as possible in ignorance."[56]

And again:

> "Certain domains belong to men alone and Indian women learn early not to encroach. Kit knew he would not have to remind Premala a second time."[57]

Evidently, Mira enjoys the best of both worlds, yet she fails to rise above or bypass the political barriers presented by Govind and his like. In fact, what Markandaya wants to suggest here reminds one of the great Foster's own intentions in **A Passage to India:** it is that the time has not yet come for a happy meeting of individuals, howsoever enlightened, who are pitted against racial barriers. Mira and Richard have no option. But Mira has no illusion either, as she says sadly: "You belong to one side—if you don't, you belong to the other. It is as simple as that; even children understand it. And in between? There is no in between."[58]

The cruel, inexorable nature of the end of this relationship is extremely poignant and renders the vision of Indian womanhood truly tragic.

Like this novel, her other three novels also—**Possession, The Coffer Dams,** and **The Nowhere Man** are done round a woman's crisis, deepened further because of a dual setting—England in India. Of the three, it is perhaps **The Nowhere Man** which presents a maturer and surer form of man-woman relationships than elsewhere. To take the author's own words:

> "They had come together and in the process had solved and restored each other. But it was a muted process, more an easing of aches than a violent build up of pleasure, which did not demand the constant stimulus of touch and presence of young love. Even when they lay together, it was with a degree of serenity: looking on, as it were, on something which had once been wet and wild, but now was calm."[59]

The inescapable implication here is that what can really solve the problems of society, the tensions of East-West confrontation and man-woman hostilities is a pervasive and imaginative sense of humanity, a harmonious concord between one person and another.

Even though examples can be easily multiplied and more cases can be brought in for examination, the conclusion reached so far may remain unaltered, which is that it is the woman, endowed with greater sensitiveness than man, who is more intensely aware of the malaise in all man-woman relationships. Indeed, she need not waste away her womanliness for nurturing the feminist movement. Ultimately, every woman, in East or West, or anywhere else for that matter, is more precious than the movement known as feminism.

References

1. Shantha Krishnaswamy, *The Woman in Indian Fiction in English,* New Delhi: Ashish Publishing House, 1984, 'Abstract', p-vii.
2. In the Sanskrit original it reads thus: *'Triya charitram purushasya bhagyam devo na janati kuto manushyah'.*

3. Vidyapati (15th century A.D.)
4. Shantha Krishnaswamy, *The Woman in Indian Fiction in English,* p. 5.
5. Madhu Trehan and Sunil Sethi, "Indian Women: a Time for Reckoning", *India Today* (August 1-15, 1980) p. 33.
6. Name of the heroine of Ibsen's play, *A Doll's House.*
7. Name of the heroine of Jainendra Kumar's novel, *Sunita.*
8. Said by Manu, a famous codifier of Hindu laws of the 6th century, B.C. quoted in *Status of Women in India—a Synopsis of the Report of the National Committee,* New Delhi: Indian Council of Social Science Research, 1975, pp. 13-4.
9. Meenakshi Mukherjee, *The Twice-Born Fiction,* London: Heinemann, 1971, p. 29
10. *Ibid.,* p. 23.
11. Shantha Krishnaswamy, *The Woman in Indian Fiction in English,* p. 5.
12. Simon de Beauvoir, *The Second Sex,* London: Penguin, 1979, p. 29
13. Shantha Krishnaswamy, *The Woman in Indian Fiction in English,* p. 19.
14. *Ibid.,* p. 19.
15. Mao Tse-Tung, "Women" in Quotations from the Chairman, Peking: Foreign Languages Press, 1961, Chapter 31; also quoted in *The Woman in Indian Fiction in English,* p. 8.
16. Raja Rao, *The Serpent and the Rope,* Delhi: Orient Paperbacks, 1968, p. 178.
17. Elizabeth Hardwick, *Seduction and Betrayal, Woman and Literature,* New York: 1974, Random House, p. 9.
18. *Ibid.,* pp. 13-4.
19. Quoted by Elizabeth Hardwick, *Seducation and Betrayal,* p. 19.
20. *Ibid.,* p. 29.
21. *Ibid.,* p. 121.
22. Quoted in *Seduction and Betrayal* p. 109.
23. *Ibid.,* p. 128.
24. Quoted in *Seduction and Betrayal,* p. 130.
25. *Ibid.,* p. 138.
26. *Ibid.,* p. 139.
27. *Ibid.,* p. 182.
28. Raja Rao, *The Serpent and the Rope, op.cit.,* p. 352.
29. Quoted in *The Woman in Indian Fiction in English,* p. 33.
30. Raja Rao, *op.cit.,* p. 36.
31. *Ibid.,* pp. 31-2.
32. *Ibid.,* p. 311.
33. *Ibid.,* p. 50.
34. *Ibid.,* p. 209.
35. *Ibid.,* p. 214.

36. *The Twice-Borns Fiction, op.cit.*, p. 150.
37. *The Serpent and the Rope, op.cit.*, p. 262.
38. *The Woman in Indian Fiction in English, op.cit.*, p. 60.
39. Susan Lydon (ed.). "Liberating Woman's Orgasm" in *The New Eroticism* New York: Philip Nobik, 1970, p. 225.
40. Meenashi Mukherjee, *op.cit.*, p. 165.
41. *Ibid.*, p. 165.
42. Mulk Raj Anand, *The Old Woman and the Cow*, Bombay: Kutub-Popular, 1960, p. 284.
43. *Ibid.*, p. 284.
44. R.K. Narayan, *The Dark Room*, New Delhi; Orient Longman, 1978, p. 80.
45. William Walsh, "Nataraja and the packet of saffron": in *Readings from Commonwealth Literature*, London: Oxford, 1973, p. 54.
46. *The Woman in Indian Fiction in English, op.cit.*, p. 129.
47. R.K. Narayan, *The Guide*, New Delhi, Orient Longman, 1978, p. 223.
48. *The Woman in Indian Fiction in English, op.cit.*, p. 135.
49. Susan Lydon, *The New Eroticism*, pp. 225-6.
50. Anita Desai, *Cry the Peacock*, Calcutta: Rupa and Co. 1978, p.9.
51. *Ibid.*, p. 129.
52. Arun Joshi, *The Last Labyrinth*, New Delhi: Orient Longman, 1981, pp 38-09.
53. *Ibid.*, pp. 107-8.
54. *Ibid.*, p. 121.
55. *The Twice-Born Fiction*, p. 66.
56. *The Woman in Indian Fiction in English*, p. 189.
57. *Ibid.*, p. 189.
58. *Ibid.*, p. 191.
59. Kamla Markendeya, *The Nowhere Man*, New Delhi: Orient Longman, 1975, p. 70.

PART III
ARCHIVES—DATA AND REFERENCES

18

The Indian Woman : a Statistical Panorama

*J. P. Singh, Sangeet Kumar and Dilip K. Singh**

Compilation of statistical information on the Indian woman seems to be a quite useful exercise, as one can readily understand the existing realities about the position of woman objectively on the basis of these data. Herein we have attempted to collate the latest data from various sources. The Indian census reports from 1961 to 1991, however, form the main source of our data. In the main, it is an effort to bring out the dominant demographic characteristics of the Indian woman.

For a long time the expectation of life at birth of women had been lower than that of men, but now the situation has reversed. The women have now recorded a slightly higher expectancy of life at birth (62 years) than men (61 years). This is largely on the line of other societies in the world. However, the infant mortality rates for women, as compared to men, continue to be higher.

Males continue to outnumber females. Kerala is the only state where females outnumber males. The sex ratio (F/M) of Indian population continues to be heavily in favour of males. At

* J.P. Singh is Chairman, Institute of Population and Integrated Development Patna-800013, Sangeet Kumar is Research Scholar in Sociology, Patna University, Patna-800005 and Dilip Kumar Singh is Lecturer in Sociology, A.B. Singh College (B.B.A. Bihar University), Lalganj, Vaishali, (Bihar).

the 1991 census the sex ratio of India was 929, suggesting a shortage of 71 females per 1000 population, which is in a clear contrast with the situation obtaining in major parts of the world. A higher rate of mortality for females at infancy, childhood and motherhood is the main cause for continuing imbalance in the sex ratio.

Child marriage is still in practice, to some extent, particularly in rural parts of the country. Though the age at marriage is steadily increasing, more so in urban areas, there continues to be a large difference in the age at marriage between the sexes. According to 1981 census, the singulate mean age at marriage for males is 23 years as against 18 years for females in the country.

In matters of education women continue to be lagging behind men due to the gross neglect of female edcuation. The difference between the level of male and female literacy is quite considerable. At the 1991 census, for instance, only 39 percent women were recorded literate as against 53 percent for males. The situation was quite the worst at the beginning of this century; that is, the level of literacy was about nine percent for males and less than one percent for females. Kerala and Mizoram are the only states where females have recorded about 80 percent or above level of literacy rate, while all other major states, except Tamil Nadu and Maharashtra, tended to have shown a level of literacy lower than 50 percent at the 1991 census.

India is characterised by a low female work participation rate. At the 1991 census, the work participation rate for females was about 23 percent as against 52 percent for males. In general the female work participation rate had declined during 1901-1971 and it showed an increasing trend from 1971 onwards only, but the increase was more perceptible in rural than in urban areas. One of the potential reasons for low female work participation rate is the fact that the household work of women is not recorded as 'work' by the census authorities.

Among the states, there are considerable variations in the female work participation rate. States of South India generally have recorded a higher female work participation rate than those of North India, while the states of North-eastern region have a still higher rate than those of all other regions in the country.

Females are either not encouraged or preferred in job market for various socio-cultural reasons. A workforce rate of 23 percent for females is mainly because they tend to preponderate in the primary sector. In the poorer section of society both males and females work together outside their homes as cultivators, agricultural labourers or daily wagers to eke out a living. In secondary and tertiary sectors females have always remained in a microscopic minority, and the chance of upswing in the current scenario is quite remote in near future due to mounting unemployment in the country.

Table-1: Some Demographic Attributes of Female Population in India, 1981

State	*Literacy rate among females aged 15+ 1981*	*Work rate 1981*[1]	*Percent females employ-eed 1981*[2]	*Percent ST & SC 1981*[3]	*Sex Ratio (females/ males) 1981*	*Percent married females 1981*[4]	*Contra-ceptive use rate 1980*[5]
India*	25.7	14.0	16.0	23.7	934	80.5	22.3
1 Andhra Pradesh	20.0	27.0	12.0	20.7	975	84.1	26.7
2 Bihar	13.2	9.1	8.4	23.2	946	88.6	12.3
3 Gujarat	33.2	11.0	19.4	21.6	942	76.3	32.8
4 Haryana	21.6	4.7	26.3	19.0	870	80.6	30.3
5 Karnataka	28.2	19.0	19.0	20.0	963	76.1	22.9
6 Kerala	70.8	12.8	43.9	11.0	1,032	60.6	29.4
7 Madhya Pradesh	15.9	22.3	8.2	37.7	941	87.1	21.1
8 Maharashtra	34.6	24.0	13.5	16.6	937	79.8	35.2
9 Orissa	21.2	10.7	15.6	37.5	981	77.4	24.8
10 Punjab	32.4	2.3	64.0	26.7	879	69.4	25.0
11 Rajasthan	12.0	9.3	14.8	29.4	919	88.5	13.3
12 Tamil Nadu	34.7	22.4	17.5	19.4	977	72.7	28.6
13 Uttar Pradesh	13.9	5.4	11.7	21.4	885	88.4	11.6
14 W. Bengal	33.3	5.8	38.4	28.0	911	74.7	22.0

1. Female main workers percent of female population.
2. Non-agricultural and non-household industry female workers percent of total female main workers.
3. Scheduled Tribe and Scheduled Caste females percent of total females.
4. Currently married females percent of total females aged 15-44.
5. Percentage of couples, in reproductive age group 15-44, effectively protected against conception.

* Excludes Assam.

Source : O.P. Sharma and Robert D. Retherford, *Recent Literacy Trends in India*, 1987, Occasional Paper No. 1 of 1987, New Delhi; Office of the Registrar General and Census Commissioner, India, pp. 42-43.

Table-2: Birth and Death Rates and Expectation of Life at Birth (Census Estimates)

	Rate per 1000 population @		*Expectation of life at birth (in years)*	
Decades	*Birth*	*Death*	*Males*	*Females*
1901-11	49.2	42.6	22.6	23.3
1911-21	48.1	47.2	19.4	20.9
1921-31	46.4	36.3	26.9	26.6
1931-41	45.2	31.2	32.1	31.4
1941-51	39.9	27.4	32.4	31.7
1951-61	41.7	22.8	41.9	40.6
1961-71	41.2	19.0	46.4	44.7
1971-81*	37.2	15.0	50.9+	50.0+
1994@@	29.0	10.0	61.0	62.0

@ By reverse survival method.

* Provisional.

\+ Based on Sample Registration System,1980.

@@ UN, *ESCAP Population Data Sheet*, Bangkok, 1994.

Source: Registrar General, India.

Table-3: Distribution of Population and Sex Ratio (Female/Male) In India, 1981-91

State/ Union Territory	Population 1991 Persons	Male	Females	Sex Ratio 1981	1991
India	843,930,861	437,597,929	406,332,932	934	929
States					
1 Andhra Pradesh	66,304,854	33,623,738	32,681,116	975	972
2 Arunachal Pradesh	858,392	461,242	397,150	862	861
3 Assam	22,294,562	11,579,693	10,714,869	910	925
4 Bihar	86,338,853	45,147,280	41,191,573	946	912
5 Goa	1,168,622	593,563	575,059	975	969
6 Gujarat	41,174,060	21,272,388	19,901,672	942	936
7 Haryana	16,317,715	8,705,379	7,612,336	870	874
8 Himachal Pradesh	5,111,079	2,560,894	2,550,185	973	996
9 Jammu and Kashmir	7,718,700	4,014,100	3,704,600	892	923
10 Karnataka	44,817,398	22,861.409	21,955,989	963	960
11 Kerala	29,011,237	14,218,167	14,793,070	1,032	1,040
12 Madhya Pradesh	66,135,863	34,232,048	31,903,814	941	932
13 Maharashtra	78,706,719	40,652,056	38,054,663	937	936
14 Manipur	1,826,714	931,511	895,203	971	961
15 Meghalaya	1,760,626	904,308	856,318	954	947
16 Mizoram	686,217	356,672	329,545	919	924
17 Negaland	1,215,573	643,273	572,300	863	890
18 Orissa	31,512,070	15,979,904	15,532,166	981	972
19 Punjab	20,190,795	10,695,136	9,495,659	879	888
20 Rajasthan	43,880,640	22,935,895	20,944,745	919	913
21 Sikkim	403,612	214,723	188,889	835	880
22 Tamil Nadu	55,638,318	28,217,947	27,420,371	977	972
23 Tripura	2,744,827	1,410,545	1,334,282	946	946
24 Uttar Pradesh	138,760,417	73,745,994	65,014,423	885	882
25 West Bengal	67,982,732	35,461,898	32,520,834	911	917
Union Territories					
1 A & N Islands	277,989	152,737	125,252	760	820
2 Chandigarh	640,725	357,411	283,314	769	793
3 Dadra and Nagar Haveli	138,542	70,927	67,615	974	953
4 Daman & Diu	101,439	51,452	49,987	1,062	972
5 Delhi	9,370,475	5,120,733	4,249,742	808	830
6 Lakshadweep	51,681	26,582	25,099	975	944
7 Pondicherry	789,416	398,324	391,092	985	982

Notes:

1. In 1981, census was not conducted in Assam. Based on the 1971 Census population and the 1991 Census provisional results, the population of Assam for 1981 has been interpolated.
2. As a consequence of the revised estimates for Assam for the year 1981, the total population of India as of 1981 has been estimated as 683,329,097 as against earlier published figures of 685,184,692.
3. As a consequence of the revised figures, the decadal growth rate for India during 1971-81 has been estimated as 24.66 percent.
4. The 1991 Census has not yet been conducted in Jammu and Kashmir. The figures are as per projections prepared by the Standing Committee of Experts on Population Projections, October, 1989.
5. Sex ratio is defined as number of females per 1,000 males.

Source: Census of India 1991, *Provisional Population Totals*, Series—1, *India*, Paper 1 of 1991, p. 71.

Table-4: Infant Mortality Rates by Sex, India, 1972-87

Year	*Rural*		*Urban*		*Total*	
	Males	*Females*	*Males*	*Females*	*Males*	*Females*
1972	141	161	85	85	132	148
1973	141	144	88	90	132	135
1976	133	146	78	82	124	134
1977	136	146	80	82	126	135
1978	132	143	74	75	123	131
1979	129	131	73	71	119	121
1980	123	125	65	65	113	115
1981	119	119	63	62	110	111
1982	114	114	70	60	106	104
1983	113	114	69	63	105	105
1984	113	114	68	64	104	104
1985	106	107	56	62	96	98
1986	+	+	+	+	96	97
1987	+	+	+	+	95	96

+ Not Available.

Source: Registrar General, India—*Sample Registration System*.

Table-5: Infant Mortality Rates in Indian States by Sex, 1987

State	*Males*	*Females*
India	95	96
Andhra Pradesh	80	77
Assam	103	100
Bihar	99	104
Gujarat	90	106
Haryana	79	95
Himachal Pradesh	77	87
Jammu and Kashmir	74	69
Karnataka	79	71
Kerala	27	28
Madhya Pradesh	122	118
Maharashtra	73	59
Orissa	137	113
Punjab	60	66
Rajasthan	97	107
Tamil Nadu	70	82
Uttar Pradesh	126	128
West Bengal	73	68

Source : *Sample Registration System*, 1987, Office of Registrar General, India.

Table 6 : Projected Child Population (0-14) By Sex In India, 1981-2001

State	1981		1986		1991		1996		2001	
	M	F	M	F	M	F	M	F	M	F
India	140321	131679	148151	140415	152784	144965	157998	149670	157606	149556
1 Andhra Pradesh	10,370	10,136	10,787	10,617	10,792	10,528	11,240	10,882	10,911	10,553
2 Assam	4,475	4,215	4,850	4,547	5,000	4,794	5,288	5,035	5,459	5,186
3 Bihar	14,941	14,209	15,912	15,370	16,497	16,059	18,157	17,529	19,100	18,612
4 Gujarat	6,876	6,475	7,067	6,734	7,050	6,789	6,889	6,612	6,554	6,297
5 Haryana	2,830	2,531	3,089	2,185	3,195	2,932	3,179	2,907	2,828	2,588
6 Karnataka	7,412	7,285	7,878	7,675	8,081	7,758	8,127	7,723	7,710	7,366
7 Kerala	4,505	4,454	4,632	4,498	4,686	4,528	4,707	4,500	4,613	4,474
8 M. P.	10,869	10,418	11,655	11,140	12,139	11,391	12,689	11,864	12,263	11,501
9 Maharashtra	12,179	11,492	12,630	11,970	12,135	11,474	11,839	11,078	11,474	10,731
10 Orissa	5,246	5,243	5,456	5,344	5,518	5,285	5,707	5,369	5,651	5,318
11 Punjab	3,277	2,927	3,378	3,056	3,228	2,965	3,016	2,825	2,808	2,650
12 Rajasthan	7,572	7,074	8,418	7,930	9,239	8,746	10,231	9,724	10,806	10,293
13 Tamil Nadu	8,537	8,295	8,804	8,480	8,866	8,486	8,886	8,475	8,602	8,196
14 U. P.	24,907	21,929	26,784	24,061	28,150	25,605	30,418	27,974	32,244	29,944
15 W. B.	10,704	10,483	11,111	10,840	11,352	11,030	11,714	11,176	11,352	10,801

Source: Census of India1981, Occasional Papers No. 4 of 1988, *Report of the Expert Committee on the population projections.*

Table-7: Selected Nuptiality Indicators for States in India, 1971 and 1981

	Census Year	No. of married females between 15-44 years (in 000's)	Proportion married females in age groups			Singulate mean age at marriage		Rate of married couples per 1000 population
			15-44	15-19	20-24	M	F	
1 Andhra	1981	9,680	84.0	56.2	90.2	23.0	17.3	181
Pradesh	1971	7,846	85.3	66.9	92.7	22.7	16.2	180
2 Bihar	1981	12,612	88.5	63.9	93.5	21.5	16.5	180
	1971	10,556	90.4	76.2	95.2	19.8	15.3	187
3 Gujarat	1981	5,711	76.4	26.7	83.1	23.1	19.5	168
	1971	4,366	80.7	39.5	88.6	22.3	18.4	164
4 Haryana	1981	2,111	82.8	47.6	89.2	21.6	17.8	163
	1971	1,620	87.4	61.0	93.9	20.5	16.6	161
5 Karnataka	1981	6,012	76.1	36.2	78.9	25.9	19.2	162
	1971	4,794	80.4	49.6	86.8	25.0	17.8	164
6 Kerala	1981	3,705	60.7	14.1	57.9	27.2	21.8	146
	1971	2,981	63.1	18.1	64.2	26.7	21.0	140
7 Madhya	1981	9,169	87.0	62.2	91.7	20.6	16.6	176
pradesh	1971	7,433	91.0	77.9	95.4	19.7	15.0	178
8 Maha-	1981	10,554	79.7	38.2	83.8	24.2	18.8	168
rashtra	1971	8,631	83.8	53.1	88.1	23.6	17.5	171
9 Orissa	1981	4,346	77.3	30.8	86.6	24.2	19.1	165
	1971	3,835	85.4	56.7	92.3	22.6	17.3	175
10 Punjab	1981	2,450	69.2	13.4	68.0	24.4	21.1	146
	1971	1,938	73.6	22.3	77.6	23.3	20.2	143
11 Rajasthan	1981	5,980	88.6	64.3	94.7	20.3	16.1	175
	1971	4,600	91.2	75.5	96.6	19.5	15.1	179
12 Tamil	1981	8,134	72.6	22.8	75.5	26.0	20.2	168
Nadu	1971	6,974	76.0	26.8	81.2	25.9	19.6	169
13 Uttar	1981	18,980	88.4	60.7	93.5	21.0	16.7	171
Pradesh	1971	15,639	90.8	72.9	95.3	19.3	15.4	177
14 West	1981	8,718	75.1	37.5	78.4	25.7	19.2	160
Bengal	1971	6,740	79.2	51.4	85.0	24.3	17.9	152
All	1981*	112,172	80.5	43.4	84.5	23.3	18.3	169
India	1971	93,144	83.9	55.4	88.8	22.4	17.2	170

* Excludes Assam.

Source: Registrar General, India.

Table-8: Number of Ever-Married (Married, Divorced and Widowed) Children (10-14 Years) and their Proportion to Total Children in India, 1971 and 1981

Year	Area	Number of ever married children		Proportion of ever married to total children (%)	
		Males	Females	Males	Females
1971	Rural	15,87,237	35,09,789	5.41	13.57
	Urban	68,020	2,41,592	0.95	3.76
1981@	Rural	-	-	3.14	7.90
	Urban	-	-	1.01	2.19

Note: @ Excludes Assam

Sources: 1. K.S. Natrajan, "Child in India—a Demographic Profile (Mimeograph) 1970", Tables A—19 to 22.

2. Census of India 1981, Series-1, India, Paper 2 of 1983, *Key Population Statistics Based on 5 Percent Sample Data, P. 6*

Table-9: Percent Distribution of Currently Married Women by Age at Marriage, Level of Education in India, 1984

Sl. No.	Level of education	Age at Marriage (years)					
		Rural Areas			Urban Areas		
		Below 18	18-20	21+	Below 18	18-20	21+
1.	Illiterate	66.3	25.5	8.2	63.5	28.1	8.4
2.	Literate but below Primary	54.6	33.0	12.4	53.7	34.5	11.8
3.	Primary but below Matric	49.8	35.5	14.7	47.9	37.4	14.7
4.	Matric but below Graduate	32.3	39.7	28.0	26.8	43.0	30.2
5.	Graduate and above	16.9	31.1	52.0	10.1	32.7	57.2
6.	All levels	63.5	27.2	9.3	52.4	33.0	14.6

Source: Census of India, Occasional Paper No. 2 of 1988, *Advance Report on Age at Marriage Differentials in India*, 1984.

Table-10: Crude Literacy Rate in India by Sex, 1901-91

Year	Literacy rate		Change in percent points	
	Males	Females	Males	Females
1901	9.8	0.6	-	-
1911	10.6	1.1	0.8	0.5
1921	12.2	1.8	1.6	0.7
1931	15.6	2.9	3.4	1.1
1941	24.9	7.3	9.3	4.4
1951	25.0(27.2)	7.9(8.9)	0.1	0.6
1961	34.4(40.4)	12.9(15.3)	9.4	5.0
1971	39.5(46.0)	18.7(22.0)	5.1	5.8
1981	46.9(53.4)	24.8(28.5)	7.4	6.1
1991*	53.2(63.9)	32.6(39.4)	6.3	7.8

* Excluding Assam and Jammu and Kashmir.

Note: Litercy rates under parantheses from 1951 to 1981 relate to population aged 5 and above, but the literacy rates for 1991 relate to population aged 7 and above.

Source: 1. O.P. Sharma and Robert D. Retherford, *Recent Literacy Trends in India, 1987*, Occasional Paper No. 1 of 1987, New Delhi: Office of the Registrar General & Census Commissioner, India, p. 7
2. Census of India, 1991, *Provisional Population Total*, Series-1, India, Paper-1 of 1991, p. 59.

Table-11 : Literacy Rates in India in Rural and Urban Areas by Sex, 1961-91

Residence	Year	Males	Females
Literacy rates			
Rural	1961	28.9	8.4
	1971	33.8	13.1
	1981	40.8	18.0
	1991	47.4	25.4
Urban	1961	57.4	34.4
	1971	61.2	42.0
	1981	65.8	47.8
	1991	69.3	54.0
Change in percent points			
Rural	1961-71	4.9	4.7
	1971-81	7.0	4.9
	1981-91	6.6	7.4
Urban	1961-71	3.8	7.6
	1971-81	4.6	5.8
	1981-91	3.5	6.2
Rural-urban gap			
	1961	28.5	26.0
	1971	27.4	28.9
	1981	25.0	29.8
	1991	21.9	28.6

Source: K.G. Jolly, "Strategies to Attain Universal Literacy in India by 2001," Demography-India, Vol. 20, No. 1, 1991, p. 144.

Table-12: Crude Literacy Rates of Females for State and Union Territories, 1961-91

State Union Territory	1961	1971	1981	1991
India	12.9	18.7	24.8	32.6
States				
1. Andhra Pradesh	12.0	15.8	20.4	28.1
2. Bihar	6.9	8.7	13.6	18.6
3. Gujarat	19.1	24.8	32.3	41.2
4. Haryana	9.2	14.9	22.3	33.6
5. Himachal Pradesh	9.5	20.2	31.5	44.0
6. Jammu and Kashmir	4.3	9.3	15.9	—
7. Karnataka	14.2	21.0	27.7	37.3
8. Kerala	38.9	54.3	65.7	75.4
9. Madhya Pradesh	6.7	10.9	15.5	23.2
10. Maharashtra	16.8	26.4	34.8	43.8
11. Manipur	15.9	19.5	29.1	39.4
12. Meghalaya	21.2	24.6	30.1	36.5
13. Nagaland	11.3	18.7	33.9	45.5
14. Orissa	8.6	13.9	21.1	29.1
15. Punjab	17.4	25.9	33.7	42.7
16. Rajasthan	5.8	8.5	11.4	16.6
17. Sikkim	4.3	8.9	22.2	38.4
18. Tamil Nadu	18.2	26.9	35.0	44.9
19. Tripura	10.2	21.2	32.0	41.0
20. Uttar Pradesh	7.0	10.6	14.0	21.0
21. West Bengal	17.0	22.4	30.3	39.0
Union Territories				
1. A & N Islands	19.4	31.1	42.1	53.9
2. Arunchal Pradesh	1.4	3.7	11.3	23.0
3. Chandigarh	42.0	54.3	59.3	61.0
4. Dadra & Nagar Haveli	4.1	7.8	16.8	21.5
5. Delhi	42.5	47.7	53.1	56.0
6. Goa,Daman & Diu	23.0	35.1	47.6	58.8
7. Lakshadweep	11.0	30.6	44.6	57.8
8. Mizoram	34.7	46.7	54.9	64.1
9. Pondicherry	24.6	34.6	45.7	56.5

Note : Excludes Assam in the case of 1961, 1971 and 1981 censuses and Assam and Jammu and Kashmir in the case of 1991 census. Herein, for the purpose of comparison, literacy rates from the 1991 census are calculated on the basis of population of all ages on the line of earlier practices.

Source: 1. Census of India, 1971 and 1981, *Primary Census Abstract: General Population*, Series-1, India, Part II B [i] Census of India, 1991, *Provisional Population Totals*, Series-1, India, Paper-1 of 1991.

Table-13: Male Female Differential in Literacy Rates For States and Union Territories, 1961-1991

State/ Union Territory	Mule-female difference in literacy rates				Female-male ratio of literacy rates			
	1961	1971	1981	1991	1961	1971	1981	1991
India*	21.5	20.8	22.1	20.5	37.5	47.3	52.9	61.4
States								
1 Andhra Pradesh	18.2	17.4	18.9	18.7	39.8	47.5	51.9	60.1
2 Bihar	22.9	21.9	24.5	23.8	23.1	28.5	35.7	43.9
3 Gujarat	22.0	21.4	22.1	20.3	46.4	53.7	59.3	67.0
4 Haryana	20.0	22.4	25.9	22.3	31.5	39.9	45.2	60.1
5 Himachal Pradesh	22.8	23.0	21.7	18.6	29.4	46.8	59.1	70.3
6 Jammu and Kashmir	12.7	17.5	20.4	—	25.1	34.7	43.8	—
7 Karnataka	22.0	20.7	21.1	19.1	39.3	50.4	56.8	66.1
8 Kerala	16.1	12.3	9.5	5.6	70.8	81.5	87.3	93.1
9 Madhya Pradesh	20.3	21.8	24.0	23.9	24.9	33.5	39.3	49.3
10 Maharashtra	25.2	24.6	24.0	20.8	39.9	51.8	59.2	67.8
11 Manipur	29.2	26.5	24.2	18.8	35.3	42.4	54.5	67.7
12 Meghalaya	11.2	9.6	7.8	5.3	65.4	72.0	79.4	87.4
13 Nagaland	12.4	16.4	16.2	10.5	47.2	53.3	67.7	81.2
14 Orissa	26.0	24.4	26.0	23.4	24.9	36.4	44.8	55.4
15 Punjab	17.3	14.5	13.5	12.4	50.2	64.1	71.4	77.5
16 Rajasthan	17.9	20.3	24.9	27.6	24.6	29.4	31.5	37.5
17 Sikkim	15.4	16.5	21.7	16.1	21.7	35.1	50.5	70.4
18 Tamil								

Nadu	26.4	24.9	23.3	19.1	40.8	51.9	60.1	70.2
19 Tripura	19.4	19.0	19.7	17.2	34.4	52.7	61.9	70.4
20 Uttar Pradesh	20.3	20.9	24.7	24.0	25.7	33.5	36.2	46.7
21 West Bengal	23.1	20.4	20.4	17.6	42.4	52.4	59.7	68.9
Union Territories								
1 A & N Islands	23.1	20.5	16.6	13.5	45.7	60.2	71.8	80.0
2 Arunachal Pradesh	10.8	14.1	17.6	18.3	11.6	20.8	39.1	55.7
3 Chandigarh	15.0	12.6	9.7	9.7	73.7	81.2	86.0	86.3
4 Dadra & Nagar Haveli	10.7	14.3	19.5	21.7	27.5	35.4	46.2	49.8
5 Delhi	18.2	16.0	15.3	13.8	70.0	74.9	77.6	80.3
6 Goa, Daman & Diu	16.0	19.2	18.0	15.1	59.0	64.5	72.5	79.5
7 Lakshadweep	24.8	25.9	20.6	13.8	30.7	54.1	68.4	80.7
8 Mizoram	18.7	13.8	9.6	6.3	65.0	77.2	85.2	91.1
9 Pondicherry	25.8	22.7	20.1	15.5	48.9	60.4	69.4	78.5

* Excludes Assam.

Note: For the purpose of comparison, the literacy rates for the 1991 Census are calculated on the basis of population of all ages on the line of earlier practices.

Source: 1.Census of India, 1971 and 1981, *Primary Census Abstract : General Population*, Series-1, India, Part II B (i) 2. Census of India, 1991, *Provisional Population Totals*, Series-1, India, Paper-1 of 1991.

Table 14: Percent Distribution of Literates by Highest Educational Level Completed for Major States (Females), 1971-81

	State	Year	Total literates	Less than primary	Primary	Middle	Matri-culation or higher secondary	Graduate and above
				Higheat educational level completed				
	State							
	India*	1971	100.0	36.6	38.2	15.6	8.2	1.4
		1981	100.0	33.4	34.0	16.8	12.8	3.0
1	Andhra	1971	100.0	33.0	46.5	13.6	6.2	0.7
	Pradesh	1981	100.0	23.4	44.9	18.5	11.4	1.8
2	Bihar	1971	100.0	47.4	24.1	22.3	5.2	1.0
		1981	100.0	42.1	22.8	22.5	10.8	1.8
3	Gujarat	1971	100.0	55.6	27.6	7.2	8.5	1.1
		1981	100.0	46.5	28.3	8.1	14.4	2.7
4	Haryana	1971	100.0	34.0	37.3	17.7	9.1	1.9
		1981	100.0	36.3	31.7	13.2	14.8	4.0
5	Karnataka	1971	100.0	21.9	47.7	19.2	10.3	0.9
		1981	100.0	29.7	32.8	20.9	14.3	2.3
6	Kerala	1971	100.0	32.1	42.9	16.5	7.8	0.7
		1981	100.0	29.2	32.9	24.3	12.0	1.6
7	Madhya	1971	100.0	49.1	30.2	10.7	8.2	1.8
	Pradesh	1981	100.0	45.6	28.7	12.2	9.8	3.7
8	Mahara-	1971	100.0	35.5	35.6	19.7	7.8	1.4
	shtra	1981	100.0	31.7	31.0	20.7	13.4	3.2
9	Orissa	1971	100.0	20.1	63.5	13.5	2.4	0.5
		1981	100.0	19.8	55.6	15.5	8.0	1.1
10	Punjab	1971	100.0	32.8	41.4	12.4	11.8	1.6
		1981	100.0	28.1	35.9	14.7	17.4	3.9
11	Rajasthan	1971	100.0	48.8	29.4	11.4	8.7	1.7
		1981	100.0	39.6	30.4	14.3	11.6	4.1
12	Tamil	1971	100.0	40.4	35.9	15.4	7.7	0.6
	Nadu	1981	100.0	32.9	36.1	14.4	14.9	1.7
13	U. P.	1971	100.0	36.2	40.7	12.1	9.1	1.9
		1981	100.0	37.6	32.9	12.7	12.4	4.4
14	W. Bengal	1971	100.0	32.2	38.6	17.7	9.3	2.2
		1981	100.0	29.6	41.0	14.5	11.4	3.5

* Excludes Assam.

Source: O.P. Sharma and Robert D. Retherford, *Recent Literacy Trends in India*, 1987, Occasional Paper No.1 of 1987, New Delhi : Office of the Registrar General and Census Commisioner, India, p 38.

Table-15: Percentage of Children Attending School by Residence Age Group and Sex in States/Union Territories, 1981

Sl. No.	State/ Union Territory	Age Group	Males		Females	
			Rural	Urban	Rural	Urban
1.	Andhra Pradesh	5-9	42.3	65.1	44.6	73.9
		10-14	44.6	73.9	21.1	59.2
2.	Bihar	5-9	30.1	38.7	14.8	47.0
		10-14	52.4	75.5	19.4	60.0
3.	Gujarat	5-9	45.3	60.2	33.0	55.5
		10-14	66.0	81.1	40.6	70.5
4.	Haryana	5-9	42.2	64.4	22.9	59.1
		10-14	69.2	79.9	28.4	70.0
5.	Himachal Pradesh	5-9	56.9	75.7	44.9	72.4
		10-14	83.3	90.7	54.1	86.3
6.	Jammu and Kashmir	5-9	31.6	59.4	20.4	51.9
		10-14	59.8	71.6	27.0	59.9
7.	Karnataka	5-9	43.5	61.6	30.7	57.0
		10-14	52.4	74.2	27.9	63.0
8.	Kerala	5-9	74.4	79.7	74.2	79.6
		10-14	87.3	84.4	83.3	88.2
9.	Madhya Pradesh	5-9	33.1	59.2	15.4	51.5
		10-14	49.4	79.1	15.6	63.7
10.	Maharashtra	5-9	52.0	69.1	39.0	64.8
		10-14	67.3	84.7	39.9	75.3
11.	Manipur	5-9	38.3	59.5	32.2	54.0
		10-14	69.2	87.1	51.5	75.3
12.	Meghalaya	5-9	24.1	71.2	24.8	69.4
		10-14	40.0	84.4	41.9	81.4
13.	Nagaland	5-9	37.8	74.0	33.0	70.0
		10-14	66.7	85.4	57.6	82.1
14.	Orissa	5-9	47.2	61.9	31.6	53.8
		10-14	53.9	73.7	27.2	59.1
15.	Punjab	5-9	51.3	66.0	44.4	60.2
		10-14	67.0	77.0	45.6	75.0
16.	Rajasthan	5-9	32.3	55.1	9.5	42.3
		10-14	54.2	76.5	10.3	51.4

17.	Sikkim	5-9	42.2	67.4	34.1	63.7
		10-14	69.1	78.5	40.5	74.9
18.	Tamil Nadu	5-9	59.7	72.2	47.9	68.3
		10-14	59.8	77.4	34.3	65.7
19.	Tripura	5-9	43.0	69.4	37.6	65.5
		10-14	65.4	89.5	50.5	83.2
20.	Uttar Pradesh	5-9	30.0	46.8	13.6	39.3
		10-14	56.6	65.2	18.8	52.1
21.	West Bengal	5-9	35.5	59.3	27.2	53.7
		10-14	55.3	77.0	38.1	68.6
	Union Territories					
22.	Andaman & Nicobar Islands	5-9	62.5	77.9	57.8	72.1
		10-14	79.5	87.3	69.5	85.3
23.	Arunachal Pradesh	5-9	30.1	62.0	18.3	51.4
		10-14	50.1	76.9	27.0	64.2
24.	Chandigarh	5-9	60.0	75.6	60.3	72.8
		10-14	76.3	84.4	64.1	83.3
25.	Dadra & Nagar Haveli	5-9	49.3	77.5	32.8	67.1
		10-14	51.6	78.6	27.7	62.2
26.	Delhi	5-9	62.8	70.8	52.6	66.7
		10-14	86.1	83.9	60.9	78.1
27.	Goa, Daman & Diu	5-9	69.3	74.8	63.2	71.7
		10-14	85.9	88.6	72.3	80.7
28.	Lakshadweep	5-9	69.9	67.7	66.2	60.5
		10-14	93.0	93.7	83.3	78.9
29.	Mizoram	5-9	57.1	81.9	57.2	82.3
		10-14	80.5	94.5	74.0	92.7
30.	Pondicherry	5-9	67.4	75.6	57.4	71.4
		10-14	75.2	80.4	49.5	68.5
	India	5-9	39.8	61.8	25.9	55.8
		10-14	57.6	77.0	29.2	65.4

Notes: 1. This table is based on 20 percent sample data for major states and union territories and on 100 percent sample data for minor states and union territories. The state having more than one crore population is considered as a major state.

2. 1981 Census figures exclude Assam.

Source : Office of the Registrar General, India.

Table-16: Elementary Education In India-Progress of Enrolment

(Million Persons)

Year	Middle Level (Class I-V) (Age 6-11 Years)		Middle Level (Class VI-VIII) (Age 11-14 Years)	
	Boys	Girls	Boys	Girls
1950-51	13.8	5.4	2.6	0.5
1955-56	17.5	7.7	3.4	0.9
1960-61	23.6	11.4	5.1	1.6
1965-66	32.2	18.3	9.7	2.8
1970-71	35.7	21.3	9.4	3.9
1975-76	40.7	25.0	11.0	5.0
1976-77	42.7	26.4	11.4	5.3
1977-78	43.2	26.9	12.0	5.7
1978-79	44.0	28.2	12.1	6.0
1979-80	44.2	27.3	13.0	6.3
1980-81	45.3	28.5	13.9	6.8
1981-82	46.7	29.4	14.7	7.2
1982-83	48.6	30.9	15.7	7.9
1983-84	50.4	32.2	16.6	8.6
1984-85	51.9	33.7	17.2	9.0
1985-86	52.2	35.2	17.7	9.6
1986-87 (p)	53.8	36.1	18.6	10.2
1987-88 (p)	55.1	37.8	19.2	10.7
1988-89 (p)	57.1	38.6	19.7	11.2
(7th plan Target)	55.0	41.0	25.1	16.5
Enrolment as percentage of the corresponding age group				
1950-51	60.6	24.8	20.6	4.6
1960-61	82.6	41.4	33.2	11.3
1970-71	92.6	59.1	46.5	20.8
1975-76	95.7	62.0	47.0	23.3
1978-79	100.2	67.8	49.4	26.0
1979-80	99.3	65.0	52.0	26.4
1980-81	95.8	64.1	54.3	28.6
1981-82	98.9	66.2	56.0	29.7
1982-83	103.0	69.7	58.3	31.8
1983-84	106.9	72.6	60.6	33.2
1984-85	110.3	75.9	61.3	34.1
1985-86	111.1	79.2	61.8	35.3
1986-87(P)	111.8	79.2	66.5	38.9
1987-88(P)	113.1	81.7	68.9	40.6
1988-89(P)	115.7	82.5	70.8	42.3
(7th Plan Target)	122.3	97.4	80.5	52.1

P=Provisional.

Source : Ministry of Human Resource Development (Dept. of Education).

Table-17: Drop-Out Rates at Primary and Middle Stage of Schools By Sex In India, 1986-87

State/ Union Territory	Class I-V (primary)		Class I-VIII (Middle)	
	Boys	Girls	Boys	Girls
States				
1. Andhra Pradesh	57.7	62.2	78.0	85.1
2. Assam	62.0	66.9	70.3	73.2
3. Bihar	64.1	68.2	77.2	84.7
4. Gujarat	41.3	48.6	58.6	67.9
5. Haryana	26.9	32.8	29.8	48.3
6. Himachal Pradesh	30.9	32.4	15.2	31.0
7. Jammu and Kashmir	39.7	38.2	46.9	57.4
8. Karnataka	49.5	62.9	67.3	77.6
9. Kerala	0.4	1.3	19.1	18.3
10. Madhya Pradesh	38.4	49.2	51.8	69.8
11. Maharashtra	37.4	47.6	87.4	72.1
12. Manipur	72.0	73.8	76.6	80.5
13. Meghalaya	64.3	69.8	86.3	86.9
14. Negaland	29.1	18.4	78.3	79.2
15. Orissa	49.8	53.5	61.5	74.0
16. Punjab	38.8	40.1	60.3	67.7
17. Rajasthan	49.1	56.6	59.0	69.8
18. Sikkim	62.4	62.9	66.1	65.4
19. Tamil Nadu	19.9	25.1	44.9	55.2
20. Tripura	62.5	62.5	71.1	71.3
21. Uttar Pradesh	45.5	46.5	50.5	64.2
22. West Bengal	61.2	64.7	78.2	79.6
Union Territories				
1. A & N Island	24.0	27.5	31.6	41.3
2. Arunachal Pradesh	65.5	62.5	78.1	75.5
3. Chandigarh	8.2	1.7	13.4	16.3
4. D & N Haveli	37.8	50.2	71.6	75.0
5. Delhi	8.2	20.6	15.1	30.1
6. Goa, Daman & Diu	9.4	13.0	23.7	32.8
7. Lakshadweep	19.0	21.4	41.0	46.9
8. Mizoram	40.2	40.9	77.0	77.1
9. Pondicherry	–12.7	–6.7	–9.8	24.3
India	46.9	51.2	61.4	70.2

Note: The large variation in drop-out rate is due to the enrolment of classes A and B which was shown under pre-primary up to the 1981-82 has been reported under classes I and II respectively from the 1982-83 onwards.

Source: Department of Education, Ministry of Human Resources Development, New Delhi.

Table-18: Population of Literate Females in 1991 and Female Literacy Rates for 1981 and 1991

State/ Union Territory	Literate population aged 7 years and above	Percentage of Literates to estimated population aged 7 years and above	
		1981	1991
India* (Includes Jammu & Kashmir)	131,562,883	29.7	39.4
1. Andhra Pradesh	9,165,396	24.2	33.7
2. Arunachal Pradesh	91,456	14.0	29.4
3. Assam	3,769,414	N.A.	43.7
4. Bihar	7,678,025	16.5	23.1
5. Goa	341,606	55.2	68.2
6. Gujarat	8,194,861	38.5	48.5
7. Haryana	2,558,951	26.9	40.9
8. Himachal pradesh	1,122,343	37.7	52.5
9. Jammu and Kashmir	N.A.	19.5	N.A.
10. Karnataka	8,205,971	33.2	44.3
11. Kerala	11,149,750	75.6	86.9
12. Madhya Pradesh	7,390,910	19.0	28.4
13. Maharashtra	16,607,460	41.0	50.5
14. Manipur	352,710	34.6	48.6
15. Meghalaya	312,138	37.1	44.8
16. Mizoram	211,284	68.6	78.1
17. Nagaland	260,522	40.3	55.7
18. Orissa	4,519,585	25.1	34.4
19. Punjab	4,055,366	39.6	49.7
20. Rajasthan	3,474,997	14.0	20.8
21. Sikkim	71,277	27.3	47.2
22. Tamil Nadu	12,317,190	40.4	52.3
23. Tripura	547,164	38.0	50.0
24. Uttar Pradesh	13,602,592	17.2	26.0
25. West Bengal	12,665,922	36.1	47.1
Union Territories			
1. A and N Islands	67,510	53.1	66.2
2. Chandigarh	173,087	69.3	73.6
3. Dadra and Nagar Heveli	14,491	20.4	26.1
4. Daman and Diu	25,529	46.5	61.4
5. Delhi	2,378,555	62.6	68.0
6. Lakshadweep	14,516	55.3	70.9
7. Pondicherry	222,305	53.0	65.8

* The 1991 Census was not conducted in Jammu and Kashmir. The population figures are as per projections prepared by the Standing Committee of Experts on population projections, October, 1989.

NA. Stands for 'not available'

Source : Census of India 1991, Series-1, *Provisional Population Totals*, Paper-1 of 1991, *India*, pp. 72-73

Table-19: States and Union Territories arranged in a Descending Order of Literacy Rate, 1991

Males		*Females*	
State/Union	*Literacy rate*	*State/Union Territory*	*Literacy rate*
Kerala	94.5	Kerala	86.9
Lakshadweep	87.1	Mizoram	78.1
Daman and Diu	85.6	Chandigarh	73.6
Goa	85.5	Lakshadweep	70.9
Mizoram	84.1	Goa	68.2
Pondicherry	83.9	Delhi	68.0
Chandigarh	82.7	A & N Islands	66.2
Delhi	82.6	Pondicherry	65.8
A & N Islands	79.7	Daman & Diu	61.4
Tamil Nadu	74.9	Nagaland	55.7
Maharashtra	74.8	Himachal Pradesh	52.5
Himachal Pradesh	74.6	Tamil Nadu	52.3
Manipur	73.9	Maharashtra	50.5
Gujarat	72.5	Tripura	50.0
Tripura	70.1	Punjab	49.7
Haryana	67.8	Manipur	48.6
Karnataka	67.3	Gujarat	48.5
West Bengal	67.2	Sikkim	47.2
Nagaland	66.1	West Bengal	47.2
Sikkim	64.3	Meghalaya	44.8
India	63.9	Karnataka	44.3
Punjab	63.7	Assam	43.7
Orissa	62.4	Haryana	40.9
Assam	62.3	India	39.4
Madhya Pradesh	57.4	Orissa	34.4
Andhra Pradesh	56.2	Andhra Pradesh	33.7
Uttar Pradesh	55.4	Arunachal Pradesh	29.4
Rajasthan	55.1	Madhya Pradesh	28.4
Bihar	52.6	Dadra & Nagar Heveli	26.1
Dadra and Nagar Haveli	52.1	Uttar Pradesh	26.0
Meghalaya	51.6	Bihar	23.1
Arunachal Pradesh	51.1	Rajasthan	20.8

Note : These figures are not comparable to literacy rates of the earlier censues, as the population aged seven years and above only was taken into consideration to calculate the literacy rate in the 1991 Census.

Source : Census of India, Series-1, *Provisional Population Totals,* Paper-1 of 1991, *India* pp 72-73.

Table-20: Percentage Distribution of Female Workers by Industrial Categories In Major Indian States, 1971 & 1981

State	Year	Cultivators	Agricultural labourers	Live stock forestry, fishing, etc.	Mining and Quarrying	Manufacturing, processing servicing and repairs H	Manufacturing, processing servicing and repairs OTH	Construction	Trade and commerce	Transport, storage and communication	Other services
India	1971	29.8	50.9	1.9	0.4	4.2	2.8	0.6	1.8	0.5	7.1
	1981	33.2	46.2	1.8	0.4	4.6	3.5	0.8	2.0	0.4	7.0
1 Andhra	1971	19.4	63.1	1.0	0.3	4.2	2.3	0.9	2.6	0.3	6.0
Pradesh	1981	23.8	59.1	0.8	0.2	5.1	2.5	0.6	2.5	0.2	5.2
Bihar	1971	17.3	73.6	0.4	1.1	2.4	0.8	0.2	0.9	0,2	3.0
	1981	25.5	63.3	0.6	0.9	2.8	1.5	0.2	1.2	0.1	3.9
3 Gujarat	1971	33.8	48.4	0.9	0.4	2.1	3.0	1.2	1.6	0.4	8.3
	1981	30.2	48.1	2.2	0.2	2.5	3.6	1.1	2.3	0.8	9.1
4 Haryana	1971	37.0	25.9	1.4	0.5	4.0	6.0	2.4	1.4	0.4	21.0
	1981	49.3	2.0	0.4	0.03	2.4	3.8	1.3	1.5	0.4	18.8
5 Karnataka	1971	23.4	49.0	4.5	0.5	6.4	3.6	1.3	2.6	1.2	7.5
	1981	24.7	49.7	3.6	0.4	6.5	4.9	0.8	2.7	0.4	6.2
6 Kerala	1971	4.6	49.1	5.4	0.2	8.1	12.3	0.3	2.0	1.0	17.0
	1981	4.9	43.6	6.2	0.3	7.6	12.8	0.7	3.3	1.6	18.9
7 Madhya	1971	41.1	48.7	0.6	0.4	3.6	0.9	0.4	0.8	0.1	3.3
pradesh	1981	47.3	40.6	0.7	0.5	3.9	1.5	1.0	1.1	0.1	3.4
8 Maharashtra	1971	33.8	51.5	0.6	0.2	2.9	2.7	0.7	1.5	0.5	5.5
	1981	38.5	45.6	0.9	0.2	2.4	3.0	1.2	1.8	0.4	5.9
9 Orissa	1971	20.0	52.5	1.9	1.7	8.0	2.0	0.3	3.0	0.7	9.6
	1981	24.5	54.2	1.6	1.2	5.7	2.4	0.8	2.5	0.2	6.8
10 Punjab	1971	5.6	10.9	0.7	0.01	7.2	9.2	0.8	2.8	0.9	61.9
	1981	5.9	25.3	1.4	0.03	4.9	9.3	1.2	4.5	0.8	40.6
11 Rajasthan	1971	63.9	20.8	3.3	0.4	3.0	1.3	0.6	0.7	0.2	5.8
	1981	66.7	15.7	3.5	0.8	2.8	2.5	0.9	1.0	0.3	5.8
12 Tamil Nadu	1971	18.9	54.4	3.4	0.3	6.0	4.4	0.9	2.8	0.7	8.2
	1981	22.7	53.4	2.3	0.1	6.3	5.4	0.7	2.6	0.4	6.0
13 Uttar	1971	42.6	44.5	0.5	0.05	3.9	1.0	0.1	0.9	0.2	6.2
Pradesh	1981	47.8	35.2	0.3	0.05	5.2	2.2	0.3	1.1	0.2	7.6
14 West	1971	12.1	44.5	11.7	0.7	4.7	4.8	0.3	2.3	1.9	17.6
Bengal	1981	14.7	38.4	9.2	0.7	7.5	7.8	0.5	2.5	0.8	16.9

Source: Census of India, 1981, *Comparative Primary Census Abstract, 1971 & 1981*, Series-1, *India*, Paper-2 of 1986.

Table-21: Age Composition of Main Workers by Sex and Residence in India, 1971-1981

Age Group	*T/R/U*	*Males*		*Females*	
		1971	*1981*	*1971*	*1981*
0-14	T	5.3	4.2	9.2	8.4
	R	6.1	4.9	9.6	8.9
	U	2.1	1.8	5.0	4.7
15-19	T	9.4	9.8	11.0	12.4
	R	9.9	10.6	11.4	12.8
	U	6.9	7.0	8.2	9.0
20-24	T	11.8	12.6	12.3	12.8
	R	11.4	12.3	12.1	12.8
	U	13.9	13.5	13.5	13.0
25-29	T	12.9	13.2	12.9	12.5
	R	12.3	12.5	12.8	12.2
	U	15.2	15.6	14.4	14.8
30-39	T	23.1	22.5	22.9	22.4
	R	22.3	21.1	22.7	21.9
	U	26.8	26.5	25.3	26.1
40-49	T	17.9	18.2	16.9	17.3
	R	17.5	17.7	16.6	17.2
	U	19.7	19.8	18.5	18.7
50-59	T	11.4	11.6	9.6	9.4
	R	11.6	11.8	9.5	9.4
	U	10.5	10.8	10.0	9.3
60+	T	8.4	7.9	5.3	4.8
	R	9.1	8.8	5.3	4.8
	U	5.4	5.0	5.1	4.4

Sources: (1) Census of India, 1981, *General Economic Table* (B-1 to B-5) Part III-A.

(2) Census of India, 1971, *General Economic Tables*, Part B(i).

Table-22: Percent Distribution of Female Main Workers by Three Sectors of Economy by Rural-Urban Residence for India and 14 Major States, 1971 and 1981

State	T/R/U	Primary		Secondary		Tertiary	
		1971	1981	1971	1981	1971	1981
India	T	83.0	81.6	7.7	9.1	9.3	9.4
	R	90.0	89.4	5.5	6.5	4.5	4.1
	U	24.8	23.7	25.8	28.1	49.4	48.2
Andhra Pradesh	T	83.8	83.8	7.4	8.2	8.8	8.0
	R	88.3	88.6	5.6	6.4	2.7	5.0
	U	33.9	34.2	27.2	27.3	38.9	38.5
Bihar	T	92.4	90.3	3.5	4.8	4.1	5.0
	R	94.9	93.4	2.9	4.2	2.2	2.5
	U	41.8	35.1	15.4	15.1	42.8	49.8
Gujarat	T	83.4	81.1	6.2	6.9	10.3	12.0
	R	94.0	91.7	3.0	4.2	3.0	4.1
	U	21.6	21.6	25.6	22.3	52.9	56.1
Haryana	T	64.9	71.8	12.3	8.5	22.8	19.6
	R	79.3	85.7	11.4	6.5	9.3	7.8
	U	12.9	10.5	15.9	17.4	71.3	72.2
Karnataka	T	77.4	78.5	11.3	13.0	11.3	8.6
	R	86.2	87.8	7.6	8.7	6.2	3.5
	U	28.8	28.6	31.9	35.8	39.4	35.7
Kerala	T	59.3	55.2	20.8	21.0	19.9	23.8
	R	64.8	615	20.3	20.5	15.0	18.0
	U	20.6	17.4	24.0	23.6	55.4	59.1
Madhya Pradesh	T	90.8	89.1	4.9	6.5	4.3	4.5
	R	94.8	93.7	3.6	4.7	1.7	1.6
	U	29.5	29.8	24.9	28.7	45.6	41.5
Maharashtra	T	86.2	85.0	6.3	6.9	48.9	8.1
	R	94.8	94.2	3.4	3.8	1.9	1.9
	U	24.7	21.6	26.7	27.7	48.6	50.8
Orissa	T	76.3	81.5	10.4	8.9	13.4	9.6
	R	80.5	86.0	10.0	8.1	9.5	5.8
	U	23.9	28.9	14.3	17.7	61.9	53.5
Punjab	T	17.2	32.3	17.2	14.8	65.6	53.0
	R	34.2	53.6	22.7	16.0	43.2	30.4
	U	2.4	6.1	12.4	13.3	85.2	80.7
Rajasthan	T	88.4	86.4	4.8	6.4	6.8	6.9
	R	93.9	93.2	3.0	4.1	3.0	2.7
	U	24.7	26.8	25.5	27.6	49.8	45.7
Tamil Nadu	T	77.0	78.8	11.3	12.3	11.7	9.0
	R	87.4	88.5	6.9	7.4	5.6	4.0
	U	29.7	27.7	31.4	37.4	39.9	34.9
Uttar Pradesh	T	87.6	83.4	5.0	7.6	7.3	8.9

	R	92.6	90.8	3.9	5.4	3.5	3.8
	U	12.6	14.9	23.2	28.3	64.2	56.7
West Bengal	T	69.0	63.7	9.9	16.3	21.1	20.1
	R	84.8	78.1	7.5	14.5	7.7	7.3
	U	5.7	6.0	19.2	23.4	75.1	70.6

Sources : (1) Census of India, 1971, *General Economic Tables*, Part II-B(i),1975 and (2) Census of India, 1981, *General Economic Tables*, Part III-A(i), 1987.

Table-23: Percentage of Main Workers by Completed Education Level by Sex and Rural-Urban Residence for India, 1971 and 1981

			Educational Level							
Year	*T R U*	*P M F*	*Illiterate*	*Literate without educational level*	*Primary*	*Middle*	*Matric*	*Non-technical Diploma*	*Technical Diploma*	*Graduate and above*
1971	T	P	63.0	9.9	13.6	6.8	5.1	0.2	0.2	1.3
		M	57.4	11.3	15.7	8.0	5.9	0.2	0.2	1.4
		F	88.9	3.2	3.8	1.3	1.7	0.2	0.2	0.7
	R	P	69.0	9.6	12.8	5.2	2.7	0.2	0.1	0.3
		M	68.7	11.2	15.0	6.3	3.1	0.2	0.7	0.4
		F	91.7	3.0	3.5	0.9	0.5	0.1	0.0	0.1
	U	P	35.2	11.3	17.0	13.9	16.5	0.1	0.6	5.5
		M	31.6	12.0	18.2	15.0	17.1	0.1	0.6	5.5
		F	65.5	5.1	6.2	4.7	11.1	0.4	1.1	5.8
1981	T	P	57.5	9.1	13.8	7.9	8.5	0.1	0.4	2.7
		M	50.6	10.3	16.0	9.5	10.0	0.1	0.4	3.0
		F	84.4	4.1	5.1	1.9	2.4	0.1	0.3	1.5
	R	P	65.5	9.3	13.2	6.6	5.2	0.05	0.2	0.9
		M	57.7	10.9	15.6	8.0	6.4	0.15	0.2	1.1
		F	88.2	3.9	4.8	1.6	1.0	0.05	0.2	0.3
	U	p	30.4	8.1	16.3	13.2	21.2	0.1	1.0	9.6
		M	26.9	8.5	17.5	14.3	22.2	0.1	1.0	9.4
		F	56.5	5.3	7.6	4.6	13.2	0.3	1.3	10.9

Source : K.C. Suri, J.G. Bauer and J.R. Rele, *Analysis of Work Force in India*, Occasional Paper No. 8 of 1988, Office of the Registrar General and Census Commissioner, India, p. 20.

Table - 24 : Distribution of Female Main Workers by Industrial Categories in India by Resience in each Industrial Category, 1971-81

Industrial Category	*Females*					
	Rural			*Urban*		
		Percent change in employment			*Percent change in employment*	
	1971	*1981*	*71-81*	*1971*	*1981*	*71-81*
I. Cultivators	32.7	37.1	60.2	4.2	4.7	80.0
II. Agricultural labourers	54.3	50.2	30.7	17.5	16.6	52.5
III. Livestock, forestry, fishing, etc.	2.6	1.9	2.4	2.1	1.8	39.5
IV. Mining and quarrying	0.3	0.3	31.5	1.0	0.7	12.2
V. Manufacturing :						
(a) Household industry	3.6	3.8	50.3	10.9	10.5	69.6
(b) Other than household industry	1.6	2.1	92.5	12.9	14.6	82.2
VI. Construction	0.4	0.6	107.6	2.9	3.1	72.6
VII. Trade and commerce	1.0	1.1	55.9	8.2	8.9	74.3
VIII. Transport, storage and communication	0.1	0.1	15.3	3.2	2.2	12.2
IX. Other services	3.4	2.9	19.1	38.1	37.0	56.6
Total	100.0	100.0	43.0	100.0	100.0	62.2

Note: India excludes Assam. The 1981 figures are based on the 20% sample data.

Sources:(1) Census of India, 1971, *General Economic Tables*, part II-B(i), 1975.

(2) Census of India, 1981, *General Economic Tables*, part III-A(i), 1987.

Table-25: Percentage of Female Main Workers in India (Other than Cultivators and Agricultural Labourers) by 8 Major Occupational Divisions, 1971-1986

	Occupational Division	T/R/U	Females 1971	Females 1981	Percent change 1971-81
1	Professional, technical	T	14.7	15.7	65.8
	and related workers	R	9.8	10.1	53.8
		U	21.2	22.5	72.9
2	Administrative, executive	T	0.4	0.5	119.4
	and managerial workers	R	0.3	0.2	–0.3
		U	0.5	1.0	255.7
3	Clerical and	T	3.5	5.2	126.8
	related workers	R	1.0	1.3	96.7
		U	6.8	9.7	132.7
4	Sales workers	T	7.6	7.3	49.7
		R	7.0	7.1	50.8
		U	8.3	7.5	48.4
5	Service workers	T	16.1	13.2	26.0
		R	13.3	9.9	11.0
		U	20.0	17.0	39.1
6	Farmers, fishers, hunters	T	10.2	8.8	34.1
	loggers and related workers	R	15.9	14.3	33.4
		U	2.7	2.3	39.1
7	8 & 9 Production and related	T	46.3	46.5	55.6
	workers, transport equipment	R	51.5	53.8	55.4
	operators and labourers	U	39.6	37.7	55.8
10	Workers not classified by	T	1.1	2.7	282.5
	occupations	R	1.2	3.1	292.1
		U	1.9	2.2	267.1
	All workers	T	100.0	100.0	54.9
		R	100.0	100.0	48.6
		U	100.0	100.0	63.3

Source : Census of India, 1981, Part II-Special, 1983. Census of India, 1971, Part II p (iii), 1977.

Table-26: Percent Share of Female Job Seekers and the Rate of Job Seekers in India and its 14 Major States by Residence, 1981

		Percent share of job seekers/available			*Rate of seeking/ available(%)**		
State	*Sex*	*Total*	*Rural*	*Urban*	*Total*	*Rural*	*Urban*
India	T	100.0	100.0	100.0	3.0	2.4	4.7
	M	100.0	100.0	100.0	3.2	2.5	5.4
	F	100.0	100.0	100.0	2.6	2.3	3.9
Andhra Pradesh	F	4.1	3.6	5.0	1.3	1.0	2.4
Bihar	F	7.6	9.2	4.5	1.9	1.7	3.3
Gujarat	F	3.7	3.2	4.7	1.9	1.6	2.7
Haryana	F	1.2	1.1	1.3	1.7	1.4	2.9
Kerala	F	23.1	27.6	14.4	15.1	14.7	17.3
Madhya Pradesh	F	4.6	4.6	4.7	1.6	1.3	2.7
Maharashtra	F	8.0	6.3	11.3	2.2	1.7	3.2
Karnataka	F	4.0	2.9	6.3	1.9	1.2	3.5
Orissa	F	1.1	2.3	1.0	1.2	1.1	2.1
Punjab	F	1.9	1.1	1.0	1.2	1.1	1.4
Rajasthan	F	4.4	5.5	2.2	2.2	2.3	1.9
Tamil Nadu	F	7.4	5.7	10.8	2.6	2.0	4.0
Uttar Pradesh	F	3.4	2.9	4.4	0.6	0.4	1.4
West Bengal	F	20.6	19.9	21.9	6.7	5.7	9.7

Source: Census of India, 1981, *General Economic Tables* (B9-B10).

* Ratio of those seeking/available for work to the relevant population times 100.

Table-27: Employment in the Organised Sector* by zones/States/ Union Territories as on 31st March, 1989 (Provisional)

Zone/ State/ Union Territory	*Total Employment*			*Women Employment*			*Percentage of Women employment to total employment*		
	Public Sector	*Private Sector*	*Total*	*Public Sector*	*Private Sector*	*Total*	*Public*	*Private*	*Total*
I.North Zone	2957857	890274	3848131	356179	115022	471201	12.0	12.9	12.2
1. Haryana	391112	196062	587174	52796	15700	68496	13.5	8.0	11.7
2. Punjab	550258	214618	764876	81132	21236	102368	14.7	9.9	13.4
3. H.P.	251270	27202	278472	27808	2908	30716	11.1	10.7	11.0
4. Chandigarh	57594	15656	73250	8594	2642	11236	14.9	16.9	15.3
5. Delhi	614475	202179	816654	75740	25064	100804	12.3	12.4	12.3
6. Rajasthan	899439	225070	1124509	91618	45737	137355	10.2	20.3	12.2
7. Jammu & Kashmir	193709	9487	203196	18491	1735	20226	9.5	18.3	10.0

II. Central Zone	3484966	772890	4257856	285537	71124	356661	8.2	9.2	8.4
8. M.P.	1376244	237023	1613267	131244	25392	156636	9.5	10.7	9.7
9. U.P.	2108722	535867	2644589	154293	45732	200025	7.3	8.5	7.6
III. North-Eastern Zone	757268	53628919	3557	100199	245262	345461	13.2	45.7	26.7
10. Assam	476809	518589	995398	54116	238417	292533	11.3	46.0	29.4
11. Meghalaya	58156	4556	62712	9546	1775	11321	16.4	39.0	18.1
12. Manipur	50309	859	51168	7104	234	7338	14.1	27.2	14.3
13. Mizorm	29026	1334	30360	6433	434	6867	22.2	32.5	22.6
14. Nagaland	58898	1594	690492	10028	463	10491	17.0	29.0	17.3
15. Tripura	84070	9357	93427	12972	3939	16911	15.4	42.1	18.1
IV. Eastern Zone	3584158	1259209	4843367	252979	164671	417650	7.1	13.1	8.6
16. Bihar	1394717	259030	1653747	95481	17460	112941	6.8	6.7	6.8
17. Orissa	623250	101376	724626	45866	11667	57533	7.4	11.5	7.9
18. W.Bengal	1566191	898803	2464994	111632	135544	247176	7.1	15.1	10.0
V.Western	3206342	2061623	5267965	436597	233730	670327	13.6	11.3	12.7
19. Gujarat	931584	683901	1615485	133954	64724	198678	14.4	9.5	12.3
20. Maharashtra	2214354	1349403	3563757	290964	163646	454610	13.1	12.1	12.8
21. Goa	60404	28319	88723	11679	5360	17039	19.3	18.9	19.2
VI. Southern Zone	4497005	1946035	6443040	752799	526877	1279676	16.7	27.1	19.9
22. A.P.	1325034	356163	1681197	134785	71751	206536	10.2	20.1	12.3
23. Karnatka	987523	398032	1385555	146696	75894	222590	14.9	19.1	16.1
24. Kerala	602248	494002	1096251	172328	212571	384899	28.6	43.0	35.1
25. Pondicherry	41398	9185	50583	6417	1065	7482	15.5	11.6	14.8
26. Tamil .N	1540802	688652	2229454	292573	165596	45869	19.0	24.0	20.6
27. A & N	28452	3247	31699	2808	98	2906	9.9	3.0	9.2
G.Total	18516048	7469567	25985615	2187098	13567884	3543882	11.8	18.2	13.6

* Includes all establishments in the public sector irrespective of the size of employment and those non-agricultural establishments in the private sector employing 10 or more persons.

** The Union Territory of Andaman & Nicobar Island is outside the zonal classification as per the State Reorganisation Act, 1956.

Note: Sikkim, Arunachal Pradesh, Dadar & Nagar Haveli and Lakshadweep are not covered under Employment Market Information programme.

Source:- Family Welfare programme in India, *Year book 1989-90,* Ministry of Health and Family Welfare, Government of India, New Delhi, p. 166.

Table-28: Proportion and Growth Rate of Female Workers in India, 1981-91

Sl. No.	*State/ Union Territory*	*Proportion Workers*		*Growth Rate*
		1981	*1991*	*1981-91*
	*India**	14.1	16.5	44.2
1.	Andhra Pradesh	27.0	30.4	39.4
2.	Arunachal Pradesh	40.5	36.1	21.0
3.	Bihar	9.1	10.5	40.1
4.	Goa	15.3	16.7	26.2
5.	Gujarat	11.0	14.2	54.8
6.	Haryana	4.7	6.4	74.0
7.	Himachal Pradesh	18.7	19.7	27.2
8.	Karnataka	18.9	23.0	46.5
9.	Kerala	12.8	12.8	15.3
10.	Madhaya Pradesh	22.3	23.1	30.3
11.	Maharashtra	24.0	26.7	39.3
12.	Manipur	34.6	31.6	16.7
13.	Meghalaya	33.3	33.3	31.4
14.	Mizoram	32.3	34.4	48.4
15.	Nagaland	42.4	36.7	37.8
16.	Orissa	10.7	12.3	36.8
17.	Punjab	2.3	4.2	122.0
18.	Rajasthan	9.3	13.3	82.6
19.	Sikkim	34.7	30.1	14.3
20.	Tamil Nadu	22.4	26.3	34.9
21.	Tripura	8.9	10.3	54.1
22.	Uttar Pradesh	5.4	8.2	91.2
23.	West Bengal	5.8	8.1	73.6
	Union Territories			
1.	Andaman and Nicobar Islands	5.1	8.2	150.4
2.	Chandigarh	8.9	10.4	68.5
3.	Dadra and Nagar Heveli	26.1	31.2	57.8
4.	Daman & Diu	11.6	12.1	28.5
5.	Delhi	6.5	7.4	72.9
6.	Lakshadweep	5.6	5.9	33.9
7.	Pondicherry	11.0	14.4	74.3

* Excludes Assam and Jammu & Kashmir.

Soure : Census of India, 1991, *Provisional Population Totals: Workers and Their Distribution*, Series-1, *India*, Paper 3 of 1991 pp. 22-24.

Table 29: Percentage Distributions of Female Workers in India by Rural and Urban, 1981 and 1991

State/ Union Territory	Total Percentage of workers		Rural Percentage of workers		Urban Percentage of workers	
	1981	1991	1981	1991	1981	1991
India*	19.7	22.8	23.1	27.2	8.3	9.7
1 Andhra Pradesh	33.5	34.8	40.0	42.9	11.8	12.5
2 Arunachal Pradesh	45.7	39.6	47.6	42.9	11.6	14.0
3 Bihar	13.5	15.7	14.6	17.1	4.8	5.9
4 Goa	21.9	20.5	24.9	23.8	15.1	15.5
5 Gujarat	20.7	27.1	26.8	36.5	6.5	8.8
6 Haryana	10.6	11.3	12.3	13.2	4.4	5.4
7 Himachal Pradesh	31.9	34.8	33.4	36.6	11.3	14.1
8 Karnataka	25.3	29.3	30.7	36.3	11.8	13.1
9 Kerala	16.6	16.9	17.7	17.9	11.8	14.0
10 Madhya Pradesh	30.6	32.5	35.8	39.1	9.6	10.3
11 Maharashtra	30.6	33.0	40.8	45.8	10.1	11.6
12 Manipur	39.5	37.5	43.4	41.4	28.6	27.4
13 Meghalaya	37.5	36.7	42.0	41.1	16.1	17.1
14 Mizoram	37.7	43.9	42.8	47.7	21.9	39.6
15 Nagaland	43.2	39.2	48.3	42.6	10.9	21.8
16 Orissa	19.8	20.8	21.8	22.7	9.5	8.3
17 Punjab	6.2	6.8	6.9	7.0	4.2	6.2
18 Rajasthan	21.1	27.0	25.0	32.8	5.9	7.1
19 Sikkim+	37.6	52.7	41.4	55.8	15.6	19.1
20 Tamil Nadu	26.5	30.9	33.5	39.2	12.0	14.5
21 Tripura	12.8	14.3	13.3	15.2	8.7	9.4
22 Uttar Pradesh	8.1	12.9	9.0	14.7	3.5	5.3
23 West Bengal	8.1	11.7	8.9	13.5	5.6	6.5
Union Territories						
1 Andman and Nicobar Islands	10.8	12.9	12.0	14.0	7.2	9.6
2 Chandigarh	9.1	10.5	3.6	5.1	9.5	11.1
3 Dadra and Nagar Haveli	41.3	48.9	42.3	51.0	26.8	24.4
4 Daman & Diu	22.6	23.1	26.4	29.4	16.1	16.2
5 Delhi	6.8	7.7	8.7	6.3	6.7	7.8
6 Lakshadweep	9.2	7.5	11.3	6.9	6.6	7.9
7 Pondicherry	13.5	15.5	18.1	23.1	9.3	11.2

* Excludes Assam and Jammu and Kashmir

\+ The decline in the number of workers in the urban areas of Sikkim may be due to the reorganization of five major towns by excluding certain portions from them which were added to the adjoining village after the 1981 Census.

Source: Same as for Table 28.

Table-30: Total Female Workers by Rural and Urban in India, 1991

State/ Union Territory	Total Rural Urban	Total population	Total workers	Main workers	Marginal workers
1	2	3	4	5	6
India	Total	402,813,817	91,397,489	66,189,434	25,208,055
(Excludes Jammu & Kashmir where 1991 Census was not held)					
	Rural	301,204.357	81,507,087	57,431,521	24,075,566
	Urban	101,609,460	9,890,402	8,757,913	1,132,489
India	Total	392,098,948	89,115,791	64,627,863	24,487,928
(Excluding Assam andJammu & Kashmir)					
	Rural	291,616,645	79.324,754	55,954,891	23,369,863
	Urban	100,482,303	9,791,037	8,672,972	1,118,065
States					
1. Andhra	Total	32,716,653	11,390,161	9,960,182	1,429,979
Pradesh	Rural	24,006,149	10,302,347	8,952,812	1,349,535
	Urban	8,710,504	1,087,814	1,007,370	80,444
2. Arunachal					
Pradesh	Total	397,150	157,300	143,519	13,781
	Rural	352,119	150,981	137,445	13,536
	Urban	45,031	6,319	6,074	245
3. Assam	Total	10,714,869	2,281,698	1,561,571	720,127
	Rural	9,587,712	2,182,333	1,476,630	705,703
	Urban	1,127,157	99,365	84,941	14,424
4. Bihar	Total	41,191,573	6,461,878	4,310,371	2,151,507
	Rural	35,981,227	6,154,146	4,052,175	2,101,971
	Urban	5,210,346	307,732	258,196	49,536
5. Goa	Total	575,059	117,762	96,230	21,532
	Rural	343,600	81,916	63,613	18,303
	Urban	231,459	35,846	32,617	3,229
6. Gujarat	Total	19,903,241	5,389,492	2,823,909	2,565,583
	Rural	13,160,268	4,797,824	2,402,094	2,385,730
	Urban	6,742,973	591,668	421,815	169,853
7. Haryana	Total	7,612,336	859,321	490,770	368,551
	Rural	5,732,587	757,386	399,362	358,024
	Urban	1,879,749	101,935	91,408	10,527
8. Himachal					
Pradesh	Total	2,550,185	887,204	502,648	384,556

	Rural	2,348,654	858,829	479,864	378,965
	Urban	201,531	28,375	22,784	5,073
9. Karnataka	Total	21,959,855	6,428,184	5,057,878	1,370,397
	Rural	15,285,906	5,553,119	4,235,795	1,317,324
	Urban	6,673,949	875,065	821,992	53,073
10. Kerala	Total	14,802,437	2,501,536	1,901,924	599,612
	Rural	10,901,249	1,955,480	1,463,056	42,424
	Urban	3,901,188	546,056	438,868	107,188
11. Madhya Pradesh	Total	31,903,814	10,379,433	7,362,895	3,016,538
	Rural	24,663,844	9,635,216	6,711,290	2,923,926
	Urban	7,239,970	744,217	651,605	92,612
12. Maharashtra	Total	38,061,961	12,568,538	10,146,570	2,421,968
	Rural	23,824,803	10,919,855	8,649,539	2,270,316
	Urban	14,237,158	1,648,683	1,497,031	151,652
13. Manipur	Total	895,203	335,715	282,617	53,098
	Rural	646,084	267,462	226,249	41,213
	Urban	249,119	68,253	56,368	11,885
14. Meghalaya	Total	856,318	314,169	285,264	28,905
	Rural	700,056	287,503	259,421	28,082
	Urban	156,262	26,666	25,843	823
15. Mizoram	Total	329,545	144,812	113,454	31,358
	Rural	176,454	84,142	70,488	13,654
	Urban	153,091	60,670	42,966	17,704
16. Negaland	Total	572,300	224,647	210,100	14,547
	Rural	479,651	204,472	191,517	12,955
	Urban	92,649	20,175	18,583	1,592
17. Orissa	Total	15,532,166	3,238,842	1,911,574	1,327,268
	Rural	13,567,459	3,076,228	1,771,640	1,304,588
	Urban	1,964,707	162,614	139,934	22,680
18. Punjab	Total	9,495,659	643,521	395,446	248,075
	Rural	6,703,367	470,315	235,187	235,128
	Urban	2,792,292	173,206	160,259	12,947
19. Rajasthan	Total	20,944,745	5,657,746	2,794,069	2,863,677
	Rural	16,241,442	5,322,517	2,532,202	2,790,315
	Urban	4,703,303	335,229	261,867	73,362
20. Sikkim	Total	189,605	100,005	57,072	42,933

	Rural	173,784	96,985	54,284	42,701
	Urban	15,821,	3,020	2,788	232
21.Tamil Nadu	Total	27,420,371	8,468,513	7,214,803	1,253,710
	Rural	18,145,197	7,118,897	5,967,059	1,151,838
	Urban	9,275,174	1,349,616	1,247,744	101,872
22. Tripura	Total	1,334,282	190,999	137,587	53,412
	Rural	1,129,314	171,780	119,833	51,947
	Urban	204,968,19,219	17,754	1,465	
23.Uttar Pradesh	Total	65,132,844	8,379,751	5,366,247	3,013,504
	Rural	52,333,564	7,701,411	4,780,961	2,920,450
	Urban	12,799,280	678,340	585,286	93,054
24. West Begal	Total	32,520,834	3,795,943	2,623,244	1,172,699
	Rural	23,933,371	3,241,373	2,114,126	1,127,247
	Urban	8,587,463	554,570	509,118	45,452
Union Territory					
1. Andaman &	Total	125,788	16,179	10,345	5,834
Nicobar	Rural	93,250	13,068	7,330	5,738
Island	Urban	32,538	3,111	3,015	96
2. Chandigarh	Total	283,314	29,812	29,522	290
	Rural	25,614	1,317	1,285	32
	Urban	257,700	28,495	28,237	258
3. Dadar &	Total	67,522	33,004	21,097	11,907
Nagar	Rural	62,245	31,718	20,266	11,452
Haveli	Urban	5,277	1,286	831	455
4 Daman & Diu	Total	49,987	11,525	6,058	5,467
	Rural	25,931	7,629	3,426	4,203
	Urban	24,056	3,896	2,632	1,264
5. Delhi	Total	4,249,742	326,097	313,410	12,687
	Rural	425,469	27,937	21,758	5,279
	Urban	3,824,273	299,060	291,652	7,408
6.Lakshadweep	Total	25,099	1,878	1,484	394
	Rural	11,073	768	599	169
	Urban	14,026	1,110	885	225
7. Pondicherry	Total	399,360	61,824	57,665	4,159
	Rural	142,914	33,033	30,215	2,818
	Urban	256,446	28,791	27,450	1,341

Source : Same as for Table 28.

Table-31 : Distribution of Districts by Proportion of Agricultural Workers (Cultivators and Agricultural Labourers Taken Together) of Female Main Workers in Rural Areas, 1991

State/ Union Territory	A	B	C	D	E	F
India*	446	84	38	108	134	82
States						
1. Andhra Pradesh	22	1	1	13	7	—
2. Arunachal Pradesh	11	—	1	4	4	2
3. Assam	23	13	3	5	2	—
4. Bihar	42	1	—	6	25	10
5. Goa	2	2	—	—	—	—
6. Gujarat	19	2	2	7	7	1
7. Haryana	16	3	1	9	3	—
8. Himachal Pradesh	12	-1	5	1	5	
9. Karnataka	20	4	1	3	12	—
10. Kerala	14	13	—	1	—	—
11. Madhaya Pradesh	45	2	—	4	14	25
12. Maharashtra	29	—	—	4	12	13
13. Manipur	8	2	—	2	4	—
14. Meghalaya	5	—	1	1	1	2
15. Mizoram	3	—	—	—	1	2
16. Nagaland	7	—	—	2	1	4
17. Orissa	13	2	1	8	2	—
18. Punjab	12	10	1	1	—	—
19. Rajasthan	27	—	1.	4	16	6
20. Sikkim	4	1	1	1	1	—
21. Tamil Nadu	20	3	2	7	8	—
22. Tripura	3	1	1	1	—	—
23. Uttar Pradesh	63	9	14	16	12	12
24. West Bengal	16	8	5	3	—	—
Union Territories						
1. Andaman & Nicobar Islands	2	2	—	—	—	—
2. Chandigarh	1	1	—	—	—	—
3. Dadar and Nagar Haveli	1	—	—	—	1	—
4. Daman & Diu	2	2	—	—	—	—
5. Delhi	1	1	—	—	—	—
6. Lakshadweep	1	1	—	—	—	
7. Pondicherry	2	—	1	1	—	—

* Excludes Assam and Jammu and Kashmir.
A : Total number of districts.
B : 70.00 per cent or less.
C : 70.01-80.00 per cent.
D : 80.01-90.00 per cent.
E : 90.01-95.00 per cent.
F : 95.01 per cent and above.
Source: Same as for Table 28.

Table-32 : States and Union Territories Arranged in a Descending Order of Their Proportion of Other Workers of Rural Female Main Wokers, 1991

Rank in 1991	*State/ Union Territory*	*1991*	*1981*	*Rank in 1981*
1.	Lakshadweep	95.7	39.8	6
2.	Chandigarh	92.9	82.9	1
3.	Delhi	73.6	66.2	2
4.	Daman and Diu	63.2	40.2	5
5.	Andaman and Nicobar Islands	51.5	63.7	3
6.	Goa	44.6	39.4	7
7.	Kerala	44.2	38.1	8
8.	Punjab	33.1	42.0	4
9.	West Bengal	21.9	25.6	9
10.	Tripura	19.1	19.4	10
11.	Sikkim	16.8	11.5	13
12.	Pondicherry	14.1	15.0	11
13.	Meghalaya	13.1	11.2	15
14.	Gujarat	13.0	9.6	17
15.	Karnataka	12.8	11.3	14
16.	Haryana	12.1	12.8	12
17.	Manipur	10.5	5.3	23
18.	Tamil Nadu	10.4	9.0	20
19.	Orissa	9.4	10.9	16
	India*	8.8	8.9	
20.	Dadra and Nagar Haveli	8.3	9.4	18
21.	Arunachal Pradesh	7.4	4.2	27
22.	Andhra Pradesh	7.0	7.8	21
23.	Himachal Pradesh	6.7	5.2	24
24.	Uttar Pradesh	6.4	5.8	22
25.	Nagaland	6.1	3.2	30
26.	Mizoram	5.6	3.7	29
27.	Rajasthan	5.0	9.3	19
28.	Maharashtra	4.7	4.9	26
29.	Bihar	4.3	5.0	25
30.	Madhya Pradesh	3.4	4.1	28

* Excludes Assam and Jammu and Kashmir.

Source: Same as for Table 28.

Table-33 : States and Union Territories Arranged in Descending Order of their Proportion of Other Workers of Urban Female Main Workers, 1991

Rank in 1991	*State/ Union Territory*	*1991*	*1981*	*Rank in 1981*
1	Andaman and Nicobar Islands	98.5	98.6	2
2	Chandigarh	98.5	99.0	1
3	Sikkim	96.1	93.3	5
4	Delhi	95.8	97.8	3
5	Tripura	93.5	96.4	4
6	Daman and Diu	93.2	90.3	7
7	Meghalaya	88.6	89.0	9
8	Himachal Pradesh	87.5	84.1	11
9	Punjab	86.3	90.9	6
10	Haryana	85.1	86.4	10
11	Goa	83.1	83.6	12
12	West Bengal	83.1	89.6	8
13	Arunachal Pradesh	77.8	72.0	17
14	Lakshadweep	77.7	70.8	18
15	Pondicherry	75.6	73.2	15
16	Gujarat	75.4	74.4	14
17	Maharashtra	73.6	73.1	16
18	Kerala	72.6	79.0	13
19	Orissa	70.2	69.8	20
	India*	69.2	68.3	
20	Karnataka	69.0	60.4	25
21	Tamil Nadu	67.0	61.8	24
22	Uttar Pradesh	65.8	66.9	22
23	Rajasthan	63.8	65.6	23
24	Bihar	61.2	67.1	21
25	Dadra and Nagar Haveli	61.1	42.2	29
26	Madhya Pradesh	58.8	59.7	26
27	Nagaland	55.2	70.1	19
28	Andhra Pradesh	54.2	54.5	27
29	Mizoram	47.8	52.4	28
30	Manipur	36.6	29.4	30

* Excludes Assam and Jammu and Kashmir.

Source: Same as for Table 28.

Table-34: States and Union Territories Arranged in a Descending Order of Their Proportion of Rural Female Marginal Workers with Ranks in 1991 and 1981

Rank in 1991	*State/ Union Territory*	*1991*	*1981*	*Rank in 1981*
1	Sikkim	24.6	3.4	25
2	Dadra and Nagar Haveli	18.4	15.6	1
3	Gujarat	18.2	13.4	5
4	Rajasthan	17.2	14.4	2
5	Daman and Diu	16.2	13.9	4
6	Himachal Pradesh	16.1	14.0	3
7	Madhya Pradesh	11.9	10.0	7
8	Orissa	9.6	10.0	6
9	Maharashtra	9.5	9.5	8
10	Karnataka	8.6	8.4	10
	India*	8.0	7.0	
11	Mizoram	7.7	6.0	14
12	Manipur	6.4	4.5	21
13	Tamil Nadu	6.4	5.7	15
14	Haryana	6.2	7.4	13
15	Andaman and Nicobar Islands	6.2	7.6	12
16	Bihar	5.8	5.0	19
17	Andhra Pradesh	5.6	8.0	11
18	Uttar Pradesh	5.6	3.1	26
19	Goa	5.3	8.4	9
20	West Bengal	4.7	2.7	27
21	Tripura	4.6	4.3	23
22	Kerala	4.5	4.3	22
23	Meghalaya	4.0	5.0	18
24	Arunachal Pradesh	3.9	5.4	1
25	Punjab	3.5	5.2	17
26	Nagaland	2.7	0.8	29
27	Pondicherry	2.0	3.7	24
28	Lakshadweep	1.5	4.9	20
29	Delhi	1.2	2.7	28
30	Chandigarh	0.1	0.4	30

* Excludes Assam and Jammu and Kashmir.

Source: Same as for Table 28.

Table-35: State and Union Territories Arranged in Descending Order of Their 1991 Female Work Participation Rate

Rank in 1991	*State/ Union Territory*	*Female Work Participation Rate 1991*	*1981*	*Rank in 1981*
1	Sikkim	52.7	37.6	6
2	Dadra and Nagar Heveli	48.9	41.3	3
3	Mizoram	43.9	37.7	5
4	Arunachal Pradesh	39.6	45.7	1
5	Nagaland	39.3	43.2	2
6	Manipur	37.5	39.5	4
7	Meghalaya	36.7	37.5	7
8	Andhra Pradesh	34.8	33.5	8
9	Himachal Pradesh	34.8	31.9	9
10	Maharashtra	33.0	30.6	11
11	Madhya Pradesh	32.5	30.6	10
12	Tamil Nadu	30.9	26.5	12
13	Karnataka	29.3	25.3	13
14	Gujarat	27.1	20.1	17
15	Rajasthan	27.0	21.1	16
16	Daman and Diu	23.1	22.6	14
	India*	22.7	19.7	
17	Orissa	20.9	19.8	18
18	Goa	20.5	21.9	15
19	Kerala	16.9	16.6	19
20	Bihar	15.7	13.5	20
21	Pondicherry	15.5	13.4	21
22	Tripura	14.3	12.9	22
23	Uttar Pradesh	12.9	8.1	27
24	Andaman and Nicobar Islands	12.9	10.8	23
25	West Bengal	11.7	8.1	28
26	Haryana	11.3	10.6	24
27	Chandigarh	10.5	9.1	26
28	Delhi	7.7	6.8	29
29	Lakshadweep	7.5	9.2	25
30	Punjab	6.8	6.2	30

* Excludes Assam and Jammu and Kashmir.

Source: Same as for Table-28.

19

The Indian Woman: a Select Bibliography

*Prabhash P. Singh**

Ahmad, Karuna Chanana, *Gandhi, Women's Roles and the Freedom Movement*, New Delhi: Nehru Memorial Museum and Library, 1984.

—, *Social Context of Women's Education in India 1921-81* (Tentative Formulations), New Delhi: Nehru Memorial Museum and Library, 1990 (Occasional Papers on History and Society (First Series No. VI).

—, Education of girls: a sociological perspective, *Kurukshetra*, 1990, 38 (12): 23-25.

Ahooja-Patel, Krishna, 'Gender-sensitive development: a political imperative', *Mainstream*, 1991, 129(31): 28-29.

Aleem, Shamim, *Women Police and Social Change*, New Delhi: Ashish Publishing House, 1991.

Arora, Anand *The Women Elite in India*, New Delhi : Radiant Publications, 1990.

Arputhamurthy, Savitri, *Women, Work and Discrimination*, New Delhi: Ashish Publishing House, 1990.

Arunachalam, Jaya, 'Women and their role in development of co-operatives', *Co-operative Perspective*, 1991, 20(2): 124-42.

Asha, C.B. and Subrahamanian, K.A., 'Problems of elderly women', *Indian Journal of Community Guidance Service*, 1990, 7(3): 61-87.

* The author is Assistant Librarian at the A.N. Sinha Institute of Social Studies, Patna - 800 001

Asharfi, Talat Ara, *Muslim Women in Changing Perspective*, New Delhi: Commonwealth Publishers, 1992.

Ashirvad, N., *'Drive against illiteracy:* quest for a new approach': *Yojna*, 1990, 34(28): 15-16.

Awasty, Indira, *Rural Women of India*, Delhi: B.R. Publishing Corportation, 1982.

Badruddin, 'Women workers in Assam tea plantations', *Social Welfare*, 1990, 37 (2): 29.

Bajpai, Shalleja, 'The lesser sex', *The Indian Express*, 28 Oct., 1990.

Balasubramanyan, Vimal, 'Women do not need quota', *Mainstream*, 1991, 29(30): 22-28.

Banerjee, Debdas, *Development and Women: Some Experience of Mulberry Silk Production in West Bengal*, Calcutta: Centre for Studies in Social Science, 1992.

Banerjee, Narayan 'Family postures Vs. family reality: strategies for survival and mobility', *Samya Shakti* 1989-90, (4-5): 192-212.

Banerji, Himani, 'Fashioning a self-educational proposal for and by women in popular magazines in colonial Bengali, *Economic and Political Weekly*, 1991, 26(43): 50-52.

Bardhan, Kalpana, 'Women's work in relation to family strategies in South and South-East Asia', *Samya Shakti*, 1989-90,(4-5) 83-120.

Barr, Pat, *The Dust in the Balance: British Women in India', 1905-1945*, London: Hamilton, 1989.

Bhagat, R.B., 'Status of women and age at marriage in India', *Social Change*, 1990, 20(2): 20-25.

Bhagyalakshmi. J., 'Girl child: unwanted, neglected and suffering', *Kurukshetra*, 1990, 38(12): 42-49.

Bhasin, Kamla, 'Girl child or fish among crocodiles', *Kurukshetra*, 1990, 38(12): 29-31.

Bhasin, Kamla and Menon, Ritu, 'The problem', *Seminar*, 1988, (342): 12-13.

Bhaskaran, V., 'National workshop on prostitutes and their children', *Social Welfare*, 1990, 37(4): 17-19.

Bhatia, Kiran Sharma, 'Silent conflicts', *Seminar*, 1991, (382): 39-42.

Bhatt, Ela, 'Structural reform; view from the other side', *Economic Times*, 17 Jan, 1992 : 6.

Bhatt, K.N., *Place of Women' Development Question in Indian*

Planning: A Socio-economic and Historical Perspective of the Problems, Allahabad: Govind Ballabh Pant Social Science Institute, 1989.

Bhatt, R., 'Women's co-operatives' *Co-operative Perspective*, 1989, 26(2): 121-127.

Bhoite, Anuradha, *Women Employees and Rural Development: Problems of Employed Women in Rural Area*, Delhi: Gyan Publishing House, 1987.

Caplan, Patricia, *Class and Gender in India*: Women and Their *Organisation in a South Indian City*, New York: Tavistock Publications, 1985.

Chakraborti, Sreemati, 'Peasant woman's struggle and patriarchy', *Teaching Politics*, 1990, 15(1-2): 91-100.

Chambers, Jenny, 'Inner rebillions, *Seminar*, 1991,(382) : 26-33.

Chandra, Shanta Kohli, *Development of Women Entrepreneurship in India: study of Public Policies and Programmes*, New Delhi: Mittal Publications, 1991.

Chandra, Shivanandanam, 'Frustration reaction patterns in women criminals and girls delinquents,' *Indian Journal of Criminology*, 1991, 18(1) : 28-35.

Chandrasekhar, B.K. and Inbanathan, Anand, 'Profile and participation of women: Zila Parishad and mandal panchayat members: The case of Karnataka', *Journal of Rural Development, 1991*, 10(5) : 575-589.

Chatterji, Jyotsna, 'Education and training of girl child : some suggestions,' Kurukshetra, 1990, 38(12): 26-28.

Chatterji, Shoma, 'Increasing abuse of male power,' *Free Press Journal*, 19 August, 1990 : 6.

----,'Women politicians: still behind times', *Free Press Journal*, 13 Jan., 1991: 10.

----,'Women: Fishing in troubled waters,' *Economic Times* (Suppl.), 19 Dec. 1991: VI: 1-3

Chaturvedi, Geeta, *Women Administrators of India: a Study of Socio-economic Background and Attitudes of Women Administrators of Rajasthan*, Jaipur: R.B.S.A. Publishers, 1985.

Chaudhary, Pratima K., *Changing Values among Young Women*, Delhi: Amar Prakashan, 1988.

Chauhan, Indira, *Dilemma of Working Women Hostellers with Special Reference to Maharashtra*, Delhi: B.R. Publishing Corporation, 1986.

Chowdhary, Ritu Parna, 'Status of Indian women through the ages,' *Assam Tribune*, 30 Oct., 1990: 3.

Chowdhary, D. Paul, 'What do we need to reduce their drudgary?' *Kurukshetra*, 1990, 38 (12): 34-38.

Dable, Isabelle, *The School Education of Girls*, Paris: UNESCO, 1980.

Darley, S.A., 'Big time careers for the little women: a dual role dilemma,' *Journal of Social Issues*, 1976, 32(3): 85-92.

Das Gupta, Abhijit, 'Causes of prostitution and methods of prevention, '*Social Welfare*, 1990, 37(3): 9-12.

Das-Hazarika, B., 'Female talent and challenges,' *Assam Tribune*, 17 June 1990.

Dass, Rajata and Chopra, Romila, 'Prostitution: how to deal with it,' *Social Welfare*, 1990, 37(3): 2-3.

Datta, V.N., *Sati*: a *Historical, Social and Philosophical Enquiry into the Hindu Rite of Widow Burning*, New Delhi: Manohar Books, 1988.

Desai, Neera, 'Social movements: struggle for Indian women's emancipation', *Indian Journal of Social Research*, 1988, (29): 335-360.

Deshpande, Anjali, 'Hazards of work in informal sector', *Mainstream*, 1989, 27(31): 13-14.

Deshpande, Nirmala, 'Participation of women in political system,' *Kurukshetra* 1989, 37(5): 56.

Devi, M. Indira, *Women Education, Employment, Family Living : a Study of Emerging Hindu Wives in Urban India*, Delhi: Gyan Publishing House, 1987.

Dex, Shirlex, *The Sexual Division of Work: Conceptual Revolution in Social Sciences*, New York: Harvestar Press, 1985.

Dhagamwar, Vasudha, 'Saint, victim or criminal', *Seminar*, 1988 (342): 34-39.

Diaz, S.M., 'Domestic violence in the Indian setting', *Indian Journal of Criminology*, 1991, 19(2): 92-96.

Duerst-Lahti, Georia, 'But women play the game too: communication control and influence in administrative decision-making', *Administration and Society*, 1990, 22(2): 182-205.

Dutta, Dipali and Verma, S.K., 'Free and independent but trapped,' *Social Welfare*, 1990, 36(12): 4-5.

Farooqui, Vimla, 'Constitute national commission for women', *New Age*, 1991, 39(48): 4.

Fruzzetti, Lina, *The Gift of a Virgin: Women, Marriage and Ritual in a*

Bengali Society, New Delhi: Oxford University Press, 1990.

Gallagher, Margaret, *Unequal Opportunities: the Case of Women and the Media*, Paris: UNESCO, 1981.

Gandhi, Nandita and Shah, Nandita, 'Opening doors: making space for women,' *Administrator*, 1989, 34(3): 16-20.

Gautam, D.N. and Trivedi, B.V., *Unnatural Deaths of Married Women with Special Reference to Dowry Deaths: a Sample Study of Dowry*, New Delhi: Govt. of India press, 1986.

Ghadially, Rehana, *Women in Indian Society*, New Delhi: Sage Publications, 1988.

Ghosh, Bahinisikha, *Indian Population Problem: a Household Economic Approach*, New Delhi: Sage Publications, 1990.

Gothoskar, Sujata, 'Struggles for working women: emerging issues,' *Janata*, 1991, 45(36-40) : 21-25.

Gray, J.D., 'The married professional women: an examination of her role conflicts and coping strategies, '*Psychology of Women Quarterly*, 1983, 7(3): 235-243.

Gulati, Leela, *Profiles of Female Poverty: a Study of Five Poor Working Women in Kerala*, Delhi: Hindustan Publishing Corporation, 1981.

----, *Women in the Urban Industrial Labour Force in India*, Trivandrum: Centre for Development Studies, 1981.

----, *Women in Fishing Villages on the Kerala Coast: Demographic and Socio-economic Impacts of a Fisheries Development Project*, Geneva: ILO, 1983.

----, *Women in the Unorganised Sector: With Special Reference to Kerala*, Trivandrum: Centre for Development Studies, 1983.

----, *Fisher Women on the Kerala Coast, Geneva*; ILO, 1984.

Gupta, G.R. and Ganguli, H.C., 'Marriage-work interaction: a study on Indian women, '*Indian Journal of Clinical Psychology*, 1982, (9): 113-123.

Gupta, Vishwa Nath, 'Women labour in tea plantation, '*Social Welfare*, 1990, 37 (2): 2-3.

Hale, Sylvia, 'Status of women in India,' *Public Affairs*, 1989, 6(2): 364-381.

Hari, M., 'Modernisation, status of women and fertility, '*Journal of Family Welfare*,' 1991, 37(2): 62-67.

Harish, Economic Development and Role of Indian Women, New Delhi: Commonwealth Publisher, 1991.

Hate, Chandrakala A., *Changing Status of Women in Post Independence India*, Bombay: Allied Publishers Pvt. Ltd., 1969.

Herman, J.B. and Gyllstrom, K.K., 'Working man and women: inter- and intra-role conflict', *Psychology of Women Quarterly*, 1977, 1 (4): 319-333.

Holahan, C.H. and Gilbert, L.A., 'Conflict between major life roles: men and women in dual career couples, '*Human Relations*, 1979, 32(6): 451-467.

India, Ministry of Labour, *Socio-economic Conditions of Women Workers of Mines*, Simla: Govt. of India Press, 1979.

----, Ministry of Labour and Rehabilitation, *Statistical Profile of Women Labour*, Simla: Controller of Publications, 1983.

----, Ministry of Labour and Rehabilitation, *Socio-economic Conditions of Women Workers in Textile, Khandsari and Sugar Products Industries*, Delhi: The Controller of Publications, 1985.

----, Ministry of Labour, *Socio-economic Conditions of Women Workers in Manufacturers of Chemical and Chemical Products (except tea, coffee and sugar, industries)*, Delhi: Controller of Publications, 1986.

----, Department of Women and Children, *National Perspective Plan for women 1988-2000 A.D.*, New Delhi: Publications Division, 1988.

----, Ministry of Labour, *Socio-economic Conditions of Women Workers in Revolution of Tobacco, Zarda and Cigarettes, Brick Kilns, Files, Stone Dressing and Stone Crushing, Electric and Miniature Lamp, Audio and Television, Fountain Pens and Ball Pens Industries*, Simla: Govt of India Press, 1988.

Indian Council of Social Science Research, *Status of Women in India*, New Delhi: ICSSR, 1975.

Ismail, Razia, 'India's girl child: daughter of denial', *Kurukshetra*, 1990, 138(12): 39-47.

Israney, S.M., 'Status of women in the academic work: Indian context; *University News*, 1989, 27 (23): 11 - 14.

Jain, Devaki, 'Women's opinion on national issues: need of the hour,' *Indian Express*, 11 Jan., 1991:4.

Jain, Rakesh, 'Let's stop discrimination against the girl', *Social Welfare*, 1990, 36(10-11): 23.

Jain, Suman, 'National commissions on women: economic implications', *Yojana*, 1991, 35(6): 24 - 25.

Jaiswal, R.P., *Professional Status of Women*, Jaipur: Rawat Publication, 1993.

Jeffery, Patricia, *Frogs in a Well: Indian Women in Purdah*, Delhi: Vikas Publishing House, 1979.

Jejeebhoy, Shireen J., 'Female literacy in India: the situation in 1991,' *Journal of Family Welfare*, 1991, 37(7): 23-24.

Jena, Vandana Kumari, 'Women and development,' *Indian Journal of Public Administration*, 1989, 36(4): 911-927.

Jha, Rama, *Women and the Indian Print Media: Portrayal and Performance*, Delhi: Chanakaya Publications, 1991.

Jose, A.V., (ed.), *Limited Options: Women Workers in Rural India*, Geneva: ILO, 1989.

Joseph, Ammu and Sharma, Kalpana, 'Between the lines: women issues in English language newspapers', *Economic and Political Weekly*, 1991, 26 (47): WS 75-80.

Josh, Pushpa, *Gandhi on Women*, New Delhi : Navajivan Trust, 1988.

Joshi, S.R., *Invisible Barriers: Women at Senior Levels in Indian Television in* UNESCO: *Women and Media-decision Making: the Invisible Barriers, Paris*: UNESCO, 1987.

Joshi, Uma, 'Communication strategy for women's development', *Social Welfare*, 1990, 36 (12): 8-9.

—, 'Imperatives of women's uplift,' *Yojana*, 1990, 34 (4): 21-22.

Jumani, Usha, *Dealing with Poverty: Self-employment for Poor Rural Women*, New Delhi: Sage Publications, 1991.

Jyothi, Rani and Rajaiah, B., Female population, literacy and employment: some observations', *Indian Journal of Social Welfare*, 1988, 49 (3): 245-251.

Kalpagam, U., *Female Labour in Small Industry: The Case of Export Garments*, Madras: Madras Institute of Development Studies, 1981.

Kamala Raman, J., 'Women and Development', *Janata*, 1991, 45(36): 47-48.

Kamalraj, M., 'Women in salt industry', *Khadi Gramadyog*, 1990, 36(14): 411-418.

Kanhere, Usha S., *Women and Socialisation: a Study of Their Status and Role in Lower Castes in Ahmedabad*, Delhi : Mittal Publications, 1987.

Kannan, Jayam and Ilango. P., 'Health hazards of women working in bidi industries,' *Social Welfare*, 1990, 37(12) : 10-11.

Kapoor Savita,'Condensed courses of education and vocational training for women', *Social Welfare*, 1990, 37(7): 2-3.

Katan., S.S., 'A case study of Amravati city: the income, wages and working conditions of women workers in the unorganised sector', *Social Welfare*, 1989, 36 (2) : 29-31.

Karim, Wazir Jahan, 'Consumption status, production and classes of goods: the gender function', *Samya Shakti*, 1989-90, (4-5): 175-91.

Karkal, Malini and Pandey, Divya, *Studies on Women and Population: a Critique*, Bombay: Himalaya Publishing House, 1989.

Karlekar, Malavika, *Poverty and Women's work : a Study of Sweeper Women in Delhi*, New Delhi: Vikas Publishing House, 1982.

—, *Voices From Within: Early Personal Narratives of Bengali Women*, Delhi: OUP, 1991.

Kasturi, Leela, *et al.* (eds.), *Women Workers in India : Studies in Employment and Status*, Delhi: Chanakya Publications, 1980.

Kaur, Indrajeet, *Status of Hindu Women in India*, Allahabad: Chugh Publications, 1983.

Kaur, Manmohan, *Role of Women in Freedom Movement 1857-1957*, Delhi: Sterling Publishers Private Ltd. 1968.

—, *Women in India's Freedom Struggle*, New Delhi: Sterling Publishers, 1985.

Kaushik, Sushila (ed.), *Women in Society: Women's Oppression and Perspective*, New Delhi: Vikas Publishing House, 1985.

—,'Women, women's issues and Ninth General Election', *Teaching Politics*, 1989, 15(3-4): 105-115.

Kelkar, Govind, *Women and Development Programmes in Contemporary Rural China and India*, New Delhi: Nehru Memorial Museum and Library, 1991 (Occasional Papers on History and Society, First Series No. XXXVI).

—,*Violence Against Women*, New Delhi: Manohar Publications, 1992.

—, and Gala, Chetna, *Women Question in Bodh Gaya Movement*, New Delhi: Nehru Memorial Museum and Library, 1991 (Occasional Papers on History and Society, Second Series No. XII).

Khan, Asif, 'Advancing the status of women', *Amrit Bazar Patrika*, 6 Oct, 1990: 3.

—, Aiding women to join export trade', *Amrit Bazar Patrika*, 7 Oct., 1990:4.

—, 'Putting women back on the road to progress', *Amrit Bazar Patrika*, 1 Jan. 1990: 4.

Khan, Gulnaz, A., *Women's Studies in India: a Directory of Research Institutions*, New Delhi : Ashish Publishing House, 1993.

Khan, M.E., *Relationship Between Productive and Reproductive Role of women*, New Delhi: Operations Research Group, 1983.

Khan, M.E. *et. al.*, 'Working pattern of women and its impact on health and nutrition: some observations from the urban poor', *Journal of Family Welfare*, 1990, 36(2): 3-22.

Khan, Mumtaz Ali and Ayesha, Noor, *Status of Rural Women in India: Study of Karnataka*, New Delhi: Uppal Publishing House, 1982.

Khanna, Girija and Varghese, M.A. *Indian Women Today*, New Delhi: Vikas Publishing House, 1978.

Khullar, Mala, 'Who needs child care?' *Seminar*, 1991, (382): 19-22.

Kohli, Anita, 'Depriving girls of the right to think', Patriot 22 June, 1990.

Koll, P.P., 'Socio-economic conditions of bidi workers in Solapur district', *Social Change*, 1990, 20(2): 76-81.

Kosambi, Meera, 'Images of women and the faminine in Maharashtra', *Economic and Political Weekly*, 1991, 26(25): 1519-1524.

Krishna Chaitanya, 'Bihar Government's discrimination against women teachers', *Economic and Political Weekly*, 1991, 26(51): 2925.

Krishna Kumari, N.S., *Status of Single Women in India*, New Delhi: Uppal Publishing House, 1987.

Krishnamurti, J., *Women in Colonial India: Essays on Survival: Work and the State*, Delhi: Oxford University Press, 1990.

Krishnaraj, Maithreyi and Ahmad, Karuna Chanana (eds.) *Gender and the Household Domain*, New Delhi: Sage Publications, 1990.

—, and Pandey, Divya, 'Women artist change by not changing themselves,' *Shamya Shakti*, 1989-90, (4-5): 143-155.

Kulshreshtha, Indira, 'Technological change, women and educational reform in India', *Teacher Today*', 1990, 32(4): 9-13.

----, *Women's Studies in School Education*, New Delhi: Sterling Publishers Pvt. Ltd., 1989.

Kumar, D. Narendra and Himachalam, D., 'Women entrepreneurship development in India: problems and prospects', *Monthly Commentary on India Economic Conditions*, 1991, 32(19): 15-19.

Kumar, Ravindra, 'Nehru and the status of Indian women', *Secular Democracy*, 1989, 22(5): 20-21.

Kumar, Radha, 'The women's movement', *Seminar*, 1989 (335): 21-25.

Kumar, T. Vijay and Ramamohan, K.,'Role of education in the

improvement of women's status,' *Progress of Education'*, 1991, 65(1): 24-26.

Kumari, Ranjana, *Women Headed Household in Rural India*, New Delhi: Radiant Publications, 1989.

Lakshmi, C.S., 'Mother, mother community and mother politics in Tamil Nadu', *Economic and Political Weekly*, 1990, 25(42-43): WS 72-WS 83.

Lal Das, D.K. 'Sex discrimination against women at work', *Social Change*, 1988, 18(3): 71-79.

Lateef, Shaheeda, *Muslim Women in India: Political and Private Realities* 1890-1980, New Delhi : Kali for Women.

Leslie, Julia, (ed.), *The Perfect Wife*, London: Oxford University Press, 1989.

Loomba, Ania, 'Women work and cinema', *Seminar*, 1991 (382): 39-42.

Madhok, V.K., 'Widening women's role in armed forces', *Indian Express*, 12 Nov. 1990.

Madhu Kishwar, 'It is only a family affair?', *Illustrated Weekly of India*, 1990, 111(43): 32-35.

Madhu Nainan, 'Women welfare schemes', *Lok Rajya*, 1990, 46(4): 26-28.

Mahila Vikash Sangh, *Women and Development Planning: Case Study of Nauhatta Block*, New Delhi: Vikas Publishing House, 1988.

Majumdar, Reba, 'Education: an investment low priority and small returns for women', *University News*, 1991, 29(28): 10-13.

Mallik, Padmaja, 'Working women: adjustment in home life and work life', *Psychological Research Journal*, 1989.

Mandal, Tirtha, *Women Revolutionaries of Bengal* 1905-1939, Calcutta: Minerva Associates Publications, 1991.

Manikyamba, P., *Women in Panchayatiraj Structures*, New Delhi: Gyan Publishing House, 1989.

Manimekhalal, N. and Sundari, S., 'Female labours force in the unorganised sector of mat industries: some evidences', *Indian Journal of Social Work*, 1991, 62(2): 195-203.

Mankidy, Aruna, 'Women employees: a new variable in industrial relations in the banking industry', *Management and Labour Studies*, 1989, 14(2): 101-106.

Mann, K., *Tribal Women in a Changing Society*, Delhi: Mittal Publications, 1987.

Manohar, K. Murali (ed.), *Socio-economic Status of Indian Women*, Delhi: Seema Publications, 1983.

Marak, Caroline R., 'Women in Garo Hills : the winds of change'. *Social Welfare*, 1991, 38(3): 14-17.

Mathew, Elsy, 'Let the working women relax', Social Welfare, 1990, 26(12): 6-7.

Mathur, Kanchan and Rajan, S., *Prevention of Atrocities Against Women: Case Studies from Rajasthan*, Jaipur: Institute of Development Studies, 1988.

Mathuraja, C., 'Rural women in Indian agriculture', *Khadi Gramodyog*. 1990, 36 (8): 339-344.

Mazumdar, Aurobindo, 'Commission not enough for women', *Assam Tribune*, 5 Oct., 1990.

Mazumdar, Vina, (ed.), *Role of Rural Women in Development*, Bombay: Allied Publishers, 1978.

—, *National Specialised Agencies and Women's Equality: Khadi and Village Industries Commission*, New Delhi: Centre for Women's Development Studies, 1988.

—, 'Reservations for women', *Economic and Political Weekly*, 1989, 24(50): 2795-2796.

—, *Women Workers in India*, Delhi: Chanakya Publications, 1990.
Mehta, Hansa, *Indian Women*, Delhi: Butala & Company, 1981.

Mehta, Rama, *Socio-legal Status of Women in India*, Delhi: Mittal Publications, 1987.

Mehta, Vimla, *Attitude of Educated Women Towards Social Issues*, New Delhi: National Publishing House, 1979.

Menon, M. Indu, *Status of Muslim Women in India: a Case Study of Kerala*, New Delhi: Uppal Publishing House, 1981.

Mies, Maria, *Indian Women and Patriarchy*, New Delhi: Concept Publishing House, 1980.

Minault, Gail (ed.), *Extended Family: Women and Political Participation in India and Pakistan*, Delhi: Chanakya Publications, 1981.

Mishra, A.R., *Plan of Development of Women and Children in Rural Areas in Etawah District*, Allahabad: G.B. Pant Social Science Institute, 1986.

Mishra, Bimlesh Kumar, 'Women workers deserve a better deal'. 1990, *Yojana*; 34(12) Jly-1-15: 19-22.

Mishra, R.B. and Singh, Chandrapal, *Indian Women: Challenges and*

Changes, New Delhi: Commonwealth Publishers, 1992.

Mishra, Syamashree and Mishra, Subrata, 'Occupational structure of women in Orissa', *Social Change*, 1990, 20(2): 70-75.

Mishra, Lakshmi, *Women's Issues: an Indian Perspective*, New Delhi: Northern Book Centre, 1992.

Misra, Rekha, *Women in Mughal India 1526-1748 A.D.*, Delhi: Munshiram Manoharlal, 1967.

Mitra, Krishna, 'Rehabilitation of rescued women and girls; *Social Welfare*, 1990, 37(2): 22.

Mitra, Roma and Mitra, N.R., 'Participation of women in Bihar Polity', *Journal of Constitutional and Parliamentary Studies*, 1990, 24(1-4): 176-186.

Mitra, S.M., *Position of Women in Indian Life*, New Delhi: Neeraj Publishing House, 1981.

Moodie, A.D. (ed.), *Concept of Work in Indian Society*, New Delhi: Manohar Publications, 1988.

Mukherjee, Amitava, 'Crumbs for women workers', *National Herald*, 6 Nov., 1990.

—,'Why do women workers get such a raw deal?, *Free Press Journal*, 6 Nov., 1990.

Mukherjee, Anindita and Verma, Neelam, *Socio-economic Backwardness in Women*, New Delhi: Ashish Publishing House, 1987.

Nabar, Vrinda, 'Feminism and literature: an Indian perspective', *Indian Horizons*, 1990, 39(3-4): 53-58.

Nagaraj, Bhargavi, 'Recognition of the role of women : still a long way to go', *Decan Herald*, 8 March, 1990.

Nagraj, K., *Female Workers in Rural Tamil Nadu: a Preliminary Report*, Geneva: I.L.O., 1988.

Nair, G. Ravindran, 'Image of the girl child: a report of the workshop on the girl child', *Social Welfare*, 1990, 37(1): 4-8.

Nanda, B.R., (ed.), *Indian Women from Purdah to Modernity*, New Delhi: Vikas Publishing House, 1976.

Narasimhan, Gita and Iyer, Lalitha,'Attitude towards women managers' *Economic and Political Weekly*, 1990, 25(44): 2451-2552.

Narayan Suchindra, *Impact of Agriculture on Rural Women of Bihar: a Programme run by Mahila Vikash Sangh*, Patna: A.N. Sinha Institute of Social Studies, 1985.

Natrajan, K. and Jayaratham, M., 'Entrepreneurship: a means to women development', *Khadi Gramodyog*, 1991, 37(12): 457-460.

National Commission on Self-employed women, Occupational Health Issues of Women in Unorganised Sector, New Delhi: The National Commission on Self-employed Women, 1985.

National Institute of Urban Affairs, *Women and Urbanisation*, New Delhi: NIUA, 1989.

—, *Women Vendors in India's Urban Centres*, New Delhi: NIUA 1989.

—, *Gender Bias in Employment: Women in Urban Informal Sector*, New Delhi: NIUA, 1990.

—, *The Role of Women in Urban Informal Sector*, New Delhi: NIUA, 1990.

Nayak, Madhab, 'Women entrepreneurs: need for supportive services', *Social Welfare*, 1991, 38(2): 4-7.

Nayyar, Rohini, *Rural Labour Markets and Employment of Women in Punjab and Haryana*, Geneva: ILO, 1988.

Nehru, Syham Kumari (ed.), *Our Cause*: a *Symposium*, Allahabad: Kitabistan, (nd.).

Nuna, Sheel C., *Women and Development*, New Delhi: NIEPA, 1990.

Omvedt, Gail, *We will Smash this Prison: Indian Women in Struggle*, New Delhi: Orient Longman Ltd., 1979.

----, 'Women and Ecology', *Economic and Political Weekly*, 1990, 25(22): 1223.

Padmanabhan B.S., 'Justice for women: still a far cry', *Telegraph*, 13 Jan., 1991.

—, 'Gender justice: Long way to go', *National Herald*, 18 Jan., 1991.

Padmavathi, A., 'Problem of domestic violence', *Legal News and Views*, 1991, 5(7): 202-3.

Pakrasi, Kanti B., *Female Infanticide in India*, Calcutta: Firma K.L.M. 1970.

Panda, Snehlata, *Determinants of Political Participation: Women and Public Activity*, Delhi: Ajanta Publications, 1990.

Pande, Mrinal, 'Prime time thoughts of a woman', *Mainstream (Annual Number)*, 8 Oct., M88: 42.

—, 'Status of women', *Mainstream*, 1990, 28 (20): 4-6.

----, Family politics', *Seminar*, 1991, (382): 23-25.

Pande, P.N. and Papola, T.S., *Women Khadi Workers: a Study of*

Economic Conditions and Status of Woman Spinners in Uttar Pradesh, Lucknow: Giri Institute of Development Studies, 1985.

Pandey, Rekha, *Women from Subjugation to Liberation*, Delhi: Mittal Publications, 1989.

Pandit, K.L. and Pradhan, A., 'Unemployment among educated women and entrepreneurial qualities: a case study', *University News*, 1990 28 (19): 5-10.

Pant, A.D., *et al.*, *Women and Children Development Promotion at Maha Kumbh*, Allahabad: G.B. Pant Social Science Institute, 1988.

Papa, B. Regina, 'Women and social transformation', *Kurukshetra*, 1991, 39(7): 18-21.

Papola, T.S., *Women Workers in an Urban Labour Market: a Study of Segregation and Discrimination in Employment in Lucknow*, Lucknow: Giri Institute of Development Studies, 1982.

—, *Women Workers in an Indian Urban Labour Market*, Geneva: ILO, 1983.

Paramjit, S. Judte, *Scheduled Caste Women in Work Force in Rural Punjab*, Surat: Centre for Social Studies, 1990.

Parikh, Indira J. and Garg, Pulin K., *Indian Women: an Inner Dialogue*, New Delhi: Sage Publications, 1989.

Patel, Bella C., 'Women and health service', *Social Welfare*, 1991, 38(3): 4-8.

Patel, Vibhuti, 'Getting a foothold in politics', *Janata*, 1991, 45(36-40): 17-19.

Patkar, Pritpai, 'Children of prostitutes: a perspective', *Legal News and Views*, 1990, 4(7): 10-15.

Patnayak, Rama, 'Education for women's equality', *Kurukshetra*, 1991, 39(4): 52-56.

Phudki, Y.D., *Women in Maharashtra*, New Delhi: Maharashtra Information Centre, 1989.

Phyllis, S., 'Women Labourers in salt-pans at Tuticorin', *Social Welfare*, 1991, 38(2): 15.

Pillai, J.K., 'Development and advancement of women in Management', *University News*, 1990, 28(9): 1-3.

—, 'Empowering women in India: new roles for education', *University News*, 1990, 28(47): 1-5.

Prasad, Jeonne, 'Women in media: will they be allowed to reach the too? *Free Press Journal*, 11 Nov., 1990.

Prasad, M.N., 'Do women in IAS face discrimination?;' *Monthly Public Opinion Survey*, 1990, 35(10-11): 21-24.

Punalekar, S.P., *Female Casual Labourers in Urban Gujarat: a Case Study*, Surat: Centre for Social Studies, 1990.

Quadeer, Imrana, 'Roop Kanwar and Shah Bano', *Seminar*, 1988 (342): 31-33.

Radhakrishna, G.S., 'Andhra women take anti-liquor fight to dens,' *Telegraph*, 23 Oct., 1992.

Rahi, A.L., 'Empowering the women,' Tribune, 14 Jan., 1990.

Rajalakshmi, V., *Political Behaviour of Women in Tamil Nadu*, New Delhi: Inter-India Publication, 1985.

Ralu, Saraswati, 'Gender and deprivation: a theme revisited with geographical perspective', *Economic and Political Weekly*, 1991, 25 (46): 2827-29.

Rama, K.G., 'Shelter for single women: an urban need', *Social Welfare*, 1990, 37(1): 9.

Ramachandran, Chitra, *Maternal Employment and Educational Development of Children*, New Delhi: Commonwealth Publishers, 1989.

Ramanamma, A., *Graduate Employed Women in Urban Setting Patna: Dastana Ramachandra & Co.*, 1979.

Ramanathan, Gayatri, 'National Commission for women: a ray of hope' *Mainstream*, 1990, 28 (49) 29-30.

Ramdas, Lalita, 'Women and literacy: a quest for justice', *Prospects*, 1989, 19(4): 519-530.

Ramu, G.N., *Women, Work and Marriage in Urban India: a Study* of *Dual and Single Earner Couples*, New Delhi: Sage Publications, 1989.

—, 'Men do not cry and men do not cook and clean: a study of house work among urban couples', *Samya Shjakti*, 1989-90, (4-5): 156-174.

Rani, G. Vidya, *Status of Women Employees in Government*, New Delhi: Mittal Publications, 1989.

Rani, T. Jyothi and Reddy, T.P., 'Development programmes in economies: perspectives; *Mainstream*, 1990, 28(40): 9-10.

Rao, Amla Rama, 'Health status of the prostitue and their children', *Social Welfare*, 1990, 37(3): 20-23.

Rao, N.J. Usha, 'A generation apart: women in the national

movement', *Samya Shakti*, 1989-90, (4-5): 254-264.

—, *Women in Developing Society*, New Delhi: Ashish Publishing House, 1990.

Ray, Bharati, 'Bangali women and politics of joint family 1900-1947', *Economic and Political Weekly*, 1991, 26(52): 3015-3021.

Ray, Renuka, *et al.*, *Role and Status of Women in Indian Society*, Calcutta: Firma K.L.M., 1978.

Reddy, C. Raghunadha, *Changing Status of Educated Working Women: a Case Study*, Delhi: B.R. Publishing Corporation, 1986.

Reddy, T. Chandramohan, *et al.*, 'Some structural determinants of union participation among woman workers', *Social Action*, 1991, Vol. 41(2): 205-212.

Rekha, Mehra and Sardamoni, K., *Women and Rural Transformation*, New Delhi: Concept Publishing House, 1983.

Roy, Aruna, 'Women's view', *Seminar*, 1990, (376): 31-35.

Sabina, R.G.S., 'Women: a force to reckon with, *Legal News and Views*, 1991, 5(6): 169-170.

Sachchidananda and Sinha, R.P., *Women's Rights: Myth and Reality* Jaipur: Printwell Publishers, 1984.

Savara, Mira, *Changing Trends in Women's Employment: a Case Study of Textile Industry in Bombay*, Bombay: Himalaya Publishing House, 1986.

—, Schenk-Sandhergen, Loes, 'Employment of women: its scope in a bilateral development project in North Bengal', *Economic and Political Weekly*, 1991, 26(17): WS 27-33.

Sahai, S.N., *Women in Changing Society*, Delhi: Mittal Publications, 1984.

Sahay, Sushama Prasad, *Tribal Women Labourers: Aspects of Economic and Physical Exploitation*, Delhi: Gyan Publishing House, 1988.

Saikia, P.D., *Indian Rural Women: a Study on Role and Status of Rural Women in Assam*, Delhi: Mittal Publications, 1986.

Sangari, Kumkum, 'Perpetuating the myth', *Seminar*, 1988 (342) : 24-30.

—, and Vaid, Sudesh, (eds.) *Relating Women: Essays in Colonial History*, New Delhi: Kali for Women, 1989.

Saraswati, Ramabai, *High Caste Hindu Women*, New Delhi: Inter-India Publications, 1984.

Savita, Singal and Srinivasan, Kamla, 'Rural women participation in paid work: their satisfaction and felt needs', *Khadi Gramodyog*, 1991, 37(9): 344-351.

Saxena, M.B., 'Panchayats and women', *Kurukshetra*, 1989, 37(5): 56-59.

Sekaran, Uma and Leong, Fredirick, T.L. (eds.), *Women Power: Managing in Times of Demographic Turbulence*, New Delhi: Sage Publications, 1992.

Sen, G., *Paddy Production, Processing and Women Workers in India: the South Vs. the Northeast*, Trivandrum: Centre of Development Studies, 1983.

Sen, G. and Sen, Chiranjib, *Women's Domestic Work and Economic Activity: Results from the National Sample Survey*, Trivandrum: Centre for Development Studies, 1984.

Sengupta, Padmini, *Story of Women of India*, New Delhi: Indian Book Company, 1974.

Senthlathalban, K. *et al.*, 'Reactions to wife beating: an opinion survey among students', *Indian Journal of Criminology*, 1991 19(1): 21-29.

Sethi, Rajmohini, 'Role of non-formal educational schemes in the education and employment of women', *Guru Nanak Journal of Sociology*, 1987 (10-12): 147-54.

Shah, Kalpana, *Women's Liberation and Voluntary Action*, Delhi: Ajanta Publications, 1984.

Shah, Vidyaben, 'Role of working girl child in household economy', *Social Welfare*, 1990, 37(1): 3.

Shantha Mohan, 'New education policy: its relevance to women', *Religion and Society*, 1989, 36 (3): 3-10.

Shariff, Abusaleh, *Women Workers and Problems of Child Care (Mimeo)* Ahmedabad: The Gujarat Institute of Area Planning, 1989.

—, 'Women workers: gender equality and female autonomy', *Social Welfare*, 1990, 20(2): 44-51.

Sharma, Kalpana, 'Women's Commission: flawed framework, '*Times of India*, 30 Jan., 1990.

—, 'Christian women press for change', *Times of India*, 20 Jan., 1990.

—, 'Giving Indian women coverage to choose', *Times of India*, 9 Jan., 1990.

—, 'Women are not fundamentalist', *Times of India*, 13 Nov., 1990: 6.

Sharma, R.D. 'Society apethic to crime against women', *Times of India*, 12 Nov. 1989.

—, 'Crime against women is on rise', *Times of India*, 15 May, 1990.

Sharma, Radha Krishana, *Nationalism, Social Reform and Indian Women*, Patna: Janaki Parkashan, 1981.

Sharma, Savitri, *Women Students in India: Status and Personality*, New Delhi: Concept Publishing House, 1979.

Sharma, Ursula, *Women's Work, Class and the Urban Household: a Study of Simla*, London: Tavistock, 1987.

Shashi, S.S., *Tribal Women of India*, Delhi: Sundeep Publications, 1978.

Shirwadkar, Swati, 'Education and development of women in Maharashtra', *Social Change*, 1990, 20(2): 36-40.

Showeb, M., *Social Background, Activity and Status of Women Spinners*, Varanasi: Gandhian Institute of Studies, 1989.

—, 'Women Khadi spinners: a study in economic self-sufficiency of rural women', *Khadi Gramodyog*, 1991, 31(11): 428-433.

Shridevi, S., *Century of Indian Womenhood*, Mysore: Rao & Raghvan, 1965.

Singh, A.N., 'Women's education and its need', *Kurukshetra University Research Journal*, 1989 (23): 101-103.

Singh, Abha, 'Spatial temporal changes in urban female working population of Varanasi city region', *National Geographer*, 1989, 109-164.

Singh, Andrea-Menefee and Kelles-Viitanen, Anita, *Invisible Hands: Women in Home Based Production*, New Delhi: Sage Publications, 1987.

Singh Daljit, 'Role of women in army', *Hindustan Times*, 13 Feb., 1991.

Singh, H.M., 'Problems of rural women labourers: a study', *Kurukshetra University Research Journal*, 1989, (23): 73-76.

Singh, Hira, 'Critical analysis of existing law relating to prostitution', *Social Welfare*, 1980, 37(3): 4-8.

Singh, Indu Prakash, *Women, Law and Social Change in India*, New Delhi: Radiant Publishers, 1989.

Singh, J.P., *et al.* (eds.), *Tribal Women and Development, Rajasthan*: Tribal Area Development Department, 1985.

Singh, K.P. *Status of Women and Population Growth in India*, New Delhi: Munshiram Manoharlal Pvt. Ltd., 1979.

Singh, Nalini, 'Area of darkness', *Indian Express*, 29 July, 1991.

Singh, Narendra P. and Sengupta, Rita, *Potential Women Entrepreneurs*, Gurgaon: Management Development Institute, 1985.

Singh, Prabhash P., *Women in India: a Statistical Panorama*, New Delhi: Inter-India Publications, 1990.

Singh, R.R., 'National Commission needs much more power', *Times of India*, 9 Aug. 1990.

Singh, Sukhmani, 'Protectors of predators, '*Illustrated Weekly of India*, 1990, 111(39): 34-37.

Singh, Y.N. 'Health needs of prostitutes', *Social Welfare*, 1990, 37(4): 20-21.

Sinha, Pushpa, *Role Conflict Among the Working Women*, Patna: Janaki Prakashan, 1987.

Sinha, Ramesh P. and Verma, S.D., *Situation Analysis of Women and Children in North Bihar*, Delhi: South Central Asia Region.

Sinha, Saritha, 'Women's education in India: the myth and the reality', *Southern Economist'*, 1991, 30(11): 15-18.

Smith-Sreen, Poonam and Smith-Sreen, John, 'Insights from women diary farmers in India: what do they gain from participation?, *Social Action*, 1991. 1991 Oct. - Dec. 41(4) : 416-27.

Sood, Sushma, (ed.), *Violence Against Women*, Jaipur: Arihant Publishers, 1990.

Srinivasan, Viji, *Women's Work Experience*, New Delhi: Haranand Publication, 1992.

Srivastava, Suresh C., 'Equal remuneration for men and women', *Journal of the Indian Law Institute*, Jan-March 1990: 82-92.

Srivastava, T.N., *Women and the Law*, New Delhi: Intellectual Publishing House, 1985.

Subamma, Malladi, *Islam and Women*, New Delhi: Sterling Publishers, 1988.

Sumaraj, Leena, *Women and Medical Care*, New Delhi: Ashish Publishing House, 1991.

Sundar, Pushpa, *Credit for Self-employment of Women*, Delhi: Ford Foundation, 1983.

Sundaram, K., *Inter-State Variations in Work Force Participation Rates of Women in India: a Analysis*, Geneva: ILO, 1988.

Sundari, S. and Manimekhalal, 'Women workers in the paddy processing industries', *Social Welfare*, 1990, 36(10-11): 14-17.

Talwar, Usha, *Social Profile of Working Women*, Jodhpur: Jain Brothers, 1984.

Thakur, Laxmi, 'Socio-economic status of slum women', *Social Change*, 1988, 18(3): 90-96.

Thakur, Vijay, 'Negation or neutralization of gender and sexist bias in school curriculla', *Religion and Society*, 1989, 36(3): 25-31.

Thapar, Romila, 'In history', *Seminar*, 1988, 342: 14-19.

Thomas, Gracious, 'Impact of environmental destruction on tribal women: areas of social work intervention', *University News*, 1991, Vol. 29(41): 7-10.

Thomas, M.E. and Khan, M.Z., 'Women and development in Wayand,' *Social Change*, 1990, 20(2): 25-35.

Tikoo, Prithvi Nath, *Indian Women: a Brief Socio-cultural Survey*, Delhi: B.R. Publishing Corporation, 1985.

Tiwari, G.G., *Women's Role in Social Forestry in Uttar Pradesh*, Allahabad: G.B. Pant Social Science Institute, 1990.

Tripathi, P., 'Women workers in urban unorganised sector', *Social Welfare*, 1989, 36(2): 20-23.

Tripathi, Raj Mani, *Role and Participation of Females in Urban Labour Force of Avadh Region of Uttar Pradesh*, Allahabad: G.B. Pant Social Science Institute, 1991.

Trivedi, Harshad R., *Scheduled Caste Women Studies in Exploitation: with Reference to Superstition, Ignorance and Poverty*, Delhi: Concept Publishing House, 1976.

Uma, Alladi, *Women and Her Family—Indian and Afro-American: a Literary Perspective*, New Delhi: Sterling Publishers, 1989.

Uniyal, Lalit, 'Women and development: some reflections', *Mainstream* (Annual Number), 27 Oct. 1990: 109-115.

Unni, Jeemol, 'Work participation of women in India', *Economic and Political Weekly*, 1990, 25(10): 497-498.

Vaid, Suresh, 'Politics of widow immolation', *Seminar*, 1988, (342): 20-23.

Vandana Shiva, *Staying Alive: Women, Ecology and Survival in India*, New Delhi: Kali for Women, 1988.

Varalakshmi, G. and Kamala, K., 'Role of women in Indian economic development', *Economic Studies* (Annual Number), 1990, 29(1): 25-32.

Venkatasubramanian, V., 'Training for rural women in dairying for rural development, *Khadi Gramodyog*, 1991, 37(8): 322-324.

Verghese, Jamila, *Her Gold and Her Body*, New Delhi: Vikas Publishing House, 1986.

Verma, Amita and Kapadia, Shagufa, 'Women's studies in universities: planning developmental programmes for women's', *Journal of the Maharaja Sayaji Rao University of Baroda*, 1986, 35-36(1): 57-71.

Verma, S.K. and Valulla, Saida, 'Self-employed women in Gujarat', *Social Welfare*, 1991, 38(2): 8-10.

Verma, Satya, 'Mahila Mandals in Himachal Pradesh,' *Social Welfare*, 1991, 26(4-5): 10-12.

Verma, Sudhir, 'Policy planning for women's development at provincial level: the case of Rajasthan', *Development*, 1990 (1): 95-98.

Vinze, Medha Dubhashi, *Women Entrepreneurs in India: a Socio-economic Study of Delhi 1975-1985*, Delhi: Mittal Publications, 1987.

Visaria, Pravin and Unni, Jeemol, *Self-employed Women, Population and Human Resource Development* (Mimeo). Ahmedabad: Gujarat Institute of Development Research, 1992.

Vohra, Gautam, *Women in Bihar: a Study of Their Role in Tasar Silk Production*, New Delhi: Vikas Publishing House, 1988.

Vohra, Roopa and Sen, Arun K., *Status, Education and Problems of Indian Women*, Delhi: Akshat Publications, 1985.

Wickremasinghe, Kamala, 'Women in management', *SLIDA News letter*, 1989, 1(2): 1-10.

Winston, Fern, 'Movement for women's equality at the turn of the decade', *Political Affairs*, 1990, 69(3): 13-15.

Young, Kate, 'Employment opportunities and constraint for women from here to 2000', *Development*, 1990, (1): 13-15.

Young Women Christian Association, *Place to Live: a Study on Housing for Women*, Bombay: Allied Publishers (n.d).

Index